A Guide and Reference

W9-ALU-220

reference

HOW TO
WRITE
ANYTHING

THIRD EDITION

HOW TO WRITE ANYTHING

A Guide and Reference

John J. Ruszkiewicz

UNIVERSITY OF TEXAS AT AUSTIN

BEDFORD/ST. MARTIN'S

Boston ◆ New York

For Bedford/St. Martin's

Vice President, Editorial, Macmillan Higher Education Humanities:
Edwin Hill
Editorial Director for English and Music: Karen Henry
Publisher for Composition and Business and Technical Writing:
Leasa Burton
Executive Editor: Molly Parke
Developmental Editor: Sarah Macomber
Senior Production Editor: Deborah Baker
Assistant Production Manager: Joe Ford
Marketing Manager: Emily Rowin
Editorial Assistant: Rachel Childs
Copyeditor: Jennifer Greenstein
Indexer: Steve Csipke
Director of Rights and Permissions: Hilary Newman
Senior Art Director: Anna Palchik
Text Design: Anna Palchik
Cover Design: Billy Boardman
Composition: Cenveo Publisher Services
Printing and Binding: RR Donnelley and Sons

Manufactured in the United States of America.

9   8   7   6   5
f   e   d   c   b

For information, write: Bedford/St. Martin's, 75 Arlington Street, Boston, MA 02116
(617-399-4000)

ISBN: 978-1-4576-9368-7 (spiral edition)
ISBN: 978-1-4576-6704-6 (adhesive edition)

Acknowledgments

Text acknowledgments and copyrights appear at the back of the book on pages A-1–3, which constitute an extension of the copyright page. Art acknowledgments and copyrights appear on the same page as the art selections they cover. It is a violation of the law to reproduce these selections by any means whatsoever without the written permission of the copyright holder.

Preface

Through its first two editions, readers of *How to Write Anything: A Guide and Reference* have been intrigued—and perhaps attracted—by its title, admittedly not a humble one. Should any book, especially one designed expressly as a guide for college writers, promise so much? The simple answer is *no*; the more intriguing one is *maybe*.

What, after all, do experienced writers do when they face an assignment? As the new Introduction to this edition explains in detail, they size up a project to figure out what *genre* of writing best meets their needs and those of readers. They locate and examine specific examples of that genre, imitating some features and modifying or rejecting others. Then they shape a work within that genre themselves, bringing appropriate rhetorical, organizational, research, and language skills to bear on their writing. It is the goal of *How to Write Anything* to guide college writers through these complex choices for their most common academic and professional assignments. In doing so, it lays out key strategies to follow in any situation that requires purposeful writing.

But rarely do different writers work in the same order, and the same writer is likely to follow different paths for different projects. So *How to Write Anything* doesn't define a single process of writing or imagine that all students using it will have the same skills and interests. Instead, a modular chapter organization and an innovative system of cross-references enables writers to find exactly the information they want at the level of specificity they need—which pretty much sums up the rationale for the book. *How to Write Anything* is both focused and flexible, marrying the resources of a full rhetoric to the efficiency of a compact handbook. That commitment to clarity and efficiency is even more evident in this latest edition.

A Guide and Reference

Parts 1 and 2 of *How to Write Anything* make up the Guide, which covers genres of writing that instructors assign in composition classes or that students encounter in other college courses. For each genre, writers are offered a framework presented as a flexible series of rhetorical choices—Exploring purpose and topic; Understanding your audience; Finding and developing materials; Creating a structure; and Choosing a style and design. The explanations here are direct, practical, and economical, encouraging students to explore a range of options within genres. If writers do need more help with a particular topic, targeted cross-references make it easy to find in the Reference section.

The Reference section (Parts 3 through 9) covers key aspects of the writing process—with separate parts devoted to Ideas; Shaping & Drafting; Style; Revising & Editing; Research & Sources; Media & Design; and Common Errors. Points mentioned in the Guide section get expanded treatment here for students who need it. For instance, writers might turn to these sections to find techniques for generating arguments, improving their sentences, or overcoming writer's block. The organization of *How to Write Anything* lets students find precisely what they need without getting bogged down in other material.

Key Features

A Flexible Writing Process and Design that Works

How to Write Anything works hard to make its materials accessible and attractive to writers accustomed to intuitive design. For instance, "How to Start" questions at the opening of each chapter in the Guide anticipate where writers get stuck and direct them to exactly what they need: One writer might seek advice about finding a topic for a report, while another with a topic already in hand wants prompts for developing that idea.

Similarly, frequent cross-references between the Guide and Reference sections target the topics that students are likely to want to know more about. The simple language and unobtrusive design of the cross-references make it easy for students to stay focused on their own writing while finding related material—no explanations necessary and minimal clutter on the page. Readings and images throughout the book are similarly highlighted and variously annotated so that readers, once again, find information they need precisely when and where they require it.

Media-savvy students know that learning occurs in more than just words, so this edition preserves one of the favorite design features of *How To Write Anything*: its context-rich "How To" Visual Tutorials. Through drawings, photographs, and screenshots, these items offer step-by-step instructions for topics, ranging from how to use a writing center productively to how to cite selected materials in both MLA and APA formats.

Writing Worth Reading—From Professionals and Students

How to Write Anything: A Guide and Reference contains an ample selection of readings, more than thirty in the Guide chapters alone, representing a wide range of genres. Selections illustrate key principles and show how genres change in response to different contexts, audiences, and—increasingly important—media. Every chapter in the Guide includes many complete examples of the genres under discussion, most of these texts annotated to show how they meet criteria set down in *How to Write Anything*. The assignments at the end of the Part 1 chapters are closely tied to the chapter readings, so students can use the sample texts both as models and as springboards for discussion and exploration.

Just as important, the models in *How to Write Anything* are approachable. The readings—some by published professionals and others by student writers— reveal the diversity of contemporary writing being done in these genres. The student samples are especially inventive—chosen to motivate undergraduates to take comparable risks with their own writing. Together, the readings and exercises suggest to writers the many creative possibilities of working in these genres.

New to This Edition

How to Write Anything was designed from the outset to be a practical, highly readable guide to writing for a generation not fond of long books. The third edition doubles down on that commitment. It's smarter, more efficient, and shorter.

- **Vibrant new Introduction.** Designed as a starting point for a course, a new Introduction explains the structure and rationale of *How to Write Anything* in practical terms students will appreciate. Concepts that play a key role in the book such as *genre, subgenres, writing processes*, and even *audiences* are defined and discussed.

- **New chapter on writing portfolios.** Because more and more courses and college programs ask students to assemble writing portfolios, *How to Write Anything* introduces a new chapter (Chapter 17) explaining exactly how to compose, select, edit, and present materials for this assignment. The chapter gives special attention to composing student reflections on their coursework.

- **New "Reading the Genre" prompts.** All major readings in Part 1 are now preceded by a brief exercise or query designed to make readers think about the reading's genre or genre strategies.

- **Improved chapter organization.** Each chapter in the Guide sections has been reviewed to enhance the clarity of its presentations. Chapter 8, Rhetorical Analyses, for example, now offers a chart to summarize key questions for such a paper. And every chapter in Part 2, Special Assignments, has a new structure that makes the discussion of the genre clearer and, in most cases, simpler.

- **Focused writing throughout the book.** *How to Write Anything* has been fine-tuned to acknowledge students' preference for brevity and clarity. Chapters get to the point quicker, examples have been tightened, and some chapters have been combined to eliminate overlap.

- **Fresh readings and images.** New readings and images throughout the book keep *How to Write Anything* topical and challenging. New materials include a literacy narrative by Allegra Goodman, a movie review of *The Hunger Games*, a student's research report on women running marathons, a Jen Sorensen editorial cartoon on student debt, and Bert and Ernie on the cover of *The New Yorker*.

Get the Most Out of Your Course with *How to Write Anything*

Bedford/St. Martin's offers resources and format choices that help you and your students get even more out of your book and course. To learn more about or to order any of the following products, contact your Bedford/St. Martin's sales representative, e-mail sales support (**sales_support@bfwpub.com**), or visit the Web site at **macmillanhighered.com/howtowrite3e/catalog**.

LaunchPad for *How to Write Anything with Readings:* Where Students Learn

LaunchPad provides engaging content and new ways to get the most out of your course. Get an **interactive e-book** combined with **unique, book-specific materials** in a fully customizable course space; then assign and mix our resources with yours.

- Multimedia selections that make the most of what the Web can do with carefully selected video and multimodal readings for each chapter in Part 1.

- **Pre-built units**—including readings, videos, quizzes, discussion groups, and more—are **easy to adapt and assign** by adding your own materials and mixing them with our high-quality multimedia content and ready-made assessment options, such as **LearningCurve** adaptive quizzing.

- LaunchPad also provides access to a **gradebook** that provides a clear window on the performance of your whole class, individual students, and even individual assignments.

- A **streamlined interface** helps students focus on what's due, and social commenting tools let them **engage**, make connections, and learn from each other. Use LaunchPad on its own or integrate it with your school's learning management system so that your class is always on the same page.

To get the most out of your course, order LaunchPad for *How to Write Anything with Readings* packaged with the print book **free** for a limited time. (LaunchPad for *How to Write Anything with Readings* can also be purchased on its own.) An activation code is required.

To order LaunchPad for *How to Write Anything with Readings* with the print book, use **ISBN 978-1-319-02431-4**.

Choose from Alternative Formats of *How to Write Anything*

Bedford/St. Martin's offers a range of affordable formats, allowing students to choose the one that works best for them. For details, visit **macmillanhighered .com/howtowrite3e/formats**.

- **Spiral-bound.** To order the spiral-bound edition of *How to Write Anything*, use **ISBN 978-1-4576-9368-7**.

- *Bedford e-Book to Go.* A portable, downloadable e-book is available at about half the price of the print book. To order the *Bedford e-Book to Go for How to Write Anything*, use **ISBN 978-1-4576-9373-1**. To order the *Bedford e-Book to Go for How to Write Anything with Readings*, use **ISBN 978-1-4576-9388-5**.

- **Other popular e-book formats.** For details, visit **macmillanhighered .com/ebooks**.

Select Value Packages

Add value to your text by packaging one of the following resources with *How to Write Anything*. To learn more about package options for any of the following products, contact your Bedford/St. Martin's sales representative or visit **macmillanhighered.com/howtowrite3e/catalog**.

LearningCurve for Readers and Writers, Bedford/St. Martin's adaptive quizzing program, quickly learns what students already know and helps them practice what they don't yet understand. Game-like quizzing motivates students to engage with their course, and reporting tools help teachers discern their students' needs. *LearningCurve for Readers and Writers* can be packaged with *How to Write Anything* at a significant discount. An activation code is required. To order LearningCurve packaged with the print book, use ISBN 978-1-319-02144-3. For details, visit **learningcurveworks.com**.

i-series This popular series presents multimedia tutorials in a flexible format—because there are things you can't do in a book.

- *ix visualizing composition 2.0* helps students put into practice key rhetorical and visual concepts. To order *ix visualizing composition* packaged with the print book, contact your sales representative for a package ISBN.

● *i-claim: visualizing argument* offers a new way to see argument—with 6 multimedia tutorials, an illustrated glossary, and a wide array of multimedia arguments. To order *i-claim: visualizing argument* packaged with the print book, contact your sales representative for a package ISBN.

Portfolio Keeping, Third Edition, by Nedra Reynolds and Elizabeth Davis provides all the information students need to use the portfolio method successfully in a writing course. *Portfolio Teaching*, a companion guide for writing instructors, provides the practical information instructors and writing program administrators need to teach using the portfolio method. To order *Portfolio Keeping* packaged with the print book, contact your sales representative for a package ISBN.

Make Learning Fun with *Re:Writing 3*

macmillanhighered.com/rewriting

New open online resources with videos and interactive elements engage students in new ways of writing. You'll find tutorials about using common digital writing tools, an interactive peer review game, Extreme Paragraph Makeover, and more—all for free and for fun. Visit **macmillanhighered.com/rewriting**.

Instructor Resources

macmillanhighered.com/howtowrite3e

You have a lot to do in your course. Bedford/St. Martin's wants to make it easy for you to find the support you need—and to get it quickly.

Teaching with **How to Write Anything: A Guide and Reference** is available as a PDF that can be downloaded from the Bedford/St. Martin's online catalog at the URL above. In addition to chapter overviews and teaching tips, the instructor's manual includes sample syllabi, classroom activities, and teaching goals.

Teaching Central offers the entire list of Bedford/St. Martin's print and online professional resources in one place. You'll find landmark reference works, sourcebooks on pedagogical issues, award-winning collections, and practical advice for the classroom—all free for instructors. Visit **macmillanhighered .com/teachingcentral.**

　　Bits collects creative ideas for teaching a range of composition topics in an easily searchable blog format. A community of teachers—leading scholars, authors, and editors—discuss revision, research, grammar and style, technology, peer review, and much more. Take, use, adapt, and pass the ideas around. Then, come back to the site to comment or share your own suggestion. Visit **bedfordbits.com.**

Acknowledgments

The following reviewers were very helpful through several drafts of this book: Patricia Baines, Middle Tennessee State University; Patricia Bonner, North Carolina A&T State University; Jonathan Bradley, Middle Tennessee State University; Bob Brown, Chippewa Valley Technical College; Diana Kaye Campbell, Forsyth Technical Community College; Tricia Capansky, University of Tennessee at Martin; Susan Chism, Greenville College; Cheri Crenshaw, Dixie State University; Linsey Cuti, Kankakee Community College; Jason DePolo, North Carolina A&T State University; Amy Eggert, Bradley University; Bart Ganzert, Forsyth Technical Community College; Carl Gerriets, Century College; Anissa Graham, University of North Alabama; Gary Hafer, Lycoming College; Elizabeth Hope, Delgado Community College; Pamela Kincheloe, Rochester Institute of Technology; Michael Leggs, Saint Paul College; Lila MacLellan, Pace University; Nicholas Mauriello, University of North Alabama; Chanomi Maxwell-Parish, Northern Michigan University; Linda Miller, Middlesex Community College; Gayle Murchison, College of William and Mary; Sein Oh, University of Illinois at Chicago; Sayanti Ganguly Puckett, Johnson County Community College; Christa Raney, University of North Alabama; Jeremy Reed, Central Methodist University; Theodore Rollins, Johnson County Community College; James Sprouse, Piedmont International University; Janette Thompson, University of Nebraska at Kearney; Patrick Tompkins, John Tyler Community College; Jonathan Torres, Front Range Community College; and Justin Williamson, Pearl River Community College.

All textbooks are collaborations, but we have never before worked on a project that more creatively drew upon the resources of an editorial team and publisher. *How to Write Anything* began with the confidence of Joan Feinberg, Director of Digital Composition, that we could develop a groundbreaking brief rhetoric. She had the patience to allow the idea to develop at its own pace and then assembled an incredible team to support it. We are grateful for the contributions of Edwin Hill, Vice President; Karen Henry, Editorial Director; and Leasa Burton, Publisher. We are also indebted to Anna Palchik, Senior Art Director and designer of the text, and Deb Baker, Senior Production Editor. Special thanks to Peter Arkle and Anna Veltfort for their drawings, Christian Wise for his photographs, and to Kate Mayhew for her help with art research. They all deserve credit for the distinctive and accessible visual style of *How to Write Anything*.

For her marketing efforts, we are grateful to the guidance offered by Emily Rowin and, of course, to the efforts of the incomparable Bedford/St. Martin's sales team. And for all manner of tasks, including coordinating permissions and manuscript preparation, we thank Rachel Childs.

Our greatest debt is to Ellen Darion, who was our original editor on this lengthy project and saw this edition through to the completion of its first draft: always confident about what we could accomplish, patient when chapters went off-track, and perpetually good-humored. If *How to Write Anything* works, it is because Ellen never wavered from our high aspirations for the book. Her hand is in every chapter, every choice of reading, and every assignment.

Succeeding Ellen as editor on this latest version, Sarah Macomber joined a project she was well familiar with—having conceived *How to Write Anything*'s much admired visual tutorials. Sarah has given thoughtful attention to every corner of the book, helping to assure that this edition is tight, lively, and imaginative. It has been a pleasure to work with her.

Finally, we are extraordinarily grateful to our former students whose papers or paragraphs appear in *How to Write Anything*. Their writing speaks for itself, but we have been inspired, too, by their personal dedication and character. These are the sort of students who motivate teachers, and so we are very proud to see their work published in *How to Write Anything*: Alysha Behn,

Jordyn Brown, Stefan Casso, Marissa Dahlstrom, Manasi Deshpande, Micah T. Eades, Wade Lamb, Desiree Lopez, Cheryl Lovelady, Shane McNamee, Matthew Nance, Lily Parish, Miles Pequeno, Heidi Rogers, Kanaka Sathasivan, J. Reagan Tankersley, Katelyn Vincent, and Susan Wilcox.

John J. Ruszkiewicz

Jay T. Dolmage

Correlation to the Council of Writing Program Administrators' (WPA) Outcomes Statement

How to Write Anything helps students build proficiency in the five categories of learning that writing programs across the country use to assess their work: rhetorical knowledge; critical thinking, reading, and writing; writing processes; knowledge of conventions; and composing in electronic environments. A detailed correlation follows.

Features of *How to Write Anything: A Guide and Reference,* Third Edition, Correlated to the WPA Outcomes Statement

Note: This chart aligns with the latest WPA Outcomes Statement, ratified in July 2014.

WPA Outcomes	Relevant Features of *How to Write Anything*
Rhetorical Knowledge	
Learn and use key rhetorical concepts through analyzing and composing a variety of texts.	Each assignment chapter in the Guide includes three texts in a wide variety of genres. Questions, headnotes, and "Reading the Genre" prompts encourage students to examine and understand the key rhetorical concepts behind each genre of writing. Writing activities and prompts guide students through composing a range of texts.
Gain experience reading and composing in several genres to understand how genre conventions shape and are shaped by readers' and writers' practices and purposes.	The Introduction provides a foundation for thinking about genre, while each assignment chapter in the Guide offers a thorough look at each genre's conventions and how those conventions have developed and changed, as well as how to apply them to students' own writing situations.
Develop facility in responding to a variety of situations and contexts, calling for purposeful shifts in voice, tone, level of formality, design, medium, and/or structure.	Each assignment chapter in the Guide offers detailed advice on responding to a particular rhetorical situation, from arguing a claim and proposing a solution to writing an e-mail or a résumé.
	See "Choosing a Style and Design" sections in Part 1 chapters, and the " Getting the Details Right" sections in Part 2 chapters for advice on situation-specific style and design.
	Part 5 features chapters on "High, Middle, and Low Style" (32); "Inclusive and Culturally Sensitive Style" (33); and "Vigorous, Clear, Economical Style" (34).
Understand and use a variety of technologies to address a range of audiences.	Chapter 48 covers digital media, including blogs, social networks, Web sites, wikis, podcasts, maps, and videos. Chapter 49 covers creating and using visuals to present data and ideas.
	Each assignment chapter includes at least one visual example of the genre that the chapter focuses on, and several of the reference chapters include Visual Tutorials featuring photographs and illustrations that provide students with step-by-step instructions for challenging topics, such as using the Web to browse for ideas. This emphasis on visuals, media, and design helps students develop visual and technological literacy they can use in their own work.
	Chapter 13 covers e-mail; Chapters 17 and 18 address portfolio and presentation software; and Chapters 38 and 40 cover finding, evaluating, and using print and electronic resources for research.

WPA Outcomes	Relevant Features of *How to Write Anything*
Rhetorical Knowledge (*continued*)	
Match the capacities of different environments (e.g., print and electronic) to varying rhetorical situations.	The text and LaunchPad include a wide range of print and multimodal genres from essays and scholarly articles to photographs, infographics, Web sites, and audio and video presentations. Rhetorical choices that students make in each genre are covered in the Guide chapters and appear in discussions of the writing context and in abundant models in the book.
Critical Thinking, Reading, and Composing	
Use composing and reading for inquiry, learning, thinking, and communicating in various rhetorical contexts.	The assignment chapters in the Guide emphasize the connection between reading and writing a particular genre: Each chapter includes model readings with annotations that address the key features of the genre. Each Part 1 chapter shows students the rhetorical choices they need to consider when writing their own papers in these genres and offers assignments to actively engage them in these choices.
	Chapter 21, "Critical Thinking," explains rhetorical appeals and logical fallacies.
	Reference chapters in Parts 3 through 8 cover invention, reading, writing, research, and design strategies that work across all genres.
Read a diverse range of texts, attending especially to relationships between assertion and evidence, to patterns of organization, to interplay between verbal and nonverbal elements, and how these features function for different audiences and situations.	Each assignment chapter in the Guide includes three texts in a wide variety of genres.
	Each of the Guide chapters also includes sections on understanding audience, creating a structure, finding and developing material (including evidence), and choosing a style and design that best reflect the genre of writing.
	Chapter 20, "Smart Reading," helps students read deeply and "against the grain," while in Chapter 21, "Critical Thinking," students learn about claims, assumptions, and evidence. Chapter 26, "Organization," gives advice on devising a structure for a piece of writing.
Locate and evaluate primary and secondary research materials, including journal articles, essays, books, databases, and informal Internet sources.	Part 7 covers research and sources in depth, with chapters on beginning your research, finding print and online sources, doing field research, evaluating and annotating sources, and documenting sources.

WPA Outcomes	Relevant Features of *How to Write Anything*
Critical Thinking, Reading, and Composing (*continued*)	
Use strategies — such as interpretation, synthesis, response, critique, and design/redesign — to compose texts that integrate the writer's ideas with those from appropriate sources.	Chapters 41 ("Annotating Sources"), 42 ("Paraphrasing Sources"), and 44 ("Incorporating Sources into Your Work") explore a variety of strategies for integrating the writer's ideas with ideas and information from sources. Chapter 12, "Synthesis Papers," shows students how to summarize, compare, and assess the views offered by different sources.
Processes	
Develop a writing project through multiple drafts.	Chapter 35, "Revising Your Own Work," discusses the importance of revising and gives detailed advice on how to approach different types of revision. Targeted cross-references throughout the text help students get the revision help they need when they need it.
Develop flexible strategies for reading, drafting, reviewing, collaboration, revising, rewriting, rereading, and editing.	The Reference's brief, targeted chapters and cross-references lend themselves to a flexible approach to writing process, with an array of strategies for students to choose from whether they're crafting an introduction or preparing to revise a first draft. Genre-specific advice in the Guide chapters helps students tailor each step of the writing process to their writing situation, while process-based chapters in the Reference offer guidance that can be applied to any type of writing.
Use composing processes and tools as a means to discover and reconsider ideas.	Each Part 1 chapter includes two sections that encourage students to use the composing process as a means of discovery. "Deciding to write . . ." covers the reasons a writer might choose a specific form of writing, while "Exploring purpose and topic" prompts students to challenge their own ideas about a subject and write to discover what they think when they look more deeply at it.
Experience the collaborative and social aspects of writing processes.	Several chapters in the Reference send students out into their worlds for advice, information, and feedback. Chapter 22, "Experts," talks about the kinds of experts — such as librarians, instructors, peers, and writing center tutors — that students can call on for help. Chapter 39, "Doing Field Research," discusses the whys and hows of interviewing and observing people as part of the research process. Chapter 36, "Peer Editing," offers advice for helping peers improve their work.
Learn to give and act on productive feedback to works in progress.	Chapter 36, "Peer Editing," encourages students to give specific, helpful advice to peers and think about peer editing in the same way they revise their own work.

WPA Outcomes	Relevant Features of *How to Write Anything*
Processes (*continued*)	
Adapt composing processes for a variety of technologies and modalities.	Chapter 48 focuses on digital media, including blogs, Web sites, wikis, podcasts, maps, and videos.
	Chapter 13 covers e-mail; Chapters 17 and 18 address portfolio and presentation software; and Chapters 38 and 40 cover finding, evaluating, and using print and electronic resources for research.
Reflect on the development of composing practices and how those practices influence their work.	The new Introduction invites students to consider their writing practices and how the choices they make during invention, drafting, research, and revision shape their process and their work.
Knowledge of Conventions	
Develop knowledge of linguistic structures, including grammar, punctuation, and spelling, through practice in composing and revising.	Part 9 (Common Errors) includes chapters on grammar, punctuation, and mechanics, while Chapters 35 and 36 provide editing and proofreading advice. Targeted cross-references throughout the text send students to these chapters as needed.
Understand why genre conventions for structure, paragraphing, tone, and mechanics vary.	Each Part 1 chapter includes a section on choosing style and design to help students understand how their choice of style, structure, tone, and mechanics is shaped by the genre in which they're writing.
Gain experience negotiating variations in genre conventions.	Models of work from several subgenres within the book's main genres show students the variations that exist within the confines of a given genre. In addition, "Reading the Genre" prompts help students identify and understand the genre conventions at work in each selection.
Learn common formats and/or design features for different kinds of texts.	Each assignment chapter in the Guide covers a format specific to the genre covered there; see "Choosing a Style and Design" in the Part 1 chapters and "Getting the Details Right" in the Part 2 chapters.
Explore the concepts of intellectual property (such as fair use and copyright) that motivate documentation conventions.	Chapter 45, "Documenting Sources," helps students understand why documentation is important and what's at stake in properly identifying and citing material used from sources.
Practice applying citation conventions systematically in their own work.	Chapters 46, "MLA Documentation and Format," and 47, "APA Documentation and Format," include detailed guidance for citing sources according to each style's conventions. Visual Tutorials in each chapter help students identify and find the information they need in order to create accurate citations.

Introduction

If a blank page or empty screen scares you, join the club. Even professional writers freeze up when facing new and unfamiliar assignments or intimidating audiences. It's only natural for you to wonder how you'll handle all the tasks you face in school or on the job—the reports, evaluations, personal statements, opinion pieces, reviews, and more. Much more. Even writing you do for pleasure has a learning curve.

So how do you get rolling? Exactly the way experienced authors do, by examining the strategies other writers have used to achieve similar goals for demanding audiences. That's not very creative, you might object. But in fact, it's the way inventive people in many fields operate. They get a feel for the shape and features, structures and strategies, materials and styles of whatever they hope to construct themselves, and then they work from that knowledge to fashion new ideas. They become masters of their *genre*. This book will introduce you to writing by taking exactly the same approach.

Understand Genres of Writing

So what is a *genre*? An old-school definition might describe it as a variety of writing we recognize by its distinctive purpose and features. For instance, a work that fits into the genre of *narrative* usually tells a story and emphasizes characterization, dialogue, and descriptions; a *report* presents reliable facts and information and relies on research and documentation; an *argument* defends a claim with reasons and evidence and uses lots of powerful language and even, sometimes, pulls at your heartstrings. *How To Write Anything* introduces you to these three familiar genres, along with five others you'll run up against throughout your academic and professional life: *evaluations, causal analyses, proposals, literary analyses,* and *rhetorical analyses.*

But if you are expecting simple formulas, templates, and step-by-step instructions for each category, guess again. No one learns to write by filling in blanks because the processes are too complicated. So this book treats genres far more dynamically—as real-life responses to ever-changing writing situations. You'll find that genres aren't arbitrary, inflexible, predictable, or dull. Instead, they change constantly—maybe the better term is *evolve*—to serve the needs of writers *and* readers. (Consider how just in the past few years personal and professional letters have metamorphosed into e-mails, text messages, and tweets.)

Though it still makes sense to draw upon patterns and models that work reliably, that's only half the process of learning to write. First you study what existing genres can teach you (and that's a lot). Then you bend the genres to fit actual assignments you get and, just as important, the kind of work you'd like to do on your own. You figure out what to say within a genre, tailor those concepts to the people you hope to influence, organize your ideas strategically, and state them powerfully in appropriate media—including visual, oral, and online formats. That's what Part 1 of *How to Write Anything* is about. It walks you through the full range of choices you face in making genres work for you—and not the other way around.

It might help to think of genres as shortcuts to success. When you learn a new genre, you don't necessarily acquire a hard-and-fast set of rules for writing; instead, you gain control over that genre's *possibilities*. Who knows where those insights might take you?

Connect Purpose to Subgenres

But let's step back a moment and think about the "specific assignments" you'll be facing, especially in school. One of the first matters to settle is always the aim or purpose of a given paper, and it is rarely just *to write* or even to compose open-ended narratives, reports, or arguments. Instead, you'll be asked or required to compose projects so narrowly focused that they actually turn broad *genres* into *subgenres*. A subgenre is simply a specialized version of a genre, one that adapts its general principles to immediate purposes: For example, you need to tell a good story to talk yourself out of an expensive parking ticket or into an honors program.

To put it more formally, you won't ordinarily compose a nonspecific report; you'll write a history term paper detailing some aspect of the Cuban Missile Crisis or a newspaper column explaining NCAA recruitment policies. You won't do a causal analysis for the exercise; you'll write a topic proposal to determine the feasibility of a thesis idea. You won't argue just for the fun of it; you'll dash off an editorial to persuade student government to fix its election code. In effect, you are encouraged to modify a genre to fit your more immediate needs. And that's a good thing.

Why? Because you can base your work in subgenres on very specific models readily available in print and online—they're materials you read and work with every day. In *How to Write Anything*, for instance, the chapter on "Evaluations" presents basic strategies for making smart judgments about people and things, explaining in detail how to establish and apply criteria of evaluation and how to present the evidence you collect. Fair enough.

But your purpose in preparing (or even reading) evaluations will often be much more focused. You'll want to know whether a restaurant is worth your dollar, a book is smart and challenging, a school program up-to-snuff academically. So you'll likely consult book, restaurant, or program reviews you've come to regard as trustworthy, probably because of how well they handle criteria of evaluation and evidence. Once you know how a genre works, you'll appreciate how its subgenres refine those moves. Suddenly, your task as a writer is easier because knowing a genre gives you a method and vocabulary for dealing with all its subgenres—and appreciating how they operate.

Subgenres, then, work the same way as genres, presenting an array of specific features and strategies for you to emulate and modify. You'll find connections between genre and subgenres throughout *How to Write Anything*. Each of the major readings in Part 1 is identified by a subgenre, and all the major writing assignments suggest that you take one of the items as a pattern to help you with a project of your own. Part 2 "Special Assignments" is entirely about subgenres crucial to people in school or entering the job market—items such as essay examinations, résumés, personal statements, and oral reports. In this section, you'll clearly see how practical and action-oriented subgenres can be. At the end of this introduction, you'll find a list of the genres and subgenres covered in *How to Write Anything*.

Choose Audiences

Remember the claim that genres serve the needs of writers *and* demanding audiences? It's very important. As an analogy, just consider how much you rely on genres to select what movies you will see: *sci-fi films, westerns, action/adventure films, romances* (a.k.a. "chick flicks"), *horror movies,* and so on. You bring expectations to films in these categories based upon your past experiences. You may be satisfied when a movie meets or exceeds your expectations, angry when a work fails to live up to genre standards, and *really* excited when a flick manages to do something new—stretches a genre the way *The Dark Knight* or *Marvel's The Avengers* did.

Readers of *your* work will react the same way, which is why you'll find sections on "Understanding Your Audience" in each of the genre chapters of *How to Write Anything*. Audiences you target with a particular genre will bring specific expectations to your work, based on their understanding of your project. For example, a highly academic genre such as a "literary analysis" usually has a narrower and more demanding readership than, let's say, a movie review you post on a blog. You've got to learn how to make genres work for their typical readers—which means understanding them or at least being aware of what they bring to the table when they read.

But as a writer working in genres, you'll also discover you have the power sometimes to define or summon audiences for your work. You might, for example, decide to write a report on bullying aimed at middle-school students; it would differ significantly from a report on the same topic aimed at parents, wouldn't it? Or you might consider how academic readers might be convinced to take a topic such as zombies in films seriously: What features in your text would signal your serious intentions to them? Your analysis of such choices is exactly what makes writing within genres exciting and challenging.

Manage Structure and Style

How to Write Anything gives as much attention to structure and style as to audience in each of the genre chapters—and for good reason. Like the treatment of audience, these elements can make genres seem familiar and comfortable, or they can stretch their boundaries to breaking, depending entirely on choices you make.

Many subgenres, for example, are rigid in their organization: You wouldn't want to experiment with the structure of a lab report or grant application. Nor would you take chances with the formal style expected in these documents. Get a little funky and you've flunked chemistry or lost your funding. Common sense, you say, and you'd be right.

But other genres have lots of give, and so chapters on these genres suggest how that flexibility creates opportunities for innovation and experimentation. For instance, not all narratives have to move in lockstep from beginning to middle to end, but if you are going to tell a story out of sequence or via flashbacks, there are consequences: You might befuddle some readers and push them away. Or think about the range of style you have in narratives—from descriptions that are elegant and formal to dialogue that tells it like it is. You might even use these choices of style to attract readers you want—that is, people who share your values or taste. Even a genre as sober as evaluation has room for enormous range in structure and style—which we signal in this edition by featuring a satire as one of the models.

Develop Writing Processes

For more than a generation now, writing has been taught in schools as a sequential process. You probably learned it that way, working steadily from finding ideas, developing them, writing a first draft, and proofreading a final one. There's nothing wrong with the model, especially the parts that encourage revision. But in working with genres, you'll discover that writing behaviors grow more complicated. Simply put, there are many processes and pathways to successful composing.

Each chapter in Part 1 of *How to Write Anything* outlines a process for creating a particular genre. Some kinds of writing require intense personal reflection, others send reporters into the field for interviews or into libraries for research, and still others may push you deep inside texts for experiences in close reading. Some genres will develop your skills with media or make you examine the clarity of charts and graphs. Others will have you playing with and repeatedly refining your choice of words.

Because of these individual demands, you'll discover that all the genre chapters in the Guide section of *How to Write Anything* (Parts 1–2) are strategically cross-referenced to supplemental materials in what's called the "Reference" section (Parts 3–9). The reference chapters are designed to support your specific needs as a writer, whatever the genre you might be exploring. If you have a problem with writer's block, you will find detailed advice to get you moving. If a genre assignment pushes you to a library catalog, a reference chapter will explain the tools and resources you'll find there and offer sensible strategies. If you have to document a paper or you've forgotten how to get pronouns to agree with fussy antecedents, you have a place to go. It's worth noting that the reference chapters are, for the most part, written in the same informal style as the rest of the book. So don't ignore them. You might even find stuff there to write about.

Invitation to Write

How to Write Anything was designed and edited to be compact and efficient. But you'll find that it has a personal voice, frank and occasionally humorous. Why? Because yet another textbook lacking style or character probably won't convince you that your own prose should speak to real audiences. And if some chapters operate like reference materials, they still aren't written coldly or dispassionately—not even the section on Common Errors.

   If *How to Write Anything* seems like an oddly ambitious title, maybe it's because learning to write should be a heady enterprise, undertaken with confidence and optimism. Give it a try.

Genres and Subgenres in *How to Write Anything*

Narratives
- Literacy narrative
- Memoir/reflection
- Graphic narrative
- Personal statement

Reports
- Research report
- Feature story
- Infographic
- Essay examination
- Annotated bibliography
- Synthesis paper
- E-mail
- Business letter
- Résumé
- Oral report

Arguments
- Support of a thesis
- Refutation
- Visual argument
- Position paper

Evaluations
- Arts review
- Satire
- Product review
- Parody
- Portfolio review
- Peer review

Causal Analyses
- Causal argument
- Research analysis
- Cultural analysis

Proposals
- Trial balloon
- Manifesto
- Visual proposal
- Topic proposal

Literary Analysis
- Thematic analysis
- Close reading
- Photographs as literary texts

Rhetorical Analysis
- Rhetorical analysis
- Close analysis of an argument
- Film analysis

Contents

guide

Part 1 Genres 2

1 Narratives 4

4   Evaluations   100

8   Rhetorical Analyses   218

11   Annotated Bibliographies   266

12   Synthesis Papers   272

reference

guide

Genres

Need a form you don't see here? Try "Special Assignments," p. 250.

How to start

- Need a **topic**? See page 10.
- Need to choose the right **details**? See page 13.
- Need to **organize the events** in your story? See page 15.

1 Narratives

chronicle events in people's lives

Chances are you've shared bits and pieces of your life story in writing many times. In doing so, you've written personal narratives. *Personal* does not mean that writers of personal narratives are always baring their souls. Instead, it suggests that they are telling stories from an individual perspective, providing details only they could know and insights only they could have.

LITERACY NARRATIVE
To work at the campus writing center, you need to submit a *literacy narrative* detailing your own experiences with writing and language.

MEMOIR/ REFLECTION
You direct your grandparents to a community group that is collecting *memoirs* from local citizens who entered the United States as immigrants.

GRAPHIC NARRATIVE
You want more people to think about bicycling to work, so you create a *visual narrative* about your experiences as an urban cyclist, posting both photographs and videos on a blog.

DECIDING TO WRITE A NARRATIVE. Narratives describe events that people want to share with readers in words or through other media, including photographs, film, songs, cartoons, and more (see the Introduction for more on choosing a genre). These stories may be about family or work experiences, growing up, personal tragedies, relationships, and so on. Expect a narrative you compose to do the following.

Tell a story. In a narrative, something usually happens. Maybe all you do is reflect on a moment when something peculiar caught your attention. Or your story could recount a series of events — the classic road-trip script. Or you might spin a tale complicated enough to resemble a movie plot, with a connected beginning, middle, and end. But your job is always to focus on some action. Otherwise you are rambling.

Introduce characters. They may be people or animals or animate objects, but a story usually needs someone or something for readers to care about. You

Telling stories — sometimes competitively — in clubs and restaurants has become a form of entertainment in cities across the United States. Marvin Joseph/ The Washington Post via Getty Images.

needn't pile on physical descriptions or build elaborate backstories. But you ordinarily need characters with names and interesting relationships who speak believable dialogue. Sometimes that fascinating person is you.

Make a point — usually.   There's usually a reason for writing a narrative. When an insurance agent asks about your recent fender bender, she expects you to explain what happened and how you are involved. Most narratives, however, will be less clinical and more reflective, enabling you to connect with readers creatively — to amuse, enlighten, and, perhaps, even to change them. ○ Some narratives are therapeutic too, helping you confront personal issues or get a weight off your chest.

Report details.   What brings a narrative to life are its details — the colors, shapes, sounds, textures, and other physical impressions that convince people a story is credible and authentic. They prove that you were close enough to an experience to have an insider's perspective and that the story really belongs to you. Don't fall back on clichés.

develop a statement
p. 362

A noteworthy subgenre of narratives explores the processes by which people learn to read or write or acquire other life-changing intellectual skills. In the following selection from a slightly longer piece originally published in the *New York Times* "Writers on Writing" series, contemporary novelist Allegra Goodman reflects on how she learned to overcome the doubts that plague many writers. Her most recent work is *The Cookbook Collector* (2010).

Reading the Genre   As you read the selection, pay attention to the way Goodman uses pronouns, especially *I/me* and *you/your*. To whom is the essay directed? Are there places where Goodman seems to be talking as much to herself as to readers? How does that move add interest to the story?

O.K., You're Not Shakespeare. Now Get Back to Work

ALLEGRA GOODMAN

They say writing is lonely work. But that's an exaggeration. Even alone at their desks, writers entertain visitors: characters of a novel, famous and not so famous figures from the past. On good days, all these come to the table. On bad days, however, only unwelcome visitors appear: The specter of the third-grade teacher who despaired of your penmanship. The ghost of the first person who told you that spelling counts. The voice of reason pointing out that what you are about to attempt has already been done — and done far better than you might even hope.

So why bother? Why even begin? It is, after all, abundantly clear that you are not Henry James. Your themes are hackneyed, your style imitative. As for your emotions, memories, insights, and invented characters, what makes you think anyone will care? These are the perfectly logical questions of the famous, petty, and implacable inner critic.

What should a writer do when the inner critic comes to call? How to silence these disparaging whispers? I have no magic cure, but here, from my own experience, is a modest proposal to combat the fiend.

> Details in the opening paragraphs introduce the general theme of the narrative: a writer's self-doubts.

Forget the past. Nothing stops the creative juices like thoughts of the literary tradition. "You'll never be John Donne!" your inner critic shrieks. Or: "*Middlemarch*! Now that was a book!" These thoughts used to fill me with gloom. Then I went to graduate school at Stanford, and I steeped myself in Shakespeare, Wordsworth, and Defoe. The experience set me free.

It happened like this. I was sitting in Green Library trying to write a story, and I looked at all the shelves of books around me, and suddenly the obvious occurred to me. All the great Romantic poets and Elizabethan playwrights and Victorian novelists that tower over me — they're dead! Oh, they still cast their shadow, but I'm alive, and they are irrefutably dead. Their language is exquisite, their scenes divine, but what have these writers done lately? Not a damn thing. Think about it. The idea should give you hope. Past masters are done. Their achievements are finite, known, measurable. Present writers, on the other hand, live in possibility. Your masterpiece could be just around the corner. Genius could befall you at any moment.

"Well," your inner critic counters gloomily, "just remember that when you're gone, your books will suffer the same fate as all the rest. They'll be relics at best. More likely, they'll just languish in obscurity." To which I have to say: So what? I won't be around to care.

Carpe diem. Know your literary tradition, savor it, steal from it, but when you sit down to write, forget about worshiping greatness and fetishizing masterpieces. If your inner critic continues to plague you with invidious comparisons, scream, "Ancestor worship!" and leave the building.

Treat writing as a sacred act. Just as the inner critic loves to dwell on the past, she delights in worrying about the future. "Who would want to read this?" she demands. "Nobody is going to publish a book like that!" Such nagging can incapacitate unpublished writers. Published writers, on the other hand, know that terrible books come out all the time. They anguish: "The reviewers are going to crucify me, and nobody will want to publish me after that."

But take a step back. What are you really afraid of here? When you come down to it, this is just a case of the inner critic masquerading as public opinion, and playing on your vanity.

I know only one way out of this trap, which is to concentrate on your writing itself, for itself. Figuring out what the public wants, or even what

> The story turns personal and its setting is specific.

> Goodman offers glimpses into her thinking as a writer.

the public is: That's the job of pollsters and publicists and advertisers. All those people study the marketplace. But the creative artist can change the world. A true writer opens people's ears and eyes, not merely playing to the public, but changing minds and lives. This is sacred work. . . .

Ultimately every writer must choose between safety and invention; between life as a literary couch potato and imaginative exercise. You must decide which you like better, the perfectionist within or the flawed pages at hand.

> Goodman's personal reflections lead to advice for would-be writers.

Perhaps you'd rather hold yourself to the impossibly high standards of writers long dead. Or perhaps you'd rather not waste time writing something that will go unpublished, unnoticed, and unread. You have received no encouragement from anyone else, and so you would never think of encouraging yourself. Or you choose to be a realist. You're smart enough to see your talent is limited, your gift too small to pursue. You can convince yourself of all this, or you can listen to your imagination instead. You can fire yourself up with words and voices. You can look out into the world teeming with stories and cast your net.

Exploring purpose and topic

▶ topic

You don't need to search for a topic when writing a narrative on your own. You know what aspects of your life you want to share on Facebook or in a journal. You also understand your audiences well enough to fit your stories to people likely to read them.

But you face tougher choices when asked to write a narrative for school. Typically, such an assignment invites you to describe an event that has shaped or changed you. Or perhaps an instructor wants a story that explores a dimension of your personality or reveals something about the communities you belong to. When no topic ideas suggest themselves, consider the following strategies.

Brainstorm, freewrite, build lists, and use memory prompts. To find a story worth recounting, pick up a yearbook, scroll through photographs, or browse your social media sites. Talk with others about their choices of subjects and share ideas on a class Web site.

Choose a manageable subject. You might be tempted to focus on life-changing events so dramatic that they can seem clichéd: deaths, graduations, car wrecks, winning hits, or first love. But for such topics to work, you have to make them fresh for readers who've probably undergone similar experiences — or seen the movie. If you can find that novel perspective (maybe a satiric or ironic one), take the risk. ○

Alternatively, try narrating a slice of life rather than the whole side of beef — your toast at a wedding rather than the three-hour reception, a single encounter on a road trip rather than the entire cross-country adventure, or just the scariest part of your encounter with Superstorm Sandy. Most big adventures contain within them dozens of more manageable tales.

A photograph can jog your memory. For example, this picture of Niki de Saint Phalle's sculpture *Sun God* got one student writing about her colorful trip to San Diego, California. *Sun God*, 1983. Concrete structure, paint, 413.4 x 177.2 x 118 inches. Stuart Collection, University of California La Jolla Campus San Diego, California, U.S.A.

get an idea
p. 331

Understanding your audience

People like to read stories, so the audiences for narratives are large, diverse, and receptive. Most of these eager readers probably expect narratives to make some point or reveal an insight. They hope to be moved by what they read, learn something from it, or perhaps be amused by it.

You can capitalize on such expectations, using stories to introduce ideas that readers might be less eager to entertain if presented more formally. As Zadie Smith puts it, "A writer hopes to make connections where the lazy eye sees only a chasm of difference." Women and members of outsider groups have long used narratives to document the adversities they face and to affirm their solidarity. But good stories also cross boundaries and win sympathetic readers from well outside the original target audience.

Of course, you might sometimes decide that the target audience of a narrative is really yourself: You can write about personal experiences to get a handle on them. Even then, be demanding. Think about how your story might sound ten or twenty years from now. Whatever the audience, you have choices to make.

Focus on people.   They are what readers care about, so give them names and define their relationships. But don't slow the action to characterize or describe them. Let your readers figure out the people you are presenting through what they do and say.

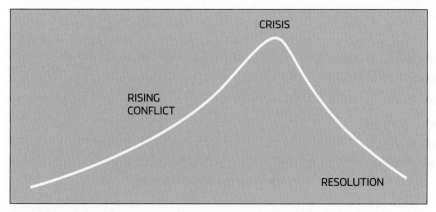

A Classic Narrative Arc   You'll need to decide where to start your story and where to stop. The plan shown in this illustration is effective because the action unfolds in a way that meets audience expectations.

Select events that will keep readers engaged.   Which events represent high points in the action or moments that could not logically be omitted? Which are the most intriguing and entertaining? Focus on these and consider cutting the others. Build toward a few major events in the story that support one or two key themes.

Pace the story.   After a brisk start, slow the narrative to fill in necessary details about characters and set up expectations for what will follow. If a person plays a role later in the story, introduce him or her briefly in the early paragraphs. If a cat matters, mention the cat. But don't dwell on incidentals: Keep the story moving.

Adjust your writing to appeal to the intended readers.   Here, for example, is a serious anecdote offered in an application to graduate school.

> During my third year of Russian, I auditioned for the role of the evil stepsister Anna in a stage production of *Zolushka*. Although I welcomed the chance to act, I was terrified because I could not pronounce a Russian *r*. I had tried but was only able to produce an embarrassing sputter. Leading up to the play, I practiced daily with my professor, repeating "ryba" with a pencil in my mouth. When the play opened, I was able to say *"Kakoe urodstvo!"* with confidence. I had discovered the power to isolate a problem, seek the necessary help, and ultimately solve it. Now I want to pass this power along to others by becoming a Russian language instructor.
>
> — Melissa Miller

But can you imagine Melissa describing her problems with the Russian *r* differently to her peers, maybe even comically? Such an adjustment would only be natural. And it's the kind of shift you have to learn to make as well.

A narrative you write for academic readers might need to be as sober and deliberate as Melissa's statement, and when writing it you might have to keep a tight rein on how you present your life. ○ But don't be too cautious. Any story has to have enough grit to make your experiences seem authentic. So pay close attention to how your instructor defines the audience you are supposed to address in a narrative assignment. If need be, ask questions.

refine your tone
p. 400

Finding and developing materials

When you write about an event soon after it occurs — for instance, in an accident report for an insurance claim — you have the facts fresh in your mind. Yet even in such cases, evidence helps back up your recollections. That's why insurance companies encourage drivers to carry a camera in their cars in case they have a collision. The photo freezes details that human memory, especially under pressure, could ignore or forget. Needless to say, when writing about events in the more distant past, other aids to memory help.

Consult documents. A journal, if you keep one, will be full of narrative possibilities. But even a daily planner or electronic calendar might hold the facts needed to reconstruct a sequence of events: Just knowing when important meetings occurred may refresh your memory.

Consult images. Not only do photographs and videos document people and places, but they may also generate ideas for personal narratives. Such prompts may revive past events and the feelings they stir up too. Visual images also remind you of physical details — locales, clothing, hairstyles — that can add authenticity to a narrative.

Talk to the people involved. A phone call home or a posting on social media might bring a wealth of information. Family and friends might remember details of a story you've forgotten (or suppressed.) They might also see events from a perspective you haven't considered.

Trust your experiences. Assigned a narrative, lots of people wonder, "What have I done worth writing about"? ○ They underestimate the quality of their own experiences. College students, for example, are incredibly knowledgeable

develop ◄
details

Photographs such as this one taken at a Fourth of July parade may help you recall not only the scene but also the moment the photo was taken, who was there, and so on. © The Orange County Register/ZUMAPress.com.

find a topic
p. 331

about high school or the local music scene or working minimum-wage jobs or dealing with narrow-minded parents. You don't have to be a salaried professional to observe life or have something to say about it.

Here's humorist David Sedaris — who has made a career writing about his very middle-class life from his unique personal perspective — describing the insecurity of many writers:

> When I was teaching — I taught for a while — my students would write as if they were raised by wolves. Or raised on the streets. They were middle-class kids and they were ashamed of their background. They felt like unless they grew up in poverty, they had nothing to write about. Which was interesting because I had always thought that poor people were the ones who were ashamed. But it's not. It's middle-class people who are ashamed of their lives. And it doesn't really matter what your life was like, you can write about anything. It's just the writing of it that is the challenge. I felt sorry for these kids, that they thought that their whole past was absolutely worthless because it was less than remarkable.

— David Sedaris, interviewed in *January Magazine*, June 2000

If every picture tells a story, what narrative does this image suggest? Consider the missing windmill blade, the worker's posture, the quiet sky, and any other details that seem important.
John J. Ruszkiewicz.

Creating a structure

Don't be intimidated by the prospect of organizing a narrative. ○ You know a lot about narrative structure from reading books or watching films or TV. Many of the plot devices there — from foreshadowing to flashback — can be adapted to stories you write. But you need to plan ahead, know how much space you have to tell a story, and then connect the incidents in your narrative with transitional devices.

organize ◄ events

Consider a simple sequence. It's a natural choice when one event follows another chronologically. Journals and diaries may have the most bare-bones sequential structures, with writers connecting one event to another by little more than a date.

> First event
>
> Next event
>
> Next event
>
> Final event

Build toward a climax. Narratives become more complicated when you present a series of incidents that lead to a *climax* or an *epiphany*. Readers usually expect one or the other in a personal narrative. A climax is the moment when the action of a story peaks, takes an important turn, or is resolved: The criminal gets caught. An epiphany is a moment of revelation or insight when a writer or character suddenly sees events in a new way: The detective realizes that he's not much different from the felon.

> First event
>
> Next event
>
> Next event
>
> Climax and/or epiphany
>
> Final event

Narratives often have both a climax and an epiphany — it's only logical for major events in life to trigger heightened awareness or illumination. To organize a story this way, decide what the pivotal event of the story will be and then figure out what elements lead up to or explain it. Delete all actions, characters, descriptions, or passages of dialogue that don't contribute to that point, however much you love them. ○ Or refocus your narrative on a moment that you do love.

connect ideas
p. 387

revise and edit
p. 422

Choosing a style and design

Narratives are usually written in approachable middle or low styles because they nicely mimic the human voice through devices such as contractions and dialogue. Both styles are also comfortable with *I*, the point of view of many stories. A middle style may be perfect for reaching academic or professional audiences. But a low style, dipping into slang and unconventional speech, may sometimes feel more authentic to more general readers. It's your choice.

Style is important because narratives get their energy and textures from sentence structures and vocabulary choices. Narratives require tight but expressive language — *tight* to keep the action moving, *expressive* to capture the gist of events. In a first draft, run with your ideas and don't do much editing. Flesh out the story as you have designed it and then go back to see if it works technically: Characters should be introduced, locations identified and colored, events clearly explained and sequenced, key points made memorably and emphatically. You'll need several drafts to get these key elements into shape.

Then look to your language and allow plenty of time to revise it. Begin with Chapter 34, "Vigorous, Clear, Economical Style." Here are some options for your narrative.

Don't hesitate to use first person — *I*. Most personal narratives are about the writer, so first-person pronouns are used without apology. ○ A narrative often must take readers where the *I* has been, and using the first-person pronoun helps make writing authentic. Consider online journalist Michael Yon's explanation of why he reported on the Iraq War using *I* rather than a more objective third-person perspective:

> I write in first person because I am actually there at the events I write about. When I write about the bombs exploding, or the smell of blood, or the bullets snapping by, and I say *I*, it's because I was there. Yesterday a sniper shot at us, and seven of my neighbors were injured by a large bomb. These are my neighbors. These are soldiers. . . . I feel the fire from the explosions, and am lucky, very lucky, still to be alive. Everything here is first person.
>
> — From Glenn Reynolds, *An Army of Davids*

And yet don't count out telling a story from a third-person point of view, even when you are writing about yourself. You may find it bracing to present yourself as someone else might see you.

define your style
p. 400

Use figures of speech such as similes, metaphors, and analogies to make memorable comparisons.   *Similes* make comparisons by using *like* or as: *He used his camera like a rifle. Metaphors* drop the *like* or *as* to gain even more power: *His camera was a rifle aimed at enemies.* An *analogy* extends the comparison: *His camera became a rifle aimed at his imaginary enemies, their private lives in his crosshairs.*

People make comparisons habitually. Some are so common they've been reduced to invisible clichés: *hit me like a ton of bricks; dumb as an ox; clear as a bell.* In your own narratives, you want similes and metaphors fresher than these and yet not contrived or strained. Here's science writer Michael Chorost effortlessly deploying both a metaphor (*spins up*) and a simile (*like riding a roller coaster*) to describe what he experiences as he awaits surgery.

> I can feel the bustle and clatter around me as the surgical team spins up to take-off speed. It is like riding a roller coaster upward to the first great plunge, strapped in and committed.
>
> — *Rebuilt: How Becoming Part Computer Made Me More Human*

In choosing verbs, favor active rather than passive voice.   Active verbs propel the action (*Estela signed the petition*), while passive verbs slow it down by an unneeded word or two (*The petition was signed by Estela*). ○

Since narratives are all about movement, build sentences around strong verbs that do things. Edit until you get down to the nub of the action. You will produce sentences as effortless as these from Joseph Epstein, describing the pleasures of catching plagiarists. ○ Verbs are highlighted in this passage; only one (*is followed*) is passive.

> In thirty years of teaching university students I never encountered a case of plagiarism, or even one that I suspected. Teachers I've known who have caught students in this sad act report that the capture gives one an odd sense of power. The power derives from the authority that resides behind the word *gotcha.* This is followed by that awful moment — a veritable sadist's Mardi Gras — when one calls the student into one's office and points out the odd coincidence that he seems to have written about existentialism in precisely the same words Jean-Paul Sartre used fifty-two years earlier.
>
> — "Plagiary, It's Crawling All Over Me," *Weekly Standard,* March 6, 2006

Need help seeing the big picture? See "How to Revise Your Work" on pp. 426–27.

improve your sentences p. 412

avoid plagiarism p. 466

> The difference between the almost right word and the right word is really a large matter — it's the difference between the lightning bug and the lightning.

—Mark Twain

Library of Congress, Prints and Photographs Division, LC-USZ62-5513.

Keep the language simple.   Your language need not be elaborate when it is fresh and authentic. Look for concrete expressions that help readers visualize a scene. And when it comes to modifiers, one strong word is usually better than several weaker ones (*freezing* rather than *very cold*; *doltish* rather than *not very bright*). In the paragraph below from a narrative about telling ghost stories, notice how simple items clearly detailed (oil lamp, soft blankets, *pan dulce*) draw you into the scene.

> When we tell scary stories, we're usually in the half-light of an old oil lamp that my Tío Fernando brings out from the storage room in back. Its flame flickers on the walls — creating dancing shadows — and the smell of oil permeates the room. We pass soft blankets around to cuddle beneath and keep terrors at bay. Snacks are set on the kitchen table for us to munch on: chips with spicy hot sauce, *pan dulce*, leftover *burritos de chile colorado* from earlier in the day. We make ourselves comfortable and settle in for a long night — one full of chills that will likely give us nightmares.
>
> — Alexandra Rayo, "The Thrill of Terror"

Develop major characters through action and dialogue.   It's usually better to portray people via their words and actions than through static descriptions: The mantra is, *show, don't tell*. Remember it! If a character is conceited or cheap, let readers see him glancing in mirrors or heading to the restroom as the lunch bill arrives.

You can also bring people to life in a story by what they say — and without much commentary from you. Just be sure your characters' lines sound natural, following the advice of author John Steinbeck: "If you are using dialogue — say it aloud as you write it. Only then will it have the sound of speech." Avoid using dialogue to explain complicated plot points. No one believes it when characters plunge into detailed (and perfectly grammatical) passages of exposition: "Oh look, the house is in flames and here comes the first of several emergency vehicles!" *No* dialogue is better than awkward dialogue.

The following is a selection from a personal narrative about a student's trip to South Africa that artfully melds precise observation, deft characterization, and believable dialogue. Note, too, how the use of the present tense makes the moment seem immediate and dramatic.

At last we arrive at the Ikageng Itereleng AIDS Ministry center, a sanctuary that emerges from a cloud of dust. It is an organization run by Carol Dyanti. She is everyone's mama, a hero to her community. From her modest building she passes out food, clothing, and school supplies to families in need. But all the families are in need. I watch as Carol embraces two bashful young women with their gazes fixed downward. She sends them away with a gallon of cooking oil and a sack of corn meal for *mieliepap*.

Carol turns to us and offers the same loving hugs.

"Those two," she tells me, "they're sisters, twelve and fourteen. They live alone now because their parents abandoned them. They can't even go to school because they must work now."

I watch them walk away. They have no smiles, no girlish giggles, or sisterly quarrels. They walk slowly, bent against a crisp winter wind.

Carol runs her organization from donations of both supplies and money from outreach groups. Some groups are local, but most are from Western countries. Oprah Winfrey, for example, has given money and vans to help Ikageng Itereleng.

"But see, she just comes in and gives money — there is no thought behind it," Carol tells me. "Sometimes we don't see any of it because of how poorly everything is managed. She is a wonderful lady, but . . ." Carol pauses. "She only sees what she wants to see. And that doesn't help us much."

— Lily Parish, "Sala Kahle, South Africa," 2013

For the record, dialogue ordinarily requires quotation marks and new paragraphs for each change of speaker. And keep the tags simple: You don't have to vary much from *he said* or *she said*.

Your Turn Good dialogue is hard to write. So practice. Write a one-page story mostly in dialogue. Tell readers what you must about your characters, but let most of the action occur within their words. Then read your story aloud over and over and revise it until the dialogue sounds authentic. Get feedback from your classmates and give them suggestions on their stories as well.

Develop the setting to set the context and mood.   Show readers where and when events are occurring if the setting makes a difference — and most of the time it will. Location (Times Square; dusty street in Gallup, New Mexico; your bedroom), as well as climate and time of day (cool dawn, exotic dusk, broiling afternoon), will help readers get a fix on the story. But don't churn out paragraphs of description just for their own sake; readers will skate right over them. ○

Use images to tell a story.   Consider the ways photos attached to a narrative might help readers grasp the setting and situation. More complex stories about your life or community can be told by combining your words and pictures in photo-essays or other media environments. ○ Or use images simply to illustrate a sequence of events. An illustrated timeline is a simple form of this sort of narrative, as are scrapbooks or high school yearbooks.

Fisherman with His Catch, a 32-Inch, 18-Pound Striped Bass Note how the photograph conveys far more than the statistics alone would. Courtesy of Sid Darion.

develop a draft
p. 367

think visually
p. 557

Examining models

MEMOIR/REFLECTION In the following essay, Miles Pequeno uses a narrative about a chess match to describe a changing relationship with his father and preserve an important memory. He wrote this paper in response to an assignment in an upper-division college writing class.

Reading the Genre An epiphany is a sudden moment of insight that may occur at some moment in a personal narrative, often in the conclusion. Would you describe Pequeno's final paragraph as an epiphany? Does it seem like an appropriate ending for the piece?

Pequeno 1

Miles Pequeno

Professor Mitchell

English 102

May 12, 20--

Check. Mate?

"Checkmate! Right? You can't move him anywhere, right? I got you again!" I couldn't control my glee. For good measure, I even grabbed my rook, which stood next to his king, and gave him a posthumous beating. The deposed king tumbled from the round table and onto the hardwood floor with a thud. The sound of sure victory. Being eight, it was easy to get excited about chess. It gave me not only at least a few minutes of Dad's attention and approval, but the comfort of knowing I'd taste victory every time. Either Dad was letting me always win, or I was the prodigy he wanted me to be. I always liked to believe it was the latter.

The relationship I had with my father was always complicated. I loved him and he loved me; that much was

> Narrative opens with dialogue and action.

For an additional reading, see **macmillanhighered.com/howtowrite3e**.
e-readings › Katerina Cizek, *Out My Window* [MULTIMEDIA DOCUMENTARY]

21

Pequeno 2

Uses particular details to explain relationship with father.

understood. But his idea of fatherhood was a little unorthodox (or maybe too orthodox, I'm not sure which). We didn't play catch in the yard, but he did make flash cards to teach me my multiplication tables when I was still in kindergarten. He didn't take me to Astros games, but he made sure I knew lots of big words from the newspaper. We were close, but only on his terms.

Using first person, Pequeno draws on personal experience to describe and characterize his father.

Save for the ever-graying hair near his temples, he looks much the same now as he did when I was little: round belly, round face, and big brown eyes that pierced while they silently observed and inwardly critiqued. His black hair, coarse and thick, and day-or-two-old beard usually gave away his heritage. He came to our suburb of Houston from Mexico when he was a toddler, learned English watching Spider-Man cartoons, and has since spent his life catching up, constantly working at moving up in the world. Even more was expected of me, the extension of his hard work and dreams for the future. I had no idea at the time, but back when I was beating him at chess as a kid, I myself was a pawn. He was planning something.

Then a funny thing happened. After winning every game since age eight, the five-year winning streak ended. I lost. This time, Dad had decided to take off the training wheels. Just as he was thrust into the real world unceremoniously with my birth when he was but eighteen years old, I was forced to grow up a little early too. The message was clear: Nothing is being handed to you anymore, Son.

Notice how a metaphor here (training wheels) blossoms into an analogy about growing up.

Pequeno 3

This abrupt lesson changed my outlook. I no longer wanted to make Dad proud; I wanted to equal or better him. I'd been conditioned to seek his attention and approval, and then the rug was pulled from beneath my feet. I awoke to the realization that it was now my job to prove that the student could become the teacher.

I spent time after school every day playing chess against the artificial intelligence of my little Windows 95 computer. I knew what problems I had to correct because Dad was sure to point them out in the days after forcing that first loss. I had trouble using my queen. Dad always either knocked her out early or made me too afraid to put her in play. The result was my king slaughtered time and time again as his bride, the queen, sat idle on the far side of the board.

Our chess set was made of marble, with green and white hand-carved pieces sitting atop the thick, round board. Dad kept the set next to the TV and, most nights, we'd take it down from the entertainment center and put it on the coffee table in front of the sofa, where we sat side by side and played chess while halfway paying attention to the television. One night after Mom's spaghetti dinner, I casually walked into the living room to find Dad sitting sipping a Corona and watching the Rockets game. Hakeem Olajuwon was having a great night. Usually, if Dad was really into something on TV, we'd go our separate ways and maybe play later. This night, I picked up the remote control from the coffee table. Off.

Provides background information that is important later in story.

Paragraph sets the physical scene for climactic chess match.

Pequeno 4

First dialogue since opening signals rising action.

"Let's play," I said resolutely. I grabbed the marble chess set, with all the pieces exactly where I had put them in anticipation of this game. The board seemed heavier than usual as I carried it to the coffee table. I sat down next to him on the sofa and stared at the pieces, suddenly going blank. The bishops might as well have been knights. I froze as Dad asked me what color I wanted. Traditionally, this had been merely a formality. I'd always picked white before because I wanted to have the first move. That was the rule: *White moves first, green next*.

"Green."

Then it all came back to me. The certainty of my declaration surprised him. He furrowed his brows slightly and leaned back just enough to show good-natured condescension.

"You sure? That means I go first."

"I'm sure. Take white."

So he began his attack. He started off controlling one side of the board, slowly advancing. The knights led the charge, with the pawns waiting in the wings to form an impenetrable wall around the royal family, who remained in their little castle of two adjacent spaces.

Every move was made with painful precision. Now and then after my moves, he'd sigh and sink a little into the sofa. He'd furrow those big black brows, his eyes darting quickly from one side of the board to the other, thinking two or three moves ahead. Some of his mannerisms this time were completely new, like the hesitation of his hand as he'd reach for a piece and then

"Combat" metaphor in next few paragraphs moves story forward.

Pequeno 5

jerk it back quickly, realizing that my strategy had shut more than a few doors for him.

Eventually I worked up the courage to thrust the queen into action. She moved with great trepidation at first, never attacking, merely sneaking down the board. In the meantime, Dad's advancing rooks and knights were taking out my line of pawns, which I'd foolishly put too far into play. Every risk either of us took was clearly calculated. Sometimes he'd mutter to himself, slowly realizing this game wasn't as usual.

Things were looking good. Even if I didn't win, I'd already won a victory by challenging him. But that wasn't what I had practiced for. It wasn't why I'd turned off the television, and it certainly wasn't why I was concentrating so hard on these white and green figurines.

I was locked in. This was more than father and son. This was an epic battle between generals who knew each other well enough to keep the other at bay. But I was advancing. Sure, there were losses, but that was the cost of war. I had a mission.

My queen finally reached his king unharmed.

"Check."

I uttered the word silently. As the game had progressed, gaining intensity and meaning, there was no conversation. In its place were sporadic comments, muttered with deference. So when I said "check," I made sure not to make a big deal of it. I said it quietly, softly. I didn't want to jinx myself with bragging, and I certainly didn't want to get too excited and break my own

Another extended analogy.

Pequeno 6

concentration. As his king scrambled for a safe hiding place, my knights continued their advance. I had planned for this stage of the game several moves before, which was apparently at least one move more than Dad was thinking ahead. Check again. More scrambling, and another check. It seemed I had him cornered. Then . . .

"Check." It wasn't the first time I had him in check, and I didn't expect it to be the last in this game.

"Mate," he whispered, faint hints of a smile beginning to show on the corners of his mouth, pushing his cheeks up slightly. I hadn't realized that I had won until he conceded defeat with that word. Raising his eyebrows, he leaned back into the cushion of the sofa. He looked a little tired.

"Mate?" I wasn't sure he was right. I didn't let myself believe it until I stared at these little marble men. Sure enough, his desperate king was cornered.

"Good game, Son."

And that was it. There was his approval right there, manifesting itself in that smile that said "I love you" and "you sneaky son of a bitch" at the same time. But I didn't feel like any more of a man than I had an hour before. In fact, I felt a little hollow. So I just kept my seat next to him, picked up the remote control again, and watched the Rockets finish off the Mavericks. Business as usual after that. I went back to my room and did some homework, but kept the chess game at the forefront of my mind.

> Note that story climax occurs mostly through dialogue.

> Father's smile signals change in father-son relationship.

Pequeno 7

Wait a second. Had he let me win? Damn it, I'd worked so hard just for him to toy with me again, even worse than when he'd let me beat him before. No, there's no way he let me win. Or maybe he did. I don't know.

I walked back into the living room.

"Rematch?"

So we played again, and I lost. It didn't hurt, though. It didn't feel nearly as bad as when he first took off the training wheels. This was a different kind of defeat, and it didn't bother me one bit. I had nothing left to prove. If I'd lost, so what? I'd already shown what I could do.

But what if he'd let me win?

Again, so what? I had made myself a better player than I was before. I didn't need him to pass me a torch. I'd taken the flame myself, like a thirteen-year-old Prometheus. After that night, I was my own man, ready for everything: high school, my first girlfriend, my parents' divorce, my first job, moving away to college, starting a career. I never lost the feeling that I could make everything work if I just chose the right moves. I still live by that principle.

GRAPHIC NARRATIVE (EXCERPT)   In *Persepolis* (2003), Marjane Satrapi uses the medium of the graphic novel to narrate the story of her girlhood in Iran. As she grew up, she witnessed the overthrow of the shah and the Islamic Revolution, and the subsequent war with Iraq. The selection on the following pages describes life under the shah.

Reading the Genre   Describe the specific devices Satrapi uses to tell her story and portray characters. What features does *Persepolis* share with prose narratives? With movies or documentaries?

HE TOOK PHOTOS EVERY DAY. IT WAS STRICTLY FORBIDDEN. HE HAD EVEN BEEN ARRESTED ONCE BUT ESCAPED AT THE LAST MINUTE.

TODAY I WENT TO REY HOSPITAL WITH MY CAMERA.

PEOPLE CAME OUT CARRYING THE BODY OF A YOUNG MAN KILLED BY THE ARMY. HE WAS HONORED LIKE A MARTYR. A CROWD GATHERED TO TAKE HIM TO THE BAHESHTE ZAHRA CEMETERY.

THEN THERE WAS ANOTHER CADAVER, AN OLD MAN CARRIED OUT ON A STRETCHER. THOSE WHO DIDN'T FOLLOW THE FIRST ONE WENT OVER TO THE OLD MAN, SHOUTING REVOLUTIONARY SLOGANS AND CALLING HIM A HERO.

HERE IS ANOTHER MARTYR.

WELL, I WAS TAKING MY PHOTOS WHEN I NOTICED AN OLD WOMAN NEXT TO ME. I UNDERSTOOD THAT SHE WAS THE WIDOW OF THE VICTIM. I HAD SEEN HER LEAVE THE HOSPITAL WITH THE BODY.

PLEASE! STOP IT! STOP IT!

WHAT? WHAT IS IT?

STOP IT!

WHO ARE YOU?

HIS WIDOW!

ARE YOU A ROYALIST?

NO, BUT MY HUSBAND DIED OF CANCER...

Assignments

1. **Literacy Narrative:** After reading Allegra Goodman's "O.K., You're Not Shakespeare. Now Get Back to Work" (p. 7), write a literacy narrative of your own, perhaps recalling how you learned to read or write. Describe books that changed you or any ambitions you might now have to pursue a writing or media career. However, you don't have to be an aspiring writer to make sense of this assignment. Remember that there are many kinds of literacy. The narrative you compose may be about your encounters with paintings, films, music, fashion, architecture, or maybe even video games. Or it may explore any intellectual passion — from mathematics to foreign policy.

2. **Memoir/Reflection:** Using Miles Pequeno's "Check. Mate?" (p. 21) as a model, compose a short narrative describing how an individual (like Pequeno's father) changed your life or made you see the world differently. Give readers a strong sense both of this person and of your relationship to him or her. Make this a paper you might want to keep.

3. **Graphic Narrative:** *Persepolis* (p. 28) demonstrates that a story can be told in various media: This graphic novel even became an animated film in 2007. Using a medium other than words alone, tell a story from your own life or from your community. Draw it, use photographs, craft a collage, create a video, record interviews, or combine other media suited to your nonfiction tale.

4. **Your Choice:** Compose a personal narrative about a subject and for an audience of your choosing. Perhaps you have to prepare a personal statement for a scholarship application or you'd like to turn some blog entries you wrote while traveling in South America into a more coherent tale. You may experiment with media too, combining prose and images in a Web project or trying your hand at creating a photo narrative.

How to start ▶
- Need a **topic**? See page 47.
- Need to **find information**? See page 50.
- Need to **organize that information**?
  See page 52.

2 Reports

provide readers with reliable information

You've been preparing reports since the second grade, when you probably used an encyclopedia to explain why volcanoes erupt or who Franklin Roosevelt was. Today, the reports you write may be more ambitious.

RESEARCH REPORT
You write a *research report* drawing from a music archive on campus to document the influence of two important blues pioneers.

FEATURE STORY
You do a *feature story* on countries that are competing for international attention by building skyscrapers or other signature buildings.

INFOGRAPHIC
You design an *infographic* to present recent data on the gender and ethnic makeup of students graduating from local high schools.

DECIDING TO WRITE A REPORT.   As you might guess, reports make up one of the broadest genres of writing. If you use Google to search the term online, you will turn up an unwieldy 4.6 billion items, opening with dictionary entries and the *Drudge Report* and moving on to sites that cover everything from financial news to morbidity studies. Such sites may not resemble the term papers, presentations, and lab reports you'll prepare for school. But they'll share at least some of the same goals (for more on choosing a genre, see the Introduction).

U.S. ENVIRONMENTAL PROTECTION AGENCY

OFFICE OF INSPECTOR GENERAL

Response to Congressional Inquiry Regarding the EPA's Emergency Order to the Range Resources Gas Drilling Company

Report No. 14-P-0044   December 20, 2013

This report was issued by the EPA's Office of Inspector General, in response to a Congressional inquiry about an EPA emergency order against a gas drilling company. The report includes an "At a Glance" page describing the report's background and results, before the detailed full report, which includes visual aids such as a map and a chemical analysis chart. U.S. Environmental Protection Agency and the Office of the Inspector General/Cover photo: Outside the Range Resources' Butler and Teal hydraulic fracturing well sites. EPA OIG photo.

Present information. People read reports to discover what they don't already know or to confirm what they do. So they'll expect what you offer to be timely and accurate. Sometimes, information you present *will*, in fact, be new (as in *news*), built upon recent events or fresh data. But just as often, your academic reports will repackage research from existing sources. *Are dogs really color-blind?* The answer to such a question is already out there for you to find — if you know where to look.

Find reliable sources. The heart and soul of any report will be reliable sources that provide or confirm information—whether they are "high government officials" quoted anonymously in news stories or scholarly articles listed in the bibliographies of college term papers. If asked to write a report about a topic new to you, immediately plan to do library and online research. O

The information in reports may also come from careful experiments and observations—as would be the case when you prepare a lab report for a biology or chemistry course. Even personal experience may provide material for reports, though observations and anecdotes of this kind usually need corroboration to be convincing.

Aim for objectivity. Writers and institutions (such as newspapers or government agencies) know that they lose credibility when their factual presentations seem incomplete or biased. Of course, smart readers understand that reports on contentious subjects—climate change, energy policy, or health-care reform, for example—may lean one way or another. In fact, you may develop strong opinions based on the research you've done and be inclined to favor certain ideas. But most readers of reports prefer to draw their own conclusions.

Present information clearly. Readers expect material in reports and reference material to be arranged (and perhaps illustrated) for their benefit. O So when you put forward information, state your claims quickly and support them with data. You'll gain no points for surprises, twists, or suspense in a report. In fact, you'll usually give away the game on the first page of most reports by announcing not only your thesis but also perhaps your conclusions.

find a topic
p. 331

think visually
p. 557

When Susan Wilcox received an open-ended assignment to write a report, she responded with a traditionally researched academic essay on a subject important to her, one that she wanted her classmates to learn more about. The essay is formally documented in MLA style.

Reading the Genre Wilcox's report prepared for an academic course draws on a wide range of sources, from personal interviews to books. What impact might this list of sources have on a reader's reception of the report?

Wilcox 1

Susan Wilcox

Professor Longmire

Rhetoric 325M

March 7, 20--

Marathons for Women

Today in America, five women are running. Two of them
live in Minnesota, one in Virginia, and two in Texas. Their
careers are different, their political views are divergent, and
their other hobbies are irrelevant, for it is running that draws
these women together. They are marathoners. Between them,
they are eighteen-time veterans of the 26.2-mile march of
exhaustion and exhilaration.

These five women are not alone; over 205,000 women in the
United States alone ran a marathon in 2010 (RunningUSA). They
sacrifice sleeping late, watching TV, and sometimes even
toenails (lost toenails are a common malady among marathon
runners) for the sake of their sport. Why do these women do this

Opening paragraphs establish a context for a report on women marathon runners, engaging readers.

Wilcox 2

to themselves? Karin Warren explains, "It started out being about losing weight and getting fit again. But I enjoyed running so much—not just how physically fit I felt afterward, but the actual act of running and how it cleared my mind and made me feel better about myself in all aspects of my life—that it became a part of who I am." The other women agree, using words like "conquer," "powerful," and "confident" to describe how running makes them feel.

However, these women know that only a generation ago, marathons weren't considered suitable for women. Tammy Moriearty and Wendy Anderson remember hearing that running could make a woman's uterus fall out; Tammy adds, "It floors me that medical professionals used to believe that." Michelle Gibson says that her friends cautioned her against running when she was pregnant (she ran anyway; it's safe). Naomi Olson has never heard a specific caution, but "lots of people think I am crazy," she says. Female runners, like their male counterparts, do have to maintain adequate nutrition during training (Third Age), but "there are no inherent health risks involved with marathon preparation and participation" (Dilworth). Unfortunately, scientists were not researching running health for women when the marathon was born, and most people thought women were too fragile to run that far. The myth that marathoning is dangerous for women was allowed to fester in the minds of race organizers around the world.

Author uses interviews with runners to define myths about women and marathoning.

Wilcox 3

Legend holds that the original marathon runner, Pheidippides, ran from the Battle of Marathon to Athens to bring news of the Athenian victory over Persia. Pheidippides died of exhaustion after giving the news, and the marathon race today is held in honor of his final journey (Lovett x). Historians doubt all the details of this legend, including that a professional runner in Greece would die after what would have been a relatively short distance for him (x-xi). Nevertheless, the myth remains. When the Olympic Games were revived in Athens in 1896, a race covering Pheidippides's route from Marathon to Athens was scheduled as the final Olympic event (xii). Even though no women were permitted to compete, a Greek woman known as Melpomene arrived on the day of the race, ready to run. Race officials denied her access to the course, so she ran alongside it, eventually finishing an hour and a half after the winner. However, the first woman known to have run the marathon distance was a different Greek woman, Stamatis Rovithi, who ran the course from Marathon to Athens in March of 1896, a few months before the Olympic Games (Lovett 126). Even without proper medical research, these two women were proof that the marathon was not too far for a woman to run.

The occasional woman would run a marathon throughout the first half of the twentieth century (Lovett 126), but never with sufficient fanfare to attract attention to her accomplishment. That changed in 1966, when Roberta Gibb

The report is organized by time and sequence.

Wilcox 4

decided to enter the Boston Marathon. At the time, Gibb would sometimes cover 40 miles on a training run, so she was shocked when her entry was returned with a note informing her that "women [are] not physiologically capable of running 26 miles" (Gibb). Gibb was not put off by such assertions; she hid in the bushes at the starting line and wore her brother's clothes to hide her gender. It was obvious to the men running around her that she was a woman, though, and buoyed by their support, Gibb took off the bulky sweatshirt she was wearing, delighting the crowd who hadn't expected to see a woman running Boston.

By the time Gibb reached the finish, the governor of Massachusetts was there to greet her. *Sports Illustrated* reported of Gibb's achievement, "[The] performance should do much to phase out the old-fashioned notion that a female is too frail for distance running" (Brown). Race officials were less pleased, insisting that Gibb "merely covered the same route as the official race while it was in progress. No girl has ever run in the Boston Marathon" (Brown). The fight was on.

The following year, another woman took on Boston, this time as an official entrant. Kathrine Switzer's coach, like so many others, thought that women couldn't handle the marathon distance (Switzer 49). He had insisted that she prove her ability before he would allow her to enter the race, and once she did so, he also insisted that she be an official registrant to avoid being suspended from collegiate athletics (70). Switzer

Wilcox 5

Officials attempt to remove Kathrine Switzer from the 1967 Boston Marathon. *Source:* Associated Press.

AP photo in the report provides visual evidence.

registered using her initials, not revealing her gender. On the day of the race, once word spread that a woman was running with a race number, officials tried to remove Switzer from the course. Her teammates protected her from the attack in full view of the press truck; once again, a woman running Boston was front-page news (Lovett 127).

Women continued to run Boston unofficially for the next four years, but it was the New York City Marathon that first moved toward equality, allowing women runners for the first time in 1971. In the face of this inclusion by the neighbor race, Boston officials relented and allowed women to enter in 1972 (Run Like a Girl). The Boston Marathon is popular enough to require qualifying times for competitors, so it holds a mystique in the

Wilcox 6

minds of many runners. On any given marathon day, many runners cross the start line hoping to finish in a Boston qualifying time.

Even after the prestigious New York and Boston races accepted women, the fight raged on for a women's Olympic marathon. Other race distances for women were also on the Olympic wish list, and Lovett notes, "Some lobbyists felt that the addition of women's races should be made gradually" (128), a notion that did not sit well with many women who were longing to compete on the world's largest stage. Marathoner Jacqueline Hansen pointed out, "They didn't ask [two-time Olympic marathon gold medalist] Frank Shorter to wait another four years" (Run Like a Girl). After years of lobbying from supporters, including Nike and the now-famous Switzer, the International Olympic Committee agreed. Joan Benoit from Maine launched herself into stardom and gained iconic status when she finished first at the inaugural Olympic marathon in 1984 (Lovett 136).

The evolution of women's running is not over. In September 2011, the governing body of running (the International Association of Athletics Federations, or IAAF) announced that beginning in 2012, women's finishing times can only be considered for world records if they are set in women-only races. The rule is in the interest of fairness: Women running with men have faster competitors to pace themselves with, while men have no such pacers (Associated Press). Runners worldwide reacted with shock, since current women's marathon world record holder

The report champions women runners, though its style generally avoids connotative language.

Wilcox 7

Paula Radcliffe would lose her time of 2:15.25, set at the 2003 London Marathon. That record would now be called a "world best," and the new official record would be shifted to 2:17.42, Radcliffe's time in the 2005 women-only London Marathon (Longman). However, under "the vehemence of protests," the IAAF has insisted that Radcliffe's faster time will be allowed to stand as the world record (Associated Press) and that this rule only applies to future races. The controversy is ongoing, and IAAF has been known to change policy before.

　　Thousands of women run today, competitively and recreationally, at distances ranging from across the front lawn to 100-mile ultramarathons. Our five women all agree that running makes their lives better, no matter what the distance. And they agree on one more thing: No one has ever told any of them that they shouldn't run just because they are women. The fight for running equality was a generation before these women, but they do not fail to be grateful for the benefits. Women run marathons because they can.

Wilcox 8

Works Cited

Anderson, Wendy. Facebook interview. 25 Feb. 2012.

Associated Press. "Paula Radcliffe to Keep Marathon Record."
　　ESPN Olympic Sports. ESPN, 9 Nov. 2011. Web. 19 Feb. 2012.

Wilcox 9

Brown, Gwilym S. "A Game Girl in a Man's Game." *Sports Illustrated*. SI Vault, 2 May 1966. Web. 19 Feb. 2012.

Dilworth, Mark. "Women Running Marathons: Health Risks." *EmpowHER*. EmpowHER Media, 23 Apr. 2010. Web. 19 Feb. 2012.

Gibb, Roberta. "A Run of One's Own." *Running Past*. Running Past, 2011. Web. 19 Feb. 2014.

Gibson, Michelle. Facebook interview. 20 Feb. 2012.

Longman, Jeré. "Still Playing Catch-Up." *New York Times*. New York Times, 5 Nov. 2011. Web. 19 Feb. 2012.

Lovett, Charles C. *Olympic Marathon: A Centennial History of the Games' Most Storied Race*. Westport: Praeger-Greenwood, 1997. Print.

Moriearty, Tammy. Facebook interview. 21 Feb. 2012.

Olson, Naomi. Facebook interview. 21 Feb. 2012.

Run Like a Girl. "History of Women's Distance Running." *Run Like a Girl Film*. Run Like a Girl, n.d. Web. 20 Feb. 2012.

RunningUSA. "RunningUSA's Annual Marathon Report." *RunningUSA*. RunningUSA, 16 Mar. 2011. Web. 19 Feb. 2012.

Switzer, Kathrine. *Marathon Woman: Running the Race to Revolutionize Women's Sports*. New York: Avalon, 2007. Print.

Third Age. "Women Running Marathons: Do Benefits Outweigh Risks?" *Third Age*. Third Age Media, 1 July 2008. Web. 19 Feb. 2012.

Warren, Karin. Facebook interview. 21 Feb. 2012.

Exploring purpose and topic

topic ◀

When you are assigned a report, carefully identify the subgenre (psychology term paper, physics lab report, article for an arts journal) and the kinds of information your report will require. Will your report merely answer a factual question about a topic and deliver basic information? Or are you expected to do a more in-depth study or compare different points of view, as you would in an investigative report? Or might the report deliver information based on your own research or experiments? Consider your various options as you select a topic.

Answer questions.   For this kind of report, include basic facts and, perhaps, an overview of key features, issues, or problems. Think of an encyclopedia entry as a model: Facts are laid out cleanly, usually under a series of headings. The discussions are generally efficient and basic, not exhaustive.

Assigned an informative piece like this, you can choose topics that might otherwise seem overly ambitious. When readers expect an overview, not expertise, you can easily write two or three fact-filled pages on "Atonal Music" or "The Battle of Salamis" by focusing on just a few key figures, events, or concepts. Given a prompt of this sort, consider a topic that introduces you to new ideas or perspectives—providing you this opportunity could, in fact, be an instructor's rationale for such an assignment.

Review what is already known about a subject.   Instructors who ask you to write five- or ten-page reports on specific subjects within a field—for example, to compare banking practices in Japan and the European Union or to describe current trends in museum architecture—doubtless know plenty about those subjects already. They want you to look at the topic in some depth to increase what *you* know. But the subject may also be one evolving rapidly because of current events, technological changes, or ongoing research.

So consider updating an idea introduced in a lecture or textbook: You might be surprised by how much you can add to what an instructor has presented. If workers are striking in Greece again, make that a focal point of your general report on European Union economic policies; if your course covers globalism, consider how a world community made smaller by jet travel complicates the response to epidemic diseases. In considering topics for in-depth reports, you'll find "research guides" especially helpful. ○ You may also want to consult librarians or experts in the field you're writing about. ○

plan a project
p. 436

ask for help
p. 350

Field research is one way to acquire new information. © The Natural History Museum/The Image Works.

Report new knowledge.   Many schools encourage undergraduates to conduct original research in college. In most cases, this work is done under the supervision of an instructor in your major field, and you'll probably choose a topic only after developing expertise in some area. For a sampling of research topics students from different schools have explored, search "undergraduate research journal" on the Web.

If you have trouble finding a subject for a report, try the brainstorming techniques suggested in Chapter 19, both to identify topic ideas and to narrow them to manageable size.

> **Your Turn**   Having trouble finding a fresh topic for a report? Let your curiosity guide you. Make a list of things you'd simply like to know more about within the general area of your topic. If you need prompts, check out HowStuffWorks.com, especially its blogs and podcasts, such as "Stuff You Missed in History Class." You'll see that almost any subject or topic area is filled with interesting nooks and crannies.

Understanding your audience

You know that you should attune any report to its potential readers. Well-informed audiences expect detailed reports that use technical language, but if your potential audience includes a range of readers, from experts to amateurs, design your work to engage them all. Perhaps you can use headings to ease novices through your report while simultaneously signaling to more knowledgeable readers what sections they might skip. ○ Make audience-sensitive moves like this routinely, whenever you are composing.

However, sometimes it's not the content that you must modify for potential readers but their perceptions of you. They'll look at you differently according to the expertise you bring to the project. What are the options?

Suppose you are the expert.   This may be the typical stance of most writers of professional reports, who smoothly present material they know well enough to teach. But knowledgeable people often make two common mistakes in presenting information. Either they assume an audience is as informed as they are, and so omit the very details and helpful transitions that many readers need, or they underestimate the intelligence of their readers and consequently bore them with trivial and unnecessary explanations. ○ Readers want a confident guide but also one who knows when—*and when not*—to define a term, provide a graph, or supply some context.

Suppose you are the novice.   In a typical report for school, you're probably dealing with material relatively new to you. Your expertise on language acquisition in childhood may be only a book chapter and two journal articles thick, but you may still have to write ten pages on the topic to pass a psychology course. Moreover, not only do you have to provide information in a report, but you also have to convince an expert reader—your instructor—that you have earned the credentials to write about this subject.

Suppose you are the peer.   For some reports, your peers may be your primary audience. That's especially true of oral presentations in class. You know that an instructor is watching your presentation and is probably grading the content—including your topic, organization, and sources. But that instructor may also be watching how well you adapt that material to the interests and capabilities of your classmates. ○

> **Tips for Writing Credible Reports**
>
> - Choose a serious subject you know you can research.
> - Model the project on professional reports in that area.
> - Select sources recognized in the field.
> - Document those sources correctly.
> - Use the discipline's technical vocabulary and conventions.

think visually p. 557

respect your readers p. 408

understand oral reports p. 322

Finding and developing materials

▶ find
information

Once you have settled on a research topic and thesis, plan to spend time gathering data. You can start with reference works such as dictionaries and encyclopedias, but you need to move quickly to resources created or used by experts in the field, including scholarly books published by university presses, articles in academic journals, government reports (also known as white papers), oral histories, and so on. Look for materials that push you well beyond what you knew at the outset of the project. Such works may intimidate you at first, but that's a signal that you are learning something new—an outcome your instructor probably intended.

To get reports right, follow these basic principles.

Base reports on the best available sources. You will embarrass yourself quickly if you don't develop procedures and instincts for evaluating sources. Look for materials—including data such as statistics and photographic reproductions—presented by reliable authors and experts and supported by major institutions in government, business, and the media. For academic papers, take your information whenever possible from journals and books published by university presses and professional organizations. O

Need help finding relevant sources? See "How to Browse for Ideas" on pp. 338–39.

With Web materials, track them back to their original sources and then assess them. Use the Google search engine for "Korean War," for instance, and you might find an item that seems generic—except that its URL indicates a military location (.mil). Opening the URL, you discover that a government institution—the Naval Historical Center—supports the site. So its information is likely to be credible but will reflect the perspectives of the Department of the Navy. That's information you need to know as you read material from the site.

Base reports on multiple sources. Don't rely on a limited or biased selection of material. You need not give equal weight to all ideas or points of view, but neither should you ignore important perspectives you disagree with. Above all, avoid the temptation to base a report on a single source, even one that is genuinely excellent. You may find yourself merely paraphrasing the material, not writing a report of your own. O

find reliable
sources p. 451

restate ideas
p. 463

Fact-check your report.   It's a shame to get the big picture in focus in a report and then lose credibility because you slip up on a few easily verifiable facts. In a lengthy project, these errors might seem inevitable or just a nuisance. But misstatements can take on a life of their own and become lore—like the initial and exaggerated reports of crime and mayhem during Hurricane Katrina. So take the extra few minutes required to get the details right.

Some Online Sites for Locating Facts and Information

- **Bartleby.com: Great Books Online** Includes online versions of key reference and literary works, from *Gray's Anatomy* to the *Oxford Shakespeare*.
- **Biography.com** A collection of twenty-five thousand brief biographies, from Julius Caesar to Miley Cyrus.
- **FedStats** *The* site for finding information gathered by the federal government. Also check out USA.gov.
- **Internet Public Library** Provides links to material on most major academic fields and subjects. Includes reference collections as well.
- **The World Factbook** Check here for data about any country—compiled by the CIA.

Creating a structure

▶ organize
 information

How does a report work? Not like a shopping mall—where the escalators and aisles are designed to keep you wandering and buying, deliberately confused. Not like a mystery novel that leads up to an unexpected climax, or even like an argument, which steadily builds in power to a memorable conclusion. Instead, reports lay all their cards on the table right at the start and harbor no secrets. They announce what they intend to do and then do it, providing clear markers all along the way.

Clarity doesn't come easily; it only seems that way when a writer has been successful. You have to know a topic in depth to explain it to others. Then you need to choose a structure that supports what you want to say. Among patterns you might choose for drafting a report are the following, some of which overlap. ○

Organize by date, time, or sequence. Drafting a history report, you may not think twice about arranging your material chronologically: In 1958, the Soviet Union launched *Sputnik*, the first Earth satellite; in 1961, the Soviets launched a cosmonaut into Earth's orbit; in 1969, the United States put two men on the moon. This structure puts information into a relationship readers understand immediately as a competition. You'd still have blanks to fill in with facts and details to tell the story of the race to the moon, but a chronological structure helps readers keep complicated events in perspective.

By presenting a simple sequence of events, you can use time to organize reports involving many kinds of information, from the scores in football games to the movement of stock markets to the flow of blood through the human heart. ○

Organize by magnitude or order of importance. Many reports present their subjects in sequence, ranked from biggest to smallest (or vice versa), most important to least important, most common/frequent to least, and so on. Such structures assume, naturally, that you have already done the research to position the items you expect to present. At first glance, reports of this kind might seem tailored to the popular media: "Ten Best Restaurants in Seattle," "One Hundred Fattest American Cities." But you might also use such a frame-work to report on the disputed causes of a war, the multiple effects of a stock market crash, or even the factors responsible for a disease.

develop a
draft p. 367

shape your
work p. 374

Organize by division.   It's natural to arrange some reports by simply breaking a subject into its major parts. A report on the federal government, for example, might be organized by treating each of its three branches in turn: executive, legislative, and judicial. A report on the Elizabethan stage might examine the individual parts of a typical theater: the "heavens," the balcony, the stage wall, the stage, the pit, and so on. Of course, you'd then have to decide in what order to present the items, perhaps spatially or in order of importance. For example, you might use an illustration to clarify your report, working from top to bottom. Simple but effective.

Organize by classification.   Classification is the division of a group of concepts or items according to specified and consistent principles. Reports organized by classification are easy to set up when you borrow a structure that is already well established—such as those that follow.

- **Psychology** (by type of study): abnormal, clinical, comparative, developmental, educational, industrial, social
- **Plays** (by type): tragedy, comedy, tragicomedy, epic, pastoral, musical
- **Nations** (by form of government): monarchy, oligarchy, democracy, dictatorship
- **Passenger cars** (by engine placement): front engine, mid-engine, rear engine
- **Dogs** (by breed group): sporting, hound, working, terrier, toy, nonsporting, herding

A project becomes more challenging when you try to create a new system — perhaps to classify the various political groups on your campus or to describe the behavior of participants in a psychology experiment. But such inventiveness can be worth the effort.

Organize by position, location, or space.   Organizing a report spatially is a powerful strategy for arranging ideas—even more so today, given the ease with which material can be illustrated. O A map, for example, is a report organized by position and location. But it is only one type of spatial structure.

think visually
p. 557

You use spatial organization in describing a painting from left to right, a building from top to bottom, a cell from nucleus to membrane. A report on medical conditions might be presented most effectively via cutaways that expose different layers of tissues and organs. Or a report on an art exhibition might follow a viewer through a virtual 3-D gallery.

The Swan Theatre
The architectural layout of this Elizabethan theater, shown in this 1596 sketch by Johannes de Witt, might suggest the structure of a report describing the theater.

Organize by definition. Typically, definitions begin by identifying an object by its "genus" and "species" and then listing its distinguishing features, functions, or variations. This useful structure is the pattern behind most entries in dictionaries, encyclopedias, and other reference works. Once the genus and species have been established, you can expand a definition through explanatory details: *Ontario* is a *province of Canada* between Hudson Bay and the Great Lakes. That's a good start, but what are its geographical features, history, products, and major cities—all the things that distinguish it from other provinces? You could write a book, let alone a report, based on this simple structure.

Organize by comparison/contrast. You probably learned this pattern in the fourth grade, but that doesn't make comparison/contrast any less potent for college-level reports. ○ You compare and contrast to highlight distinctions that might otherwise not be readily apparent. Items are often compared one at a time or feature by feature.

The images here compare two important "technologies" for reading, the scroll (below) and the codex (right). For a report contrasting these devices with the electronic screens readers use today, see page 59. *Below:* Museo Archeologico Nazionale, Naples, Italy/De Agostini Picture Library/The Bridgeman Art Library. *Right:* Museo Lazaro Galdiano, Madrid, Spain/The Bridgeman Art Library.

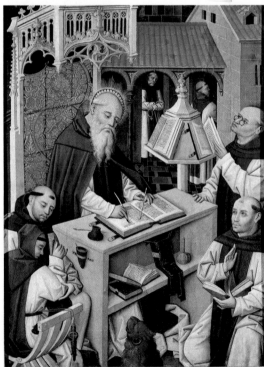

understand
evaluation p. 100

Organize by thesis statement.   Obviously, you have many options for organizing a report; moreover, a single report might use several structural patterns. So it helps if you explain early in a report what its method of organization will be. That idea may be announced in a single thesis sentence, a full paragraph (or section), or even a PowerPoint slide. ○

SENTENCE ANNOUNCES STRUCTURE

In the late thirteenth century, Native Puebloans may have abandoned their cliff dwellings for several related reasons, including an exhaustion of natural resources, political disintegration, and, most likely, a prolonged drought.

— Kendrick Frazier, *People of Chaco: A Canyon and Its Culture*

PARAGRAPH EXPLAINS STRUCTURE

In order to detect a problem in the beginning of life, medical professionals and caregivers must be knowledgeable about normal development and potential warning signs. Research provides this knowledge. In most cases, research also allows for accurate diagnosis and effective intervention. Such is the case with cri du chat syndrome (CDCS), also commonly known as cat cry syndrome.

— Marissa Dahlstrom, "Developmental Disorders: Cri du Chat Syndrome"

develop a
statement p. 362

Choosing a style and design

Reports are typically written in a formal or *high* style—free of contentious language that might make them sound like arguments. ○ To separate fact from opinion, scientific and professional reports usually avoid personal reflections as well as devices such as contractions and dialogue. Reports in newspapers, magazines, and even encyclopedias may be less formal: You might detect a person behind the prose. But the style will still strive for impartiality, signaling that the writer's opinions are (or, at least, *should* be) less important than the facts reported.

Why tone down the emotional, personal, or argumentative temper of the language in reports? It's a matter of audience. The moment readers suspect that you are twisting language to advocate an agenda or moving away from a sober presentation of facts, they will question the accuracy of your report. So review your drafts to see if a word or phrase might be sending the wrong signals to readers. Give your language the appearance of neutrality, balance, and thoughtfulness.

Present the facts cleanly. Get right to the point and answer key questions directly: *Who? What? Where? When? How? Why?* Organize paragraphs around topic sentences so readers know what will follow. Don't go off on tangents. Keep the exposition controlled and focus on data. When you do, the prose will seem coolly efficient and trustworthy.

Keep out of it. Write from a neutral, third-person perspective, avoiding the pronouns *I* and *you*. When perusing a report, readers usually don't care about the writer's personal opinion unless that writer's individual experiences are part of the story. But like all guidelines, this one has exceptions, and it certainly doesn't apply across the board to other genres of writing. Increasingly, even scientific and scholarly reports in some fields allow researchers to explain them-selves directly to readers—as you'll see in a model report on page 59.

Avoid connotative language. Maintaining objectivity is not easy because language is rife with *connotations*—the powerful cultural associations that may surround words, enlarging their meanings and sometimes imposing value judgments. Connotations make *shadowy* and *gloomy* differ from *dark*; *porcine* and *tubby*, from *overweight*. What's more, the connotations of individual words are not the same for every reader. One person may have no problem

define your
style p. 400

with a term like *slums*, but another person living in *low-income housing* may beg to differ.

Given the hotbed of protest that writing can be, don't use loaded words when more neutral terms are available and just as accurate. Choose *confident*, not *overweening* or *pompous*; try *corporate official* rather than *robber baron*—unless, of course, the more colorful term fits the context. O

Pay attention to elements of design.   Clear and effective design is particularly important in reports. O If your paper runs more than a few pages and can be divided into coherent parts, consider inserting headings to help readers appreciate its structure or locate information they need. Documents such as term papers and lab reports may even follow patterns and templates you need to use.

Many types of factual information are best presented graphically. This is especially the case with numbers and statistics. So don't hesitate to use charts, graphs, photos, illustrations, and also captions in your work. Software such as Microsoft Word allows you to create modest tables and simple graphics; you can generate more complex tables and graphs with software such as Excel, OmniGraffle or VectorDesigner. And remember that any visual items should be purposeful, not ornamental.

Many reports these days are, in fact, oral presentations that rely on presentation software such as PowerPoint, Keynote, or Prezi. You'll want to learn how to use these tools effectively.

improve your
sentences p. 412

think visually
p. 557

Examining models

In a lively feature item published in the *New York Times*, Lev Grossman outlines core differences between the three major forms the book has had over the past several millennia. Though an advocate for the familiar paper book — or codex — Grossman does a fascinating job explaining what's been gained and lost with each shift in technology. Arguably, the thesis of this piece is not stated until the final paragraph.

Reading the Genre Reports work especially well when they have "surprise value" — that is, they teach you something new. Take note of any new information you learn from Grossman's feature story. Do these details keep you reading?

From Scroll to Screen

Lev Grossman

In a playful middle style, Grossman quickly identifies the topic.

Something very important and very weird is happening to the book right now: It's shedding its papery corpus and transmigrating into a bodiless digital form, right before our eyes. We're witnessing the bibliographical equivalent of the rapture. If anything we may be lowballing the weirdness of it all.

The last time a change of this magnitude occurred was circa 1450, when Johannes Gutenberg invented movable type. But if you go back further there's a more helpful precedent for what's going on. Starting in the first century AD, Western readers discarded the scroll in favor of the codex — the bound book as we know it today.

Analogies here and throughout help readers understand key ideas.

In the classical world, the scroll was the book format of choice and the state of the art in information technology. Essentially it was a long, rolled-up piece of paper or parchment. To read a scroll you gradually unrolled it, exposing a bit of the text at a time; when you were done you had to roll it back up the right way, not unlike that other obsolete medium, the VHS tape. English is still littered with words left over from the scroll age. The first page of a scroll, which listed information about

---

For an additional reading, see **macmillanhighered.com/howtowrite3e**.
e-readings > UNICEF, *Innovations for Child Health in Uganda* [VIDEO REPORT]

where it was made, was called the "protocol." The reason books are sometimes called volumes is that the root of "volume" is *volvere*, to roll: To read a scroll, you revolved it.

Scrolls were the prestige format, used for important works only: sacred texts, legal documents, history, literature. To compile a shopping list or do their algebra, citizens of the ancient world wrote on wax-covered wooden tablets using the pointy end of a stick called a stylus. Tablets were for disposable text — the stylus also had a flat end, which you used to squash and scrape the wax flat when you were done. At some point someone had the very clever idea of stringing a few tablets together in a bundle. Eventually the bundled tablets were replaced with leaves of parchment and thus, probably, was born the codex. But nobody realized what a good idea it was until a very interesting group of people with some very radical ideas adopted it for their own purposes. Nowadays those people are known as Christians, and they used the codex as a way of distributing the Bible.

One reason the early Christians liked the codex was that it helped differentiate them from the Jews, who kept (and still keep) their sacred text in the form of a scroll. But some very alert early Christian must also have recognized that the codex was a powerful form of information technology — compact, highly portable, and easily concealable. It was also cheap — you could write on both sides of the pages, which saved paper — and it could hold more words than a scroll. The Bible was a long book.

The codex also came with a fringe benefit: It created a very different reading experience. With a codex, for the first time, you could jump to any point in a text instantly, nonlinearly. You could flip back and forth between two pages and even study them both at once. You could cross-check passages and compare them and bookmark them. You could skim if you were bored, and jump back to reread your favorite parts. It was the paper equivalent of random-access memory, and it must have been almost supernaturally empowering. With a scroll you could only trudge through texts the long way, linearly. (Some ancients found temporary fixes for this bug — Suetonius apparently suggested that Julius Caesar created a proto-notebook by stacking sheets of papyrus one on top of another.)

Structure is chronological, augmented by comparisons.

Piece is thick with information.

Over the next few centuries the codex rendered the scroll all but obsolete. In his "Confessions," which dates from the end of the fourth century, St. Augustine famously hears a voice telling him to "pick up and read." He interprets this as a command from God to pick up the Bible, open it at random, and read the first passage he sees. He does so, the scales fall from his eyes, and he becomes a Christian. Then he bookmarks the page. You could never do that with a scroll.

Right now we're avidly road-testing a new format for the book, just as the early Christians did. Over the first quarter of this year e-book sales were up 160 percent. Print sales — codex sales — were down 9 percent. Those are big numbers. But unlike last time it's not a clear-cut case of a superior technology displacing an inferior one. It's more complex than that. It's more about trade-offs.

On the one hand, the e-book is far more compact and portable than the codex, almost absurdly so. E-books are also searchable, and they're green, or greenish anyway (if you want to give yourself nightmares, look up the ecological cost of building a single Kindle). On the other hand the codex requires no batteries, and no electronic display has yet matched the elegance, clarity, and cool matte comfort of a printed page.

But so far the great e-book debate has barely touched on the most important feature that the codex introduced: the nonlinear reading that so impressed St. Augustine. If the fable of the scroll and codex has a moral, this is it. We usually associate digital technology with nonlinearity, the forking paths that Web surfers beat through the Internet's underbrush as they click from link to link. But e-books and nonlinearity don't turn out to be very compatible. Trying to jump from place to place in a long document like a novel is painfully awkward on an e-reader, like trying to play the piano with numb fingers. You either creep through the book incrementally, page by page, or leap wildly from point to point and search term to search term. It's no wonder that the rise of e-reading has revived two words for classical-era reading technologies: scroll and tablet. That's the kind of reading you do in an e-book.

The codex is built for nonlinear reading — not the way a Web surfer does it, aimlessly questing from document to document, but the way a deep reader does it, navigating the network of internal connections that

Transitions carefully mark passage of time.

Note how the paragraph structures an important comparison.

The novel *Cloud Atlas* connects six related stories.

exists within a single rich document like a novel. Indeed, the codex isn't just another format, it's the one for which the novel is optimized. The contemporary novel's dense, layered language took root and grew in the codex, and it demands the kind of navigation that only the codex provides. Imagine trying to negotiate the nested, echoing labyrinth of David Mitchell's *Cloud Atlas* if it were transcribed onto a scroll. It couldn't be done.

Final paragraph reveals the thesis of the report.

    God knows, there was great literature before there was the codex, and should it pass away, there will be great literature after it. But if we stop reading on paper, we should keep in mind what we're sacrificing: that nonlinear experience, which is unique to the codex. You don't get it from any other medium — not movies, or TV, or music, or video games. The codex won out over the scroll because it did what good technologies are supposed to do: It gave readers a power they never had before, power over the flow of their own reading experience. And until I hear God personally say to me, "Boot up and read," I won't be giving it up.

INFOGRAPHIC Infographics are visual reports designed to present data memorably and powerfully. If they do their job well, they can also make convincing arguments. So it should be no surprise that most of the infographics available on the official White House site carry partisan messages (see http://www.whitehouse.gov/share/infographics). Nonetheless, a government-sponsored item such as "Wind Technologies Market Report 2012," reproduced on the following page, can still be rich in basic facts and information—in this case helping readers to appreciate the accomplishments of a rapidly growing industry.

Reading the Genre Study the infographic that follows, paying attention to the way it presents data about growth in the energy sector. Aside from presenting numbers and information, what messages do the designers of the relatively modest chart try to convey? What visual devices do its creators use to emphasize key points about wind energy? Why is it important that "Share on Facebook" and "Share on Twitter" buttons accompany this item when viewed online?

Wind Technologies Market Report 2012

America is home to one of the largest and fastest growing wind markets in the world. Here are a few of the major milestones achieved by the U.S. wind industry in 2012.

THE BIG PICTURE

Total U.S. wind power capacity surpassed 60 gigawatts (GW) -- enough to power more than 15 million homes every year.

RECORD BREAKING GROWTH

U.S. Wind power installations were more than 90% higher than in 2011. With 13.1 GW of new capacity added, the U.S. installed more wind capacity than any other country last year.

BUILT TO LAST

72%

72% of turbine equipment installed at U.S. wind farms -- including blades, gears and generators -- was made in America.

WIND ALL-STARS

TX

IA   KS   SD

Texas added more new wind power capacity than any other state. In South Dakota, Iowa and Kansas, wind power contributes more than 20% of electricity generation.

VIABLE ENERGY

Wind power was the leading source of U.S. electric generating capacity additions in 2012 -- overtaking natural gas.

EVOLVING TECH

Since 1998, average turbine capacity has increased by 170%. Average nameplate capacity of wind turbines installed in 2012 stands at 1.94 megawatts.

JOB CREATOR

The wind sector employs more than 80,000 American workers -- from engineers to construction workers.

PRICING TRENDS

The price of wind sold under new contracts averaged 4 cents per kilowatt-hour -- that's 50% lower than in 2009.

ENERGY.GOV

Infographic by Sarah Gerrity, Courtesy of the U.S. Department of Energy.

Assignments

1. **Research Report:** Susan Wilcox, author of "Marathons for Women" (p. 39), is a runner who turned a subject personally important to her into a fully documented academic paper of general interest. Write a similar factual report based on a serious topic from your major or on a subject you would like more people to know about. Narrow your subject to a specific claim you can explore in several pages. Use trustworthy sources and document them correctly.

2. **Feature Story:** As a novelist and book critic for *Time* magazine, Lev Grossman, the author of "From Scroll to Screen" (p. 59), obviously has an enthusiast's interest in writing about technologies that affect his livelihood. Identify a topic that has a comparable impact on you and write a fact-filled story of interest to general readers modeled upon Grossman's report. It can be from any area of interest, academic or not. Perhaps you wonder how developments in biomedical engineering might alter the sports you love. Or maybe you wonder what exactly a college campus might look like in the age of MOOCs. Do the necessary research and present what you learn to a general audience. Like Grossman, you may use first person in this report and, if you are adventurous, you might try holding off on your thesis or point until the final section or paragraph. Present any sources you use responsibly, mentioning them in the body of the paper or (if your instructor prefers) citing them in traditional academic form — see Susan Wilcox's research report on page 39.

3. **Infographic:** "Wind Technologies Market Report 2012" (p. 64) not only conveys information but also offers a perspective on a new technology. Using a data source such as FedStats, The World Factbook (see p. 51), or SportsStats.com, create a factual report based upon interesting or surprising statistics or information. Be creative, perhaps using statistics pertinent to your local environment or community. You can write a paper, create a slide presentation, or even try your hand at designing an infographic.

4. **Your Choice:** Identify a *controversial* topic you would love to know more about, choosing one that has at least two clearly defined and disputed sides. Do the necessary research to find out much more about the controversy, narrowing the matter down to manageable size for a paper or oral presentation. Then either prepare a written version of the report to submit to your instructor or an oral version to share with a wider audience, perhaps your classmates if you have the opportunity. In your report, explain the controversy *without taking sides*.

How to start

- Need a **topic**? See page 77.
- Need **support for your argument**? See page 83.
- Need to **organize your ideas**? See page 86.

3 Arguments

ask readers to consider debatable ideas

It doesn't take much to spark an argument these days—a casual remark, a political observation, a dumb joke that hurts someone's feelings. Loud voices and angry gestures may follow, leaving observers upset and frustrated. But arguments aren't polarizing or hostile by nature, not when people are more interested in generating light than heat offers them. Arguments should make us smarter and better able to deal with problems in the world. In fact, you probably make such constructive arguments all the time without raising blood pressures, at least not too much.

ARGUMENT TO ADVANCE A THESIS In an op-ed for the local paper, you *argue for the thesis* that people who talk on cell phones while driving are a greater hazard than drunk drivers because they are more numerous and more callous.

REFUTATION ARGUMENT In a term paper, you use facts and logic to *refute the argument* that students with college degrees will probably earn more in their lifetimes than students with only high school diplomas.

VISUAL ARGUMENT Rather than write a letter to the editor about out-of-control salaries for NCAA football coaches, you create a *visual argument*—an editorial cartoon—suggesting that a local coach is paid more than the entire faculty.

DECIDING TO WRITE AN ARGUMENT.   Arguments come in many shapes to serve different purposes. Subsequent chapters in this section cover specialized genres of argument often assigned in the classroom, including *evaluations*, *proposals*, and *literary analyses* (for more on choosing a genre, see the Introduction). But even less formal arguments have distinctive features. In your projects, you'll aim to do the following.

Offer levelheaded and disputable claims.   You won't influence audiences by making points no one cares about. Something consequential should be at stake in an argument you offer for public consumption. Maybe you want to change reader's minds about an issue that everyone else thinks has been settled. Or maybe you want to shore up what people already believe. In either case, you need a well-defined point, either stated or implied, if you hope to influence the kind of readers worth impressing: thoughtful, levelheaded people. ○

What claim does this ad from the Utah Department of Public Safety actually make? Might anyone dispute it? Do you find the ad effective visually? Utah Department of Highway Safety. Creative Director/Art Director: Ryan Anderson, Creative Director/Copywriter: Gary Sume, Account Supervisor: Peggy Lander, Agency Richter7.

develop a
statement p. 362

Offer good reasons to support a claim.   Without evidence and support-ing reasons, a claim is just an assertion—and little better than a shout or a slogan. Slogans do have their appeal in advertising and politics. But they don't become arguments until they are backed by solid reasoning and a paper trail of evidence. No one said writing arguments is easy. Allow time for finding the facts.

Understand opposing claims and points of view.   You won't make a strong case of your own until you can *honestly* paraphrase ○ the logic of those who see matters differently. Many people find that tough to do because it forces them to consider alternative points of view. But you will seem more credible when you acknowledge these other *reasonable* opinions even as you refute them. When you face less than rational claims, rebut them calmly but firmly. Avoid the impulse to respond with an insult or a petty comment of your own.

Frame arguments powerfully—and not in words only.   Sensible opin-ions still have to dress for the occasion: You need the right words and images to move a case forward. ○ Fortunately, strategies for making effective arguments also cue you in to appeals that are less legitimate. We've all been seduced by claims just because they are stylish, hip, or repeated so often that they begin to seem true. But if such persuasion doesn't seem fair or sensible, that's all the more reason to reach for a higher standard in your own appeals.

restate ideas
p. 463

think visually
p. 557

Immediately following a U.S. Supreme Court decision striking down federal prohibitions against same-sex marriage, the *New Yorker* — famous for its memorable covers — added another to its collection. Without a word, the magazine expressed its opinion of the ruling. What elements in the cover make it an argument? How might you phrase the claim it makes visually? © New Yorker Magazine/Jack Hunter/Condé Nast.

Here's an ingenious argument that Stefan Casso, a student in a college writing class, took on as a deliberate challenge: Could he defend a thesis that — to many of his colleagues — seemed indefensible? Aristotle defined rhetoric as the art of discovering all the available means of persuasion in a given case. That's exactly what Casso has to do here. You can decide — or maybe argue — how well he did his job.

Reading the Genre   As you read Casso's essay, try to identify those places where you are most aware of being moved by the author to consider claims that you hadn't considered before or had perhaps already rejected. Can you think of other arguments that Casso might have used to defend Lance Armstrong?

Casso 1

Stefan Casso

Rhetoric 325M

April 30, 2013

Worth the Lie

At age sixty-four, Barbara Grossman was diagnosed with bone marrow cancer. With no family to help her face her upcoming struggles, Barbara was scared. She would presumably spend the remainder of her life alone in a hospital bed without any emotional support. Then, just as she began giving up hope, a ray of light pierced the abyss. In an adjacent hospital room, Barbara had caught a glimpse of a poster depicting Lance Armstrong — a cancer survivor — on his bicycle. She immediately asked for pictures of the athlete to be displayed in her room as well. After months of treatment and countless rounds of chemotherapy, Barbara's cancer went into remission. In a letter

Casso 2

to Armstrong, as reported by ESPN's Brian Triplett, Barbara wrote, "I spent minutes, hours, weeks, and months getting inspiration from your pictures. . . . I was wondering if it would be possible to shake your hand and say thank you personally for the inspiration you gave me in fighting this dreaded disease called cancer!"

> An emotional anecdote sets a context for the argument.

Browsing through a wide range of Lance Armstrong–related articles from early in this century, I discovered Barbara's account is not atypical. I found countless stories of cancer victims expressing gratitude toward Armstrong. Some attribute their recovery entirely to the inspiration they got from his uplifting story. Armstrong, diagnosed with testicular cancer at twenty-five, overcame all odds not only to beat the disease but also to become the greatest cyclist of all time. He soared to the top of his profession, winning seven straight Tours de France — a grueling race spanning twenty-one days and covering two thousand miles. As a result of his amazing performances, Lance Armstrong stole the hearts of millions, including my own, and became a living hero. But as is the case with many people placed high upon a pedestal, he fell back to earth. Hard.

> The author makes a personal connection to the Lance Armstrong story, establishing his credibility or *ethos*.

After a decade of fervently denying the use of performance-enhancing drugs, Armstrong finally admitted on January 17, 2013, that he had used them. Human growth hormone, testosterone, cortisone, and blood transfusions were part of his doping regimen, a common practice for the vast majority of cyclists in

Casso 3

the years Armstrong was competing in the Tour de France. His
defamation suits against former friends like Frankie Andreu, who
testified to hearing Armstrong speak of using banned substances,
and hostile attacks against the U.S. Anti-Doping Agency for its
public suspicions were all just an elaborate charade. One big fat lie.
I'm not here to defend Armstrong's inexplicable cheating. Rules are
rules. But do I believe his lie was worth the subsequent backlash?
In this rare case, does the end justify the means? Absolutely.

Today on lancesupport.org, people are leaving comments of
encouragement for Lance Armstrong. There are pages and
pages of commentaries dated after his admission on January 17.
And many of them had me on the verge of tears. For these
people, Lance Armstrong is not a fraud, he's a hero:

> "Your story gave me hope and gave me confidence that
> cancer can be beat." —Kim
> "Reading your book gave us courage to carry on . . .
> discussing the Tour everyday with Dad kept him going."
> —Sonia
> "I am a cancer survivor and you were giving me
> courage when I needed it most . . . my hero forever."
> — Celou

Comment upon comment tells stories of how Armstrong
delivered hope when all seemed lost. His inspiring example
provided cancer patients with the courage to undergo painful

Casso uses a
series of short
sentences
to make a
controversial
and bold claim.

Casso 4

treatments and the confidence to stay optimistic. It brought
comfort to victims' families, who could dream of a day when their
loved ones, too, could return to strength. His story even illustrated
to people with no connection to cancer how perseverance and
hard work could culminate in dreams. Armstrong had touched
these people's lives, and nothing could now take that away.

In 2007, *USA Today* ranked Lance Armstrong as the eighth
most influential person in the world over the past twenty-five
years—beating the likes of Michael Jordan, Nelson Mandela,
and Pope John Paul II. After he was struck by testicular cancer,
his merely riding a bike around a park would have been
inspirational, so it's clear why winning the Tour de France seven
consecutive times raised him to a rock-star level. If he had
confessed to taking performance-enhancing drugs after his first
win, however, his influence would have been exponentially
smaller. He would have given false hope to his fans and further
diminished cancer victims' dreams of making full recoveries.
People would have been left to look for a hero elsewhere. Maybe
they never would have found him or her. Though it evolved from
his lie, without Armstrong's inspiration, we might have lost
people like Kim, Celou, and Sonia's dad from the disease.

Despite his lies (or maybe because of them), Lance
Armstrong saved lives through his work with the Livestrong
Foundation, launched in 2003. That year marked the fourth Tour

First means of
persuasion is
to cite evidence
that Armstrong
gave hope
to cancer
survivors.

Second line
of argument
is to consider
the possible
consequences
of truth telling
early on.

Casso 5

de France win for Lance Armstrong. This same year he was given the Outstanding Male Athlete Award by the ESPYs, an annual award show hosted by ESPN. Armstrong's fame and influence had reached an all-time high. It marked the perfect time to launch his foundation, which hit the ground running. Millions of dollars poured in, and the Livestrong Foundation quickly became a nationwide institution for cancer information and support.

The Livestrong Foundation "unites, inspires, and empowers people affected by cancer." The foundation provides support to families dealing with the consequences of cancer. Foundation members provide one-on-one dialogue with victims to ensure their attitudes remain strong and positive. Unity, they believe, is the key to fighting the disease. Additionally, the Livestrong Foundation aims at enhancing knowledge about cancer. It hosts numerous awareness-spreading events across the country, resulting in plentiful donations that go directly to cancer research. With total revenue of close to $36 million in 2011, the Livestrong Foundation has established itself as one of the leading cancer-support foundations in the world.

As would have been the case with the inspiration Armstrong offered cancer victims, had he confessed to using banned substances early on in his career, all of this charitable work would have been erased. He simply would not have had the money, prominence, or backing to create Livestrong.

Most fully de-veloped line of argument fo-cuses on legacy of Armstrong's Livestrong Foundation.

Casso 6

Moreover, it is important to note how Armstrong chose to spend his money. He could have easily kept it all, bought himself five beach houses, and tried his luck at becoming a movie star. Instead, Armstrong used his fame and fortune to give back to the community, much as John D. Rockefeller did—a perceived villain in his own time.

In the early 1900s, Rockefeller, owner of Standard Oil, was among the most hated entrepreneurs in America because of his monopolistic business methods. He eventually became the richest man America had ever produced. Like Armstrong, Rockefeller chose to use his riches not only for himself but also for noble purposes. He created the Rockefeller Foundation to promote public heath and the General Education Board to support education in impoverished areas. According to the Rockefeller Archive Center, his charitable donations reached over $540 million. Rockefeller is now remembered as much as a philanthropist as a businessman—and as one of the most respected men in American history. And soon Lance Armstrong may be reconsidered, too, as a man who, despite his faults, made a real difference in the world.

Lance Armstrong will have his critics. The way in which he deceived his sport, his fans, and his country is tough for anyone to defend. But ultimately, one should look at the results of it all. Armstrong's lies led to lives being saved, whether it was through his inspiration or his foundation. Armstrong will forever

A final line of argument involves an extended analogy.

Casso 7

be remembered for his contributions to society—if not by the masses, then at least by the cancer survivors and victims' families whom he touched. Armstrong's lie was undoubtedly worth it. The end did justify the means.

Casso 8

Works Consulted

"John D. Rockefeller, 1839–1937." *Rockefeller Archive Center*.
   Rockefeller Archive Center, n.d. Web. 10 Apr. 2013.

Livestrong Foundation. *Livestrong Foundation*. Livestrong
   Foundation, n.d. Web. 17 Mar. 2013.

"Messages of Support." *Support for Lance*. Real Estate
   Webmasters, n.d. Web. 17 Mar. 2013.

Page, Susan. "Most Influential People." *USA Today*. USA Today,
   9 Sept. 2007. Web. 17 Mar. 2013.

Triplett, Brian. "Inspirations of Lance." *ESPN.com*. ESPN, 25 July
   2004. Web. 17 Mar. 2013.

Exploring purpose and topic

topic ◀

In a college assignment, you could be asked to write arguments about general topics related to courses, but you probably won't be told what your claims should be. That's your responsibility, based on your knowledge, experiences, and leanings. So choose subjects you genuinely care about—not issues the media or someone else defines as controversial. You'll do a more credible job defending your questionable choice *not* to wear a helmet when motorcycling than explaining, one more time, why the environment should concern us all. And if environmental matters do roil you, stake your claim on a well-defined ecological problem—perhaps from within your community—that you might actually influence by the power of your rhetoric. ○

If you really are stumped, the Yahoo! Directory's list of "Issues and Causes"—with topics from *abortion* to *zoos*—offers problems enough to keep pundits from MSNBC and Fox News buzzing to the end of the century. To find it, search "Society and Culture" or "Issues and Causes" on the site's main Web directory. ("Society and Culture" itself offers a menu of intriguing topic areas.) Once you have an issue or even a specific claim, your real work begins.

Learn much more about your subject.   Your first task is to do basic library and online research to get a better handle on your topic—*especially* when you think you already have all the answers. Chances are, you don't.

State a preliminary claim, if only for yourself.   Some arguments fail because writers never focus their thinking. They wander around vague topics, throwing out ideas or making contradictory assertions and leaving it to readers to assemble the random parts. To avoid this blunder, begin with a claim — a *complete* sentence that states a position you hope to defend. Such a statement will keep you on track as you explore a topic. Even a simple sentence helps:

> The college rankings published annually by *U.S. News & World Report* do more harm than good.

> People who oppose gay marriage don't know what they are talking about.

get an idea
p. 331

Arguments take many different forms, but finger-pointing is rarely a good persuasive tool. *Top:* Ghislain and Marie David de Lessy/The Image Bank/ Getty Images. *Bottom:* Courtesy of Dr. Susan Farrell.

Qualify your claim to make it reasonable. As you learn more about a subject, revise your topic idea to reflect the complications you encounter. ○ Your thesis will probably grow longer or take several sentences to explain, but the topic itself will actually narrow because of the specific issues you've identified. You'll also have less work to do, thanks to qualifying expressions such as *some, most, a few, often, under certain conditions, occasionally, when necessary,* and so on. Other qualifying expressions are highlighted below.

The statistically unreliable college ratings published by *U.S. News & World Report* usually do more harm than good to students because some claim that they lead admissions officers to award scholarships on the basis of merit rather than need.

Many conservative critics who oppose gay marriage unwittingly undermine their own core principles, especially monogamy and honesty.

Examine your core assumptions.   Claims may be supported by reasons and evidence, but they are based on assumptions. *Assumptions* are the principles and values upon which we base our beliefs and actions. Sometimes these assumptions are controversial and stand right out. At other times, they're so close to us, they seem invisible—they are part of the air we breathe. Expect to spend a paragraph defending any assumptions your readers might find questionable or controversial. ○

think critically
p. 343

develop ideas
p. 383

CLAIM

The statistically unreliable college ratings published by *U.S. News & World Report* usually do more harm than good to students because some claim that they lead admissions officers to award scholarships on the basis of merit rather than need.

ASSUMPTION

Alleviating need in our society is more important than rewarding merit.
[Probably controversial]

CLAIM

Westerners should be more willing to defend their cultural values and intellectual achievements if they hope to defend freedom against its enemies.

ASSUMPTION

Freedom needs to be defended at all costs.
[Possibly controversial for some audiences]

CLAIM

Many conservative critics who oppose gay marriage unwittingly undermine their own core principles, especially monogamy and honesty.

ASSUMPTION

People should be consistent about their principles.
[Probably not controversial]

Your Turn   Many writers have a tough time expressing their topic in a complete sentence. They will offer a tentative word or phrase or sentence fragment instead of making the commitment that a full sentence demands, especially one with subordinators and qualifiers that begin to tie their ideas together. So give it a try. Take a topic you might write about and turn it into a full-bore sentence that tells readers what your claim is and how you intend to support it.

Understanding your audience

Retailers know audiences. In fact, they go to great lengths to pinpoint the groups most likely to buy their fried chicken or hybrid cars. They then tailor their brand images and Web advertising to precisely those customers. You'll play to audiences the same way when you write arguments—if maybe a little less cynically.

Understand that you won't ever please everyone in a general audience, even if you write bland, colorless mush—because some readers will then regard you as craven and spineless. In fact, how readers imagine you, *as the person presenting an argument*, may determine their willingness to consider your claims at all.

Consider and control your ethos.   People who study persuasion describe the identity that writers create for themselves within an argument as their *ethos*—the voice and attitude they fashion to enhance their appeal. It is a powerful concept, worth remembering. Surely you notice when writers are coming across as, let's say, ingratiatingly confident or stupidly obnoxious. And don't you respond in kind, giving ear to the likable voice and dismissing the malicious one? A few audiences—like those for political blogs—may actually prefer a writer with a snarky ethos. But most readers respond better when writers seem reasonable, knowledgeable, and fair—neither insulting those who disagree with them nor making those who share their views embarrassed to have them on their side.

You can shape your ethos by adjusting the style, tone, and vocabulary of your argument: For instance, contractions can make you seem friendly (or too casual); an impressive vocabulary suggests that you are smart (or maybe just pompous); lots of name-dropping makes you seem hip (or perhaps pretentious). You may have to write several drafts to find a suitable ethos for a particular argument. ○ And, yes, your ethos may change from paper to paper, audience to audience.

revise and edit
p. 422

> **Your Turn**   Chances are you have some favorite Web sites or blogs you
> consult daily. Choose one of those sites, find an entry in it that expresses the
> ethos of the contributor(s) or the site itself, and then analyze that ethos. Is
> the character of the site friendly and down-to-earth? Arrogant and authori-
> tative? Serious and politically concerned? Point to specific features of the
> site that help create its ethos. If you don't consult blogs or Web sites, apply
> your analysis to a printed or oral text, perhaps an op-ed by a favorite colum-
> nist or a political speech by a public figure.

Consider self-imposed limits.   If you read newspapers and magazines that
mostly confirm your own political views, you might be in for a wake-up call
when you venture an opinion beyond your small circle of friends. Tread softly.
There are good reasons why people don't talk politics at parties. When you do
argue about social, political, or religious issues, be respectful of those who work
from premises different from your own.

Consider the worlds of your readers.   When arguing about topics such as
education, politics, art, economics, ethics, or even athletics, you'll quickly realize that people bring their entire lives into the discussion of such issues. Their
views are shaped, in part, by their gender, race, ethnicity, sexual orientation,
income, age, and upbringing—and more, and in ever-varying combinations.
Dealing with such considerations, you should be sensitive but not gutless. ○

> Need help support-
> ing your argument?
> See "How to Use
> the Writing Center"
> on pp. 354–55.

Men and women, for instance, whether straight or gay, may not inhabit
quite the same worlds. But, even so, you shouldn't argue, either, as if all men
and all women think the same way—or should.

People's lives are similarly defined by their economic situations—and the
assumptions that follow from privilege, poverty, or something in between.
Think it would be cool to have an outdoor pool on campus or a convenient

respect your
readers p. 408

new parking garage? You may find other students less willing than you to absorb the impact such proposals might have on their tuition. And if you intend to complain about fat cats, ridicule soccer moms, or poke fun at rednecks, is it because you can't imagine people different from you among your readers?

Obviously, age matters too: You'd write differently for children than for their parents on almost any subject, changing your style, vocabulary, and allusions. But consider that people of different ages really have lived different lives. Each generation grows up with shared attitudes, values, heroes, and villains. As a writer, you have to factor such considerations into the arguments you write.

Gender attitudes develop early, along with some argument strategies. Courtesy of Dr. Susan Farrell.

Finding and developing materials

You could write a book from the materials you'll collect researching some arguments. Since arguments often deal with current events and topics, start with a resource such as the Yahoo! Directory's "Issues and Causes" list mentioned earlier. Explore your subject, too, in *LexisNexis*, if your library gives you access to this huge database of newspaper articles. ○

develop support ◀

As you gather materials, though, consider how much space you have to make your argument. Sometimes a claim has to fit within the confines of a letter to the editor, an op-ed column in a local paper, or a fifteen-minute PowerPoint talk. Aristotle, still one of the best theorists on persuasion, thought arguments *should* be brief, with speakers limiting examples to the *minimum* necessary to make a case—no extra points for piling on. So gather big, and then select only the best stuff for your argument.

List your reasons. You'll come up with reasons to support your claim almost as soon as you choose a subject. Write those down. Then start reading and continue to list new reasons as they arise, not being too fussy at this point. Be careful to paraphrase these ideas so that you don't inadvertently plagiarize them later.

Then, when your reading and research are complete, review your notes and try to group the arguments that support your position. It's likely you'll detect patterns and relationships among these reasons, and an unwieldy initial list of potential arguments may be streamlined into just three or four—which could become the key reasons behind your claim. Study these points and look for logical connections or sequences. Readers will expect your ideas to converge on a claim or lead logically toward it. ○

Assemble your hard evidence. Gather examples, illustrations, quotations, and numbers to support each main point. Record these items as you read in some reliable way, keeping track of all bibliographical information (author, title, publication info, URL) just as you would when preparing a term paper—even if you aren't required to document your argument. You want that data on hand in case your credibility is challenged later.

If you borrow facts from a Web site, do your best to trace the information to its actual source. For example, if a blogger quotes statistics from the U.S. Department of Agriculture, find that table or graph on the USDA Web site itself and make sure the numbers reported are accurate. ○

> The whole is greater than the sum of its parts.

–Aristotle

Popperfoto/Getty Images.

refine your
search p. 442

shape your
work p. 374

analyze claims
and evidence p. 456

83

Cull the best quotations.   You've done your homework for an assignment, reading the best available sources. So prove it in your argument by quoting from them intelligently. Choose quotations that do one or more of the following:

- Put your issue in focus or context.
- Make a point with special power and economy.
- Support a claim or piece of evidence that readers might doubt.
- State an opposing point well.

Copy passages that appeal to you, but don't figure on using all of them. An argument that is a patchwork of quotations reads like a patchwork of quotations—which is to say, *boring*. Be sure to copy the quotations accurately and be certain you can document them. ○

Find counterarguments.   If you study a subject thoroughly, you'll come across plenty of honest disagreement. List all reasonable objections you can find to your claim, either to your basic argument or to any controversial evidence you expect to cite. When possible, cluster these objections to reduce them to a manageable few. Decide which you must refute in detail, which you might handle briefly, and which you can afford to dismiss. ○

Watch, for example, how in an editorial, the *New York Times* anticipates objections to its defense of a *Rolling Stone* magazine cover (August 2013) featuring accused Boston Marathon bomber Dzhokhar Tsarnaev. The *Times* concedes that merchants and consumers alike might resist the cover, but then it counterpunches:

> Stores have a right to refuse to sell products because, say, they are unhealthy, like cigarettes. . . . Consumers have every right to avoid buying a magazine that offends them, like *Guns & Ammo* or *Rolling Stone*.
>
> But singling out one magazine issue for shunning is over the top, especially since the photo has already appeared in a lot of prominent places, including the front page of this newspaper, without an outcry. As any seasoned reader should know, magazine covers are not endorsements.
>
> — The Editorial Board, "Judging Rolling Stone by Its Cover," *New York Times*, July 18, 2013

understand citation
styles p. 470

develop ideas
p. 383

Consider emotional appeals. Feelings play a powerful role in many arguments, a fact you cannot afford to ignore when a claim you make stirs people up. Questions to answer about possible emotional appeals include the following:

- What emotions might be effectively raised to support my point?
- How might I responsibly introduce such feelings: through words, images,
- color, sound?
- How might any feelings my subject arouses work contrary to my claims or reasons?

Well-chosen visuals add power to an argument. A writer trying to persuade readers not to buy fur might include this photo in an article. How would this image influence you, as a reader? Jeff Foott/Discovery Channel Images/Getty Images.

Creating a structure

▶ organize ideas

It's easy to sketch a standard structure for arguments: one that leads from claim to supporting reasons to evidence and even accommodates a counterargument or two.

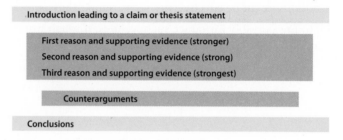

Introduction leading to a claim or thesis statement

First reason and supporting evidence (stronger)
Second reason and supporting evidence (strong)
Third reason and supporting evidence (strongest)

Counterarguments

Conclusions

The problem is that you won't read many effective arguments, either in or out of school, that follow this template. The structure isn't defective, just too simple to describe the way arguments really move when ideas matter. You won't write a horrible paper if you use the traditional model because all the parts will be in place. Thesis? Check. Three supporting reasons? Check. Counterarguments? Check. But you will sound exactly like what you are: A writer going through the motions instead of engaging with ideas. Here's how to get your ideas to breathe in an argument—while still hitting all the marks.

Make a point or build toward one.   Arguments can unfurl just as reports do, with unmistakable claims followed by reams of supporting evidence. But they can also work like crime dramas, in which the evidence in a case builds toward a compelling conclusion—your thesis perhaps. This is your call. ○ But don't just jump into a claim: Take a few sentences or paragraphs to set up the situation. Quote a nasty politician or tell an eye-popping story or two. Get readers invested in what's to come.

Spell out what's at stake.   When you write an argument, you initiate a controversy, so you'd better explain it clearly—as Stefan Casso does in "Worth the Lie" earlier in this chapter. Do you hope to fix a looming problem? Then describe your concern and make readers share it. Do you intend to correct a false notion or bad reporting? Then tell readers why setting the record straight matters. Appalled by the apathy of voters, the dangers of global warming, the infringements of free speech on campus? Explain why readers should care. ○

order ideas
p. 377

develop a statement
p. 362

Address counterpoints when necessary, not in a separate section.
Necessary is when your readers start thinking to themselves, "Yeah, but what
about . . . ?" Such doubts will probably surface approximately where your own
do—and, admit it, you have some misgivings about your argument. So take them
on. Strategically, it rarely makes sense to consign all objections to a lengthy section near the end of a paper. That's asking for trouble. Do you really want to offer
a case for the opposition just when your readers are finishing up? On the plus
side, dealing with opposing arguments (or writing a refutation itself—see p. 92)
can be like caffeine for your prose, sharpening your attention and reflexes.

Save your best arguments for the end.   Of course, you want strong
points throughout the paper. But you need a high note early on to get readers interested and then another choral moment as you finish to send them
out the door humming. If you must summarize an argument, don't let a dull
recap of your main points squander an important opportunity to influence
readers. End with a rhetorical flourish that reminds readers how compelling
your arguments are. ○

A pithy phrase, an ironic twist, and a question to contemplate can also lock
down your case. Here's Maureen Dowd, bleakly—and memorably—concluding
an argument defending the job journalists had done covering the Iraq War:

> Journalists die and we know who they are. We know they liked to cook and play
> Scrabble. But we don't know who killed them, and their killers will never be
> brought to justice. The enemy has no face, just a finger on a detonator.

—"Live from Baghdad: More Dying," *New York Times*, May 31, 2006

shape an
ending p. 391

Choosing a style and design

Arguments vary widely in style. An unsigned editorial you write to represent the opinion of a student newspaper might sound formal and serious. Composing an op-ed under your own name, you'd probably ease up on the dramatic metaphors and allow yourself more personal pronouns. Arguing a point in an alternative magazine, you might even slip into the lingo of its vegan or survivalist subscribers. Routine adjustments like these really matter when you need to attract and hold readers.

You should also write with sensitivity since some people reading arguments may well be wavering, defensive, or eager to be offended. There's no reason to distract them with fighting words if you want to offer a serious argument. Here's how political commentator Ann Coulter described a politically active group of 9/11 widows who she believed were using their status to shield their anti–Iraq War opinions from criticism:

> These broads are millionaires, lionized on TV and in articles about them, reveling in their status as celebrities and stalked by grief-arazzis. I have never seen people enjoying their husbands' deaths so much.
>
> — *Godless: The Church of Liberalism* (2006)

Any point Coulter might make simply gets lost in the viciousness of the attack.

There are many powerful and aggressive ways to frame an argument without resorting to provocative language or fallacies of argument. ○ Some of these strategies follow.

Invite readers with a strong opening.   Arguments—like advertisements—are usually discretionary reading. People can turn away the moment they grow irritated or bored. So you may need to open with a little surprise or drama. Try a blunt statement, an anecdote, or a striking example if it helps—maybe an image too. Or consider personalizing the lead-in, giving readers a stake in the claim you are about to make. The following is a remarkable opening paragraph from an argument by Malcolm Gladwell on the wisdom of banning dogs by breed. When you finish, ask yourself whether Gladwell has earned your attention. Would you read the rest of the piece?

> One afternoon last February, Guy Clairoux picked up his two-and-a-half-year-old son, Jayden, from day care and walked him back to their house in the west end of Ottawa, Ontario. They were almost home. Jayden was straggling behind, and, as his father's back was turned, a pit bull jumped over a backyard fence

avoid fallacies
p. 343

and lunged at Jayden. "The dog had his head in its mouth and started to do this shake," Clairoux's wife, JoAnn Hartley, said later. As she watched in horror, two more pit bulls jumped over the fence, joining in the assault. She and Clairoux came running, and he punched the first of the dogs in the head, until it dropped Jayden, and then he threw the boy toward his mother. Hartley fell on her son, protecting him with her body. "JoAnn!" Clairoux cried out, as all three dogs descended on his wife. "Cover your neck, cover your neck." A neighbor, sitting by her window, screamed for help. Her partner and a friend, Mario Gauthier, ran outside. A neighborhood boy grabbed his hockey stick and threw it to Gauthier. He began hitting one of the dogs over the head, until the stick broke. "They wouldn't stop," Gauthier said. "As soon as you'd stop, they'd attack again. I've never seen a dog go so crazy. They were like Tasmanian devils." The police came. The dogs were pulled away, and the Clairouxes and one of the rescuers were taken to the hospital. Five days later, the Ontario legislature banned the ownership of pit bulls. "Just as we wouldn't let a great white shark in a swimming pool," the province's attorney general, Michael Bryant, had said, "maybe we shouldn't have these animals on the civilized streets."

— "Troublemakers," *New Yorker*, February 6, 2006

Write vibrant sentences.   You can write arguments full throttle, using a complete range of rhetorical devices, from deliberate repetition and parallelism to dialogue and quotation. Metaphors, similes, and analogies fit right in too. The trick is to create sentences rich enough to keep readers hooked, yet lean enough to advance an argument. In the following three paragraphs, follow the highlighting to see how Thomas L. Friedman uses parallelism and one intriguing metaphor after another to argue in favor of immigration legislation after witnessing the diversity in a high school graduation class in Maryland. ○

There is a lot to be worried about in America today: a war in Iraq that is getting worse not better, an administration whose fiscal irresponsibility we will be paying for for a long time, an education system that is not producing enough young Americans skilled in math and science, and inner cities where way too many black males are failing. We must work harder and get smarter if we want to maintain our standard of living.

But if there is one reason to still be optimistic about America it is represented by the stunning diversity of the Montgomery Blair class of 2006. America is still the world's greatest human magnet. We are not the only country that

improve your
sentences p. 412

embraces diversity, but there is something about our free society and free market that still attracts people like no other. Our greatest asset is our ability to still cream off not only the first-round intellectual draft choices from around the world but the low-skilled, high-aspiring ones as well, and that is the main reason that I am not yet ready to cede the twenty-first century to China. Our Chinese will still beat their Chinese.

This influx of brainy and brawny immigrants is our oil well — one that never runs dry. It is an endless source of renewable human energy and creativity. Congress ought to stop debating gay marriage and finally give us a framework to maintain a free flow of legal immigration.

— "A Well of Smiths and Xias," *New York Times*, June 7, 2006

Ask rhetorical questions.   The danger of rhetorical questions is that they can seem stagy and readers might not answer them the way you want. But the device can be very powerful in hammering a point home. Good questions also invite readers to think about an issue in exactly the terms that a writer prefers. Here's George Will using rhetorical questions to conclude a piece on global warming:

In fact, the earth is always experiencing either warming or cooling. But suppose the scientists and their journalistic conduits, who today say they were so spectacularly wrong so recently, are now correct. Suppose the earth is warming and suppose the warming is caused by human activity. Are we sure there will be proportionate benefits from whatever climate change can be purchased at the cost of slowing economic growth and spending trillions? Are we sure the consequences of climate change — remember, a thick sheet of ice once covered the Midwest — must be bad? Or has the science-journalism complex decided that debate about these questions, too, is "over"?

— "Let Cooler Heads Prevail," *Washington Post*, April 2, 2006

Use images and design to make a point.   If we didn't know it already (and we did), the video and photographic images from 9/11, the *Deepwater Horizon* oil spill in the Gulf of Mexico, or the 2012–13 political protests in Egypt clearly prove that persuasion doesn't occur by words only. We react powerfully to what we see with our own eyes. Consider this image from the Associated Press of gay rights activists at a rally in St. Petersburg, Russia. The

Associated Press/Dmitry Lovetsky.

accompanying caption pointed out that police both guarded and detained activists, who were outnumbered by anti-gay protesters at the authorized gay rights rally. This image and others like it sparked debate on Russia's legislation targeting gay people and the personal safety of gay Russians.

And yet words still play a part because most images become *focused* arguments only when accompanied by commentary—as commentators routinely prove when they put a spin on news photographs or video. And because digital technology now makes it so easy to incorporate nonverbal media into texts, whether on a page, screen, or Prezi whiteboard, you should always consider how just the right image might enhance the case you want to make. ○

think visually
p. 557

Examining models

An important subgenre of arguments is the refutation, a piece that takes apart someone else's claims and sometimes seeks to correct them. In the following example of this engaging but prickly form, Bjørn Lomborg, author of *The Skeptical Environmentalist* (2001), explains where and how an influential environmental study went awry and the consequences of what he perceives as its errors. Needless to say, a refutation is, itself, an argument that deserves careful scrutiny.

Reading the Genre How did readers on *Slate.com* (where this argument was posted) react to Lomborg's refutation of *The Limits of Growth*? Spend some time checking those responses at www.slate.com/authors.bjrn_lomborg.html or, on your own, speculate how and where critics might take issue with Lomborg.

The Limits of Panic

BJØRN LOMBORG

We often hear how the world as we know it will end, usually through ecological collapse. Indeed, more than forty years after the Club of Rome released the mother of all apocalyptic forecasts, *The Limits to Growth*, its basic ideas are still with us. But time has not been kind.

The Limits to Growth warned humanity in 1972 that devastating collapse was just around the corner. But, while we have seen financial panics since then, there have been no real shortages or productive breakdowns. Instead, the resources generated by human ingenuity remain far ahead of human consumption.

But the report's fundamental legacy remains: We have inherited a tendency to obsess over misguided remedies for largely trivial problems, while often ignoring big problems and sensible remedies.

In the early 1970s, the flush of technological optimism was over, the Vietnam War was a disaster, societies were in turmoil, and economies were stagnating. Rachel Carson's 1962 book *Silent Spring* had raised fears about pollution and launched the modern environmental movement; Paul Ehrlich's 1968 title *The Population Bomb* said it all. The first Earth Day, in 1970, was deeply pessimistic.

Opening paragraphs outline Lomborg's intention to critique the legacy of *The Limits of Growth*.

For an additional reading, see **macmillanhighered.com/howtowrite3e.**
e-readings > 5 Gyres, *Understanding Plastic Pollution through Exploration, Education, and Action*
[INTERACTIVE WEB SITE]

The author summarizes his take on *The Limits of Growth*.

The genius of *The Limits to Growth* was to fuse these worries with fears of running out of stuff. We were doomed, because too many people would consume too much. Even if our ingenuity bought us some time, we would end up killing the planet and ourselves with pollution. The only hope was to stop economic growth itself, cut consumption, recycle, and force people to have fewer children, stabilizing society at a significantly poorer level.

That message still resonates today, though it was spectacularly wrong. For example, the authors of *The Limits to Growth* predicted that before 2013, the world would have run out of aluminum, copper, gold, lead, mercury, molybdenum, natural gas, oil, silver, tin, tungsten, and zinc.

Throughout the refutation, statistics play a major role.

Instead, despite recent increases, commodity prices have generally fallen to about a third of their level 150 years ago. Technological innovations have replaced mercury in batteries, dental fillings, and thermometers: Mercury consumption is down 98 percent and, by 2000, the price was down 90 percent. More broadly, since 1946, supplies of copper, aluminum, iron, and zinc have outstripped consumption, owing to the discovery of additional reserves and new technologies to extract them economically.

Similarly, oil and natural gas were to run out in 1990 and 1992, respectively; today, reserves of both are larger than they were in 1970, although we consume dramatically more. Within the past six years, shale gas alone has doubled potential gas resources in the United States and halved the price.

As for economic collapse, the Intergovernmental Panel on Climate Change estimates that global GDP per capita will increase 14-fold over this century and 24-fold in the developing world.

Lomborg speculates on why predictions in *The Limits of Growth* went awry.

The Limits of Growth got it so wrong because its authors overlooked the greatest resource of all: our own resourcefulness. Population growth has been slowing since the late 1960s. Food supply has not collapsed (1.5 billion hectares of arable land are being used, but another 2.7 billion hectares are in reserve). Malnourishment has dropped by more than half, from 35 percent of the world's population to under 16 percent.

Nor are we choking on pollution. Whereas the Club of Rome imagined an idyllic past with no particulate air pollution and happy farmers, and a future strangled by belching smokestacks, reality is entirely the reverse.

In 1900, when the global human population was 1.5 billion, almost 3 million people—roughly one in 500—died each year from air pollution, mostly from wretched indoor air. Today, the risk has receded to one death per 2,000 people. While pollution still kills more people than malaria does, the mortality rate is falling, not rising.

Nonetheless, the mind-set nurtured by *The Limits to Growth* continues to shape popular and elite thinking.

Consider recycling, which is often just a feel-good gesture with little environmental benefit and significant cost. Paper, for example, typically comes from sustainable forests, not rain forests. The processing and government subsidies associated with recycling yield lower-quality paper to save a resource that is not threatened.

Likewise, fears of overpopulation framed self-destructive policies, such as China's one-child policy and forced sterilization in India. And, while pesticides and other pollutants were seen to kill off perhaps half of humanity, well-regulated pesticides cause about 20 deaths each year in the United States, whereas they have significant upsides in creating cheaper and more plentiful food.

Indeed, reliance solely on organic farming—a movement inspired by the pesticide fear—would cost more than $100 billion annually in the United States. At 16 percent lower efficiency, current output would require another 65 million acres of farmland—an area more than half the size of California. Higher prices would reduce consumption of fruits and vegetables, causing myriad adverse health effects (including tens of thousands of additional cancer deaths per year).

Obsession with doom-and-gloom scenarios distracts us from the real global threats. Poverty is one of the greatest killers of all, while easily curable diseases still claim 15 million lives every year—25 percent of all deaths.

The solution is economic growth. When lifted out of poverty, most people can afford to avoid infectious diseases. China has pulled more than 680 million people out of poverty in the last three decades, leading a worldwide poverty decline of almost 1 billion people. This has created massive improvements in health, longevity, and quality of life.

The author blames questionable policies on assumptions The Limits of Growth fostered.

Readers are pounded with numbers and statistics.

Lomborg ends the refutation with recommendations of his own.

The four decades since *The Limits of Growth* have shown that we need more of it, not less. An expansion of trade, with estimated benefits exceeding $100 trillion annually toward the end of the century, would do thousands of times more good than timid feel-good policies that result from fearmongering. But that requires abandoning an antigrowth mentality and using our enormous potential to create a brighter future.

VISUAL ARGUMENT   Matt Bors is angry and he's not going to take it anymore, or at least that's the tenor of his "Can We Stop Worrying about Millennials Yet?" — a multipanel visual argument that appeared under the "Opinion" tab of CNN's Web site on July 9, 2013. Bors, a thirtyish, Pulitzer Prize–nominated editorial cartoonist, mocks complaints made about his generation — one that reached adulthood around the turn of the century and then ran smack into the Great Recession. Who can blame him for being ticked off?

Reading the Genre   Compare the aggressive and detailed (almost "busy") arguments Matt Bors makes in his multiple cartoon panels to the calm and wordless argument made by the *New Yorker* cover on page 69. Could you turn Bors's multipanel argument into a single image? How might it differ in aim and impact? Or would it be more interesting to translate the visual argument into a conventional essay or editorial? Consider, for example, how a written text might recreate the sarcasm in Bors's drawings.

All images pages 96–98: Matt Bors.

PEAK MILLENNIAL SLANDER OCCURRED WITH **TIME**'S JUNE 2013 COVER STORY "THE ME ME ME GENERATION." THEY WERE LATE TO THE GEN Y-BASHING PARTY, BUT THEIR TROLLING STANDS OUT AS EXEMPLARY.

CHOICE QUOTE:

"Not only do millennials lack the kind of empathy that allows them to feel concerned for others, but they even have trouble even intellectually under-standing others' points of view."

TRACKING THESE STORIES IS MADDENING. I WAS RECOVERING FROM THE TIME STORY WHEN I CAME ACROSS A WASHINGTON POST TREND PIECE THAT SEEMED TO BE A PARODY OF SOME-THING YOU WRITE WHEN YOU HAVE A DEADLINE IN THREE HOURS AND NOTHING TO SAY.

CRACKED CELLPHONE SCREENS
are point of pride for some young people

WHAT.

"Some young people say a cracked screen gives you a sort of street cred, like you've been through some real-life stuff, even if it happened on the mean streets of Bethesda. It's tough, subversive and just kinda cool."

SUDDENLY, I WAS RAGE-READING MILLENNIAL TREND PIECES EVERY DAY. PERHAPS A NEW TREND DESERVING OF ITS OWN PROFILE?

Rage Read

The new, hip thing for Gen Me? Fuming over trend pieces about themselves. "I hate you. Please stop," cartoonist Matt Bors demanded. "Stop writing this story immediately."

Enough.

IT'S TIME TO STOP WRITING GARBAGE ARTICLES ABOUT TWEETING AND TIGHT T-SHIRTS. EDITORS WHO STOP ASSIGNING TREND PIECES ON MILLENNIALS SHOULD ALL GET TROPHIES. (TO HELP DEVELOP THEIR POOR SELF-ESTEEM.)

THE STORY ABOUT YOUNG PEOPLE ISN'T WHICH COMPANY'S MARKETING PLATFORM WE'RE POSTING UPDATES ON.

THE STATUS UPDATE IS:

The Economy has been RUINED!!!

 Post

MILLENNIALS AREN'T MARRYING, BUYING HOUSES, AND HAVING KIDS LATER THAN PREVIOUS GENERATIONS BECAUSE THEY'RE SITTING AROUND TRYING TO BEAT A VIDEO GAME. THEY'RE "DELAYING ADULTHOOD" BECAUSE THE JOB MARKET IS THE WORST IT'S BEEN SINCE THE GREAT DEPRESSION.

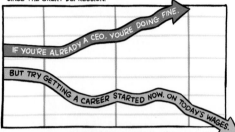

IF YOU'RE ALREADY A CEO, YOU'RE DOING FINE.

BUT TRY GETTING A CAREER STARTED NOW. ON TODAY'S WAGES.

WE ARE SAID TO BE **ENTITLED**. WE THINK WE DESERVE SOMETHING, THAT THE WORLD SHOULD HAND US SOMETHING FOR BEING HERE. WE DO. LIKE JOBS. (ARE THERE THOSE YET?) WE'RE CERTAINLY ENTITLED TO UNPAID JOBS – "INTERNSHIPS" AS THE SCAM IS KNOWN. BUT SOME OF US NEED MONEY BECAUSE STUDENT LOANS CAN'T BE PAID OFF WITH AIR.

AND THE PRICE OF EDUCATION IS A BIT HIGH THESE DAYS. SO IF YOU SAY:

IN MY DAY, WE WORKED A SUMMER JOB TO PAY FOR COLLEGE!

YOU SHOULD GET A PALLET OF $1 TRILLION IN STUDENT LOAN DEBT DROPPED ON YOUR HEAD.

IT'S PROBABLY NOT YOUR FAULT. YOU'RE PROBABLY STRUGGLING TOO. (IF YOU'RE A POLITICIAN OR INVESTMENT BANKER READING THIS, IGNORE WHAT I JUST SAID.)

MOST ECONOMIC GAINS SINCE THE RECOVERY WERE VACUUMED UP BY THE 1 PERCENT— NOT THE KIDS.

SO INSTEAD OF CONDESCENDING TO THE PEOPLE WHO WILL CARE FOR YOU WHEN YOU'RE DYING, MAYBE YOU CAN HELP NOT SHRED OUR SOCIAL SECURITY BENEFITS?

STOP HATING ON MILLENNIALS. WE DIDN'T CREATE THIS MESS. WE CAME LATE TO THE BANQUET AND WERE SERVED UP CRUMBS.

WHICH WE WILL INSTAGRAM BEFORE WE EAT.

#YUM

1. **Argument to Advance a Thesis:** Review the way Stefan Casso supports a clearly stated and controversial thesis in "Worth the Lie" (p. 70). Then write an argument that similarly provides direct support for a controversial claim in the public sphere — one that has implications for other people. Like Casso, take the time to explain the issue you are addressing and then try to offer multiple reasons to support your thesis.

2. **Refutation Argument:** Find a text with which you strongly disagree and then systematically refute it, as Bjørn Lomborg does in "The Limits of Panic" (p. 92). The text can be a position or policy promoted by a politician or public or corporate official, or it can be an argument in itself — a column, an editorial, or even a section in a textbook. Make your opposition clear, but also be fair to the position you are attempting to refute. It is especially important that your readers be able to understand whatever you are analyzing, even if they aren't familiar with it. That's a real challenge, so don't hesitate to summarize, paraphrase, or quote from the material.

3. **Visual Argument:** Study the way Matt Bors incorporates a wide range of persuasive devices in his visual argument (p. 95); he uses everything from direct quotations to stereotypes. Like many visual arguments, his piece combines images and words to make a point. Create a visual argument of your own using whatever medium you believe will convey your message most powerfully. Start with a clear point in mind ("Stop hating on Millennials!"). Then figure out how to present your claim memorably.

4. **Your Choice:** These days, most serious arguments explode across interactive online environments, where they often take on a life of their own. Working with a group, design a media project (blog, Web site, mash-up, video, etc.) to focus on an issue that members of your group believe deserves more attention. Pool your talents to develop the site technically, rhetorically, and visually. Be sure your project introduces the subject, explains its purpose, encourages interaction, and includes relevant images and, if possible, links.

How to start
- Need a **topic**? See page 106.
- Need **criteria for your evaluation**? See page 109.
- Need to **organize your criteria and evidence**? See page 112.

4 Evaluations

make a claim
about the
merit of
something

Evaluations and reviews are so much a part of our lives that you might notice them only when they are specifically assigned. Commentary and criticism of all sorts just happen.

ARTS REVIEW
You're never shy about sharing your opinions of movies, films, and restaurants, but you find it painful when you have to write an *arts review* of *Götterdämmerung* for a music appreciation course. The opera lasts longer than a football game!

SOCIAL SATIRE
Tired of self-righteous cyclists who preach eco-fundamentalism and then clog traffic with monthly Critical Mass rides, you do what any irate citizen would—you mock them in a *social satire*.

PRODUCT REVIEW
Given your work experience at a camera store, you are invited to write a *product review* for a co-op newsletter about cell phone cameras.

DECIDING TO WRITE AN EVALUATION.   It's one thing to offer an opinion, yet it's an entirely different matter to back up a claim with reasons and evidence. Only when you do will readers (or listeners) take you seriously. But you'll also have to convince them that you know *how* to evaluate a book, a social policy, a cultural trend, or even a cup of coffee by reasonable criteria. It helps if you can use objective standards to make judgments, counting or measuring varying degrees of excellence. But perhaps more often, evaluations involve people debating matters of taste—an act that draws good sense and wit into the mix. Here's how to frame this kind of argument (for more on choosing a genre, see the Introduction).

Explain your mission.   Just what do you intend to evaluate and for whom? Maybe you'll assess or rank particular products, productions, or performances or challenge opinions others have offered about them. Or maybe you want to turn social critic, making people aware of their failures or foibles. Or perhaps you see yourself as a sports pundit or fashion guru. You need to share your intentions and credentials with readers.

Every four years at the Summer Olympics, judges decide who gets a medal in gymnastics. Associated Press/Gregory Bull.

Establish and defend criteria.   *Criteria* are the standards by which objects are measured: *A good furnace should heat a home quickly and efficiently. Successful presidents leave office with the country in better shape than when they entered.* When readers are likely to share your criteria, you need to explain little about them. But when readers might object, prepare to defend your principles. ○ And sometimes you'll break new ground—as happened when critics first asked, *What is good Web design?* or *Which are the most significant social networks?* In such cases, criteria of evaluation had to be invented, explained, and defended.

Offer convincing evidence.   Evidence makes the connection between an opinion and the criteria of evaluation that support it. It comes in many forms: facts, statistics, testimony, photographs, and even good sense and keen observations. If good furnaces heat homes quickly and efficiently, then you'd have to supply data to show that a product you judged faulty didn't meet those minimal standards. (It might be noisy and unreliable to boot.)

Offer worthwhile advice.   Some evaluations are just for fun: Consider all the hoopla that arguments about sports rankings generate. But done right, most evaluations and reviews provide usable information, beneficial criticism, or even ranked choices—think restaurant or entertainment reviews on Yelp.

develop ideas
p. 383

People rely on critics of every kind of entertainment to help them decide what to read, watch, see, or hear. For many years, readers of *Entertainment Weekly* turned to Lisa Schwarzbaum for film reviews. Appraising the first of the *Hunger Games* movies, she has to accommodate avid fans of Suzanne Collins's books, as well as moviegoers entirely new to the dystopian trilogy. Both are tough audiences.

Reading the Genre   At the end of her review, you'll see that Schwarzbaum gives the movie a letter grade. Is it consistent with the full review? What role do symbols such as grades, stars, or even thumbs play in this genre?

Entertainment Weekly

Posted: April 3, 2012
Reviewed by: Lisa Schwarzbaum

The Hunger Games

Young people, selected by lottery, slaughter one another with kill-or-be-killed desperation in *The Hunger Games*. The savagery is a yearly ritual mandated by the tyrannical regime of Panem, a broken nation built, after a terrible war, on the futuristic ruins of North America. It's also broadcast on live TV, a national media event. This horrific vision of a near future in which teenagers are in peril is sickening, but the individual heroism of some who fight is also thrilling, as millions of readers can attest: Suzanne Collins's *Hunger Games* trilogy is a literary sensation. The good news now coming out of Panem, both for those who already know just how brutal the Games become and those who are new to the dystopian tale, is that the movie adaptation knows how to play too.

This *Hunger Games* is a muscular, honorable, unflinching translation of Collins's vision. It's brutal where it needs to be, particularly when children fight and bleed. It conveys both the miseries of the oppressed, represented by the poorly fed and clothed citizens of

Schwarzbaum acknowledges her mission and dual audiences.

To succeed, the film must *translate* the vision of the original book.

Panem's twelve suffering districts, and the rotted values of the oppressors, evident in the gaudy decadence of those who live in the Capitol. Best of all, the movie effectively showcases the allure of the story's remarkable, kick-ass sixteen-year-old heroine, Katniss Everdeen.

Katniss — who volunteers to fight in place of her sister as one of District 12's two unfortunate "tributes" when the little girl is chosen — is the heart and soul of the story, one of those feisty female protagonists pitched to the YA [young adult] market but appealing to adults as well. Katniss is happiest when she's hunting food for her family with the bow-and-arrow precision that is her specialty. She's a tomboy with a trademark brunet braid down her back, and she's a graceful young woman — strong, self-possessed, and unaware of her own beauty, whether dressed like a backwoods scout or dolled up for pageant display in gorgeous gowns. And Jennifer Lawrence, previously dressed as a backwoods scout in her galvanizing breakout, *Winter's Bone*, is, in her gravity, her intensity, and her own unmannered beauty, about as impressive a Hollywood incarnation of Katniss as one could ever imagine. Much of Katniss's experience throughout

A lengthy paragraph explains the film's heroine and why Jennifer Lawrence works in the role.

THE HUNGER GAMES, Jennifer Lawrence, 2012/ photo: Murray Close/© Lionsgate/Courtesy Everett Collection.

the Games — as she improvises with an ingenuity far beyond the scope of any TV *Survivor* contestant — is interior, silent. Lawrence is expressive in her stillness, and moves with athletic confidence.

Schwarzbaum explains potential differences in audience reactions to the film.

Fans of the book and moviegoers coming to the story fresh may reach different conclusions about the effectiveness of Josh Hutcherson as Peeta, the baker's son from District 12 who is at once Katniss's competitor and the boy who loves her. In the book, interesting edges rough up his niceness; he's not quite so easy to peg. But to these eyes, on screen he's been sanded down to a generic sensitive good guy, so much so that it's difficult to understand why Katniss is prickly around him. Meanwhile, so little is seen of Liam Hemsworth as Gale, Katniss's soul mate / fellow hunter, in this first episode that the uninitiated might not pay attention to the third angle of the story's romantic triangle — about the only element this high-quality pop culture phenomenon has in common with the swoons of *Twilight*.

Final line comments on differences between movies and books.

Director Gary Ross does a tight job of establishing the future-meets-*1984* vibe in Panem: the slog of daily life, the hopelessness that dulls the citizens, the fear that returns each year at the Hunger Games lottery known as the Reaping. Aided by outré costumes from designer Judianna Makovsky, he also goes to town in the Capitol sequences. Elizabeth Banks as Effie the PR handler, Woody Harrelson as Haymitch the mentor, Lenny Kravitz as Cinna the stylist, Stanley Tucci as Caesar the unctuous TV interviewer — they're all reasonable facsimiles of what's on the page, and fabulous oddities for those who are just meeting them. And if the depiction of the death-by-death progress of the Games themselves, as Katniss struggles mightily to save her own life on behalf of her sister, doesn't match the psychological tension on the page, well, thems may be the rules of the adaptation game. The movie shows how, but the book shows why. **A–**

Exploring purpose and topic

▶ topic

Most evaluations you're required to prepare for school or work come with assigned topics. But here are strategies to follow when you have a choice. ○

Evaluate a subject you know well. This is the safest option, built on the assumption that everyone is an expert on something. Years of reading *Cook's Illustrated* magazine or playing tennis might make it natural for you to review restaurants or tennis rackets. You've accumulated not only basic facts but also lots of hands-on knowledge—the sort that gives you the confidence to offer an opinion. So go ahead and demonstrate your expertise.

Evaluate a subject you need to investigate. Perhaps you are applying to law schools, looking for family-friendly companies to work for, or thinking about purchasing an HDTV. To make such choices, you'll need information. So kill two birds with a single assignment: Use the school project to explore personal or professional choices you face, find the necessary facts and data, and make a case for (or against) Arizona State, Whole Foods, or Sony.

Evaluate a subject you'd like to know more about. How do wine connoisseurs tell one cabernet from another and rank them so confidently? How would a college football championship team from the 1950s match up against more recent winning teams? Use an assignment to settle questions like these that you and friends may have debated late into the evening.

Evaluate a subject that's been on your mind. Not all evaluations are driven by decisions of the moment. Instead, you may want to make a point about social, cultural, and political matters: You believe a particular piece of health-care or immigration legislation is bad policy or find yourself disturbed by changes in society. An evaluation is often the appropriate genre for giving voice to such thoughts, whether you compose a conventional piece or venture into the realms of satire or parody.

find a topic
p. 331

Understanding your audience

Your job as a reviewer is easier when readers care about your opinions. Fortunately, most people consult evaluations and reviews routinely, often hoping to find specific information: *Is the latest Stephen L. Carter novel up to snuff? Who's the most important American architect working today? Phillies or Braves in the National League East this year?* But you'll still have to make accommodations for differing audiences—as Lisa Schwarzbaum does in her review of *The Hunger Games* (p. 103).

Write for experts.   Knowledgeable readers can be a tough group because they may bring strong, maybe inflexible, opinions to a topic. But if you know your stuff, you can take on the experts because they know their stuff too: You don't have to repeat tedious background information or discuss criteria of evaluation in detail. You can use the technical vocabulary experts share and make allusions to people and concepts they'd recognize. ○ Here are a few in-crowd sentences from a review of the football video game *Backbreaker* from an online gaming site:

> *Backbreaker* joins the sports design trend of placing emphasis on the right analog stick. It's everything from your swim/rip move on defense, to your bonecrunching hit or tackle, to juking, spinning, selecting receivers and passing. You use the right trigger as an action modifier ("aggressive mode") to go into other areas of your player's toolset. Everything is contextual to the type of player you control and it's pick-up-and-play intuitive after one trip through the tutorial.
>
> — Kotaku, "*Backbreaker* Review: The Challenger Crashes"

Write for a general audience.   General audiences need more hand-holding than specialists. You may have to spell out criteria of evaluation, provide lots of background information, and define key terms. But general readers usually are willing to learn more about a topic. Here's noted film critic Roger Ebert explaining how to watch time-travel films:

> *The Lake House* tells the story of a romance that spans years but involves only a few kisses. It succeeds despite being based on two paradoxes: time travel and the ability of two people to have conversations that are, under the terms

Need help thinking about your audience? See "How to Revise Your Work" on pp. 426–27.

improve your sentences p. 412

established by the film, impossible. Neither one of these problems bothered me in the slightest. Take time travel: I used to get distracted by its logical flaws and contradictory timelines. Now in my wisdom I have decided to simply accept it as a premise, no questions asked. A time-travel story works on emotional, not temporal, logic.

— rogerebert.com, June 16, 2006

Write for novices.   You have a lot of explaining to do when readers are absolutely fresh to a subject. Prepare to give them context and background information. For example, Digital Photography Review, a Web site that examines photographic equipment in great detail, attaches the following note to all its camera reviews: "If you're new to digital photography you may wish to read the Digital Photography Glossary before diving into this article (it may help you understand some of the terms used)." Smart reviewers anticipate the needs of their audiences.

Are buffalo dangerous?
For some audiences, you have to explain everything. John J. Ruszkiewicz.

Finding and developing materials

When you are assigned a review, investigate your subject thoroughly. Online research is easy: To figure out what others are thinking, just type the name of whatever you are evaluating into a browser, followed by the word *review* or *critic*. ○ Read what you find critically and carefully, giving close attention to reviews from reputable sources. But don't just repeat the opinions you turn up. Feel free to challenge prevailing views whenever you can make a better argument or offer a fresh perspective. To do that, focus on criteria and evidence.

develop criteria ◀

Decide on your criteria. Clarify your standards, even if you're just evaluating pizza. Should the crust be hard or soft? Should the sauce be red and spicy, or white and creamy? How thick should the pizza be? How salty? And, for all these opinions—*why*?

Didn't expect the *why*? You really don't have a criterion until you attach a plausible reason to it. ○ The rationale should be clear in your own mind even if you don't expect to explain it in the review or evaluation itself: *Great pizza comes with a soft crust that wraps each bite and topping in a floury texture that merges the contrasting flavors.* More important, any criterion you use will have to make sense to readers either on its own (*Public art should be beautiful*) or after you've explained and defended it (*Public art should be scandalous because people need to be jolted out of conformist thinking*).

Look for hard criteria. You'll seem objective when your criteria at least seem grounded in numbers or corroborated observations. Think, for example, of how instructors set measurable standards for your performance in their courses, translating all sorts of activities, from papers to class participation, into numbers. Teachers aren't alone in deferring to numbers. CNET Reviews, for instance, relies heavily on precise measurements in evaluating televisions and explains those criteria in excruciating detail on its Web site. The following is how CNET assesses just one aspect of an HDTV's performance:

> **Black luminance (0%)** *Example result: 0.0140*
> This is the measure of the luminance of "black" in fL (footlamberts), and a lower number is better. It's often referred to as MLL, for minimum luminance level, but since this measurement is taken post-calibration it may be higher than the TV's minimum. We consider the post-calibration black level most important because the calibration process aims to prevent crushing of shadow detail and "tricks"

refine your
search p. 442

develop a
statement p. 362

like dynamic contrast that can affect this measurement. The measurement is taken of a completely black screen (except for a 5% stripe on near the bottom), created by using the Quantum Data's 0% window pattern.

Good: +/− less than 0.009

Average: +/− 0.009 to 0.019

Poor: +/− 0.02 or higher

Got that? Probably not, but aren't you now inclined to take a CNET product review seriously?

Argue for criteria that can't be measured. How do you measure the success or failure of something that can't be objectively calculated—a student dance recital, Bruno Mars's latest track, or the new abstract sculpture just hauled onto campus? Look into how such topics are evaluated and discussed in public media. Get familiar with what sensible critics have to say about whatever you're evaluating and how they say it—whether it's contemporary art, fine saddles, good teaching, or successful foreign policy. If you read carefully, you'll find values and criteria embedded in all your sources. ○

In the following excerpt, for example, James Morris explains why he believes American television is often better than Hollywood films. Morris's implied criteria are highlighted.

Stated directly, Morris's criteria might sound like this: Good entertainment is intelligent; it is tailored to its medium; it does not require special effects to keep people interested; it is disciplined.

What I admire most about these shows, and most deplore about contemporary movies, is the quality of the scripts. The TV series are devised and written by smart people who seem to be allowed to let their intelligence show. Yes, the individual and ensemble performances on several of the series are superb, but would the actors be as good as they are if they were miming the action? TV shows are designed for the small screen and cannot rely, as movies do, on visual and aural effects to distract audiences. If what's being said on TV isn't interesting, why bother to watch? Television is rigorous, right down to the confinement of hour or half-hour time slots, further reduced by commercials. There's no room for the narrative bloat that inflates so many Hollywood movies from their natural party-balloon size to Thanksgiving-parade dimensions.

— "My Favorite Wasteland," *Wilson Quarterly*, Autumn 2005

read closely
p. 340

Stand by your values.   Make sure you define criteria that apply to more than just the case you are examining at the moment. Think about what makes socially conscious rap music, world-class sculpture, or a great politician. For instance, you might admire artists or actors who overcome great personal tragedies on their paths to stardom. But to make such heroics a necessary criterion for artistic achievement might look like special pleading.

Gather your evidence.   Some materials for a review will necessarily come from secondary sources. Before judging the merits of Obamacare or Truman's decision to drop atomic bombs to end World War II, expect to do a lot of critical reading in a range of sources. Then weigh the evidence before offering your opinion—being sure to credit those sources in your review. ○

Other evidence will come from shrewd observation. Sometimes you just need to be attuned to the world around you—as Jordyn Brown is in cataloging the rudeness of cell phone users (see p. 118). When reviewing a book, a movie, a restaurant, or a similar item, take notes. If appropriate, measure, weigh, photograph, or interview your subjects. (Does that gut-buster or quarter pounder measure up?) When it matters, survey what others think about an issue (a campus political flap, for example) and record such opinions. Finally, keep an open mind. Be willing to change an opinion when evidence points in directions you hadn't expected.

NO EXIT   © Andy Singer

WITH WEBSITES LIKE *"ANGIESLIST.COM,"* *"YELP,"* *"RATEMYPROFESSORS.COM"* AND PRODUCT AND VENDOR REVIEWS ON *AMAZON* AND *EBAY,* WE'RE ALL CONSTANTLY HAVING OUR PERFORMANCE APPRAISED.

CLICK

RATEMYJANITOR.COM
VIEW   FIND   RATE

Andy Singer.

read closely
p. 340

Creating a structure

Like other arguments, evaluations have distinct parts that can be arranged into patterns or structures.

Choose a simple structure when your criteria and categories are predictable. A straightforward review might announce its subject and claim, list criteria of evaluation, present evidence to show whether the subject meets those standards, and draw conclusions. Here's one version of that pattern with the criteria discussed all at once, at the opening of the piece:

Introduction leading to an evaluative claim

Criteria of evaluation stated and, if necessary, defended

Subject measured by first criterion + evidence
Subject measured by second criterion + evidence
Subject measured by additional criteria + evidence

Conclusion

And here's a template with the criteria of evaluation introduced one at a time:

Introduction leading to an evaluative claim

First criterion of evaluation stated and, if necessary, defended

Subject measured by first criterion + evidence

Second criterion stated/defended

Subject measured by second criterion + evidence

Additional criteria stated/defended

Subject measured by additional criteria + evidence

Conclusion

You might find structures this formulaic in job-performance reviews at work or in consumer magazines. Once a pattern is established for assessing computers, paint sprayers, video games, or even teachers (consider those forms you fill in at the end of the term), it can be repeated for each new subject and results can be compared.

Yet what works for hardware and tech products is less convincing when applied to music, books, political policies, or societal behaviors that are more than the sum of their parts. Imagine a film critic whose *every* review marched through the same predictable set of criteria: acting, directing, writing, cinematography, and special effects. When a subject can't (or shouldn't) be reviewed via simple categories, you decide which of its aspects and elements deserve attention. ○

Choose a focal point.   You could, in fact, organize an entire review around one or more shrewd insights, and many reviewers do. The trick is to support any stellar perception with clear and specific evidence. Consider, for example, how Lisa Schwarzbaum ties her claim that the first *Hunger Games* movie is a "muscular, honorable, unflinching translation" of the book to her portrait of Jennifer Lawrence as Katniss. Or look carefully at Jordyn Brown's scathing portrait of cell phone users (p. 118): You'll discover that what holds her satire together is a fear that too many people are missing important aspects of their lives. Brown dramatizes that problem by beginning and ending the paper at a birthday party that she and a dozen friends are just barely attending:

> This dinner was supposed to be a festive gathering to celebrate our good friend Stacey's birthday. But no one mingled or celebrated, not even Stacey. Everyone seemed to be somewhere else. They had all wandered off to Google-town, Twitter-ville, and Texting-My-Boyfriend City, and I was left there alone at the Cheesecake Factory. . . . Twelve people preferred phone activities to talking to each other and me over three-tiered red velvet cheesecake. Seriously, people. Put those phones down. You're not thinking clearly.

Compare and contrast.   Another obvious way to organize an evaluation is to examine differences. ○ Strengths and weaknesses stand out especially well when similar subjects are examined critically. When *Automobile* columnist Jamie Kitman, for example, wants to make a tongue-in-cheek case that the best American police car is one that looks most intimidating, he first has to explain his odd criterion of evaluation:

> Here [in the United States], police cars aren't meant to make us feel all fuzzy but to instill powerful sensations of fear. . . . At their best, police cars look strong, stout, capable, and most of all, mean. To the extent that they make bad people feel scared, they make those of us who ought to feel safe (because we have done nothing wrong) feel safer, while still feeling scared.

shape your
work p. 374

use comparison and
contrast p. 367

After that, it's a simple matter of comparing candidates. He dismisses Ford Tauruses and Explorers because they "don't scare enough, even with light bars on top and armed with police-academy graduates inside." GM police cruisers are even less able to terrify the citizenry: They have "the scare factor of unspoiled rice pudding." Fortunately, he has found a winner, a model already described in the column as "malevolent" and looking "pissed off, angry, and unreasonable":

> That leaves the Dodge Charger, America's indisputable reigning champion cop car, to reign longer. It's the distilled automotive essence of every TV cop who ever drove a car, from Broderick Crawford on, all rolled into one angry, authoritarian appliance. No wonder countless agencies across the country favor Chargers. They're not kidding around, and you might as well know it.

Kitman's comparison is fun, but it makes sense—scary sense—especially when visual evidence is attached.

Courtesy of the Chrysler Foundation.

Choosing a style and design

Evaluations can be composed in any style, from high to low—depending, as always, on aim and audience. ○ Look for opportunities to present evaluations visually too. They can simplify your task.

Use a high or formal style.   Technical reviews tend to be formal and impersonal: They may be almost indistinguishable from reports, describing their findings in plain, unemotional language. Such a style gives the impression of scientific objectivity, even though the work may reflect someone's agenda. For instance, here's a paragraph in formal style from the National Assessment of Educational Progress summarizing the performance of American students in science:

> Of all the racial/ethnic groups reported, Asian/Pacific Islander students had the highest percentage of fourth- and eighth-graders performing at or above the *Proficient* level in mathematics and reading in 2013. Results by gender show higher percentages of male students than female students at or above *Proficient* in mathematics at both grades in 2013. In reading, female students had higher percentages at or above the *Proficient* level than male students at both grades.
>
> — *Nation's Report Card*, 2013 Mathematics and Reading Assessment (http://nationsreportcard.gov/reading_math_2013/#/student-groups)

Use a middle style.   When a writer has a more direct stake in the work—as is typical in book or movie reviews, for example—the style moves more decisively toward the middle. You sense a person behind the writing, making judgments and offering opinions. That's certainly the case in these two paragraphs by Clive Crook, written shortly after the death of noted economist John Kenneth Galbraith: Words, phrases, and even sentence fragments that humanize the assessment are highlighted, while a contrast to economist Milton Friedman also sharpens the portrait.

> Galbraith, despite the Harvard professorship, was never really an economist in the ordinary sense in the first place. In one of countless well-turned pronouncements, he said, "Economics is extremely useful as a form of employment for economists." He disdained the scientific pretensions and formal apparatus of modern economics — all that math and number crunching — believing that it

missed the point. This view did not spring from mastery of the techniques: Galbraith disdained them from the outset, which saved time.

Friedman, in contrast, devoted his career to grinding out top-quality scholarly work, while publishing the occasional best seller as a sideline. He too was no math whiz, but he was painstakingly scientific in his methods (when engaged in scholarly research) and devoted to data. All that was rather beneath Galbraith. Brilliant, yes; productive, certainly. But he was a bureaucrat, a diplomat, a political pundit, and a popular economics writer of commanding presence more than a serious economic thinker, let alone a great one.

— "John Kenneth Galbraith, Revisited," *National Journal*, May 15, 2006

Use a low style.   Many reviewers get personal with readers, some so direct that they verge on rudeness. Consider the product reviews on Amazon.com or almost any comment section online. In contrast, the evaluations you write for academic or work assignments should be (relatively) polite and low-key in style. But you do have an enormous range of options—especially when offering social and political commentary. Then, if your evaluations turn into satire or parody, all the gloves come off. In such situations, humor or sarcasm can become powerful tools, full of insider humor, colloquial turns of phrase, bizarre allusions, and grammar on the edge. But no style is more difficult to manage. So look for models of the kinds of evaluation you want to compose. Study the ones you admire for lessons in style using language effectively.

Present evaluations visually.   Evaluations work especially well when their claims can be supported by tables, charts, graphs, or other visual elements. These allow readers to see relationships that could not be conveyed quite as efficiently in words alone. ⬤ And sometimes the images simply have more impact. Consider your response to images of real fast-food items posted on an offbeat Web site called the West Virginia Surf Report. Here's the description of the feature that appeared on the site:

Fast Food: Ads vs. Reality Each item was purchased, taken home, and photographed immediately. Nothing was tampered with, run over by a car, or anything of the sort. It is an accurate representation in every case. Shiny, neon-orange, liquefied pump-cheese, and all.

display data
p. 550

Here are several of the images the site presented of products purchased from well-known national chains:

Jeff Kay.

All you need to do is recall the carefully crafted professional photographs of these items you've seen posted in the fast-food restaurants and you can draw your own conclusion: *Caveat emptor!*

Your Turn Almost everyone reads at least one critic or type of review regularly — of restaurants, movies, TV shows, sports teams, gizmos, video games, and so on. Pick a review by your favorite critic or, alternatively, a review you have read recently and noted. Then examine its style closely. Is it formal, informal, or casual? Technical or general? Serious or humorous? Full of allusions to stuff regular readers would get? What features of the style do you like? Do you have any reservations about its style? In a detailed paragraph, evaluate only the style of the reviewer or review (not the substance of the review), organizing your work to support a clear thesis.

Examining models

SOCIAL SATIRE   Satires, which poke fun at the foibles of society in order to correct them, often require writers to draw exaggerated but recognizable portraits of people and situations. That's what Jordyn Brown attempts to do in a paper aimed at getting her friends to shut off their cell phones and pay more attention to life. If readers laugh too, that's all to the good.

Reading the Genre   To keep readers interested, satires have to be perceptive, entertaining, and funny. Can you point to specific moments in Jordyn Brown's "A Word from My Anti-Phone Soapbox" when these qualities come together? What images or ideas are you most likely to remember after reading the piece?

Brown 1

Jordyn Brown

Professor Ruszkiewicz

Rhetoric 325M

May 5, 20--

A Word from My Anti-Phone Soapbox

I sat for at least five minutes staring at the tops of the other dinner guests' heads. All twenty-four eyes (that's twelve pairs) were unwaveringly fixed on their respective laps. I didn't understand why my friends held their phones under the table. We weren't in class. Perhaps it was a subconscious admittance of shame for their inattentiveness. I sat at the dinner table confused. This dinner was supposed to be a festive gathering to celebrate our good friend Stacey's birthday. But no one mingled or celebrated, not even Stacey. Everyone seemed to be somewhere else. They had all wandered off to Google-town,

> Opening paragraph, especially its final sentence, sets the scene and the tone.

[e] For an additional reading, see **macmillanhighered.com/howtowrite3e**.
e-readings > Ivan Penn and the *Tampa Bay Times, Mandarin Chinese, Rosetta Stone Style* [PRODUCT TEST]

Brown 2

Twitter-ville, and Texting-My-Boyfriend City, and I was left there alone at the Cheesecake Factory.

Bitter frustration grew inside me because (a) my party's behavior was ridiculous and (b) I'd left my own phone in the car. Luckily, my thoughts occupied me and kept me from mounting my chair and giving my friends a stern and passionate tongue-lashing right in the middle of the restaurant. My peers disgusted me with their technological dependency. So I packaged the lecture I felt coming on at the dinner table neatly in my brain and will now recite it for you, minus the expletives.

Maybe I'm just bitter because my phone is only capable of Stone Age maneuvers like making calls and texting. But having the whole World Wide Web in your hands has ruined all of you tech fiends. Look at yourselves. You can't bear to face that terrible affliction people had to endure years ago called *boredom*. So you fill up your fancy little devices with applications, games, movies, and music to ensure that you'll never have an unoccupied moment. What a shame that would be! America's greatest pastime used to be baseball. The magic of a triple play or an out-of-the-park home run made the hours spent watching inning after inning well worth it. But now you need constant stimulation. You want to see a home run every at-bat. Your movies need to be 90 percent car chase. Your telephones are full-on pocket-sized entertainment centers. You've bastardized thrill and excitement; you can't be pleased. The movie you saw last night wasn't too slow; your world is just too fast.

The paper falls into an ancient genre called *invective*, a hearty denunciation of someone or something.

First attack focuses on the obsessive need for stimulation: "your world is just too fast."

Brown 3

Information just shouldn't be this readily available. You people can't handle it. You Urbanspoon one tasty restaurant and think you're A. A. Gill, famous British food critic. This constant tech stream has even ruined good arguments. Before, you would argue fervently for hours.

"*Top Gun* came out in '84!"

"No man, it came out in '86!"

And then you'd go round and round and, at the end of the night, no one really knew the right answer because both debaters argued so well. But, oh no, these beautiful moments are nearly extinct because some cocky know-it-all's going to whip out his iPhone, always conveniently connected to Google. And with a few strokes of his touch screen he'll find a source, take the other guy down, and crush his spirit. Braggarts today strut around like they know everything. No, it's Google that knows everything; you just have a cool phone.

And it's not just the search engines that give you phone-tech junkies balloon heads. Twitter and Facebook have you believing that people really want to know every minute detail of your life. Now, I hate to be the bearer of bad news, but unless you're Ashton Kutcher or Kim Kardashian, no one is tracking your every move every second of the day. So cut out all the Facebook statuses about your disposable-ware crisis at Target. Don't waste the space on my news feed with "Should I get paper or Styrofoam plates?" Annoying.

Second point is that technology makes us think we're smarter than we are.

Throughout, the casual style mimics speech: "what a shame that would be"; "but, oh no"; "pitiful."

Technology also makes us think we are the center of the universe.

Brown 4

And I don't care what you had for lunch. Don't TwitPic a picture of your meal, because it makes no sense. What if you'd done that ten years ago? If you had skipped into school with a picture you had gotten developed at the drugstore and gone around showing it to people, saying, "Hey guys, look what I had for dinner!" the whole fifth-grade class would have looked at you like you were insane. Twitter has made nonsense commonplace. No thought is too base to fill a tweet's 140 characters. Pitiful.

The examples throughout work if readers recognize some truth under the exaggerations.

Sad to say, these handheld devices have turned you into technologically overindulged brats. You break into temper tantrums, stomping around, pouting, throwing your Blackberries at soft surfaces, and crossing your arms in agitation whenever you hit a dead zone and can't access your precious Internet. And you have even less patience for your friends when you text or call them. After all, everything you have to say—spoken or in text—is infinitely more important than anything else in their lives. The meaning of the word urgent has evolved since the earliest days of portable and instant communication devices. Once only physicians routinely received urgent messages: "Hurry, we need you, Dr. Cardiologist, to fix this man's horrible heart." But now *urgent* can mean, "911! What do you feel like eating for dinner? I'm at the grocery store now. Hurry and call me back!!!" And I wouldn't dare let a text message from you sit in my in-box for more than an hour or I'd be in for a scolding the next time I see you.

The paragraph shows how smartphones are leading to breakdowns in social relations.

Brown 5

So, Earth to you, the people who never part from their cell phones. I'm sure you've taken several breaks while reading this rant to check your e-mail and respond to a few texts. You probably missed most of the points of my argument too, much like you're missing what's going on in the world around you. Cell phones were initially meant to connect us, broadening the time frame during which people could communicate with one another. But with all the new apps being incorporated into these devices, isolation only grows, shrinking your world and perspective. You're all constantly talking and thinking about how *you* feel and what *you* think. You don't talk to Rachel or Stephen but to the "Twitter-verse" or to Facebook at large. You communicate without any idea of who's really listening.

Twelve people preferred phone activities to talking to each other and *me* over three-tiered red velvet cheesecake. Seriously, people. Put those phones down. You're not thinking clearly.

Like most satires, this one turns serious and offers a simple solution: Turn off the phone.

PRODUCT REVIEW   Shortly after the debut of the 2013 summer film *Monsters University*, Eric Brown spent some time reviewing a promotional Web site Disney/Pixar posted for the imaginary school, a dead-ringer for real college and university home pages. (You can find it online by searching "Monsters University.") We reproduce Brown's essay from *The Chronicle of Higher Education* here. In it, Brown argues that there's a lot to admire about Disney/Pixar's make-believe college site, which itself functions as a special subgenre of evaluation.

Reading the Genre   After reading Eric Hoover's "Monsters U.'s Site Just Might Give You 'Web-Site Envy'" and perusing the MU Web site itself online, examine the home page of your current school or employer and discuss its strengths and weaknesses with colleagues.

The Chronicle of Higher Education

Posted: July 2, 2013
From: Eric Hoover

Monsters U.'s Site Just Might Give You "Web-Site Envy"

Okay, I'll admit that I've yet to see *Monsters University*, the No. 1 movie in the nation. But I've spent a good hour tooling around the promotional Web site for the fictional institution. It's scary good.

Fascinated by how this portal both mimics and mocks real-life college Web sites, I asked Ashley Hennigan, assistant director of social media strategy at Cornell University, to share her thoughts on the MU site — and what admissions officers might learn from it.

For one thing, the design is clean and consistent, a far cry from the hodgepodge, thrown-together look of some college sites. This one captures higher-education convention so well, Ms. Hennigan writes in an e-mail, that "I'm sure some universities have Web-site envy."

The first things Ms. Hennigan looks for on college Web sites are a modern design, brand continuity, and simple navigation. On those counts, she says, the Monsters U. site is a success. The home page includes a carousel of images, with news and events featured prominently, and that design is carried through the secondary pages. This, folks, is a triumph of branding.

When visiting college sites, Ms. Hennigan also looks for connections to students. Do applicants have a way of communicating with the people — er, monsters — who know the campus best? "While these monsters aren't blogging," she writes, "they are making YouTube videos and providing their own testimonials."

Thesis is simple and direct.

MU's Web site mostly measures up to a whole series of criteria.

Evidence is cited for the Web site's effectiveness.

MU's site conveys warmth, a sense of the folks students will meet on the campus (yeah, yeah, I realize these are cartoon creatures). Take the faculty profile of the inspiring Dean Hardscrabble, dean of the School of Scaring. "If you can survive a class taught by her, then the human world is a breeze," says a former MU student. Note the emphasis on teaching here; there's no mention of the dean's publishing prowess.

Ms. Hennigan says she was struck by the welcome video. "Swap out the campus and the university name, and this would be a great promo," she writes. "Hitting all of the great branding key-words — legacy, tradition, diversity, and integrity. They get bonus points for using YouTube throughout the site for recruitment." I like the array of hilarious slogans that are no more hilarious than some colleges' actual slogans ("Your future is knocking. Open the door.").

The review is playful, poking fun at genuine college Web sites.

On the admission page, there's some advice for applicants from admission counselors. The applications that stand out, one coun-selor writes, "tell a great story" about how MU will affect the life of a student: "Great students can go lots of places. We want to know that MU and the student is a great match."

Of course, like real sites, that for Monsters U omits some scary details.

Ms. Hennigan applauds that message. "I'm happy to see the scary counselor asking how attending MU will change the monster's life," she writes, "acknowledging that there are plenty of places to go and that being a great match is more important than just being a great student."

What's lacking? Oh, information about paying for all this. The financial-aid page doesn't mention the cost of attendance, and there are only vague references to meeting financial need. The par-ents' page is also thin on details about finances. "Our human par-ents would demand much more," Ms. Hennigan writes. "They want to see real numbers, financial costs, and outcome statistics."

And how much hunting should a visitor have to do? "It should take only one click off the admissions home page to find location, academic programs, and cost," Ms. Hennigan writes. "MU could up their content with these quick facts and figures." As she notes, though, there's a campus-safety page, complete with reports of specific incidents (Thursday at 12:08 AM: "Four female students report prank phone calls from an unknown male caller pretending to be a lost human.").

I laughed at the following line before realizing that it's more or less what many colleges tell families, with a straight face: "Don't let a little debt scare you and your child away from the best educational opportunity money can buy."

Perhaps no college Web site is complete without a little bragging. This factoid caught my eye: "Each year, over 26,000 high school and transfer monsters apply to MU, but only a fraction get admitted." You see, Monsters University is awesome, and it touts its acceptance rate as evidence. Can you imagine a real college doing that?

VISUAL COMPARISON How might the Insurance Institute for Highway Safety memorably celebrate its fiftieth anniversary? By crashing two cars fifty years apart in age to show how much crash safety has improved, thanks in part to the efforts of the group. The visual evidence represents a startling and memorable evaluation of their work.

Reading the Genre The pre- and post-test images in "Crash Test" leave little doubt about progress in vehicle safety. What similar image pairings might you use to evaluate either progress or decline in some other area of human life—technology, education, lifestyles, or culture? Look for images that provide specific, convincing, and maybe even measurable evidence.

Crash Test

Insurance Institute for Highway Safety

In the 50 years since U.S. insurers organized the Insurance Institute for Highway Safety, car crashworthiness has improved. Demonstrating this was a crash test conducted on Sept. 9 between a 1959 Chevrolet Bel Air and a 2009 Chevrolet Malibu. In a real-world collision similar to this test, occupants of the new model would fare much better than in the vintage Chevy.

"It was night and day, the difference in occupant protection," says Institute president Adrian Lund. "What this test shows is that automakers don't build cars like they used to. They build them better."

The crash test was conducted at an event to celebrate the contributions of auto insurers to highway safety progress over 50 years. Beginning with the Institute's 1959 founding, insurers have maintained the resolve, articulated in the 1950s, to "conduct, sponsor, and encourage programs designed to aid in the conservation and preservation of life and property from the hazards of highway accidents."

Test compares crashworthiness then and now: 1959 Chevrolet Bel Air and 2009 Chevrolet Malibu in 40 mph frontal offset test (click on photos to see larger images).

Top photo testifies to the violence of the 40-mph crash.

Watch a video of the crash test

2009 Chevrolet Malibu   1959 Chevrolet Bel Air

Malibu post-crash   Bel Air post-crash

In the crash test involving the two Chevrolets, the 2009 Malibu's occupant compartment remained intact (above left) while the one in the 1959 Bel Air (right) collapsed.

The collision demolishes the front ends of both vehicles.

But the passenger compartments tell a different story, providing clear evidence of fifty years of progress in structural design and safety.

Courtesy of Insurance Institute for Highway Safety, http://www.iihs.org.

1. **Arts Review:** Drawing on your expertise as a consumer of popular culture — the way Lisa Schwarzbaum does in her *Entertainment Weekly* review of *The Hunger Games* (p. 103) — review a movie, book, television series, musical piece, artist, or work of art for a publication that you specify. It might be the equivalent of *Entertainment Weekly* or you might aim your work at a local or student publication. Consider, too, writing a substantive piece for an online site that takes reviews — such as Amazon.com or IMDb. Write a review strong enough to change someone's mind.

2. **Social Satire:** Using the techniques of social satire modeled in "A Word from My Anti-Phone Soapbox" (p. 118), assess a public policy, social movement, or cultural trend you believe deserves serious and detailed criticism. But don't write a paper simply describing your target as dangerous, pathetic, or unsuccessful. Instead, make people laugh at your target while also offering a plausible alternative.

3. **Product Review:** Choose an item that you own, buy, or use regularly, anything from a Coleman lantern to Dunkin' Donuts coffee to a Web site, app, or social network you couldn't live without. Then write a fully developed review, making sure to name your criteria of evaluation as clearly as Ashley Hennigan does in Eric Hoover's essay on the Monsters University site (p. 123). Be attentive to your specific audience and generous with the supporting details. Use graphics if appropriate.

4. **Visual Comparison or Review:** Construct an evaluation in which a visual comparison or some other media evidence plays a major role. You might use photographs the way the West Virginia Surf Report (pp. 116–17) does. Or perhaps you can work in another medium to show, for example, how good or bad the instructions in a technical manual are, how much the brownies you baked differ from the ones pictured on the box, or how images on your school's or an employer's Web site stereotype the people who attend or work there. Be creative.

5. **Your Choice:** Evaluate a program or facility in some institution you know well (school, business, church, recreation center) that you believe works efficiently or poorly. Prepare a presentation in the medium of your choice and imagine that your audience is an administrator with the power to reward or shut down the operation.

How to start ▶
- Need a **topic**? See page 135.
- Need to identify **possible causes**? See page 140.
- Need to **organize your analysis**? See page 142.

5 Causal Analyses

explain how, why, or what if something happens

We all analyze and explain things daily. Someone asks, "Why?" We reply, "Because . . ." and then offer reasons and rationales. Such a response comes naturally.

CAUSAL ANALYSIS   An instructor asks for a ten-page *causal analysis* of the political or economic forces responsible for a major armed conflict during the twentieth century. You choose to write about the Korean War because you know almost nothing about it.

RESEARCH STUDY   You notice that most students now walk across campus chatting on cell phones or listening to music. You develop a *research study* to examine whether this phenomenon has any relationship to a recent drop in the numbers of students joining campus clubs and activities across the country.

CULTURAL ANALYSIS   Why, you wonder, in a fully illustrated *cultural analysis*, did blue jeans become a fashion phenomenon the world over? What explains their enduring popularity?

DECIDING TO WRITE A CAUSAL ANALYSIS.   From climate change to childhood obesity to high school students' poor performance on standardized tests, the daily news is full of problems framed by *how*, *why*, and *what if* questions. These are often described as issues of *cause and effect*, terms we'll use frequently in this chapter. Take childhood obesity. The public wants to know why we have a generation of overweight kids. Too many cheeseburgers? Not enough dodgeball? People worry, too, about the consequences of the trend. Will overweight children grow into obese adults? Will they develop medical problems?

We're interested in such questions because they really do matter, and we're often curious to find answers. But successful analyses of this sort call for more than a passing interest. They demand persistence, precision, and research (for more on choosing a genre, see the Introduction). Even then, you'll have to deal with a world that seems complicated or contradictory. Not every problem or issue can—or should—be explained simply. ○

Don't jump to conclusions.   Think you know why attitudes toward gay marriage changed so quickly or why people have started to resist Hollywood's summer blockbusters? Guess again. Nothing's as simple as it seems and trying to argue causes and effects to other people will quickly teach you humility—even if you *don't* jump to hasty conclusions. It's just plain hard to identify which factors, separately or working together, account for a particular event, activity, or behavior. It is tougher still to predict how what's happening today might affect the future. So approach causal arguments cautiously and prepare to use qualifiers (*sometimes, perhaps, possibly*)—lots of them. ○

Appreciate your limits.   There are rarely easy answers when investigating why things happen the way they do. The space shuttle *Columbia* burned up on reentry in 2003 because a 1.67-pound piece of foam hit the wing of the 240,000-pound craft on liftoff. Who could have imagined so unlikely a sequence of events? Yet investigators had to follow the evidence relentlessly to its conclusion, in this case working backwards—from effect to cause.

analyze claims and evidence p. 456

develop a statement p. 362

The Funnel Effect

We've all ground to a halt on freeways without obstacles in sight — no weather issues, no collisions, no ducks crossing the pavement. What gives? Highway engineers know. The Plain Dealer/Landov.

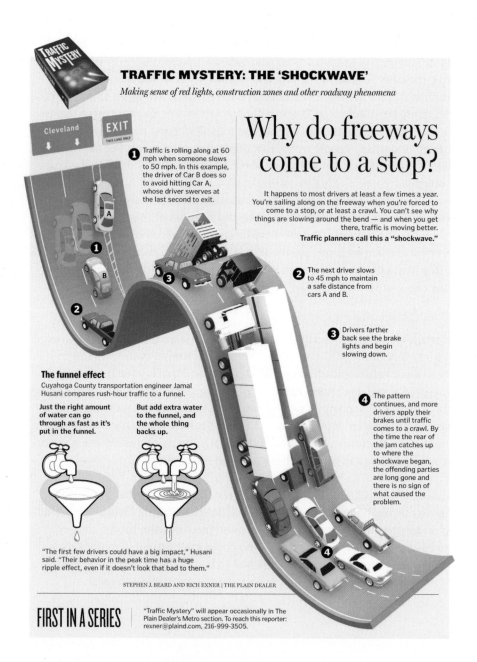

TRAFFIC MYSTERY: THE 'SHOCKWAVE'

Making sense of red lights, construction zones and other roadway phenomena

Cleveland

EXIT
THIS LANE ONLY

1 Traffic is rolling along at 60 mph when someone slows to 50 mph. In this example, the driver of Car B does so to avoid hitting Car A, whose driver swerves at the last second to exit.

Why do freeways come to a stop?

It happens to most drivers at least a few times a year. You're sailing along on the freeway when you're forced to come to a stop, or at least a crawl. You can't see why things are slowing around the bend — and when you get there, traffic is moving better.

Traffic planners call this a "shockwave."

2 The next driver slows to 45 mph to maintain a safe distance from cars A and B.

3 Drivers farther back see the brake lights and begin slowing down.

4 The pattern continues, and more drivers apply their brakes until traffic comes to a crawl. By the time the rear of the jam catches up to where the shockwave began, the offending parties are long gone and there is no sign of what caused the problem.

The funnel effect

Cuyahoga County transportation engineer Jamal Husani compares rush-hour traffic to a funnel.

Just the right amount of water can go through as fast as it's put in the funnel.

But add extra water to the funnel, and the whole thing backs up.

"The first few drivers could have a big impact," Husani said. "Their behavior in the peak time has a huge ripple effect, even if it doesn't look that bad to them."

STEPHEN J. BEARD AND RICH EXNER | THE PLAIN DEALER

FIRST IN A SERIES   "Traffic Mystery" will appear occasionally in The Plain Dealer's Metro section. To reach this reporter: rexner@plaind.com, 216-999-3505.

The fact is that you'll often have to settle for causal explanations that are merely plausible or probable because—outside of the hard sciences—you are often dealing with imprecise and unpredictable forces (especially *people*).

Offer sufficient evidence for claims.   Your academic and professional analyses of cause and effect will be held to high standards of proof—particularly in the sciences. The evidence you provide may be a little looser when you write for popular media, where some readers will tolerate anecdotal and personal examples. But even then, give readers ample reasons to believe you. Avoid hearsay, qualify your claims, and admit when you are merely speculating.

From presidents to pundits, public figures writing about current events find themselves relying on "expert opinion" that is itself open to interpretation. So do individual citizens. This short piece by Jonah Goldberg, a political commentator and global warming skeptic, typifies the dilemma. Not a scientist himself, Goldberg is in no position to make authoritative claims about the causes of climate change. But he can—and does—raise questions about how the studies are being reported to the public.

Reading the Genre   Goldberg is expressing a decidedly minority opinion in this cause-and-effect argument: The scientific consensus favoring human influence on climate change is overwhelming. If you find Goldberg credible, point to strategies in the piece he uses to establish his ethos. If you are unimpressed by his analysis, explain why he is unable to win you over.

National Review Online

Posted: September 2, 2009
From: Jonah Goldberg

Global Warming and the Sun

> The style of the analysis is colloquial, as might be expected in a blog.

On the last day of August, scientists spotted a teeny-weeny sunspot, breaking a 51-day streak of blemish-free days for the sun. If it had gone just a bit longer, it would have broken a 96-year record of 53 days without any of the magnetic disruptions that cause solar flares. That record was nearly broken last year as well.

Wait, it gets even more exciting.

During what scientists call the Maunder Minimum — a period of solar inactivity from 1645 to 1715 — the world experienced the worst of the cold streak dubbed the Little Ice Age. At Christmastime, Londoners ice-skated on the Thames, and New Yorkers (then New Amsterdamers) sometimes walked over the Hudson from Manhattan to Staten Island.

> Identifies the "Maunder Minimum" and acknowledges that its relationship to the "Little Ice Age" is controversial.

Of course, it could have been a coincidence. The Little Ice Age began before the onset of the Maunder Minimum. Many scientists think volcanic activity was a more likely, or at least a more significant, culprit. Or perhaps the big chill was, in the words of scientist Alan Cutler, writing in the *Washington Post* in 1997, a "one-two punch from a dimmer sun and a dustier atmosphere."

Well, we just might find out. A new study in the American Geophysical Union's journal, *Eos*, suggests that we may be heading into another quiet phase similar to the Maunder Minimum.

Meanwhile, the journal *Science* reports that a study led by the National Center for Atmospheric Research, or NCAR, has finally figured out why increased sunspots have a dramatic effect on the weather, increasing temperatures more than the increase in solar energy should explain. Apparently, sunspots heat the stratosphere, which in turn amplifies the warming of the climate.

Goldberg is careful to cite what will look like credible sources: *Eos, Science*.

Scientists have known for centuries that sunspots affect the climate; they just never understood how. Now, allegedly, the mystery has been solved.

Last month, in another study, also released in *Science*, Oregon State University researchers claimed to settle the debate over what caused and ended the last Ice Age. Increased solar radiation coming from slight changes in the Earth's rotation, not greenhouse-gas levels, were to blame.

Though not competent to critique the science itself, Goldberg is willing to comment on how scientific results are reported.

What is the significance of all this? To say I have no idea is quite an understatement, but it will have to do.

Nonetheless, what I find interesting is the eagerness of the authors and the media to make it clear that this doesn't have any particular significance for the debate over climate change. "For those wondering how the (NCAR) study bears on global warming, Gerald Meehl, lead author on the study, says that it doesn't — at least not directly," writes Moises Velasquez-Manoff of the *Christian Science Monitor*. "Global warming is a long-term trend, Dr. Meehl says. . . . This study attempts to explain the processes behind a periodic occurrence."

This overlooks the fact that solar cycles are permanent "periodic occurrences," a.k.a. a very long-term trend. Yet Meehl insists the only significance for the debate is that his study proves climate modeling is steadily improving.

I applaud Meehl's reluctance to go beyond where the science takes him. For all I know, he's right. But such humility and skepticism seem to manifest themselves only when the data point to something other than the mainstream narrative about global warming. For instance, when we have terribly hot weather, or bad hurricanes, the media see portentous proof of climate change. When we don't, it's a moment to teach the masses how weather and climate are very different things.

No, I'm not denying that man-made pollution and other activity have played a role in planetary warming since the Industrial Revolution.

But we live in a moment when we are told, nay lectured and harangued, that if we use the wrong toilet paper or eat the wrong cereal, we are frying the planet. But the sun? Well, that's a distraction. Don't you dare forget your reusable shopping bags, but pay no attention to that burning ball of gas in the sky — it's just the only thing that prevents the planet from being a lifeless ball of ice engulfed in darkness. Never mind that sunspot activity doubled during the twentieth century, when the bulk of global warming has taken place.

What does it say that the modeling that guaranteed disastrous increases in global temperatures never predicted the halt in planetary warming since the late 1990s? (MIT's Richard Lindzen says that "there has been no warming since 1997 and no statistically significant warming since 1995.") What does it say that the modelers have only just now discovered how sunspots make the Earth warmer?

I don't know what it tells you, but it tells me that maybe we should study a bit more before we spend billions to "solve" a problem we don't understand so well.

Goldberg complains that causal claims about climate are reported inconsistently.

Note that this analysis ends up with more questions than answers.

The analysis grows highly rhetorical here to underscore what Goldberg sees as hypocrisy in climate change explanations.

Exploring purpose and topic

To find a topic for an explanatory paper or causal analysis, begin a sentence with *why*, *how*, or *what if* and then finish it, drawing on what you may already know about an issue, trend, or problem. ○

topic ◀

> Why are fewer young Americans marrying?
>
> Why is the occurrence of juvenile asthma spiking?
>
> Why do so few men study nursing or so few women study petroleum engineering?

There are, of course, many other ways to phrase questions about cause and effect in order to attach important conditions and qualifications.

> What if scientists figure out how to stop the human aging process—as now seems plausible within twenty years? What are the consequences for society?
>
> How likely is it that a successful third political party might develop in the United States to end the deadlock between Republicans and Democrats?

A satirical infographic suggests that Twitter is destroying the environment. Courtesy CableTV.com.

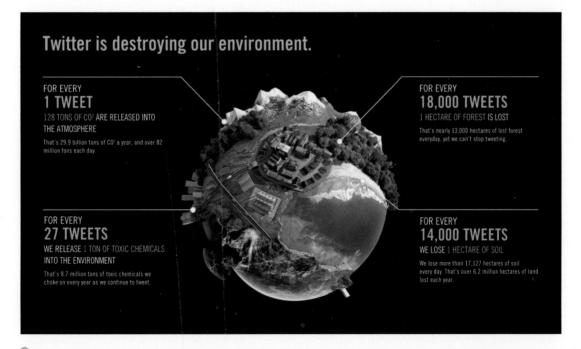

Twitter is destroying our environment.

FOR EVERY
1 TWEET
128 TONS OF CO² ARE RELEASED INTO THE ATMOSPHERE

That's 29.9 billion tons of CO² a year, and over 82 million tons each day.

FOR EVERY
18,000 TWEETS
1 HECTARE OF FOREST IS LOST

That's nearly 13,000 hectares of lost forest everyday, yet we can't stop tweeting.

FOR EVERY
27 TWEETS
WE RELEASE 1 TON OF TOXIC CHEMICALS INTO THE ENVIRONMENT

That's 8.7 million tons of toxic chemicals we choke on every year as we continue to tweet.

FOR EVERY
14,000 TWEETS
WE LOSE 1 HECTARE OF SOIL

We lose more than 17,127 hectares of soil every day. That's over 6.2 million hectares of land lost each year.

find a topic
p. 331

As you can see, none of these topics would just drop from a tree. They require cultural or technical knowledge and a willingness to speculate. Look for such cause-and-effect issues in your academic courses or professional life. Or search for them in the media—though you should shy away from worn-out subjects, such as plagiarism, credit card debt, and celebrity scandals, unless you can offer fresh insights.

To find a subject, try the following approaches.

Look again at a subject you know well.   It may be one that has affected you personally or might in the future. For instance, you may have experienced firsthand the effects of high-stakes testing in high school or you may have theories about why people your age still smoke despite the risks. Offer a hypothesis.

Look for an issue new to you.   Choose a subject you've always wanted to know more about (for example, the long-term cultural effects of the 9/11 attacks). You probably won't be able to venture a thesis or hypothesis until you've done some research, but that's the appeal of this strategy. The material is novel and you are energized. O

Examine a local issue.   Look for recent changes on campus or in the community and examine why they happened or what their consequences may be. Talk to the people responsible or affected. O Tuition raised? Admissions standards lowered? Speech code modified? Why, or what if?

Choose a challenging subject.   An issue that is complicated or vexed will push you to think harder. Don't rush to judgment; remain open-minded about contrary evidence, conflicting motives, and different points of view.

find a topic
p. 331

interview and
observe p. 447

Tackle an issue that seems settled.   If you have guts, look for a phenomenon that most people assume has been adequately explained. Tired of the way Republicans, Wall Street economists, vegans, fundamentalists, or those women on *The View* smugly explain the way things are? Pick one sore point and offer a different—and better—analysis.

Your Turn   After Richard Nixon won forty-nine states in the 1972 presidential election, the distinguished film critic Pauline Kael is reported to have said, "How can he have won? I don't know anyone who voted for him." Can you think of any times when you have similarly misread a situation because you did not have a perspective broad enough to understand all the forces in play? Identify such a situation and consider whether it might provide you with a topic for an explanatory paper. Alternatively, consider some of the times—maybe even beginning in childhood—when you have heard explanations for phenomena that you recognized as wildly implausible because they were superstitions, stereotypes, or simply errors. Consider whether you might turn one of these misconceptions into a topic for an explanatory paper.

Understanding your audience

Readers for cause-and-effect analyses and explanations are diverse, but you might notice a difference between audiences you create yourself by drawing attention to a neglected subject and readers who come to your work because your topic already interests them.

Create an audience. In some situations, you must convince readers to pay attention to the phenomenon you intend to explore. ○ Assume they are smart enough to care about subjects that might affect their lives. But make the case for your subject aggressively. That's exactly what the editors of the *Wall Street Journal* do in an editorial noting the steady *decrease* in traffic deaths that followed a congressional decision ten years earlier to do away with a national 55-mph speed limit.

This may seem noncontroversial now, but at the time the debate was shrill and filled with predictions of doom. Ralph Nader claimed that "history will never forgive Congress for this assault on the sanctity of human life." Judith Stone, president of the Advocates for Highway and Auto Safety, predicted to Katie Couric on NBC's *Today Show* that there would be "6,400 added highway fatalities a year and millions of more injuries." Federico Peña, the Clinton administration's secretary of transportation, declared: "Allowing speed limits to rise above 55 simply means that more Americans will die and be injured on our highways."

— "Safe at Any Speed," July 7, 2006

Anticipates readers who might ask, "Why does this issue matter?"

Write to an existing audience. In most cases, you'll enter cause-and-effect debates already in progress. Whether you intend to uphold what most people already believe or, more controversially, ask them to rethink their positions, you'll probably face readers as knowledgeable (and opinionated) as you are. In the following opening paragraphs, for example, from an article exploring the decline of fine art in America, notice how cultural critic Camille Paglia presumes an intelligent audience already engaged by her topic but possibly offended by her title: "How Capitalism Can Save Art."

Does art have a future? Performance genres like opera, theater, music, and dance are thriving all over the world, but the visual arts have been in slow decline for nearly forty years. No major figure of profound influence has emerged in painting or sculpture since the waning of Pop Art and the birth of Minimalism in the early 1970s.

Paglia wants readers who care about art to consider what the future holds.

develop a statement p. 362

Yet work of bold originality and stunning beauty continues to be done in architecture, a frankly commercial field. Outstanding examples are Frank Gehry's Guggenheim Museum Bilbao in Spain, Rem Koolhaas's CCTV headquarters in Beijing, and Zaha Hadid's London Aquatic Center for the 2012 Summer Olympics.

Points out that architecture is now more inventive than painting.

What has sapped artistic creativity and innovation in the arts? Two major causes can be identified, one relating to an expansion of form and the other to a contraction of ideology.

Poses causal questions knowledgeable readers will appreciate.

Painting was the prestige genre in the fine arts from the Renaissance on. But painting was dethroned by the brash multimedia revolution of the 1960s and '70s. Permanence faded as a goal of art-making.

But there is a larger question: What do contemporary artists have to say, and to whom are they saying it? Unfortunately, too many artists have lost touch with the general audience and have retreated to an airless echo chamber. The art world, like humanities faculties, suffers from a monolithic political orthodoxy — an upper-middle-class liberalism far from the fiery antiestablishment leftism of the 1960s. (I am speaking as a libertarian Democrat who voted for Barack Obama in 2008.)

Diagnoses the artistic problem: political orthodoxy.

Paglia asserts her credentials.

— "How Capitalism Can Save Art," *Wall Street Journal*, October 5, 2012

▶ consider
causes

Expect to do as much research for a causal analysis as for any fact-based report or argument. You need to be careful to show that you have thoughtfully considered what others have written on a subject. ○

Equally important is learning how exactly causal relationships work so that any claims you make about them are accurate. Causality is intriguing because it demands precision and subtlety—as the categories explained in this section demonstrate. But once you grasp them, you'll also be better able to identify faulty causal claims when you come across them. (Exposing faulty causality makes for notably powerful and winning arguments.) ○

Understand necessary causes. A *necessary cause* is any factor that must be in place for something to occur. For example, sunlight, chlorophyll, and water are all necessary for photosynthesis to happen. Remove one of these elements from the equation and the natural process simply doesn't take place. But since none of them could cause photosynthesis on their own, they are necessary causes, yet not sufficient (see *sufficient causes* below).

On a less scientific level, necessary causes are those that seem so crucial that we can't imagine something happening without them. For example, you might argue that a team could not win a World Series without a specific pitcher on the roster: Remove him and the team doesn't even get to the playoffs. Or you might claim that, while fanaticism doesn't itself cause terrorism, terrorism doesn't exist without fanaticism. In any such analysis, it helps to separate necessary causes from those that may be merely contributing factors.

Understand sufficient causes. A *sufficient cause*, by itself, is enough to bring on a particular effect. Driving drunk or shoplifting are two sufficient causes for being arrested in the United States. In a causal argument, you might need to figure out which of several plausible sufficient causes is responsible for a specific phenomenon—assuming that a single explanation exists. A plane might have crashed because it was overloaded, ran out of fuel, had a structural failure, encountered severe wind shear, and so on.

Understand precipitating causes. Think of a *precipitating cause* as the proverbial straw that breaks a camel's back. In itself, the factor may seem trivial. But it becomes the spark that sets a field gone dry for months ablaze.

refine your
search p. 442

read closely
p. 340

By refusing to give up her bus seat to a white passenger in Montgomery, Alabama, Rosa Parks triggered a civil rights movement in 1955, but she didn't actually cause it: The necessary conditions had been accumulating for generations.

Understand proximate causes.   A *proximate cause* is nearby and often easy to spot. A corporation declares bankruptcy when it can no longer meet its massive debt obligations; a minivan crashes because a front tire explodes; a student fails a course because she plagiarizes a paper. But in a causal analysis, getting the facts right about such proximate causes may just be your starting point. You need to work toward a deeper understanding of a situation. As you might guess, proximate causes may sometimes also be sufficient causes.

Understand remote causes.   A *remote cause*, as the term suggests, may act at some distance from an event but be closely tied to it. That bankrupt corporation may have defaulted on its loans because of a full decade of bad management decisions; the tire exploded because it was underinflated and its tread was worn; the student resorted to plagiarism *because* she ran out of time *because* she was working two jobs to pay for a Hawaiian vacation *because* she wanted a memorable spring break to impress her friends—a string of remote causes. Remote causes make many causal analyses challenging and interesting: Figuring them out is like detective work.

> Need help assessing your own work? See "How to Use the Writing Center" on pp. 354–55.

Understand reciprocal causes.   You have a *reciprocal* situation when a cause leads to an effect that, in turn, strengthens the cause. Consider how creating science internships for college women might encourage more women to become scientists, who then sponsor more internships, creating yet more female scientists. Many analyses of global warming describe reciprocal relationships, with CO_2 emissions supposedly leading to warming, which increases plant growth or alters ocean currents, which in turn releases more CO_2 or heat, and so on.

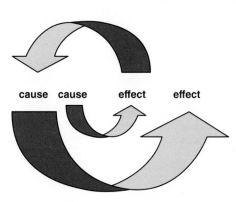

cause   cause   effect   effect

Creating a structure

organize
ideas

The introduction to a cause-and-effect argument should provide enough details for readers to see the point of your project. Spend as many paragraphs as you need to offer background information. The following brief paragraph might seem like an adequate opening for an essay on the failures of dog training. ○

> For thousands of years, humans have been training dogs to be hunters, herders, searchers, guards, and companions. Why are we doing so badly? The problem may lie more with our methods than with us.
>
> — Jon Katz, "Train in Vain," *Slate.com*, January 14, 2005

In fact, *seven* paragraphs precede this one to set up the causal claim. Those additional paragraphs help readers (especially dog owners) fully appreciate a problem many will find familiar. The actual first paragraph has author Jon Katz narrating a dog owner's dilemma.

> Sam was distressed. His West Highland terrier, aptly named Lightning, was constantly darting out of doors and dashing into busy suburban Connecticut streets. Sam owned three acres behind his house, and he was afraid to let the dog roam any of it.

By paragraph seven, Katz has offered enough corroborating evidence to describe a crisis in dogdom, a problem that leaves readers hoping for an explanation.

> The results of this failure are everywhere: Neurotic and compulsive dog behaviors like barking, biting, chasing cars, and chewing furniture—sometimes severe enough to warrant antidepressants—are growing. Lesser training problems—an inability to sit, stop begging, come, or stay—are epidemic.

Like Katz, you'll want to take the time necessary to introduce your subject and get readers invested in the issue. Then you have a number of options for developing your explanation or causal analysis.

Explain why something happened. When simply suggesting causes to explain a phenomenon, you can move quickly from an introduction that explains the phenomenon to a thesis or hypothesis. Then work through your list of factors toward a conclusion. Build toward the most convincing explanation.

shape a
beginning p. 391

> Introduction leading to an explanatory or causal claim
>
> > First cause explored + reasons/evidence
> > Next cause explored + reasons/evidence . . .
> > Best cause explored + reasons/evidence
>
> Conclusion

Explain the consequences of a phenomenon.   When exploring effects that follow from some cause, event, policy, or change in the status quo, open by describing the situation you believe will have serious consequences. Then work through those effects, connecting them as you need to. Draw out the implications of your analysis in the conclusion.

> Introduction describing a significant cause
>
> > First effect likely to follow + reasons
> > Other effect(s) likely to follow + reasons . . .
>
> Conclusion and discussion of implications

Suggest an alternative view of cause and effect.   A natural strategy is to open a causal analysis by refuting someone else's faulty claim and then offering a better one of your own. After all, we often think about causality when someone makes a claim we disagree with.

> Introduction questioning a causal claim
>
> > Reasons to doubt claim offered + evidence
> > Alternative cause(s) explored . . .
> > Best cause examined + reasons/evidence
>
> Conclusion

Explain a chain of causes.   Sometimes you'll describe causes that operate in order, one by one: A causes B, B leads to C, C trips D, and so on. In such cases, use a sequential or narrative pattern of organization, giving special attention to the links (or transitions) within the chain. ○

> Introduction suggesting a chain of causes/consequences

> First link presented + reasons/evidence
> Next link(s) presented + reasons/evidence . . .
> Final link presented + reasons/evidence

> Conclusion

People have been writing causal analysis for centuries. Here is the title page of Edward Jenner's 1798 publication, *An Inquiry into the Causes and Effects of the Variolae Vaccinae*. Jenner's research led to a vaccine that protected human beings from smallpox. © Mary Evans Picture Library/Everett Collection.

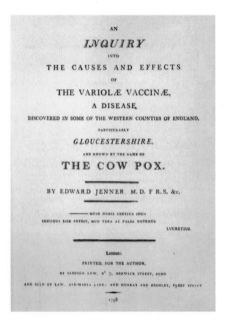

AN

INQUIRY

INTO

THE CAUSES AND EFFECTS

OF

THE VARIOLÆ VACCINÆ,

A DISEASE,

DISCOVERED IN SOME OF THE WESTERN COUNTIES OF ENGLAND,

PARTICULARLY

GLOUCESTERSHIRE,

AND KNOWN BY THE NAME OF

THE COW POX.

BY EDWARD JENNER. M. D. F.R.S. &c.

—— QUID NOBIS CERTIUS IPSIS
SENSIBUS ESSE POTEST, QUO VERA AC FALSA NOTEMUS

LUCRETIUS.

London:
PRINTED, FOR THE AUTHOR,
BY SAMPSON LOW, Nº 7, BERWICK STREET, SOHO
AND SOLD BY LAW, AVE-MARIA LANE; AND MURRAY AND HIGHLEY, FLEET STREET.

1798

shape your
work p. 374

Choosing a style and design

When you analyze cause and effect, you'll often be offering an argument or exploring an idea for an audience you need to interest. You can do that through both style and design.

Consider a middle style.   Even causal analyses written for fairly academic audiences incline toward the middle style because of its flexibility: It can be both familiar and serious. ○ Here Robert Bruegmann, discussing the causes of urban sprawl, uses language that is simple, clear, and colloquial—and almost entirely free of technical jargon.

> When asked, most Americans declare themselves to be against sprawl, just as they say they are against pollution or the destruction of historic buildings. But the very development that one individual targets as sprawl is often another family's much-loved community. Very few people believe that they themselves live in sprawl or contribute to sprawl. Sprawl is where other people live, particularly people with less good taste. Much antisprawl activism is based on a desire to reform these other people's lives.
>
> — "How Sprawl Got a Bad Name," *American Enterprise*, June 2006

Adapt the style to the subject matter.   Friendly as it is, a middle style can still make demands of readers, as the following passage from an essay by Professor Paula Marantz Cohen of Drexel University demonstrates. In it she explains how our culture is training us to expect clear and accessible explanations for subtle and complex matters, pointing to her own experience with a DVD that tries to be too helpful. Though the language is sophisticated—see the items highlighted—this is middle style at its best, making complex claims and proving them in a way that keeps knowledgeable readers interested. (You can read the entire essay on p. 221.)

> Consider some other ways we have been conditioned to expect hard explanations for soft things (e.g., works of the imagination, and moral and philosophical questions). DVDs give us "special features," that often seem to diminish our understanding of the film or our appreciation of it. The idea applies to television

define your
style p. 400

as well. After watching the last episode of [HBO's] *Girls*, I happened to let the show run on to the after-show sequence, in which creator and star Lena Dunham explained what we had just seen. Not only did her banal exegesis lessen the power of the episode, it made me less interested in her quirky persona. What had looked smart and funny, creative and irreverent, was forced into an explanatory mold and both became uninteresting and co-opted into the very sort of neatly packaged form that the show seems to oppose. I didn't want to see a counterculture icon giving me a lecture on relationship stability.

—"Too Much Information," *The American Scholar*, June 18, 2013

Use appropriate supporting media.   Causal analyses have no special design features. But, like reports and arguments, they can employ charts that summarize information and graphics that illustrate ideas. *USA Today*, for instance, uses its daily "snapshots" to present causal data culled from surveys. Because causal analyses usually have distinct sections or parts (see "Creating a structure," p. 142), they do fit nicely into PowerPoint presentations. ○

think visually
p. 557

Examining models

RESEARCH STUDY In a college research paper, Alysha Behn explores the reasons that women, despite talent and interest, so rarely pursue careers in technology and, more specifically, computer programming. Drawing heavily on research studies, Behn's causal analysis is detailed, complicated, and challenging.

Reading the Genre You may be surprised that Behn's causal argument ends on a pessimistic note, pointing out that no one-size-fits-all solution will resolve the complex issues keeping women out of technical careers. Does so tentative a conclusion weaken or add authority to the author's ethos? Does it affect how credibly she comes across to readers? (Notice that *I* does not occur in this academic paper.)

Behn 1

Alysha Behn

Professor Ruszkiewicz

Rhetoric 325M

February 20, 20--

Where Have All the Women Gone?

In 1984, 37.1 percent of computer science graduates were women. In 2009, around 11 percent of computer science graduates were women. What happened?

It's important to make clear what hasn't gone wrong. Experts dismiss the idea that men are more capable than women of succeeding at computer science, and there are no institutional barriers preventing women from pursuing a computer science degree or a tech career. In fact, rather than discriminating against women, colleges and corporations are competing desperately for female applicants. They just can't

> Opening uses statistics to identify the point of the paper.

For an additional reading, see **macmillanhighered.com/howtowrite3e**.
e-readings > *TheAtlantic.com, Think Again* [MULTIMODAL PROJECT]

147

Behn 2

find any. Women aren't pursuing careers in computer science anymore, and two decades of research hasn't found a way to stop the exodus.

The root of the problem may be the flawed way sociologists and computer scientists are researching the problem, according to Katrina Markwick, a former researcher at the Monash University Department of Education. If researchers are asking the wrong questions, it follows that the solutions they suggest are going to be ineffective.

Much of the research Markwick criticizes focused on increasing women's access to technological education through equal opportunity (EO) strategies, which try to increase women's participation in a male-dominated field without questioning the culture that made that field male dominated (Markwick 258). Equal opportunity programs focus on removing institutional barriers or encouraging a group to participate more—for example, you could instruct math teachers on how to avoid treating girls differently from boys in class, or you could organize a math- and science-oriented summer camp just for girls in order to generate interest in those fields. The problem with the EO approach is that "[these] policies were predicated on the assumption of ontological equality, a belief in the fundamental sameness of individuals, and the EO mind-set produced an acceptance that white, nondisabled, heterosexual men's experiences and interpretations of organizational life were universally applicable" (Moss and Gunn 448). In other

Behn quickly dismisses some conventional explanations.

Behn 3

words, EO programs and strategies implicitly ask women to conform—to be more like men—in order to have a career in computer science.

There's a fascinating body of research that suggests that the equal opportunity paradigm can't address all the factors turning women away from pursuing technology careers. For example, a 2008 study demonstrated that men prefer the aesthetics of Web sites designed by men, and women prefer the aesthetics of Web sites designed by women (Moss and Gunn 457-58)—and, as a result, people tend to spend more time browsing Web sites designed by a member of their own gender. Given that most computer games are made by men, it similarly follows that "young men are more attracted to playing computer games and . . . young women tend to prefer more passive purposeful games and game playing is not a major part of their leisure activities (Lang, 1999)" (Lang 221).

What's problematic about all this is that both playing with video games and tooling around on the Internet indirectly teach computer literacy. What's more, kids who don't enjoy playing with computers aren't likely to pursue careers devoted to tinkering with them. All this points to a positive feedback loop that's responsible for turning men on to technology careers and pushing women away: As more men and fewer women are responsible for designing software and hardware, fewer technological products (even products intended to look gender

A research-based paragraph explains why EO-based strategies don't attract women to tech fields.

Although this paper is documented in MLA style, the quotes include APA citations.

Behn 4

neutral, like the Apple iPad) will be designed with women's interests and aesthetic preferences in mind. Thus, fewer women will be interested in using these products, so fewer women will become skilled at using these technologies or drawn toward a career in making them.

Equal opportunity programs also don't take into account the process of socialization of gender—that is, learning from others what our gender role is—and aren't always well equipped to combat the negative lessons most women learn about themselves:

> The role socialization plays . . . cannot be underempha-
> sized in explaining the continued presence of the gender
> gap. . . . By the end of middle school, students develop
> the notion that mathematics, sciences, and computing
> fields are for white males (Clewell & Braddock, 2000).
> Furthermore, these perceptions are found to exist more
> often for girls than for boys (Trauth, 2002). (Varma 302)

Often the process of socialization is so subtle and pervasive that many women do not even notice it themselves (Varma 308). The perception that "boys are good at math" often leads counselors, parents, and teachers to subtly steer boys toward challenging math and science and away from liberal arts courses in high school, while for women the reverse holds true (Varma 306; Cheryan and Plaut). The result is that many women enter college less prepared for a computer science program than

Academic socialization steers students toward and away from tech careers.

Behn 5

their male peers. Even when male and female students are equally prepared, male students generally express more confidence in their skills, while women take as long as two years to feel that they are competent. In study after study, women have cited anxiety about performance and loss of self-confidence as a primary reason for leaving the field; in fact, some have suggested that professors have a lower opinion of female students' ability to do well than they do of their male students' (Varma 303). Thus, "Irani (2004) has argued that the act of establishing an 'identity of competence' is necessary for women to situate themselves in CS culture and verify legitimacy" (Varma 303).

Behn uses research studies to clarify and support her causal argument.

In some cases the gendered socialization is a little less subtle. The anonymity afforded by online gaming and the Internet has made unapologetic misogyny disturbingly common in gaming and Internet culture. "The Rules of the Internet," a popular document created by an anonymous poster on the online forum 4chan, include the following: "28. Always question a person's gender—just in case it's really a man. 29. In the Internet all girls are men and all kids are undercover FBI agents" (Lolrus). Such rules establish that it is the norm to be male on the Internet, and to be a woman is to be the exception to the rule. Online gaming and participation in popular Web sites like 4chan and Reddit are frequently cited as factors that attract men to computing careers, so an online culture in which

Behn 6

women are explicitly made to feel unwelcome is undoubtedly part of the problem.

Let's describe the last gendered assumption this way: Close your eyes and picture a programmer.

You probably pictured a nerdy-looking guy, perhaps with glasses, alone at his computer in a dark basement. Right? Here's the thing: The basement might be passé but the "alone" bit definitely isn't. And women show a marked aversion to programming alone (Lang 220-21). Fortunately, this is a problem we do have a solution for, and it's one that's catching on fast. Pair programming— a programming style where one partner types at the keyboard and the other partner watches closely, making suggestions and watching for errors—is an attractive solution not only because women prefer it but because the resulting code is consistently better than code written alone (Simon and Hanks 73-82). While younger companies have been eager to adopt pair programming practices, older giants like Microsoft and IBM have shown more reluctance. Furthermore, the success of pair programming will remain irrelevant until tech companies and colleges do a little PR to combat the isolated-nerd-in-a-basement image. Until then, the pair programming shift is more likely to aid retention of women in tech majors than to attract more of them to computing careers.

Markwick also criticized a second paradigm for increasing women's interest in technical fields, one emphasizing the values of femininity and suggesting solutions like a "girl friendly"

Behn offers a cultural reason that women avoid tech careers and suggests a way around the problem.

Behn resists any simple solution, noting a flaw in assumptions about women's participation in tech careers.

Behn 7

curriculum (Markwick 258-59): "This entailed 'celebrating the female side' of the gender binary and revaluing 'women's ways of knowing' (Belenky, Clinchy, Goldberger, & Tarule, 1986) . . . but it treated girls as an essentialized category, neglecting differences between girls" (Markwick 260). While this is without question a step forward from asking women to conform to the masculine norms of the computing industry, it also substitutes one false assumption—that men and women are basically the same—for another: in this case, that all women are fundamentally the same.

Few studies take into account the fact that women are not a homogeneous group (Varma 306). A solution that tries to attract women to technology careers by designing machines that appeal to women will not have much impact on minority women who can't afford that technology in the first place. Nor would a solution oriented around changing the culture of computer science classrooms do much to attract women who want a career that is known to be compatible with raising a family. A solution that tries to combat the "math is for boys" perception isn't going to make it easier for a woman to go to college if she needs to care for a young child. The list goes on. Too frequently, researchers have tried to pinpoint a single issue and define a one-size-fits-all solution, but moving women into tech careers is much more complicated than that.

Behn 8

Works Cited

Cheryan, Sapna, and Victoria C. Plaut. "Explaining
Underrepresentation: A Theory of Precluded Interest." *Sex
Roles* 63.7-8 (2010): 475-88. Print.

Lang, Catherine. "Twenty-First Century Australian Women and
IT: Exercising the Power of Choice." *Computer Science
Education* 17.3 (2007): 215-26. Web. 15 Feb. 2012.

Lolrus. "Rules of the Internet." *Internet Meme Database: Know
Your Meme*. Know Your Meme, 2010. Web. 19 Feb. 2012.

Markwick, Katrina. "Under the Feminist Post-structuralist Lens:
Women in Computing Education." *Journal of Educational
Computing Research* 34.3 (2006): 257-79. Web. 15 Feb. 2012.

Moss, G. A., and R. W. Gunn. "Gender Differences in Website
Production and Preference Aesthetics: Preliminary
Implications for ICT in Education and Beyond." *Behaviour &
Information Technology* 28.5 (2009): 447-60. *Computer
Source*. Web. 15 Feb. 2012.

Simon, Beth, and Brian Hanks. "First Year Students'
Impressions of Pair Programming in CS1." *ICER '07:
Proceedings of the Third International Workshop on
Computing Education Research* (2007): 73-85. *ACM Digital
Library*. Web. 20 Feb. 2012.

Varma, Roli. "Why So Few Women Enroll in Computing? Gender
and Ethnic Differences in Students' Perception." *Computer
Science Education* 20.4 (2010): 301-16. Web. 15 Feb. 2012.

Documentation
style used is
MLA.

CULTURAL ANALYSIS   Ambitiously accounting for why people act as they do is one of the pleasures of writing causal arguments — providing that the answers offered are not too pat or predictable. (See Paula Marantz Cohen's comments on resisting "hard explanations for soft things" on p. 145.) Lance Hosey aims big in this short and entertaining cultural analysis that originally appeared in the *New York Times*.

Reading the Genre   Much of this analysis functions like a report: Hosey reviews what scientists have learned about human reactions to aesthetic stimuli. But what do you take from his conclusion — that great design could really be a matter of "diligent and informed study"? Does science trump art, now that technicians know the formulas for aesthetic pleasure? Or are scientists mere stragglers here, trailing after artists and architects who centuries ago learned how to make beautiful objects?

Why We Love Beautiful Things

Lance Hosey

February 15, 2013

The causal question is raised and, surprisingly, Hosey suggests answers may be on the horizon.

Great design, the management expert Gary Hamel once said, is like Justice Potter Stewart's famous definition of pornography — you know it when you see it. You want it, too: brain scan studies reveal that the sight of an attractive product can trigger the part of the motor cerebellum that governs hand movement. Instinctively, we reach out for attractive things; beauty literally moves us.

Yet, while we are drawn to good design, as Mr. Hamel points out, we're not quite sure why.

This is starting to change. A revolution in the science of design is already under way, and most people, including designers, aren't even aware of it.

German scientists explain why we respond positively to natural shades and shapes.

Take color. Last year, German researchers found that just glancing at shades of green can boost creativity and motivation. It's not hard to guess why: We associate verdant colors with food-bearing vegetation — hues that promise nourishment.

This could partly explain why window views of landscapes, research shows, can speed patient recovery in hospitals, aid learning in classrooms, and spur productivity in the workplace. In studies of call

△

centers, for example, workers who could see the outdoors completed tasks 6 to 7 percent more efficiently than those who couldn't, generating an annual savings of nearly $3,000 per employee.

In some cases the same effect can happen with a photographic or even painted mural, whether or not it looks like an actual view of the outdoors. Corporations invest heavily to understand what incentivizes employees, and it turns out that a little color and a mural could do the trick.

Simple geometry is leading to similar revelations. For more than two thousand years, philosophers, mathematicians, and artists have marveled at the unique properties of the "golden rectangle": subtract a square from a golden rectangle, and what remains is another golden rectangle, and so on and so on — an infinite spiral. These so-called magical proportions (about 5 by 8) are common in the shapes of books, television sets, and credit cards, and they provide the underlying structure for some of the most beloved designs in history: the façades of the Parthenon and Notre Dame, the face of the *Mona Lisa*, the Stradivarius violin, and the original iPod.

Experiments going back to the nineteenth century repeatedly show that people invariably prefer images in these proportions, but no one has known why.

Then, in 2009, a Duke University professor demonstrated that our eyes can scan an image fastest when its shape is a golden rectangle. For instance, it's the ideal layout of a paragraph of text, the one most conducive to reading and retention. This simple shape speeds up our ability to perceive the world, and without realizing it, we employ it wherever we can.

Certain patterns also have universal appeal. Natural fractals — irregular, self-similar geometry — occur virtually everywhere in nature: in coastlines and riverways, in snowflakes and leaf veins, even in our own lungs. In recent years, physicists have found that people invariably prefer a certain mathematical density of fractals — not too thick, not too sparse. The theory is that this particular pattern echoes the shapes of trees, specifically the acacia, on the African savanna, the place stored in our genetic memory from the cradle of the human race. To paraphrase one biologist, beauty is in the genes of the beholder — home is where the genome is.

Proportions matter too — for deeply imbedded reasons.

Beauty seems built in.

Parthenon.
Funkystock/age footstock.

Pollock. *No. 1A*, 1948 (oil on canvas), Jackson Pollock (1912–1956)/Museum of Modern Art, New York, NY, USA/Photo © Boltin Picture Library/The Bridgeman Art Library; © 2014 The Pollock-Krasner Foundation/ Artists Rights Society (ARS), New York.

Life magazine named Jackson Pollock "the greatest living painter in the United States" in 1949, when he was creating canvases now known to conform to the optimal fractal density (about 1.3 on a scale of 1 to 2 from void to solid). Could Pollock's late paintings result from his lifelong effort to excavate an image buried in all of our brains?

We respond so dramatically to this pattern that it can reduce stress levels by as much as 60 percent — just by being in our field of vision. One researcher has calculated that since Americans spend $300 billion a year dealing with stress-related illness, the economic benefits of these shapes, widely applied, could be in the billions.

It should come as no surprise that good design, often in very subtle ways, can have such dramatic effects. After all, bad design works the other way: Poorly designed computers can injure your wrists, awkward chairs can strain your back, and over-bright lighting and computer screens can fatigue your eyes.

> Conclusion suggests that beauty is as much science as art.

We think of great design as art, not science, a mysterious gift from the gods, not something that results just from diligent and informed study. But if every designer understood more about the mathematics of attraction, the mechanics of affection, all design — from houses to cell phones to offices and cars — could both look good and be good for you.

1. **Causal Analysis:** Like Jonah Goldberg in "Global Warming and the Sun" (p. 132), you've probably been curious about or even skeptical of some causal claims made routinely. It might just be college faculty complaining about why students browse the Web during classes. Or, more seriously, maybe you belong to a group that has been the subject of causal analyses verging on prejudicial. If so, refute what you regard as some faulty analysis of cause and effect by offering a more plausible explanation.

2. **Research Study:** Using Alysha Behn's research essay "Where Have All the Women Gone?" (p. 147) as a model, write a paper based on sources that examines an issue or problem in your major or in some area of special concern to you. The issue should be one that involves questions of how, why, or what if. Base your analysis on a variety of academic or public sources, fully documented. Draw on interviews if appropriate to your subject.

3. **Cultural Analysis:** In "Why We Love Beautiful Things" (p. 155), Lance Hosey answers a daunting causal question with research-based studies. Be ambitious yourself and pose a similar open-ended question, perhaps one that is somewhat narrower, about an aspect of culture or society you might be in a position to address. Pick a subject that genuinely puzzles you. Why, for example, have commercials become as important a part of the Super Bowl as the game itself? Why do women like shoes? What exactly makes a video go viral? As much as possible, try to find serious evidence to support your causal argument.

4. **Your Choice:** Politicians and pundits alike are fond of offering predictions, some hopeful, but many dire. The economy, they might suggest, is about to boom or slide into depression; sports dynasties are destined to blossom or collapse; printed books will disappear; American teens will grow even fonder of vinyl records and old audio equipment. Identify one such prediction about which you have some doubts and develop a cause-and-effect analysis to suggest why it is likely to go awry. Be sure to explain in detail what factors you expect will make the prediction go wrong. If you are brave, offer an alternative vision of the future.

How to start

- Need a **topic**? See page 166.
- Need to come up with a **solution**? See page 170.
- Need to **organize your ideas**? See page 172.

6 Proposals

define a problem and suggest a solution

Proposals are written to solve problems. Typically, you'll make a proposal to initiate an action or change. At a minimum, you hope to alter someone's thinking—even if only to recommend leaving things as they are.

TRIAL BALLOON
Degree programs at your school have so many complicated requirements that most students take far more time to graduate than they expect—adding thousands of dollars to their loans. As a *trial balloon*, you suggest that the catalog include accurate "time-to-degree" estimates for all degree programs and certificates.

MANIFESTO
Packaging is getting out of hand and you've had enough. People can barely open the products they buy because everything is zipped up, shrink-wrapped, blister-packed, containerized, or child-protected. So you write a *manifesto* calling for saner and more eco-friendly approaches to product protection.

VISUAL PROPOSAL
You create a PowerPoint so members of your co-op can visualize how much better your building's study area would look with a few inexpensive tweaks in furniture, paint, and lighting. Your *visual proposal* gets you the job of implementing the changes.

DECIDING TO WRITE A PROPOSAL.   *Got an issue or a problem? Good—let's deal with it.* That's the logic driving most proposals, both the professional types that pursue grant money and the less formal propositions that are part of everyday life, academic or otherwise. Like evaluations and some explanations, proposals are another form of argument (for more on choosing a genre, see the Introduction).

Although grant writing shares some elements of informal proposals, it is driven by rigid formulas set by foundations and government agencies, usually covering things like budgets, personnel, evaluation, outcomes, and so on. Informal proposals are much easier. Though they may not funnel large sums of cash your way, they're still important tools for addressing problems. A sensible proposal can make a difference in any situation—be it academic, personal, or political.

In offering a proposal, you'll need to make many of the moves outlined below. In a first-round pitch, for example, you might launch a trial balloon to test whether an idea will work at all, roughing out a scheme with the details to

Use Only What You Need How do you persuade people in a community to save water? Denver Water created an innovative multimedia ad campaign to sell its proposal cleverly to its community. Courtesy of Denver Water.

follow. A more serious plan headed for public debate and scrutiny would have to punch the ticket on more of the items.

Define a problem.   Set the stage for a proposal by describing the specific situation, problem, or opportunity in enough detail that readers *get it*: They see a compelling need for action. In many cases, a proposal needs to explain what's wrong with the status quo.

Make specific recommendations.   This is the trial balloon. Don't just complain that someone else has botched a situation or opportunity: Explain what you propose to do about the problem. The more concrete your solution is, the better.

Target the proposal.   To make a difference, you have to reach people with the power to change a situation. That means first identifying such individuals (or groups) and then tailoring your proposal to their expectations. Use the Web or library, for example, to get the names and contact information of government or corporate officials. ○ When the people in power *are* the problem, go over their heads to more general audiences with clout of their own: voters, consumers, women, fellow citizens, the elderly, and so on.

Consider reasonable alternatives.   Your proposal won't be taken seriously unless you have weighed all the workable possibilities, explaining their advantages and downsides. Only then will you be prepared to make a case for your own ideas.

Make realistic recommendations.   You need to address two related issues: *feasibility* and *implementation*. A proposal is feasible if it can be achieved with available resources and is acceptable to the parties involved. And, of course, a feasible plan still needs a plausible pathway to completion: *First we do this; then we do this.*

plan a
project p. 436

The following proposal originally appeared in *Time* (August 21, 2005). Its author, Barrett Seaman, doesn't have the space to do much more than alert the general public (or, more likely, parents of college students) to the need for action to end alcohol abuse on campuses. Still, he does offer a surprising suggestion — a trial balloon for dealing with bingeing. Although many readers might reject his idea initially, the proposal does what it must: It makes a plausible case and gets people thinking.

Reading the Genre   One of the major tasks in writing a proposal argument is defining the problem. How much of Seaman's essay is concerned with explaining the problem of binge drinking on campus? To whom is this information addressed?

How Bingeing Became the New College Sport

BARRETT SEAMAN

In the coming weeks, millions of students will begin their fall semester of college, with all the attendant rituals of campus life: freshman orientation, registering for classes, rushing by fraternities and sororities, and, in a more recent nocturnal college tradition, "pregaming" in their rooms.

Defines problem he intends to address: bingeing known as "pregaming."

Pregaming is probably unfamiliar to people who went to college before the 1990s. But it is now a common practice among eighteen-, nineteen-, and twenty-year-old students who cannot legally buy or consume alcohol. It usually involves sitting in a dorm room or an off-campus apartment and drinking as much hard liquor as possible before heading out for the evening's parties. While reporting for my book *Binge*, I witnessed the hospitalization of several students for acute alcohol poisoning. Among them was a Hamilton College freshman who had consumed twenty-two shots of vodka while sitting in a dorm room with her friends. Such hospitalizations are routine on campuses across the nation. By the Thanksgiving break of the year I visited Harvard, the university's health center had admitted nearly seventy students for alcohol poisoning.

Proposal draws on research the author has done.

When students are hospitalized — or worse yet, die from alcohol poisoning, which happens about three hundred times each year — college

163

Points out that current solutions to college drinking don't work.

Explains factors responsible for the spike in alcohol abuse.

presidents tend to react by declaring their campuses dry or shutting down fraternity houses. But tighter enforcement of the minimum drinking age of twenty-one is not the solution. It's part of the problem.

Over the past forty years, the United States has taken a confusing approach to the age-appropriateness of various rights, privileges, and behaviors. It used to be that twenty-one was the age that legally defined adulthood. On the heels of the student revolution of the late '60s, however, came sweeping changes: The voting age was reduced to eighteen; privacy laws were enacted that protected college students' academic, health, and disciplinary records from outsiders, including parents; and the drinking age, which had varied from state to state, was lowered to eighteen.

Then, thanks in large measure to intense lobbying by Mothers Against Drunk Driving, Congress in 1984 effectively blackmailed states into hiking the minimum drinking age to twenty-one by passing a law that tied

Do current strict drinking laws in the United States actually encourage students to abuse alcohol? In 2008, a coalition of presidents from one hundred colleges recommended lowering the drinking age to eighteen.
AP Photo/Israel Leal.

compliance to the distribution of federal-aid highway funds—an amount that will average $690 million per state this year. There is no doubt that the law, which achieved full fifty-state compliance in 1988, saved lives, but it had the unintended consequence of creating a covert culture around alcohol as the young adult's forbidden fruit.

Drinking has been an aspect of college life since the first Western universities in the fourteenth century. My friends and I drank in college in the 1960s—sometimes a lot but not so much that we had to be hospitalized. Veteran college administrators cite a sea change in campus culture that began, not without coincidence, in the 1990s. It was marked by a shift from beer to hard liquor, consumed not in large social settings, since that is now illegal, but furtively and dangerously in students' residences.

Points out that current law makes it harder to deal with bingeing.

In my reporting at colleges around the country, I did not meet any presidents or deans who felt that the twenty-one-year age minimum helps their efforts to curb the abuse of alcohol on their campuses. Quite the opposite. They thought the law impeded their efforts since it takes away the ability to monitor and supervise drinking activity.

What would happen if the drinking age was rolled back to eighteen or nineteen? Initially, there would be a surge in binge drinking as young adults savored their newfound freedom. But over time, I predict, U.S. college students would settle into the saner approach to alcohol I saw on the one campus I visited where the legal drinking age is eighteen: Montreal's McGill University, which enrolls about two thousand American undergraduates a year. Many, when they first arrive, go overboard, exploiting their ability to drink legally. But by midterms, when McGill's demanding academic standards must be met, the vast majority have put drinking into its practical place among their priorities.

Offers specific proposal tentatively, posed as question.

Proposal stands up to tests of feasibility, acceptability, and practicality.

A culture like that is achievable at U.S. colleges if Congress can muster the fortitude to reverse a bad policy. If lawmakers want to reduce drunk driving, they should do what the Norwegians do: Throw the book at offenders no matter what their age. Meanwhile, we should let the pregamers come out of their dorm rooms so that they can learn to handle alcohol like the adults we hope and expect them to be.

States his thesis and then offers precedents for students behaving more responsibly with lower drinking age.

Exploring purpose and topic

▶ topic

Most people will agree to a reasonable proposal—as long as it doesn't cost them anything. But moving audiences from *I agree* to *I'll actually do something about it* takes a powerful act of persuasion. And for that reason, proposals are typically structured as arguments, requiring all the strategies used in that genre. ○

Occasionally, you'll be asked to solve a particular problem in school or on the job. Having an assigned topic makes your task a little easier, but you can bet that any such problem will be complex and open to multiple solutions. Otherwise, there would be no challenge to it.

When choosing a proposal topic on your own, keep in mind the following concerns. ○

Look for a genuine issue. Spend the first part of your project defining a problem readers will care about. You may think it's a shame no one retails Prada close to campus, but your classmates probably care more about out-of-control student fees or the high price of housing. Go beyond your own concerns in settling on a problem.

Need help deciding what to write about? See "How to Browse for Ideas" on pp. 338–39.

Look for a challenging problem. It helps if others have tried to fix it in the past but failed—and you are able to figure out why. Times change, attitudes shift, technology improves: Factors like these might make what once seemed like an intractable problem more manageable now. Choose a serious topic to which you can bring fresh perspectives.

Look for a soluble problem. Challenges *are* good, but impossible dreams are for Broadway musicals. Parking on campus is the classic impasse—always present, always frustrating. Steer clear of problems no one has ever solved, unless you have a *really* good idea.

Look for a local issue. It's best to leave "world peace" to beauty pageant contestants. Instead, investigate a problem in your community, where you can interview affected people or search local archives. ○ Doing so also makes it easier to find an audience you can influence, including people potentially able to improve the situation. You're far more likely to get the attention of your dean of students than the secretary of state.

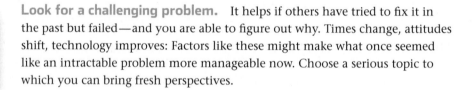

understand
argument p. 66

find a
topic p. 331

interview and
observe p. 447

FISCAL CLIFF FIX

Columbus Dispatch editorial cartoonist Nate Beeler offers a proposal for solving the country's budget woes. Nate Beeler, courtesy of Cagle Cartoons.

Your Turn   In 46 BCE, Julius Caesar used his authority as dictator to impose a new calendar on Rome because the old one had fallen five months out of sync with the seasons. Play Caesar today by imagining what problems you would fix if you could simply impose your will. Make a list. Narrow your more grandiose schemes (free pizza for all) to more plausible ones (less rowdiness in the student section at football games), and then consider which items on your roster could be argued rationally and compellingly in a short paper. Compare your list with those of other students and discuss workable proposal topics.

Understanding your audience

While preparing a proposal, keep two audiences in mind—one fairly narrow and the other more broad. The first group includes people who could possibly do something about a problem; the second consists of general readers who could influence those in the first group by bringing the weight of public opinion down on them. And public opinion makes a difference.

Writers calibrate proposals for specific readers all the time. Grant writers, especially, make it a point to learn what agencies and institutions expect in applications. Quite often, it takes two or three tries to figure out how to present a winning grant submission. You won't have that luxury with most academic or political pieces, but you can look for examples of successful proposals and study them.

Appeal to people who can make a difference. For example, a personal letter you prepare for the dean of students to protest her policies against displaying political posters in university buildings (including dormitories) should have a respectful and perhaps legalistic tone, pointing to case law on the subject and university policies on freedom of speech. You'd also want to assure the dean of your goodwill and provide her with sound reasons for loosening the restrictions.

Rally people who represent public opinion. No response from the dean of students on the political poster proposal you made? Then take the issue to the public, perhaps via an op-ed or letter in the student paper. Keeping the dean still firmly in mind, you'd now also write to stir up student and community opinion. Your new piece could be more emotional than your letter and less burdened by legal points—though still citing facts and presenting solid reasons for giving students more leeway in expressing political beliefs on campus. ○

The fact is that people often need a spur to move them—that is, a persuasive strategy that helps them imagine their role in solving a problem. Again, you'd be in good company in leading an audience to your position. As shown on page 169, when President John F. Kennedy proposed a mission to the moon in 1962, he did it in language that stirred a public skeptical about the cost and challenges of such an implausible undertaking.

refine your
tone p. 400

JFK Aims High   In 1962, the president challenged Americans to go to the moon; today American astronauts ride to the International Space Station on a Russian Soyuz. © Corbis.

There is no strife, no prejudice, no national conflict in outer space as yet. Its hazards are hostile to us all. Its conquest deserves the best of all mankind, and its opportunity for peaceful cooperation may never come again. But why, some say, the moon? Why choose this as our goal? And they may well ask why climb the highest mountain? Why, thirty-five years ago, fly the Atlantic? Why does Rice play Texas?

We choose to go to the moon. We choose to go to the moon in this decade and do the other things, not because they are easy, but because they are hard, because that goal will serve to organize and measure the best of our energies and skills, because that challenge is one that we are willing to accept, one we are unwilling to postpone, and one which we intend to win, and the others, too.

— Rice Stadium "Moon Speech," September 12, 1962

Finding and developing materials

▶ consider
   solutions

Proposals might begin with whining and complaining (*I want easier parking!*), but they can't stay in that mode long. They require sober thought and research. What makes proposals distinctive, however, is the sheer variety of strategies a single document might employ. To write a convincing proposal, you may need to narrate, report, argue, evaluate, and analyze. Here's how to develop those various parts.

Define the problem.   Research the existing situation thoroughly enough to explain it concisely to readers. To be sure you've got the basics of your topic down cold, run through the traditional journalist's questions—*Who? What? Where? When? Why? How?* When appropriate, interview experts or people involved with an issue; for instance, in college communities, the best repositories of institutional memory will usually be staff. ○ Search for any documents with hard facts on the matter that might convince skeptical readers. For instance, if you propose to change a long-standing policy, find out when it was created, by whom, and for what reasons.

The Journalist's Questions

Who?	What?
Where?	When?
Why?	How?

Examine prior solutions.   If a problem is persistent, other people have tried to solve it—or maybe they even caused it. In either case, do the research necessary to figure out, as best you can, what happened in these previous efforts. But expect controversy. You may have to sort through contentious and contradictory narratives. Once you know the history of an issue, shift into an evaluative mode to figure out why earlier strategies faltered. ○ Then explain them to readers so that they can later compare these failed approaches to your own proposal and appreciate its ingenuity.

Outline a proposal.   Coming up with a sensible proposal may take more creativity than you can muster. So consider working collaboratively, when that's an option. ○ Brainstorm aggressively with classmates and be sure to write down ideas as they emerge. Be specific about details, especially numbers and costs.

interview and
observe p. 447

understand
evaluation p. 100

collaborate
p. 428

Defend the proposal.   Any ideas that threaten the status quo will surely raise hackles. That's half the fun of proposing change. So advance your position by using all the tools of argument available to you—logical, factual, and, yes, emotional. Present yourself as smart and competent. Anticipate objections, because readers invested in the status quo will offer them in spades. Above all, show that your idea will work and that it is *feasible*—that it can be achieved with existing or new resources. For example, you might actually solve your school's traffic problems by proposing a monorail linking the central campus to huge new parking garages. But who would pay for the multimillion-dollar system?

And yet, you shouldn't be put off too easily by the objection that *we can't possibly do that*. A little chutzpah is not out of line—it's part of the problem-solving process.

Figure out how to implement the proposal.   Readers will need assurances that your ideas can be put into action: Show them how. ○ Figure out exactly what will happen: where new resources will come from, how personnel can be recruited and hired, where brochures or manuals will be printed, and so on. Provide a timetable if you can.

think critically
p. 343

Creating a structure

organize
ideas

Proposals follow the thought processes most people go through in dealing with issues, and some of these problems raise more complications than others. ○ Generally, the less formal the proposal, the fewer structural elements it will have. So adapt the following template to your needs, using it as a checklist of *possible* issues to consider in framing a proposal.

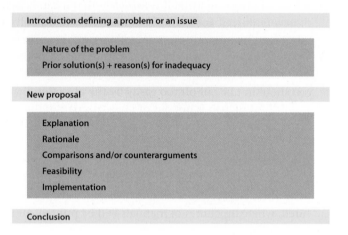

Introduction defining a problem or an issue

Nature of the problem
Prior solution(s) + reason(s) for inadequacy

New proposal

Explanation
Rationale
Comparisons and/or counterarguments
Feasibility
Implementation

Conclusion

You might use a similar structure whenever you need to examine what effects—good or bad—might follow some action, event, policy, or change in the status quo. Once again, you'd begin with an introduction that fully describes the action you believe will have significant consequences; then you explain those consequences to readers, showing how they are connected. Finally, a conclusion could draw out the implications of your analysis.

shape your
work p. 374

Choosing a style and design

Proposals do come in many forms and, occasionally, they may be frivolous or comic. But whenever you suggest changing people's lives or spending someone else's money, show a little respect and humility.

Use a formal style. Professional proposals—especially those seeking grant money—are typically written in a high style, formal and impersonal, almost as if the project would be jeopardized by reviewers detecting the slightest hint of enthusiasm or personality. ○ Academic audiences are often just as poker-faced. So use a formal style in proposals you write for school when your intended readers are formidable and "official"— professors, deans and provosts, or administrators (and pay attention to their titles!).

Observe the no-nonsense tone Thao Tran adopts early in an academic essay whose title alone suggests its sober intentions: "Coping with Population Aging in the Industrialized World."

Leaders of industrialized nations and children of baby boomers must understand the consequences of population aging and minimize its economic effects. This report will recommend steps for coping with aging in the industrialized world and will assess counterarguments to those steps. With a dwindling workforce and rising elderly population, industrialized countries must take a multistep approach to expand the workforce and support the elderly. Governments should attempt to attract immigrants, women, and elderly people into the workforce. Supporting an increasing elderly population will require reforming pension systems and raising indirect taxes. It will also require developing pronatalist policies, in which governments subsidize child-rearing costs to encourage births. Many of these strategies will challenge traditional cultural notions and require a change in cultural attitudes. While change will not be easy, industrialized nations must recognize and address this trend quickly in order to reduce its effects.

> Point of view is impersonal: *This report* rather than *I*.

> Purpose of proposal is clearly explained.

> Premises and assumptions of proposal are offered in abstract language.

Use a middle style, when appropriate. Shift to a middle style when you need to persuade a general audience or whenever establishing a personal relationship with readers might help your proposal.

It is possible, too, for styles to vary within a document. Your language might be coldly efficient as you scrutinize previous failures or tick off the advantages of your specific proposal. But as you near the end of the piece, you might decide another style would better reflect your vision for the future or

define your
style p. 400

your enthusiasm for an idea. Environmentalist David R. Brower offered many technical arguments to explain why his radical proposal for draining Lake Powell would make commercial sense. But he concluded his appeal on a more emotional note:

> The sooner we begin, the sooner lost paradises will begin to recover — Cathedral in the Desert, Music Temple, Hidden Passage, Dove Canyon, Little Arch, Dungeon, and a hundred others. Glen Canyon itself can probably lose its ugly white sidewalls in two or three decades. The tapestries can reemerge, along with the desert varnish, the exiled species of plants and animals, the pictographs, and other mementos of people long gone. The canyon's music will be known again, and "the sudden poetry of springs," Wallace Stegner's beautiful phrase, will be revealed again below the sculptured walls of Navajo sandstone. The phrase, "as long as the rivers shall run and the grasses grow," will regain its meaning.

Place names listed have poetic effect.

Lush details add to emotional appeal of proposal.

Final quotation summarizes mission of proposal.

Pay attention to elements of design.   Writers often incorporate images, charts, tables, graphs, and flowcharts to illustrate what is at stake in a proposal or to make comparisons easy. Images also help readers imagine solutions or proposals and make those ideas attractive. The SmartArt Graphics icon in the Microsoft Word Gallery opens up a range of templates you might use to help readers visualize a project. O

Your Turn   The style of proposals varies dramatically, depending on audience and purpose. Review the proposals in this chapter offered as models — including the visual items. Then explain in some detail exactly how the language of one of those items works to make its case. You can focus on a whole piece, but you may find it more interesting just to explicate a few sentences or paragraphs or one or two visual details. For example, when does Barrett Seaman (p. 163), Nate Beeler (p. 167), Katelyn Vincent (p. 175), or Jen Sorensen (p. 182) score style points with you? Be ready to explain your observation orally.

think visually
p. 557

Examining models

MANIFESTO Proposals often arise from a critical look at contemporary culture. Here, Katelyn Vincent draws upon her own experiences to argue, finally, that technology is taking up too much of our lives. She dramatizes the issue by describing her own struggle to survive for twelve hours without the Internet.

Reading the Genre The narrative structure Vincent uses in "Technology Time-Out" is not typical of more formal proposals, especially those that follow the pattern outlined on p. 172. But as she tells the story of her twelve hours without the Internet, which elements of a typical proposal do you find in the essay? How well does Vincent's proposal make a case for taking a break from technology?

Vincent 1

Katelyn Vincent

Professor Ruszkiewicz

Composition 2

November 11, 20--

Technology Time-Out

"Are you sure you want to shut down?" A gray box has popped up and is waiting for my answer. No, I think to myself, I'm really not—and it's true. I have become so reliant on my computer that the thought of willingly turning it off during the day feels strange, almost wrong. And these days, it seems that everyone else shares the same addiction. The other day, when my roommate's Internet was down for a few hours, she had a mild panic attack. I thought it was silly—until I realized I would have had the same reaction if something similar had happened to me. Now, I consider myself to be a reasonably independent

For an additional reading, see **macmillanhighered.com/howtowrite3e.**
e-readings > Michael Pollan, *Celebrate School Lunch* [VIDEO]

175

Vincent 2

The problem of
Web addiction
is identified,
connecting the
essay to a wide
audience.

person, and the thought of being so dependent on something—
especially a *machine*—horrified me. So I made a resolution—
to avoid the Internet for twelve hours.

The gray box still waits. A blue button flashes on the
screen in front of me, and the words "Shut Down" pulsate
before my eyes, daring me to make my decision. Giving in to my
curiosity, I click and watch as the luminous rectangle in front of
me fades slowly to black. That was easy enough, I think to
myself. Maybe I can handle this after all.

Vincent shifts
to present
tense to inten-
sify the action.

Looking for something to do now that my primary source
of entertainment (and procrastination) has dissolved into
nothingness, I realize that it is eight o'clock and I have not eaten
anything since breakfast. In the kitchen, I reach for the Fruity
Cheerios on the top shelf of the pantry—a food staple since I
started college—and am this close to pouring when I realize
that *making* dinner might actually be fun. Heck, I haven't made
myself a real dinner in several weeks, and since I usually spend
this time Facebook-stalking casual acquaintances from third
grade and reading random health articles on a too-familiar 9 × 13
glowing screen, today I have the time to spare. Eagerly, I pull
out the pasta box that has been sleeping on my shelf for the
past four months and get to work. You know what would be
great with this, I think—some chicken. Mmm, I know, they have
an amazing chicken pasta recipe on Allrecipes.com, I'll just go
and . . . dammit. Never mind, I'll improvise. Surprisingly, the

The details are
homey and
believable.

Vincent 3

chicken doesn't turn out horribly. My dinner is no "Nicole's Tailgate Party Chicken Salad," but an alarmingly strong lemon taste gives me a zesty kick in the mouth. And to be honest, the fact that dinner is warm and homemade makes it infinitely better than Fruity Cheerios.

After dinner I again find myself bored—and wondering how many people have commented on my Facebook status. Wait a minute—why am I so concerned about this? Am I really so lame that my happiness depends on what people comment on my Facebook posts? God, I hope not. Trying to distract myself from this disturbing thought, I pull out my textbook to study—and once again, something doesn't feel right. I realize it has been over an hour since I checked Hotmail, Facebook, or MSN. My hand itches to press the power button and start clicking and clacking away—my prestudy ritual. Who knows how many e-mails, Facebook notifications, and important articles are popping up without my knowledge? What if I am missing something hugely important? Still, determined to stick it out, I dig in my backpack and stare into *Corporate Finance*, Second Edition. After three minutes, all I can think about is how much I would love to put in my headphones and crank up Pandora.com and my Michael Bublé playlist. This is going to be a long night.

I guess, not surprisingly, I am more focused on *Corporate Finance* than I have ever been, which isn't saying much, but

> The strategy is to describe symptoms of Internet addiction that readers will recognize.

Vincent 4

Without getting technical, a full paragraph examines the limits of multitasking and the potential consequences for college students.

still—I'm impressed. I have turned off my cell phone and iPod as well, and before I know it I have read two whole sections of the book and done a chapter's worth of questions. Not bad for two hours of studying. Afterwards, I delve into marketing and manage to read an entire chapter from that book as well. I have to say, it feels good to accomplish something and not have to stress about it. And I actually think I learned something—a feeling I don't always get from studying, which for me is usually marked more by frantic memorization than any real retention of information. I guess part of the reason for my inability to recall is that studying for me usually means multitasking between chapter skimming, shopping for new boots on Amazon.com, and watching online clips from an old episode of *Glee*. I usually switch back and forth between book and computer, spending about five minutes (max) on the book before some arbitrary whim or want enters my head and I have to go online and check it out before I can resume studying. It's gratifying to do something well for a change.

The paragraph ends with a clever but important insight, driving home a key theme of the paper.

It's also kind of nice not to be in continuous contact with the rest of the world, I think to myself. What with e-mail, Facebook, calling, and texting, I feel as if I am constantly communicating with everyone I know. I can text my mom, talk on the phone with my sister, Facebook-chat with my friend, and e-mail my professor—all at the same time! While establishing relationships with other people is fine, it is also enjoyable to

Vincent 5

spend some time alone once in a while: I feel as though I haven't been truly alone in ages. Even while studying finance, I realize I am calmer than I have been in weeks. For a change, I get the chance to recharge *my* batteries instead of just my Mac's.

The next morning I am back to Fruity Cheerios and instinctively reach for the power button on my Mac as soon as I wake up. Still moving around in the foggy space of sleepiness, it takes me a moment to realize that my self-imposed sentence is not up. So much for checking my e-mail and Weather.com before I head out. Then again, I realize, I go to bed so late that it doesn't really make sense that I would have gotten any new e-mails since the last time I checked—most normal people are in bed between the hours of 2 and 6 AM, after all. Why do I have to check everything in the morning again? I have done it for so long that I guess it's just habit by now. I could be using those twenty minutes to spend more time getting ready or, even better, sleeping. I guess the only Web site it really makes sense to check in the morning is Weather.com, and even that's not a complete necessity.

The extra moments give me more time to get ready, and those seemingly insignificant twenty minutes turn my usually hectic morning routine into a much calmer transition between sleep and class. For the first time this semester, I am *not* lathering myself into a frenzy, *not* frantically applying lip gloss on my way out, and *not* running to catch the bus that's about to

Vincent realizes that technology has complicated her life and, by implication, the lives of her readers.

Vincent 6

leave (there goes my exercise). In fact, my entire morning is pretty mellow, and I don't even think about getting online again until lunchtime. By then, the twelve hours is up—but the only reason I get online is to register for classes. Why mess with a good thing?

As it turns out, the "hugely important" somethings I was missing during my online off-time consisted of one offer for a free colon cleanse, two "Take this quiz!" pop-ups on Facebook, a new MSN article on the latest *Dancing with the Stars* results, and only one actual, legitimate e-mail—from my mother. Granted, I do get some important e-mails from time to time, but when I think about it, how many of them actually require that I respond immediately? Most likely, none.

So what did I learn from all this? That I *am* addicted to technology and our online world—and I have a feeling I am not too different from the rest of society. I couldn't go twelve hours Internet free without driving myself a little crazy. But at the same time, this addiction of ours is one that we, to some degree, have been forced into. While Amazon and Pandora are, admittedly, somewhat superfluous, the use of e-mail as the primary means of communication and Facebook as the major place of social interaction nowadays means that those who ignore them are left behind. We can't just decide to ignore technology completely; it has become a part of our world and something that we have to deal with daily, whether we want to or not.

> The humor here is yet another gesture to win over readers, who have probably received similar e-mails.

> The essay concedes that most of us can't ignore technology: Turning off the Web entirely is not feasible.

Vincent 7

But at the same time, it shouldn't be our *whole* world. After all, if our online world becomes our entire universe—what happens when the computer crashes? We crash with it. The only way to ensure that doesn't happen is to distance ourselves, when possible, from that which is slowly sucking us into dependency. We need to take some time to learn how to do things on our own, take time to do things well again, take time for ourselves, and, ultimately, just take time to learn that easier doesn't always mean better.

In highly rhetorical language, Vincent makes a call for independence and change.

VISUAL PROPOSAL   Jen Sorensen is an editorial cartoonist fond of four-panel spreads with political messages. The medium requires that messages be expressed economically, so Sorensen uses broad strokes to criticize a proposal affecting student loans.

Reading the Genre   Only one character in Sorensen's cartoon "Loan Bone" speaks. What do her words suggest about possible real solutions to the problem of student debt? You may want to compare the brief proposal here to the more extended visual argument by Matt Bors on page 95.

Loan Bone

First panel identifies a specific problem.

Victims and villains are clearly identified.

Solutions offered are deliberately implausible.

1. **Trial Balloon:** In calling for reducing the drinking age, Barrett Seaman's "How Bingeing Became the New College Sport" (p. 163) offers a solution to alcohol abuse that some might call "politically incorrect" — lowering the drinking age. Indeed, many politicians or school officials would probably be reluctant to support such a proposal — even if it might make people more responsible. Choose an issue that you think needs as radical a rethinking as college-age drinking and write a research-based proposal of your own. Like Seaman, be sure to offer your ideas in language calm and persuasive enough to make responsible adults at least consider them.

2. **Manifesto:** You probably identify with at least some of the issues Katelyn Vincent presents in "Technology Time-Out" (p. 175) and with the manifesto she enunciates in her final paragraphs. Look for a problem that others might similarly recognize, describe the issue in enough detail to explain why adjustments may be necessary or desirable, and then make a compelling call for change.

3. **Visual Proposal:** Both editorial cartoonists in this chapter — Nate Beeler and Jen Sorensen — offer enough "data" in their drawings (pp. 167 and 182) to lead readers to perceive problems and draw their own conclusions. But it's not as easy as it looks. Try your hand at creating a visual proposal of your own that accomplishes the same.

4. **Your Choice:** Proposals are usually practical documents, serving a specific need. Identify such a need in your life and address it through a clear, fact-based proposal. For example, you might write to your academic adviser or dean suggesting that a service-learning experience would be a better senior project for you than a traditional written thesis — given your talents and interests. Or perhaps you might write to a banker (or wealthy relative) explaining why loaning you money to open a barbecue restaurant would make sound fiscal sense, especially since no one else in town serves decent brisket and ribs. In other words, write a paper to make your life better.

How to start

● Need to **find a text to analyze**? See page 190.

● Need to come up with **ideas**? See page 194.

● Need to **organize your ideas**? See page 200.

7 Literary Analyses

**respond
critically
to cultural
works**

Unless you're an English major, the papers you write for Literature 101 may seem as mechanical as chemistry lab reports—something done just to get a degree. But hardly a day goes by when you don't respond strongly to some literary or cultural experience, sharing your insights and opinions about the books, music, and entertainment you love. It's worth learning to do this well.

THEMATIC INTERPRETATION   After discussing Rudolfo Anaya's novel *Bless Me, Ultima* with classmates in a contemporary novels course, you write a *thematic interpretation* of the work, arguing that it fits into the category of mythic coming-of-age story.

CLOSE READING   Unconvinced by a teacher's casual suggestion that the Anglo-Saxon author of "The Wanderer" (c. tenth century CE) was experiencing what we now call "alienation," you write a *close reading* of the poem to show why the modern concept doesn't fit the poem.

ANALYSIS OF A VISUAL TEXT   Rather than roll your eyes like your companions, you take abstract art seriously. So you study El Anatsui's sculpture (on p. 185) and then write a *visual analysis* to explain what you see in the work to someone who "doesn't get it."

DECIDING TO WRITE A LITERARY ANALYSIS. In a traditional literary analysis, you respond to a poem, novel, play, or short story. That response can be interpretive, looking at theme, plot, structure, characters, genre, style, and so on. Or it can be critical, theoretical, or evaluative—locating works within their social, political, historic, and even philosophic neighborhoods. Or you might approach a literary work expressively, describing how you connect with it intellectually and emotionally. Or you can combine these approaches or imagine alternatives—reflecting new attitudes and assumptions about media.

Other potential media for analysis include films, TV shows, popular music, comic books, and games (for more on choosing a genre, see the Introduction). Distinctions between high and popular culture have not so much dissolved as ceased to be interesting. After all, you can say dumb things about *Hamlet* and smart things about *Game of Thrones*. Moreover, every genre of artistic expression—from sonnets to opera to graphic novels—at some point struggled for respectability.

Duvor Cloth (Communal Cloth)
The Ghanaian artist El Anatsui builds his remarkable abstract sculptures from street materials, including metal fragments and bottle caps. He explains, "I believe that artists are better off working with whatever their environment throws up." El Anatsui (Ghanaian, born 1944), *Duvor Cloth (Communal Cloth)*, 2007, aluminum and copper wire, 13 × 17 ft. Indianapolis Museum of Art, Ann M. Stack Fund for Contemporary Art, 2007.25. © El Anatsui/The Bridgeman Art Library.

What matters is the quality of a literary analysis and whether you help readers appreciate the novel *Pride and Prejudice* or, maybe, the video game *Red Dead Redemption*. Expect your literary or cultural analyses to do *some* of the following.

Begin with a close reading.   In an analysis, you slow the pace at which people in a 24/7 world typically operate to examine a text or object meticulously. You study the way individual words and images connect in a poem, or how plot evolves in a novel, or how complex editing shapes the character of a movie. In short, you study the *calculated* choices writers and artists make in creating their works. ○

Make a claim or an observation.   The point you want to make about a work won't always be argumentative or controversial: You may be amazed at the simplicity of Wordsworth's Lucy poems or blown away by Jimi Hendrix's take on "All Along the Watchtower." But more typically, you'll make an observation that you believe is worth proving either by research or by evidence you discover within the work itself.

Use texts for evidence.   An analysis helps readers appreciate the complexities in creative works: You direct them to the neat stuff in a poem, novel, drama, or song. For that reason, you have to pay attention to the details—words, images, textures, techniques—that support your claims about a literary or cultural experience.

Present works in context.   Works of art respond to the world; that's what we like about them and why they sometimes change our lives. Your analysis can explore these relationships among texts, people, and society.

Draw on previous research.   Your response to a work need not match what others have felt. But you should be willing to learn from previous scholarship and criticism—readily available in libraries or online. ○

read closely
p. 340

plan a
project p. 436

In "Great Expectations: What Gatsby's Really Looking For," literary critic William Deresiewicz tries once again to explain the enduring appeal of a book almost everyone reads either in high school or college, F. Scott Fitzgerald's *The Great Gatsby* (1925). His essay appeared in *The American Scholar* just shortly after yet another film version premiered in spring 2013, with Leonardo DiCaprio in the title role.

Reading the Genre Chances are you have written literary papers in school, analyzing poems or books. Does Deresiewicz's essay feel like the papers you have prepared? In what ways is it similar and, perhaps more important, how is it different? How do you account for the differences?

Great Expectations

What Gatsby's Really Looking For

WILLIAM DERESIEWICZ

I recently reread *The Great Gatsby*, for obvious reasons. (And no, I haven't worked up the stomach to see the movie yet.) Here's what I discovered: It's about the American Dream. I know, I know, but the real question is, what is the American Dream about? What is Gatsby really after? It isn't money, and it isn't Daisy, and it isn't money as a way of getting Daisy. Don't believe that Tin Pan Alley sentimentality—all the crap that Gatsby spouts about "the secret place above the trees" and "the tuning fork that had been struck upon a star"—which even Nick refers to as "appalling." Money is a way of getting Daisy, but Daisy is a way of getting something else.

Gatsby wants to arrive. He wants admission to the inner circle. He wants acceptance into what we'd later call—in the twilight of their power, once we could afford to laugh at them—the WASPs, our homegrown aristocracy. He wants what Tom and Nick, who graduated from "New Haven," represent. He's from the West; he wants to make it to the East—a dichotomy Fitzgerald maps onto the local spaces of his two Long Island towns, the famous Eggs. Money's not the point; it's only a prerequisite. Gatsby is already

> Opening teases readers to discover what *Gatsby* is really about.

> Argues Gatsby wants entry to elite society.

fabulously wealthy by the time the novel starts. But he can't cross over anyway, and not because Daisy is married. That would be an incidental obstacle, as everyone makes clear, if only she were willing.

The problem is he can't pull off the act. Wolfsheim buys it — "I saw right away he was a fine-appearing, gentlemanly young man, and when he told me he was an Oggsford I knew I could use him good" — but people like the Buchanans can tell the difference. Gatsby's downfall comes when Daisy finally goes to one of his parties and sees how vulgar they are. Since he doesn't have access to the aristocracy, he substitutes the world of celebrity, that simulacrum of it that emerged around this time (and that's replaced it altogether now). "She was appalled by West Egg, this unprecedented 'place' that Broadway had begotten upon a Long Island fishing village." (West Egg, as everybody would have understood, was a thinly veiled version of Great Neck, which was being colonized by showbiz types like Sid Caesar and the Marx Brothers. Gatsby's association with Jews, the ultimate crass arrivistes, goes deeper than his gangster friend.) It's not that Gatsby's money's dirty; it's that he hasn't had a chance to wash the newness off it yet. The process takes at least a generation. Daddy gets rich; Junior goes to "New Haven," to learn how to act like the rich.

> Explains in detail the East/West divides in the novel.

We talk about money, in America, but we're thinking about status (which we never talk about). For all of our well-known materialism, I believe we love money as much as we do just because, in the absence of a real aristocracy, it's always been our route to status. There's only so much you can buy. I sometimes wonder if the drive for endless accumulation is nothing but an evolutionary anachronism, a vestige of the time when resources had to be stockpiled, because you never knew when they might become scarce. But then I remember about status, of which it's never possible to have enough. That is the secret American hunger: a legacy, no doubt, of our colonial past, the long centuries during which we looked across the ocean — east — for affirmation. We want to get from nowhere, which is where we are (Gatsby is from North Dakota, more or less synonymous with nowhere), to that ever-elusive somewhere, full of orchids and ease and gold and girls.

> Argues that status matters more than money to Americans.

Five pages from the end of the book, Fitzgerald delivers his sociological punch line: "I see now that this has been a story of the West, after all — Tom and Gatsby, Daisy and Jordan and I, were all Westerners, and perhaps we possessed some deficiency in common which made us subtly unadaptable to Eastern life." Even the novel fails to make it East. Even Tom and Daisy feel like frauds. There is no arrival, it seems — or not, at least, for such as us.

Cites the text to clinch the argument.

A Different Kind of Criticism Lisa Brown has done a series of cartoon-style book reviews for the *San Francisco Chronicle.* This is her take on *The Great Gatsby.* © 2013 Lisa M. Brown.

Exploring purpose and topic

► find a
text

In most cases, you write a literary analysis to meet a course requirement, a paper usually designed to improve your skills as a reader of literature and art. Such a lofty goal, however, doesn't mean you can't enjoy the project or put your own spin on it.

Your first priority is to read any assignment sheet closely to find out exactly what you are asked to do. Underline any key words in the project description and take them seriously. Typically, you will see terms such as *compare and contrast*, *classify*, *analyze*, or *interpret*. They mean different things, and each entails a different strategy.

Once you know your goal in writing an analysis, you may have to choose a subject. ○ It's not unusual to have your instructor assign a work (*Three pages on* The House on Mango Street *by Friday*). But just as often, you'll select a work to study from within a range defined by the title of the course: Mexican American Literature; Major Works of Dostoyevsky; Banned Books. Which should you choose?

Choose a text you connect with.   It makes sense to spend time writing about works that move you, perhaps because they touch on an aspect of your life or identity. You may feel more confident studying them because of who you are and what you've experienced.

Choose a text you want to learn more about.   In the backs of their minds, most people have lists of works and artists they've always wanted to explore. So turn an assignment into an opportunity to sample one of them: *Beowulf*; *The Chronicles of Narnia*; or the work of William Gibson, Leslie Marmon Silko, or the Clash. Or use an assignment to push beyond the works that are from within your comfort zone, or familiar to your own experience: Examine writers and artists from cultures different from your own and with challenging points of view.

Choose a text you don't understand.   Most students write about accessible works that are relatively new: Why struggle with a hoary epic poem when you can just watch *The Lord of the Rings* on DVD? One obvious reason may be

get an
idea p. 331

to figure out how works from unfamiliar times still powerfully connect to our own; the very strangeness of older and more mysterious texts may even rouse you to ask better questions. You'll pay more attention to literary texts that puzzle you.

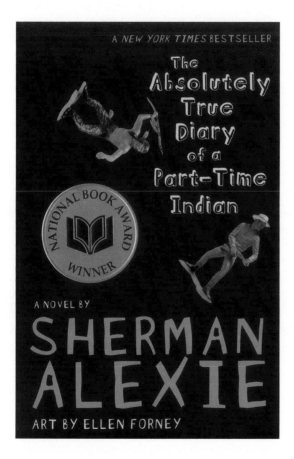

Cover of Sherman Alexie's Award-Winning Novel *The Absolutely True Diary of a Part-Time Indian* How much do you know about Native American fiction or film? Use an assignment as an opportunity to learn more. *The Absolutely True Diary of a Part-Time Indian*, by Sherman Alexie, art by Ellen Forney, published by Little Brown and Company, Books for Your Readers, Hachette Book Group, Inc. Used with permission.

Understanding your audience

Unless you write book reviews or essays for a campus literary magazine, the people reading your analyses of works of art and culture are most likely a professor and other students in your course. But in either situation, assume a degree of expertise among your readers. Understand, too, that people who read literary and cultural analyses on their own expect to learn something. So make good use of their time.

Clearly identify the author and works you are analyzing.   It seems like common sense, but this courtesy is neglected in many academic papers because students assume that *the teacher must know what I'm doing.* Don't make this mistake. Also briefly recap what happens in the works you are analyzing—especially with texts not everyone has read recently. ○ Follow the model of good reviewers, who typically review key story elements before commenting on them. Such summaries give readers their bearings at the beginning of a paper. Here's James Wood introducing a novel by Marilynne Robinson that he will be reviewing for the *New York Times*.

> *Gilead* is set in 1956 in the small town of Gilead, Iowa, and is narrated by a seventy-six-year-old pastor named John Ames, who has recently been told he has angina pectoris and believes he is facing imminent death. In this terminal spirit, he decides to write a long letter to his seven-year-old son, the fruit of a recent marriage to a much younger woman. This novel is that letter, set down in the easy, discontinuous form of a diary, mixing long and short entries, reminiscences, moral advice, and so on.

Define key terms.   Literary analyses use many specialized and technical expressions. Your instructor will doubtless know what an *epithet*, *peripeteia*, or *rondel* might be, but you need to define terms like these for wider audiences—your classmates, for instance. Alternatively, you can look for more familiar synonyms.

sum up
ideas p. 460

Don't aim to please professional critics.   Are you tempted to imitate the style of serious academic theorists you've encountered while researching your paper? No need—your instructor probably won't expect you to write in that way, at least not until graduate school.

Your Turn   In "Great Expectations: What Gatsby's Really Looking For" (p. 187), William Deresiewicz summarizes the familiar novel only minimally for his audience—the readers of a journal titled *The American Scholar*. What adjustments might he have to make for a more general—or, let's say, a less academic—audience? Did you find yourself lost or confused when reading the essay and, if so, where?

Finding and developing materials

▶ develop
  ideas

With an assignment in hand and works to analyze, the next step—and it's a necessary one—is to establish that you have a reliable "text" of whatever you'll be studying. In a course, a professor may assign a particular edition or literary anthology for you to use, making your job easier.

This Bedford/St. Martin's edition of *Frankenstein* provides important textual information and background. Look for texts with such material when studying classic novels, poems, and plays. © Bedford/St. Martin's.

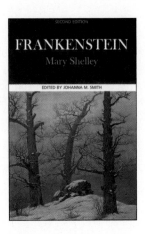

Be aware that many texts are available in multiple editions. (For instance, the novel *Frankenstein* first appeared in 1818, but the revised third edition of 1831 is the one most widely read today.) For classical works, such as the plays of Shakespeare, choose an edition from a major publisher, preferably one that includes thorough notes and perhaps some critical essays. When in doubt, ask your professor which texts to use. Don't just browse the library shelves.

Other kinds of media pose interesting problems as well. For instance, you may have to decide which version of a movie to study—the one seen by audiences in theaters or the "director's cut" on a DVD. Similarly, you might find multiple recordings of classical music: Look for widely respected performances. Even popular music may come in several versions: studio (*American Idiot*), live (*Bullet in a Bible*), alternative recording (*American Idiot: The Original Broadway Cast Recording*). Then there is the question of drama: Do you read a play on the page, watch a video when one is available, or see it in a theater? Perhaps you do all three. But whatever versions of a text you choose for study, be sure to identify them in your project, either in the text itself or on the works cited page. ○

Establishing a text is the easy part. Once that's done, how do you find an angle on the subject? ○ Try the following strategies and approaches.

understand citation
styles p. 470

find a topic
p. 331

Examine the text closely.   Guided by your assignment, carefully read, watch, or examine the selected work(s) and take notes. Obviously, you'll treat some works differently from others. You can read a Seamus Heaney sonnet a dozen times to absorb its nuances, but it's unlikely you'd push through Rudolfo Anaya's novel *Bless Me, Ultima* more than once or twice for a paper. But, in either case, you'll need an effective way to keep notes or to annotate what you're studying.

Honestly, you should count on a minimum of two readings or viewings of any text, the first one to get familiar with the work and find a potential approach, the second and subsequent ones to confirm your thesis and to find evidence for it. And do read the actual novel or play, not some "no fear" version.

Focus on the text itself.   Your earliest literature papers probably tackled basic questions about plot, character, setting, theme, and language. But these are exactly the kinds of issues that fascinate many readers. So look for moments when the plot of the novel you're analyzing establishes its themes or study how characters develop in response to specific events. Even the setting of a short story or film might be worth writing about when it becomes a factor in the story: Can you imagine the film *Casablanca* taking place in any other location?

Questions about language always loom large in literary analyses. How does word choice shape the mood of a poem? How does a writer create irony through diction or dialogue? Indeed, any technical feature of a work might be studied and researched, from the narrators in novels to the rhyme schemes in poetry.

Focus on meanings, themes, and interpretations.   Although tracing themes in literary works seems like an occupation mostly for English majors, the impulse to find meanings is irresistible. If you take any work seriously, you'll discover angles and ideas worth sharing with readers. Maybe *Seinfeld* is a modern version of *Everyman*, or *O Brother, Where Art Thou?* is a retelling of the *Odyssey* by Homer, or maybe not. Open your mind to possible connections: What have you seen like this before? What structural patterns do you detect? What ideas are supported or undercut?

Focus on authorship and history.   Some artists stand apart from their creations, while others cannot be separated from them. So you might explore closely how a work mirrors the life, education, and attitudes of its author. Is the author writing to represent his or her gender, race, ethnicity, or class? Or does the work repudiate its author's identity, class, or religion? What psychological forces or religious perspectives drive the work's characters or themes?

Similarly, consider how a text embodies the assumptions, attitudes, politics, fashions, and even technology of the times during which it was composed. A work as familiar as Jonathan Swift's "A Modest Proposal" still requires readers to know at least a *little* about Irish and English politics in the eighteenth century. How does Swift's satire expand in scope when you learn a little more about its environment?

Focus on genre.   Literary genres are formulas. Take a noble hero, give him a catastrophic flaw, have him make bad choices, and then kill him off: That's tragedy—or, in the wrong hands, melodrama. With a little brainstorming, you could identify dozens of other genres and subcategories: epics, sonnets, historical novels, superhero comics, grand opera, soap opera, and so on. Artists often create works that fall between genres, sometimes producing new ones. Readers, too, bring clear-cut expectations to a text: Try to turn a 007 action-spy thriller into a three-hankie chick flick, and you've got trouble in River City.

You can analyze genre in various ways. For instance, track a text backward to discover its literary forebears—the works an author used for models. Even works that revolt against older genres bear traces of what their authors have rejected. It's also possible to study the way artists combine different genres or play with or against the expectations of audiences. Needless to say, you can also explore the relationships of works within a genre. For example, what do twentieth-century coming-of-age stories such as *A Separate Peace*, *The Catcher in the Rye*, and *Lord of the Flies* have in common?

Focus on influences.   Some works have an obvious impact on life or society, changing how people think or behave: *Uncle Tom's Cabin, To Kill a Mockingbird, Roots, Schindler's List*. TV shows have broadened people's notions of family; musical genres such as jazz and gospel have created and sustained entire communities.

But impact doesn't always occur on such a grand scale or express itself through social movements. Books influence other books, films other films, and so on—with not a few texts crossing genres. For better or worse, books, movies, and other cultural productions influence styles, fashions, and even the way people speak. Consider *Breaking Bad*, *Glee*, or *Game of Thrones*. You may have to think outside the box, but projects that trace and study influence can shake things up.

Focus on social connections.   In recent decades, many texts have been studied for what they reveal about relationships between genders, races, ethnicities, and social classes. Works by newer writers are now more widely read in schools, and hard questions are asked about texts traditionally taught: What do they reveal about the treatment of women or minorities? Whose lives have been ignored in "canonical" texts? What responsibility do such texts have for maintaining repressive political or social arrangements? Critical analyses of this sort have changed how many people view literature and art, and you can follow up on such studies and extend them to texts you believe deserve more attention.

Find good sources.   Developing a literary paper provides you with many opportunities and choices. Fortunately, you needn't make all your decisions on your own. Ample commentary and research are available on almost any literary subject or method, both in print and online. ○ Your instructor and local librarians can help you focus on the best resources for your project, but the following boxes list some possibilities.

refine your
search p. 442

Literary Resources in Print

Abrams, M. H., and Geoffrey Harpham. *A Glossary of Literary Terms*. 11th ed. Boston: Wadsworth Cengage, 2014.

Beacham, Walton, ed. *Research Guide to Biography and Criticism*. Washington: Beacham, 1990.

Birch, Dinah, ed. *The Oxford Companion to English Literature*. 7th ed. Oxford: Oxford UP, 2009.

Crystal, David. *The Cambridge Encyclopedia of Language*. 3rd ed. New York: Cambridge UP, 2010.

Encyclopedia of World Literature in the 20th Century. 3rd ed. Farmington Hills: St. James, 1999.

Gates, Henry Louis, Jr., et al. *The Norton Anthology of African American Literature*. 3rd ed. New York: Norton, 2014.

Gilbert, Sandra M., and Susan Gubar. *The Norton Anthology of Literature by Women: The Traditions in English*. 3rd ed. New York: Norton, 2007.

Greene, Roland, et al. *The Princeton Encyclopedia of Poetry and Poetics*. 4th ed. Princeton: Princeton UP, 2012.

Harmon, William, and Hugh Holman. *A Handbook to Literature*. 12th ed. New York: Prentice, 2012.

Harner, James L. *Literary Research Guide: A Guide to Reference Sources for the Study of Literature in English and Related Topics*. 5th ed. New York: MLA, 2008.

Hart, James D., and Phillip W. Leininger. *The Oxford Companion to American Literature*. 6th ed. New York: Oxford UP, 1995.

Howatson, M. C. *The Oxford Companion to Classical Literature*. 3rd ed. New York: Oxford UP, 2011.

Leitch, Vincent, et al. *The Norton Anthology of Theory and Criticism*. 2nd ed. New York: Norton, 2010.

Sage, Lorna. *The Cambridge Guide to Women's Writing in English*. Cambridge: Cambridge UP, 1999.

Literary Resources Online

Annual Bibliography of English Language and Literature (ABELL) (subscription)

The Atlantic (http://www.theatlantic.com) (for culture and reviews)

Browne Popular Culture Library (http://www.bgsu.edu/colleges/library/pcl)

The Complete Works of William Shakespeare (http://shakespeare.mit.edu)

Eserver.org: Accessible Writing (http://eserver.org)

A Handbook of Rhetorical Devices (http://www.virtualsalt.com/rhetoric.htm)

Internet Public Library: Literary Criticism (http://www.ipl.org/div/litcrit/)

Literary Resources on the Net (http://andromeda.rutgers.edu/~jlynch/Lit)

Literature Resource Center (Gale Group — subscription)

MLA on the Web (http://www.mla.org)

New York Review of Books (http://www.nybooks.com/)

New York Times Book Review (http://www.nytimes.com/pages/books)

The Online Books Page (http://onlinebooks.library.upenn.edu)

Yahoo! Arts: Humanities: Literature (http://dir.yahoo.com/arts/humanities/literature/)

Creating a structure

▶ organize ideas

Build the structure for your literary analysis around the particular observation, claim, or point you hope to make. Your project will be organized like a report if you're interested in sharing information and explaining what is already known. Or it will develop like an argument if your thesis offers fresh claims or veers toward controversy. ○ What matters most, however, is that you organize your work in ways that make sense to readers.

Imagine a structure.   Analyses of literature and culture can head in various directions. One analysis might present a string of evidence to support a thematic claim; another might examine similarities and differences between two or more works; yet another might explore an open-ended question, with ideas emerging expressively, rather than demonstrating a single point. Consider how the following claims might lead to very different structures:

> **STUDY OF THEME**
> In *Bless Me, Ultima*, the youngster Antonio has to reconcile his mystical beliefs with Ultima's prediction that he will become a "man of learning."

> **CONTRAST OF GENRES**
> The movie version of Annie Proulx's short story "Brokeback Mountain" actually improves on the original work, making the narrative more appealing, moving, and believable.

> **CULTURAL ANALYSIS**
> One likely impact of digital technology will be to eliminate traditional barriers between art, entertainment, and business — with books becoming films that morph into games that inspire commercial art and even music.

Here are three simple forms a literary analysis might take, the first developing from a thesis stated early on, the second comparing two works to make a point, and the third building toward a conclusion rather than opening with a traditional thesis. ○

Introduction leading to a claim
First supporting reason + textual evidence
Second supporting reason + textual evidence
Additional supporting reasons + textual evidence

Conclusion

understand
argument p. 66

develop a
statement p. 362

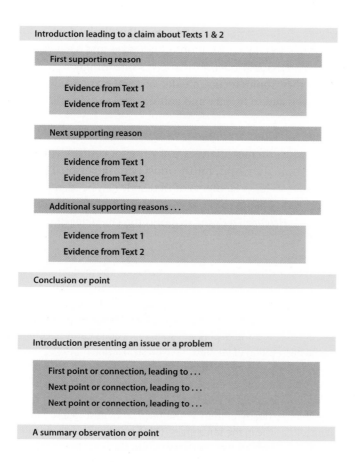

Introduction leading to a claim about Texts 1 & 2

First supporting reason

Evidence from Text 1
Evidence from Text 2

Next supporting reason

Evidence from Text 1
Evidence from Text 2

Additional supporting reasons . . .

Evidence from Text 1
Evidence from Text 2

Conclusion or point

Introduction presenting an issue or a problem

First point or connection, leading to . . .
Next point or connection, leading to . . .
Next point or connection, leading to . . .

A summary observation or point

Work on your opening.   Be sure that the introductory paragraphs of your literary or cultural analyses identify the works you are examining, explain what you hope to accomplish, and provide necessary background information (including brief plot summaries, for example). ◯ Always provide enough context so that the project stands on its own and would make sense to someone other than the instructor who assigned it.

shape a
beginning p. 391

Choosing a style and design

Literary analyses are traditional assignments still typically done in an academic style and following specific conventions of language and MLA documentation. ○ But such analyses also lend themselves surprisingly well to new media, especially when their topics focus on video or aural texts. So style and media can be important issues in literary and cultural projects.

Use a formal style for most assignments.   As the student example in this chapter suggests, literary analyses you write for courses will be serious in tone, formal in vocabulary, and, for the most part, impersonal—all markers of a formal or high style. ○ Elements of that style can be identified in this paragraph from an academic paper in which Manasi Deshpande analyzes Emily Brontë's *Wuthering Heights*. Here she explores the character of its Byronic hero, Heathcliff:

Examines Heathcliff from the perspective of a potential reader, not from her own.

Complex sentences smoothly incorporate quotations and documentation.

Related points are expressed in parallel clauses.

Vocabulary throughout is accessible but formal. No contractions are used.

In witnessing Heathcliff's blatantly violent behavior, the reader is caught between sympathy for the tormented Heathcliff and shock at the intensity of his cruelty and mistreatment of others. Intent on avenging Hindley's treatment of him, Heathcliff turns his wrath toward Hareton by keeping him in such an uneducated and dependent state that young Cathy becomes "upset at the bare notion of relationship with such a clown" (193). Living first under Hindley's neglect and later under Heathcliff's wrath, Hareton escapes his situation only when Catherine befriends him and Heathcliff dies. In addition, Heathcliff marries Isabella only because Catherine wants to "'torture [him] to death for [her] amusement'" and must "'allow [him] to amuse [himself] a little in the same style'" (111). Heathcliff's sole objective in seducing and running away with Isabella is to take revenge on Catherine for abandoning him. Heathcliff's sadism is so strong that he is willing to harm innocent third parties in order to punish those who have caused his misery. He even forces young Cathy and Linton to marry by locking them in Wuthering Heights and keeping Cathy from her dying father until she has married Linton, further illustrating his willingness to torture others out of spite and vengeance.

cite in
MLA p. 472

define your
style p. 400

Use a middle style for informal or personal papers.   Occasionally, for example, you may have to write brief essays called *response* or *position papers*, in which you record your immediate reactions to poems, short stories, or other readings. In these assignments, an instructor may want to hear your voice and may even encourage exploratory reactions. Here is Cheryl Lovelady responding somewhat personally to a proposal to revive the Broadway musical *Fiddler on the Roof*:

> How can a play set in a small, tradition-bound Jewish village during the Russian Revolution be modernized? I would argue that *Fiddler on the Roof* is actually an apt portrayal of our own time. Throughout the show, the conflicted main character, Tevye, is on the brink of pivotal decisions. Perplexed by his daughters' increasingly modern choices, Tevye prays aloud, "Where do they think they are, America?" Tevye identifies America as a symbol of personal freedom — the antithesis of the tradition that keeps his life from being "as shaky as a fiddler on the roof." Forty years after the play's debut, America has become startlingly more like the Anatevka Tevye knows than the America he envisions. Post-9/11 America parallels Anatevka in a multitude of ways: Political agendas ideologically separate the United States from most of the world; public safety and conventional wisdom are valued over individual freedoms; Americans have felt the shock of violence brought onto their own soil; minority groups are isolated or isolate themselves in closed communities; and societal taboos dictate whom people may marry.

Question focuses paragraph. Reply suggests strong personal opinion.

Basic style remains serious and quite formal: Note series of roughly parallel clauses that follow colon.

Follow the conventions of literary analysis.   One of those norms is to set the action in a novel, poem, or movie in the present tense when you describe or summarize it: "Hamlet kills his uncle just moments before he himself dies."

Another convention is to furnish the dates of birth and death for any major authors or artists you mention in an analysis. Similarly, give a year of publication or release date for any major works of art you mention. The dates usually appear in parentheses.

> Joan Didion (b. 1934) is the author of *Play It as It Lays* (1970), *Slouching Towards Bethlehem* (1968), and *The Year of Magical Thinking* (2005).

Finally, since you'll be frequently citing passages from literary works as well as quoting critics and reviewers, thoroughly review the rules for handling quotations. ○ All quoted materials need to be appropriately introduced and, if necessary, modified to fit smoothly into your sentences and paragraphs.

use quotations
p. 466

A 1964 production of the musical *Fiddler on the Roof*. United Artists/Photofest.

Cite plays correctly. Plays are cited by act, scene, and line number. In the past, passages from Shakespeare were routinely identified using a combination of Roman and Arabic numerals. But currently, MLA recommends Arabic numerals only for such references.

FORMER STYLE

Hamlet's final words are "The rest is silence" (*Ham*. V.ii.358).

CURRENT STYLE

Hamlet's final words are "The rest is silence" (*Ham*. 5.2.358).

Explore alternative media. You can be creative with literary and cultural projects, depending on the tools and media available to you. ○ For example, an oral presentation on a literary text can be handled impressively using presentation software such as PowerPoint or Prezi. Or Google Maps might be used to trace the physical locations or journeys in literary works. Naturally, if your project is to be submitted in electronic form, you can incorporate photographs, images, or the spoken word into your project, as appropriate. "Appropriate" means that the media elements genuinely enrich your analysis.

go multimodal
p. 542

Examining models

CLOSE READING In "Insanity: Two Women," Kanaka Sathasivan examines a poem (Emily Dickinson's "I felt a Funeral, in my Brain") and a short story (Charlotte Perkins Gilman's "The Yellow Wallpaper") to discover a disturbing common theme in the work of these two American women writers. The essay, written in a formal academic style, uses a structure that examines the works individually, drawing comparisons in a final paragraph. Note, in particular, how Sathasivan manages the close reading of the poem by Emily Dickinson, moving through it almost line by line to draw out its themes and meanings. Here's the text of "I felt a Funeral, in my Brain."

I felt a Funeral, in my Brain,
And Mourners to and fro
Kept treading — treading — till it seemed
That Sense was breaking through —

And when they all were seated,
A Service, like a Drum —
Kept beating — beating — till I thought
My Mind was going numb —

And then I heard them lift a Box
And creak across my Soul
With those same Boots of Lead, again,
Then Space — began to toll,

As all the Heavens were a Bell,
And Being, but an Ear,
And I, and Silence, some strange Race
Wrecked, solitary, here —

And then a Plank in Reason, broke,
And I dropped down, and down —
And hit a World, at every plunge,
And Finished knowing — then —

For an additional reading, see **macmillanhighered.com/howtowrite3e**.
e-readings › Erik Didriksen, *Pop Sonnet: Royals* [PARODY]

205

You can find the full text of "The Yellow Wallpaper" by searching online by the title. One such text is available at the University of Virginia Library Electronic Text Center: http://etext.virginia.edu/toc/modeng/public/GilYell.html.

Reading the Genre   Like any skillful academic paper, Sathasivan's "Insanity: Two Women" follows a great many conventions in structure, style, and mechanics. Go through the essay paragraph by paragraph and list as many of these moves as you can identify — right through the works cited page. Compare your list with those produced by several classmates.

Sathasivan 1

Kanaka Sathasivan

Professor Glotzer

English 102

March 3, 20--

Insanity: Two Women

The societal expectations of women in the late nineteenth century served to keep women demure, submissive, and dumb. Although women's rights had begun to improve as more people rejected these stereotypes, many women remained trapped in their roles because of the pressures placed on them by men. Their suppression had deep impacts not only on their lives but also on their art. At a time when women writers often published under male aliases to gain respect, two of America's well-known authors, Emily Dickinson (1830-1886) and Charlotte Perkins

Works to be analyzed are set in context: late nineteenth century.

Sathasivan 2

Gilman (1860-1935), both wrote disturbing pieces describing the spiritual and mental imprisonment of women. In verse, Dickinson uses a funeral as a metaphor for the silencing of women and the insanity it subsequently causes. Gilman's prose piece "The Yellow Wallpaper" (1899) gives us a firsthand look into the mental degradation of a suppressed woman. These two works use vivid sensory images and rhythmic narration to describe sequential declines into madness.

In "I felt a Funeral, in my Brain" (first published in 1896), Dickinson outlines the stages of a burial ceremony, using them as metaphors for a silenced woman's departure from sanity. The first verse, the arrival of Mourners, symbolizes the imposition of men and society on her mind. They are "treading" "to and fro," breaking down her thoughts and principles, until even she is convinced of their ideas (Dickinson 3, 2). The Service comes next, representing the closure—the acceptance of fate. Her "Mind was going numb" as the sounds of the service force her to stop thinking and begin accepting her doomed life. These first two verses use repetition at parallel points as they describe the Mourners as "treading—treading" and the service as a drum "beating—beating" (Dickinson 3, 7). The repetition emphasizes the incessant insistence of men; they try to control threatening women with such vigor and persistence that eventually even the women themselves begin to believe men's ideas and allow their minds to be silenced.

Sathasivan 3

As the funeral progresses, the Mourners carry her casket from the service. Here Dickinson describes how they scar her very Soul using the "same Boots of Lead" which destroyed her mind (Dickinson 11). From the rest of the poem, one can infer that the service took place inside a church, and the act of parting from a house of God places another level of finality on the loss of her spirituality. While the figures in the poem transport her, the church's chimes begin to ring, and, as if "all the Heavens were a Bell / And Being, but an Ear," the noise consumes her (Dickinson 13-14). In this tremendous sound, her voice finally dissolves forever; her race with Silence has ended, "Wrecked," and Silence has won (Dickinson 16). Finally, after the loss of her mind, her soul, and her voice, she loses her sanity as they lower her casket into the grave and bury her. She "hit a World, at every plunge, / And Finished knowing" (Dickinson 19-20). The worlds she hits represent further stages of psychosis, and she plunges deeper until she hits the bottom, completely broken.

Like Dickinson, Gilman in "The Yellow Wallpaper" also segments her character's descent into madness. The narrator of the story expresses her thoughts in a diary written while she takes a vacation for her health. Each journal entry represents another step toward insanity, and Gilman reveals the woman's psychosis with subtle hints and clues placed discreetly within

With simple transition, turns to Gilman's short story.

Sathasivan 4

the entries. These often take the form of new information about the yellow room the woman has been confined to, such as the peeled wallpaper or bite marks on the bedpost. The inconspicuous presentation of such details leads the reader to think that these artifacts have long existed, created by someone else, and only now does the narrator share them with us. "I wonder how it was done and who did it, and what they did it for," she says, speaking of a groove that follows the perimeter of the walls (Gilman 400). Here, Gilman reuses specific words at crucial points in the narration to allude to the state of her character's mental health. In this particular example, both the narrator and the maid use the word "smooch" to describe, respectively, the groove in the wall and yellow smudges on the narrator's clothes (Gilman 400). This repetition indicates that she created the groove in the room, a fact affirmed at the end of the story.

Gilman's narrator not only seems to believe other people have caused the damage she sees but also imagines a woman lives trapped within the paper, shaking the pattern in her attempts to escape. "I think that woman gets out in the daytime!" the narrator exclaims, recounting her memories of a woman "creeping" about the garden (Gilman 400, 401). Again, Gilman uses repetition to make associations for the reader as the narrator uses "creeping" to describe her own exploits. As in the previous example, the end of the story reveals that the

Uses present tense to describe action in "The Yellow Wallpaper."

Sathasivan 5

woman in the paper is none other than the narrator, tricked by her insanity. This connection also symbolizes the narrator's oppression. The design of the wallpaper trapping the woman represents the spiritual bars placed on the narrator by her husband and doctor, who prescribes mental rest, forbidding her from working or thinking. Even the description of the room lends itself to the image of a dungeon or cell, with "barred" windows and "rings and things in the walls" (Gilman 392). Just as the woman escapes during the daytime, so, too, does the narrator, giving in to her sickness and disobeying her husband by writing. Finally, like the woman in the paper breaking free, the narrator succumbs to her insanity.

Both Dickinson's and Gilman's works explore society's influence on a woman's mental health. Like Dickinson's character, Gilman's narrator has also been compelled into silence by a man. Although she knows she is sick, her husband insists it isn't so and that she, a fragile woman, simply needs to avoid intellectual stimulation. Like a Mourner, "treading—treading," he continually assures her he knows best and that she shouldn't socialize or work. This advice, however, only leads to further degradation as her solitude allows her to indulge her mental delusions. When the narrator attempts to argue with her husband, she is silenced, losing the same race as Dickinson's character.

Draws attention to common themes and strategies in the two works.

Sathasivan 6

In both these pieces, the characters remain mildly aware of their declining mental health, but neither tries to fight it. In Dickinson's poem, the woman passively observes her funeral, commenting objectively on her suppression and burial. Dickinson uses sound to describe every step, creating the feel of secondary sensory images—images that cannot create a picture alone and require interpretation to do so. Gilman's narrator also talks of her sickness passively, showing her decline only by describing mental fatigue. In these moments she often comments that her husband "loves [her] very dearly" and she usually accepts the advice he offers (Gilman 396). Even on those rare occasions when she disagrees, she remains submissive and allows her suppression to continue. In contrast to Dickinson, Gilman uses visual images to create this portrait, describing most of all how the narrator sees the yellow wallpaper, an approach that allows insight into the narrator's mental state.

Both Dickinson and Gilman used their writing to make profound statements about the painful lives led by many women in the nineteenth century. Through repetition, metaphor, symbolism, and sensory images, both "I felt a Funeral, in my Brain" and "The Yellow Wallpaper" describe a woman's mental breakdown, as caused by societal expectations and oppression. The poetry and prose parallel one another and together give insight into a horrific picture of insanity.

Notes difference in technique between authors.

Concludes that writers use similar techniques to explore a common theme in two very different works.

Sathasivan 7

Works Cited

Dickinson, Emily. "I felt a Funeral, in my Brain." *Concise
Anthology of American Literature*. 7th ed. Ed. George
McMichael. Boston: Longman, 2011. 1139. Print.

Gilman, Charlotte Perkins. "The Yellow Wallpaper." *The
American Short Story and Its Writer, An Anthology*. Ed. Ann
Charters. Boston: Bedford, 2000. 391-403. Print.

MLA documentation style used for in-text notes and works cited.

PHOTOGRAPHS AS LITERARY TEXTS   Photography attained its status as art in the twentieth century. Even documentary photographs not originally conceived as works of art became prized for their striking depictions of the human condition. Three artists recognized for such work are Dorothea Lange (1895–1965), Walker Evans (1903–1975), and Gordon Parks (1912–2006). During the Great Depression and subsequent years, they produced photographs for the Farm Security Administration (FSA) intended to record all aspects of American life. But their best portraits of people and places often reach beyond the immediate historical context, as the following three images demonstrate. Note how these photographs present and frame their subjects, encouraging viewers to expand and interpret their meanings.

Reading the Genre   If you have a smartphone, chances are you take "documentary" photographs all the time to record what you do and see and whom you meet. How do these photographs differ from those by Lange, Evans, and Parks? How would you define serious "documentary photography," and have you taken any shots that fall into that category?

Dorothea Lange, *Jobless on Edge of Pea Field, Imperial Valley, California* (1937). Library of Congress, Prints and Photographs Division/FSA/OWI Collection.

Walker Evans, *Burroughs Family Cabin, Hale County, Alabama* (1936).
Library of Congress, Prints and Photographs Division/FSA/OWI Collection, LC-USF342-
T01-008133.

Gordon Parks, *American Gothic* (1942). Library of Congress, Prints and Photographs Division/ FSA/OWI Collection.

Assignments

1. **Thematic Interpretation:** Review William Deresiewicz's "Great Expectations: What Gatsby's Really Looking For" (p. 187). Then try your hand at similarly describing a theme or issue explored in a literary or cultural work you particularly admire. Perhaps you have a take on Neil Gaiman's *Sandman* series that you want to share or you view a more conventional work (*Tom Sawyer*; *The Scarlet Letter*) in ways that other readers typically do not. Because of its magazine audience, Deresiewicz's essay is relatively short and has no documentation. Your essay might follow the same format, but be respectful in acknowledging sources informally.

2. **Close Reading:** In "Insanity: Two Women" (p. 205), Kanaka Sathasivan does a close, almost line-by-line analysis of Emily Dickinson's "I felt a Funeral, in my Brain"; then she compares the themes and strategies of the poem to those she finds in Charlotte Perkins Gilman's "The Yellow Wallpaper." For a project of your own, do *either* a close reading of a favorite short poem or song *or* a comparison of two works from different genres or media.

For the close reading, tease out all the meanings and strategies you can uncover and show readers how the text works. For the comparison, be sure to begin with works that interest you because of some important similarity: They may share a theme or plot, or even be the *same* work in two different media—*Game of Thrones* in novel and television forms, for instance.

3. **Analysis of a Visual Text:** Photographers Dorothea Lange, Walker Evans, and Gordon Parks (pp. 213–16) recorded images documenting the long-term effects of the Great Depression. In a short paper, describe the specific scenes you would photograph today if you hoped to leave as important a documentary legacy as Lange, Evans, and Parks. To make the project manageable, focus on your local community. Showcase your own images in a photo-essay.

4. **Your Choice:** Write a paper about any work of poetry or fiction that you wish more people would read. Use your essay to explain (or, if necessary, defend) the qualities of the work that make it worth someone's serious attention.

How to start ▶
- Need to **find a text to analyze**? See page 224.
- Need to come up with **ideas**? See page 227.
- Need to **organize your ideas**? See page 230.

8 Rhetorical Analyses

examine in detail the way texts work

Rhetorical analyses foster the kind of careful reading that makes writers better thinkers. Moreover, they're everywhere in daily life, especially in politics and law. In fact, they're hard to avoid, especially if you spend much time reading new media.

RHETORICAL ANALYSIS

You've seen too many slick TV spots touting smartphones that do everything but wash dishes. Your own new phone doesn't work quite so well. You decide to write a *rhetorical analysis* of the ads to explain why consumers (like you) fall so easily for questionable claims.

CLOSE READING OF AN ARGUMENT

For an assignment in a writing class, you do a *close reading of an argument* a politician makes in an important campaign speech. You want to discover exactly how and why he manages to sound so much more persuasive than most Washington pols.

CULTURAL ANALYSIS

Management has heard that the mostly blue-collar customers of a clothing store where you work don't like its Web site. You understand the problem: The models online all frolic at expensive resorts while looking ridiculously thin, young, and upper class. You write a brief *cultural analysis* of the situation, suggesting changes to align the store's online presence to the diversity of its actual customers.

DECIDING TO WRITE A RHETORICAL ANALYSIS.   You react to what others say or write all the time. Sometimes an advertisement, a speech, or maybe a cultural image grabs you so hard that you want to take it apart to see how it works. Put those discoveries into words and you've composed a *rhetorical analysis* (for more on choosing a genre, see the Introduction).

"Twinkies" At first glance, this editorial cartoon by Nate Beeler of the *Columbus Dispatch* might seem just a riff on the return of Hostess Twinkies to the marketplace in 2013. But how exactly do the images in the panel mesh with the remark made by one of its characters: "There is something seriously wrong with America"? What exactly is going on here — rhetorically? Nate Beeler, courtesy of Cagle Cartoons.

Rhetoric is the art of using language and media to achieve particular ends. In rhetorical analyses, you identify the specific techniques that writers, speakers, artists, or advertisers use to be persuasive and then assess their effectiveness objectively. ○ You take a rhetorical analysis one step further when you cast neutrality aside and offer good reasons for endorsing or disagreeing with a particular argument—in effect making a case of your own. Such a detailed inspection of a text is sometimes called a *critical analysis*.

When you write a rhetorical analysis, you'll make the following moves.

Take words and images seriously.   When you compose rhetorical analyses, hold writers to high standards because their choices have consequences. Fair and effective techniques of persuasion deserve to be identified and applauded. And crooked ones should be ferreted out, exposed, and sent packing. It takes practice to distinguish one from the other—which is what rhetorical analyses provide.

Spend time with texts.   You cannot evaluate the techniques of a writer, speaker, or artist until you know them inside out. But we blow through most of what we read (and see) without much thought. Serious rhetorical analysis does just the opposite: It makes texts move like bullets in *The Matrix*, their motion slowed and their trajectories magnified for careful study. ○

Pay attention to audience.   When you do a rhetorical analysis, understanding for *whom* a text is written can be as important as *what* it says. In fact, audiences determine the content, shape, and language of most arguments.

Mine texts for evidence.   Find and cite any rhetorical moves that casual readers of a text are likely to miss. Point to subtle or ironic language, overblown emotional appeals, intricate logic, or covert bigotry. Moves such as these will be the best support for your claims in a rhetorical analysis. Expect to quote often. ○

understand
argument p. 66

read closely
p. 340

use quotations
p. 466

In "Too Much Information," an essay originally published in *The American Scholar* (June 18, 2013), Professor Paula Marantz Cohen of Drexel University examines what happens to us as a result of living in a society that insists on answering, indeed *anticipating*, all the questions we might have in our daily lives. Her article is a rhetorical analysis because it demonstrates how modes of communication shape—and then sometimes diminish—our capacity to think. But Cohen also explores why we now demand immediate answers to complex questions—which is why you will find a selection from this piece quoted in the chapter on causal analyses (see p. 145).

Reading the Genre   The title and subtitle of Cohen's essay likely start you thinking about the problem she identifies. Is information overload an issue you have encountered yourself? After reading the piece, consider whether you find Cohen's discussion convincing. Do your own experiences tend to confirm her thesis, or might you be inclined to challenge it—perhaps from a generational point of view?

Too Much Information

The Pleasure of Figuring Things Out for Yourself

PAULA MARANTZ COHEN

Cohen identifies a question that puzzles her.

When did we start wanting everything explained to us? Why can't we be content with indeterminate meaning and subjective interpretation?

Part of the explanatory drive comes, I believe, from the nature of higher education. The cost of college is so great that students and their parents feel they should get their money's worth—which is to say, get answers to all the difficult questions.

Another reason is the Internet. The other day, a colleague came into my office disgusted. He had asked his students to write a paragraph about the symbolism of the flower pot in Raymond Carver's story "Popular Mechanics." The answers that came back were similar, he said, not because students had copied from each other, but because they had all Googled "Popular Mechanics," "Carver," "flower pot," and "symbolism," scanned what came up,

She looks to media habits for an answer.

> She finds more examples of media hustling to serve our curiosity — inadequately.

and found the "answer." They had no idea that this wasn't the way to proceed. They figured that the question had a singular answer, much in the way a math problem has an answer.

Consider some other ways we have been conditioned to expect hard explanations for soft things (e.g., works of the imagination, and moral and philosophical questions). DVDs give us "special features" that often seem to diminish our understanding of the film or our appreciation of it. The idea applies to television as well. After watching the last episode of [HBO's] *Girls*, I happened to let the show run on to the after-show sequence, in which creator and star Lena Dunham explained what we had just seen. Not only did her banal exegesis lessen the power of the episode, it made me less interested in her quirky persona. What had looked smart and funny, creative and irreverent, was forced into an explanatory mold and both became uninteresting and co-opted into the very sort of neatly packaged form that the show seems to oppose. I didn't want to see a counterculture icon giving me a lecture on relationship stability.

Museums are another example. I usually bypass the audiotapes that accompany a special exhibit. I don't like the didactic tone — being told what to feel about this or that picture, or the development of this or that artist. Biographical information about the artist, some gossip about his or her circle, what other artists have been influenced by this one — yes. But to be told that this is X's most accomplished work, or that Y shows particular genius here, or that the depiction of the young girl in the corner is especially moving in what it says about isolation and alienation — no thanks. Such commentary also frequently appears on the cards used to identify paintings on the wall. Along with the date and a few details as to where the work was painted, we are now likely to get a mini-dissertation on how the green background is a statement about the artist's wish to return to the bucolic farm of his boyhood. Driving the trend is the assumption that people want more information — they want to get their money's worth.

> Cohen exposes how habitual the move to provide information has become, a key insight.

I recently received an e-mail from a student asking if she could use No Fear Shakespeare for my Shakespeare class. I had no idea what No Fear Shakespeare was, though the phrase made me shudder in anticipation. I soon learned that it gives you Shakespeare's play on one side and "regular" English on the other.

I don't think there's a genuine pedagogical impulse behind our explanatory culture. It's more about selling more product—in this case, cultural product. And it's about control. I'm not a conspiracy theorist, believing that some Big Brother is trying to control my every move, but I do think the tendency of a capitalist economy is to know where consumers are (which includes how we think) all the time in order to sell us stuff. This is why movie theaters bombard us with commercials and movie-related tidbits even before the endless previews begin. It's also why the TV now runs continually in doctors' offices. And why, as a friend of mine pointed out, we need to have signs on the highway telling us that a "Scenic Overlook" is coming up, as though prescribing in advance what is photoworthy—and also to have a kiosk available to sell us throwaway cameras, Kleenex, and bags of chips.

She then analyzes the motives for selling "cultural product."

All this chattery explanation seems designed to refuse us a moment of peace in which to think for ourselves. Despite my jab at capitalism, the problem is more existential than economic. It's like the sort of chanting that goes on in a house of worship. The effect is soothing but also distracting. It keeps us from focusing on the difficult, unanswerable questions associated with the human condition—from gazing into the abyss and learning about the best use of our lives and the best way to face our eventual deaths. We may be getting explanations a mile a minute but we're not getting wisdom.

The analysis argues that "chattery explanation" preempts deeper thinking.

Exploring purpose and topic

▶ find a text

Make a difference.   Done right, rhetorical analyses can be as important as the texts they examine. They may change readers' opinions, open their eyes to new ideas, or keep an important argument going. They may also draw attention to rhetorical strategies and techniques worth imitating or avoiding.

When you write an angry letter to the editor complaining about bias in news coverage, you won't fret much about defining your purpose and topic—they are given. But when responding to a course assignment, particularly when you can choose a text on your own to analyze rhetorically, you've got to establish the boundaries. Given a choice, select a text to analyze with the following characteristics.

Choose a text you can work with.   Find a gutsy piece that makes a claim you or someone else might actually disagree with. It helps if you have a stake in the issue and already know something about it. The text should also be of a manageable length so that you can explore it coherently within the limits of the assignment.

Choose a text you can learn more about.   Some items won't make much sense out of context. So choose a text or series of texts that you can study and research. ○ It will obviously help to know who created it; where it first appeared; and when it was written, presented, or produced. This information is just as important for visual texts, such as advertisements, posters, and films, as for traditional speeches or articles.

Need help deciding what to write about? See "How to Browse for Ideas" on pp. 338–39.

Choose a text with handles.   Investigate arguments that do interesting things. Maybe a speech uses lots of anecdotes or repetition to generate emotional appeals; perhaps a photo-essay's commentary is more provocative than the images; a print ad may arrest attention by its simplicity but still be full of cultural significance. You've got to write about the piece. Make sure it offers you adventurous things to say.

plan your research p. 436

Choose a text you know how to analyze.   Stick to printed texts if you aren't sure how to write about ads or films or even speeches. But don't sell yourself short. You can pick up the necessary vocabulary by reading models of rhetorical and critical analysis. Moreover, you don't always need highly technical terms to describe poor logic, inept design, or offensive strategies, wherever they appear. Nor do you need special expertise to describe cultural trends or detect political motives.

Your Turn   You don't need a highbrow or sophisticated topic for a successful rhetorical analysis, as Professor Cohen's look at Google, DVDs, and No Fear Shakespeare suggests (p. 221). It's a much better strategy to dissect a text that genuinely interests you and then make an audience as intrigued by it as you are. If you take something seriously (zombies, for example; see p. 238), chances are that your readers will too. So begin an open-ended assignment by listing the sorts of texts you work with regularly. Even text messages and tweets can be studied rhetorically if you approach them from a new angle.

Understanding your audience

Some published rhetorical analyses are written for ready-made audiences already inclined to agree with the authors. Riled up by an offensive editorial or a political campaign, people these days may even seek out and enjoy mean-spirited, over-the-top criticism, especially on the Web. But the rhetorical and critical analyses you write for class should be relatively restrained because you can't predict how your readers might feel about the arguments you are critiquing. So assume that you are writing for a diverse and thoughtful audience, full of readers who prefer reflective analysis to clever put-downs. You don't have to be dull or passionless. Just avoid the easy slide into rudeness. ○

The Shelter Pet Project Advertisements featuring animals appeal to audiences, especially when they involve animal care or welfare. Here's a pitch to adopt shelter pets that may be — like humans — a little less than perfect. The Humane Society of the United States, Maddie's Fund ®, and the Ad Council.

respect your
readers p. 408

Finding and developing materials

ideas ◄

Before you analyze a text of any kind, do some background research. Discover all you can about its author, creator, publisher, sponsor, and so on. For example, you would need to know if a TV commercial you intend to examine has aired only on sports networks or lifestyle programs on cable. Figure out, too, the contexts in which an argument occurs. If you reply to a *Wall Street Journal* editorial, know what events sparked that item and investigate the paper's editorial slant.

Read the piece carefully just for information first, highlighting names or allusions you need to look up; there's very little you can't uncover these days via a Web search. When you think you understand the basics, you are prepared to approach the text rhetorically. Persuasive texts are often analyzed according to how they use three types of rhetorical appeal. Typically, a text may establish the character and credibility of its author (*ethos*), generate emotions in order to move audiences (*pathos*), and use evidence and logic to make its case (*logos*).

Consider the ethos of the author.   Ethos—the appeal to character—may be the toughest argumentative strategy to understand. Every text and argument is presented by someone, whether an individual, a group, or an institution. Audiences, whether they realize it or not, are influenced by that self-presentation: They are swayed by writers or speakers who come across as knowledgeable, honest, fair-minded, and believable. They are less friendly to people or institutions that seem to be deceptive, untrustworthy, or incompetent.

Here Michael Ruse describes a witness whose frank words established his ethos in a 1981 court case dealing with requiring creation science in Arkansas schools.

> The assistant attorney general was trying to tie him into knots over some technical point in evolutionary biology. Finally, the man blurted out, "Mr. Williams, I'm not a scientist. . . . I am an educator, and I have my pride and professional responsibilities. And I just can't teach that stuff [meaning creationism] to my kids."
>
> — "Science for Science Teachers," *Chronicle of Higher Education*, January 13, 2010

Look for such moments in texts—though such frank testimony will be rare. Instead, you may find indications of writers' authority and competence (or lack thereof) in how they describe their credentials, how they use sources, how they address readers, or how they use language. Even the absence of a "self" in a piece, as is typically the case in a scientific paper or academic article, can suggest a persuasive objectivity and rigor. Writers also bring their careers and reputations to a piece, and that stature may be enhanced (or diminished) by where they publish, yet another aspect of ethos.

Consider how a writer plays to emotions. *Pathos*—the emotional appeal— is usually easy to detect but sometimes difficult to assess. Look for places where a text generates strong feelings to support its points, win over readers, or influence them in other ways. Then consider how appropriate the tactic is for advancing a particular argument. The strategy is legitimate so long as raising emotions such as pity, fear, pride, outrage, and the like fits the moment and doesn't move audiences to make choices based upon distorted perceptions of the facts. Columnist Peggy Noonan, for example, routinely uses emotions to make her political points.

> We fought a war to free slaves. We sent millions of white men to battle and destroyed a portion of our nation to free millions of black men. What kind of nation does this? We went to Europe, fought, died, and won, and then taxed ourselves to save our enemies with the Marshall Plan. What kind of nation does this? Soviet communism stalked the world and we were the ones who steeled ourselves and taxed ourselves to stop it. Again: What kind of nation does this?
>   Only a very great one.
>
> —"Patriots, Then and Now," *Wall Street Journal*, March 30, 2006

Obviously, patriotic sentiments like these can be a smoke screen in some political debates. Your challenge in a rhetorical analysis is to point out emotional appeals and to determine whether they move audiences to act humanely or manipulate them into making bad or even stupid choices.

Consider how well reasoned a piece is. *Logos*—the appeal to reason and evidence—is most favored in academic texts. In a rhetorical analysis, you look carefully at the claims a text offers and whether they are supported by facts, data, testimony, and good reasons. What assumptions lie beneath the argument? That's a crucial query.

Ask questions about evidence too. Does it come from reliable sources or valid research? Is it up-to-date? Has it been reported accurately and fully? Has due attention been given to alternative points of view and explanations? Has enough evidence been offered to make a valid point? You might pose such objections, for example, when Peter Bregman, an expert on leadership training in business, makes an especially controversial argument.

A *study* of 829 companies over thirty-one years showed that diversity training had "no positive effects in the average *workplace*." Millions of dollars a year were spent on the training resulting in, well, nothing. Attitudes — and the diversity of the organizations — remained the same.

It gets worse. The researchers — Frank Dobbin of Harvard, Alexandra Kalev of Berkeley, and Erin Kelly of the University of Minnesota — concluded that "In firms where training is mandatory or emphasizes the threat of lawsuits, training actually has negative effects on management diversity."

— "Diversity Training Doesn't Work," *Harvard Business Review Blog Network*, March 12, 2012

Clearly, you have your work cut out for you: Suddenly you are dealing not solely with Bregman but also with the study he cites (and a link in his blog posting takes you right to it). The bottom line is that the logic of every major claim in a text may need such scrutiny in a rhetorical analysis. You are simultaneously fact-checker and skeptic.

Questions for a Rhetorical Analysis

Consider the topic.	What is **fresh** or striking about the topic? How well defined is it? **Does the piece make a point?** Could it be clearer? Is **the topic** important? Relevant? Controversial? Is the subject covered comprehensively or selectively **and with obvious biases**? What is the level of detail?
Consider the audiences of the text.	To whom is the piece addressed? How **well** is the text **adapted** to its audience? Who is **excluded** from the audience and how can you tell? What does the text offer its audience: information, controversy, entertainment? What does it **expect** from its audience?
Consider the author.	What is the author's relationship to the material? Is the writer or creator personally **invested** or **distant**? Is the author an expert, a knowledgeable amateur, or something else? What does the author **aim** to accomplish?
Consider the medium and design.	What is the medium or **genre** of the text: essay, article, editorial, advertisement, book excerpt, poster, video, podcast, or other format? How well does the medium **fit** the subject? How might the material look different in another medium? How do the various **elements** of design — such as arrangement, color, fonts, images, white space, audio, video, and so on — support the medium or genre?
Examine the language.	What is the **level** of the language: formal, informal, colloquial? What is the **tone** of the text — logical, sarcastic, humorous, angry, condescending?
Consider the occasion.	Why was the text created? To what circumstances or situations does it respond, and what might **public reaction** to it be? What problems does it solve or create? What pleasure might it give? Who benefits from the text?

Creating a structure

▶ organize
ideas

In a rhetorical analysis, you'll make a statement about how well the argumentative strategy of a piece works. Don't expect to come up with a thesis immediately or easily: You need to study a text closely to figure out how it works and then ponder its strengths and weaknesses. Draft a tentative thesis and then refine it throughout the process of writing until you have a thought-provoking claim you can prove. O

Your thesis should do more than just list rhetorical features: *This ad has good logical arguments and uses emotions and rhetorical questions.* Why would someone want to read (or write) a paper with such an empty claim? The following thesis promises a far more interesting rhetorical analysis:

> The latest government antidrug posters offer good reasons for avoiding
> steroids but do it in a visual style so bland that most students will ignore them.

Once you have a thesis or hypothesis, try sketching a design based on a thesis / supporting reason / evidence plan. Focus on those features of the text that illustrate the points you wish to make. You don't have to discuss every facet of the text.

> **Introduction leading to a claim**
>
> > **First supporting reason + textual evidence**
> > **Second supporting reason + textual evidence**
> > **Additional supporting reasons + textual evidence**
>
> **Conclusion**

In some cases, you might perform a line-by-line or paragraph-by-paragraph deconstruction of a text. This structure shows up frequently online. Such analyses practically organize themselves, but your commentary must be smart, accurate, and stylish to keep readers on board.

> **Introduction leading to a claim**
>
> > **First section/paragraph + detailed analysis**
> > **Next section/paragraph + detailed analysis**
> > **Additional section/paragraph + detailed analysis**
>
> **Conclusion**

develop a
statement p. 362

Choosing a style and design

The style of your rhetorical analyses will vary depending on audience, but you always face one problem that can sometimes be overcome by clever design: sharing the work you are analyzing with readers. They have to know what you are talking about.

Consider a high style.   Rhetorical and critical analyses for school usually need a formal or high style. ○ Keep the tone respectful, the vocabulary technical, and the perspective impersonal—avoiding *I* and *you*. Such a style gives the impression of objectivity and seriousness and enhances your ethos as a critic.

Consider a middle style.   Rhetorical and critical analyses appearing in the public arena—rather than in the classroom—are often less formal. To win over readers not compelled to read their stuff, writers turn to the middle style, which gives them ample options for expressing strong opinions and feelings (sometimes including anger, outrage, and contempt). Public writing is full of distinctive personal voices—from Stephen Carter and Paul Krugman to Naomi Klein and Peggy Noonan—offering opinions, making judgments, and advancing agendas. The ethos of middle style is often more cordial and sympathetic than that of high style, if somewhat less authoritative and commanding. You win the assent of readers by making them like and trust you.

Make the text accessible to readers.   Your rhetorical analysis should be written *as if readers do not have the text you are analyzing in hand or in front of them*. One way to achieve that clarity is to summarize and quote selectively from the text as you examine it, or to provide visual images that are captioned or annotated. You can see examples of this technique in Matthew James Nance's essay on pages 232–38 and in J. Reagan Tankersley's analysis on pages 239–48. Of course, you can always also attach photocopies or images of any short items you are analyzing or provide Web links to them. With other types of subjects—such as movies, advertising campaigns, and so on—simply describe or summarize the content of the work. Whatever you examine, always be sure to identify authors (or creators), titles, places/modes of publication, and dates in your paper.

define your
style p. 400

Examining models

For a class assignment on rhetorical analysis, Matthew James Nance chose as his subject the award-winning feature article "Can't Die for Trying" by journalist Laura Miller — who later would serve as mayor of Dallas. In the essay, Nance explains in detail how Miller manages to present the story of a convicted killer who wants to be executed to readers who might have contrary views about capital punishment. Nance's analysis is both technical and objective. He does an especially good job of helping readers follow the argument of "Can't Die for Trying," a fairly long and complicated article.

Reading the Genre Nance skillfully handles an important technical feature of many rhetorical analyses: quotations. Read this piece with a focus on the ways he introduces material from Laura Miller's "Can't Die for Trying." Note how smoothly he merges her words with his and how strategically he introduces quotations to make or confirm his analyses.

Nance 1

Matthew James Nance

Professor Norcia

English 2

June 14, 20--

A Mockery of Justice

In 1987, David Martin Long was convicted of double homicide and sentenced to death. He made no attempt to appeal this sentence and, surprisingly, did everything he could to expedite his execution. Nonetheless, due to an automatic appeals process, Long remained on Texas's Death Row for twelve years before he was finally executed. For various

Sets scene carefully and provides necessary background information.

For an additional reading, see **macmillanhighered.com/howtowrite3e**.
e-readings › Nickolay Lamm, *The History of Music* [INFOGRAPHIC]

Nance 2

reasons, including investigations into whether he was mentally ill, the state of Texas had continued to postpone his execution date. In 1994, when David Long was still in the middle of his appeals process, *Dallas Observer* columnist Laura Miller took up his case in the award-winning article "Can't Die for Trying." In this article, Miller explores the enigma of a legal system in which a sociopath willing to die continues to be mired in the legal process. The article is no typical plea on behalf of a death-row inmate, and Miller manages to avoid a facile political stance on capital punishment. Instead, Miller uses an effective combination of logical reasoning and emotional appeal to evoke from readers a sense of frustration at the system's absurdity.

> Miller defies expectations and Nance explains why in his thesis.

> Long paragraph furnishes detailed evidence for Miller's two premises.

To show that David Martin Long's execution should be carried out as soon as possible, Miller offers a reasoned argument based on two premises: that he wants death and that he deserves it. Miller cites Long's statement from the day he was arrested: "I realize what I did was wrong. I don't belong in this society. I never have. . . . I'd just wish they'd hurry up and get this over with" (5). She emphasizes that this desire has not changed, by quoting Long's correspondence from 1988, 1991, and 1992. In this way, Miller makes Long's argument seem reasoned and well thought out, not simply a temporary gesture of desperation. "'Yes, there are innocent men here, retarded men, insane men, and men who just plain deserve another

Nance 3

chance,' Long wrote [State District Judge Larry] Baraka in April 1992, 'But I am none of these!'" (5). Miller also points out his guilty plea, and the jury's remarkably short deliberation: "The jury took only an hour to find Long guilty of capital murder—and forty-five minutes to give him the death penalty" (5). Miller does not stop there, however. She gives a grisly description of the murders themselves, followed by Long's calculated behavior in the aftermath:

> He hacked away at Laura twenty-one times before going back inside where he gave Donna fourteen chops. The blind woman, who lay in bed screaming while he savaged Donna, got five chops. Long washed the hatchet, stuck it in the kitchen sink, and headed out of town in Donna's brown station wagon. (5)

Miller's juxtaposition of reasoned deliberation with the bloody narrative of the murders allows her to show that Long, in refusing to appeal, is reacting justly to his own sociopathy. Not only is it right that he die; it is also right that he does not object to his death.

In the midst of this reasoned argument, Miller expresses frustration at the bureaucratic inefficiency that is at odds with her logic. She offers a pragmatic, resource-based view of the situation:

> Of course, in the handful of instances where a person is wrongly accused . . . this [death-penalty activism] is noble, important work. But I would argue that in others—David Martin Long in particular—it is a sheer waste of taxpayer dollars. And a mockery of justice. (6)

Provides both summaries and quotations from article so that readers can follow Miller's argument.

To clarify Miller's point, Nance adds a phrase in brackets to the quotation.

Nance 4

Miller portrays the system as being practically incompatible with her brand of pragmatism. The figures involved in Long's case are painted as invisible, equivocal, or both. For instance, in spite of Long's plea, Judge Baraka was forced to appoint one of Long's attorneys to start the appeals process. "The judge didn't have a choice. Texas law requires that a death-penalty verdict be automatically appealed. . . . [This] is supposed to expedite the process. But the court sat on Long's case for four long years" (5). Miller also mentions Danny Burn, a Fort Worth lawyer in association with the Texas Resource Center, one of the "do-good . . . organizations whose sole feverish purpose is to get people off Death Row. . . . No matter how airtight the cases" (6). Burn filed on Long's behalf, though he never met Long in person. This fact underscores Miller's notion of the death-row bureaucracy as being inaccessible and, by extension, incomprehensible.

This parade of equivocal incompetence culminates in Miller's interview with John Blume, another activist who argued on Long's behalf. Miller paints Blume as so equivocal that he comes across as a straw man. "As a general rule," says Blume, "I tend to think most people who are telling you that are telling you something else, and that's their way of expressing it. There's something else they're depressed or upset about" (6). The article ends with Miller's rejoinder: "Well, I'd wager, Mr. Blume, that something is a lawyer like you" (6). Whereas the article up to this point has maintained a balance between

> Notice how smoothly quotations merge into Nance's sentences.

Nance 5

reason and frustration, here Miller seems to let gradually building frustration get the best of her. She does not adequately address whether Blume might be correct in implying that Long is insane, mentally ill, or otherwise misguided. She attempts to dismiss this idea by repeatedly pointing out Long's consistency in his stance and his own statements that he is not retarded, but her fallacy is obvious: Consistency does not imply sanity. Clearly, Miller would have benefited from citing Long's medical history and comparing his case with those of other death-row inmates, both mentally ill and well. Then her frustrated attack on Blume would seem more justified.

Miller also evokes frustration through her empathetic portrayal of Long. Although the article is essentially a plea for Long to get what he wants, this fact itself prevents Miller from portraying Long sympathetically. Miller is stuck in a rhetorical bind; if her readers become sympathetic toward Long, they won't want him to die. However, the audience needs an emotional connection with Long to accept the argument on his behalf. Miller gets around this problem by abandoning sympathy altogether, portraying Long as a cold-blooded killer. The quotation "I've never seen a more cold-blooded, steel-eyed sociopath ever" (5) is set apart from the text in a large font, and Miller notes, "This is a case of a really bad dude, plain and simple. . . . Use any cliché you want. It fits" (5). Miller here opts for a weak appeal, evoking from the audience the same negative emotion that

Nance makes a clear judgment about Miller's objectivity — then offers evidence for his claim.

Nance examines the way Miller deals with the problem she has portraying a cold-blooded killer to readers.

Nance 6

Long feels. She gives voice to Long's frustration over his interminable appeals: "Long stewed. . . . Long steamed. . . . Long fumes . . ." (6). She also points out Long's fear of himself: "I fear I'll kill again" (6). Clearly, the audience is meant to echo these feelings of frustration and fear. This may seem like a weak emotional connection with Long, but perhaps it is the best Miller could do, given that a primary goal of hers was to show that Long deserves death.

Laura Miller won the H. L. Mencken Award for this article, which raises important questions about the legal process. Part of its appeal is that it approaches capital punishment without taking a simplistic position. It can appeal to people on both sides of the capital punishment debate. The argument is logically valid, and for the most part, the emotional appeal is effective. Its deficiencies, including the weak emotional appeal for Long, are ultimately outweighed by Miller's overarching rationale, which calls for pragmatism in the face of absurdity.

Nance 7

Work Cited

Miller, Laura. "Can't Die for Trying." *Dallas Observer* 12 Jan.
1994: 5-6. Print.

CULTURAL ANALYSIS   Rhetorical analyses can illuminate cultural trends. In "Humankind's
Ouroboros," J. Reagan Tankersley explores the phenomenon of zombies from a historical and cultural perspective. He argues that these disembodied creatures increasingly popular in movies and, more recently,
television series, have come to represent what the public in general fears most in any given era. Hence,
zombies embody our anxieties. The paper includes shots from *Dracula*, *Night of the Living Dead*, *28 Days
Later*, and *The Walking Dead*.

Reading the Genre   Arguably, what makes Tankersley's essay a rhetorical analysis is the way it
connects zombie films and television series to the changing, culturally shared fears of audiences who
watch them. How plausible do you find his argument? Does it explain how these films work rhetorically
to you?

Tankersley 1

J. Reagan Tankersley

Professor Wilkes

Composition 1

November 24, 20--

Humankind's Ouroboros

Arguably, what we fear is perhaps the greatest indicator of how we behave as human animals. Fear is the emotion with the greatest impact on our fight or flight instincts; our animal brain is exposed when we decide to cover our eyes or keep on watching. It is why both lanes of traffic slow when there's been an accident: One lane brakes due to the obstruction; drivers in the other lane linger because they all want to see what happened, knowing it could've been them.

Horror films act in the same way. The monster movie of the Golden Age of Hollywood was the first sign that people can't always look away from what scares them. And it was lucrative. The horror genre remains one of the most prolific and profitable of the eleven classic genres of film, beginning with such titles as *Frankenstein* and *Dracula*. Within this body of works, none seems more prevalent today than the zombie movie, with the possible exception of highly sexualized vampire and werewolf dramas. Yet, despite a singular ability to scare audiences, the zombie movie has never been a solid form in itself. The zombies

Tankersley 2

of Classical Hollywood are strikingly different from those seen in the summer blockbusters of the past few years. More than any other monster, the zombie is able to evolve according to what will scare us the most, depending on where we stand in our own history. So the ever-evolving design of the zombie is an arguably strong tether to our fears, to how we react as humans.

The first film considered to be a zombie movie was released in 1932, in the heart of the Classical Hollywood era, and starred the master of the monster film, Bela Lugosi. While *White Zombie* is a long stretch from the zombie films of today, it broke ground on the very concept of "zombification." The plot involves a plantation owner from Haiti who, using witchcraft to win his love interest, accidentally turns her into a zombie obeying his every command.

A scene from *Dracula*. Everett Collection.

Tankersley introduces his thesis: that zombies in films embody the current fears of our society.

Tankersley 3

This plot hints at the roots of the zombie concept, which lie in voodoo legends, the word *zombie* originating in West Africa. The film was also the first to present on screen something akin to our modern image of the zombie: After she becomes a zombie, the love interest of the film is pale white, with the look of a corpse.

The film of that era that best predicted the future of the zombie film was the aptly named *Things to Come*, released in 1936. This adaptation of H. G. Wells's novel of the same name does not directly focus on zombies; however, its epic storyline includes a viral plague, which causes the infected to wander aimlessly, spreading the contagion on contact—an essential plot point in the large-scale zombie films of today. Both of these films reflect the concerns of the horror audience of the 1930s: fear of the mystical and fear of the future. *White Zombie* played to an uneasiness with voodoo magic, which some people associated with postslavery African American culture. *Things to Come* captured the signature pessimism of H. G. Wells during an era of economic recession in the troubled period between two great wars.

Zombies took a backseat in the horror genre following the fall of Classical Hollywood. Moreover, the new medium of television did not allow for such sensational and scary subject matter. Things changed, however, with the rise of the New American Cinema in the 1960s, a school of filmmaking that promoted noncontinuous editing and deliberately explicit images. George A. Romero, considered the father of the modern

The analysis explores the historical roots of today's zombie films.

zombie, released *Night of the Living Dead* to horrify audiences in 1968. Romero is given this lofty title simply because he introduced what is considered the paradigmatic zombie, that is, the walking corpse who exists only to eat the flesh of the living. The film broke many cinematic taboos of the time, especially with a sequence involving a zombified child eating her parents. The shocking imagery from this scene sent tremors through the film community. This reimagining of the zombie played to an audience perhaps changed by the televised violence of the Vietnam War era; certainly, the explicit images of cannibalistic corpses brought the horror genre to a much higher level than the monster films of the previous age.

Romero's cult masterpiece was followed by a slew of mediocre-to-downright-horrible zombie films, all produced in the wake of *Night*'s success. These cheap imitations were quelled only briefly by Romero's next project, *Dawn of the Dead*, which debuted in 1978. Although it was released just ten years after the original, the film altered the nature of the zombie to again depict the current fears of the audience. With the demoralizing end of the Vietnam War, Americans adopted a more critical view of their national values. Romero's film, which takes place primarily in a shopping mall, became a direct commentary on growing levels of consumerism in America. Romero heightened his societal critique by increasing the scale of the zombie outbreak, presenting images of zombies—once people

Tankersley focuses on the visual imagery of modern zombie films.

Tankersley 5

A scene from *Night of the Living Dead*. Everett Collection.

themselves—mindlessly consuming other people in a shopping mall, of all places. This level of rebuke represents a paradigm shift in the zombie film: It shows that the fear we experience from zombies comes not just from the gore and frightening images. Rather, it is from the fact that zombies *are* society, without its rules or adornments. Zombies became mindless consumers, a description increasingly given to society itself.

Romero's cinematic shift to a larger-scale zombie drama with social commentary failed to have much impact until recently. Between the original *Dawn of the Dead* and Zack Snyder's remake in 2004, there was again a very long train of awful zombie films. It wasn't until 2002, with the release of *28 Days Later*, that the zombie film again became a genre to be reckoned with. Danny Boyle's foray into the zombie film is most

Presents the post–Vietnam War zombie as a metaphor for consumerism.

Tankersley 6

notable for its sweeping views of an abandoned London, providing a postmortem view of society destroyed by an infection. Not only did Boyle manage to make the catastrophe seem brutally real through such heart-wrenching images as a notice board plastered with missing persons reports, but he also revolutionized the zombie as a species. His ghouls—the result of animal testing gone horribly wrong—were more realistic and more frightening, leaving their infected victims with something similar to rabies. The defining differences between Boyle's zombies and those of the past, however, were their ability to run and their virus's aggressive capacity to infect on contact, transforming a victim into the undead in a matter of seconds. This gave the zombie genre a much-needed boost, especially since previous films were often criticized for featuring antagonists who could barely walk. Boyle's new zombies could sprint for longer periods than normal humans, due to a lack of physical pain, leaving the protagonists with no safe place to hide for long.

Boyle's film made another point: that zombie films can be constructed around more than just spooky lighting, token characters, cheap scares, and nauseating images. He achieved this goal by focusing on the living characters: Their personal fears and their realization that all the people they loved were gone raised the question of what there was to survive for. This approach made the fear of zombies as much internal as external; the fear becomes personal to each individual audience member.

Tankersley analyzes the physical details of 28 *Days Later*.

Tankersley 7

A scene from *28 Days Later*. Mary Evans Picture Library/© 20th Century Fox/
Everett Collection.

A scene in which the protagonist finds his parents—who
committed suicide before the infection spread to them—is
all one needs to understand the real terror that an event
as widespread as a zombie infection would create.

Numerous films after *28 Days Later* have approached
the human dimension of the zombie film similarly, ensuring
that audiences would effectively place themselves in dire

Tankersley 8

A scene from *The Walking Dead*. *The Walking Dead*, foreground, left to right, Norman Reedus, Andrew Lincoln in "Seed" (Season 3, Episode 1, aired October 14, 2012), 2010–, photo: Gene Page/© AMC/courtesy Everett Collection.

emotional situations. Of course, there remain the blood-filled blockbusters, such as the *Resident Evil* franchise, but Boyle's film, and some that followed, gave a film buff something to appreciate in a zombie movie. This greater sophistication is evident in what is currently the zombie production to see, *The Walking Dead*, a television series on AMC. The story has its origin in a popular comic book series, but the television show, directed by Frank Darabont (*The Shawshank Redemption*), follows in Boyle's footsteps, exploring the internal dramas of the characters as much as the physical threat of the zombies. The series, still in release, has so far been lauded by zombie enthusiasts, primarily because it pulls back

Tankersley 9

to the traditional zombies of Romero's age, the aimlessly hobbling, sunken-eyed corpses. Thus far, the show appears to have found a place in the zombie canon.

The zombie began as a mysterious creature of mystical origin, with no will of its own. It quickly evolved into the flesh-eating monster that many associate with the term today. And, although it has recently become the product of viral testing and chemical warfare, the textbook zombie remains unwavering in its basic mission—to scare people. At the beginning of the twentieth century, audiences feared the unknown, whether that was mysticism or troubling political events. In the post-Vietnam War era, people began to question themselves, doubting their values and wondering if they were still the good guys that American leaders made them out to be. And finally, with the increasing threat of terrorism, people have returned to fearing the possibilities the future might bring. Now, *The Walking Dead* has moved beyond even this horror, with the source of its zombie infection completely unnamed. In the zombie films of the past ten years, it is clear that what we fear most is ourselves. We fear what people next to us may be capable of if their reason is taken from them by some man-made virus, unknown pathogen, or something else entirely. We all know that deep down, people are capable of heinous acts, and it is only reason that can stop them. But when reason is lost, human society has every faculty to consume itself.

Tankersley explains how zombie films are currently evolving.

The conclusion finally explains the visual image offered in the title of the paper: the serpent that devours itself.

Tankersley 10

Works Consulted

Dirks, Tim. "Main Film Genres." *The Greatest Films: The "Greatest" and the "Best" in Cinematic History*. AMC, 2010. Web. 15 Nov. 2011.

The Internet Movie Database (*IMDb*). Amazon, n.d. Web. 15 Nov. 2011.

"List of Zombie Films." *Wikipedia*. Wikimedia Foundation, 13 Nov. 2010. Web. 15 Nov. 2011.

1. **Rhetorical Analysis:** Using Paula Marantz Cohen's "Too Much Information" (p. 221) as a model, write an essay in which you examine how some modes of communication, media platforms, or habits of thought are shaping the way you encounter the world. If that sounds awfully abstract, consider what Cohen discusses in her essay — everything from students' use of Google to the star's comments following an episode of HBO's *Girls*. You might find a subject in your addiction to apps, your reliance on tweeting, or your grandparents' inability to translate emojis.

2. **Close Reading of an Argument:** Browse recent news or popular-interest magazines or Web sites (such as *Time*, *The Atlantic*, *GQ*, the *New Yorker*, and so on) to locate a serious article you find especially well argued and persuasive. As Matthew James Nance does in "A Mockery of Justice" (p. 232), study the piece carefully enough to understand the techniques it uses to influence readers. Then write a rhetorical analysis in which you make and support a specific claim about the rhetorical strategies of the piece.

3. **Cultural Analysis:** Identify a cultural phenomenon (TV talent shows), theme (men who won't grow up), trend (divorce parties), or type of image (disaster photos) and examine the way it either influences society or reflects the way that people are thinking or behaving. Make the analysis rhetorical by focusing on questions related to audience, social context, techniques of persuasion, or language. Help readers see your subject in a new light or from a fresh perspective. Use J. Reagan Tankersley's "Humankind's Ouroboros" (p. 238) as a starting point.

4. **Your Choice:** Fed up by the blustering of a talk-show host, political figure, op-ed columnist, local editorialist, or stupid advertiser? Try an item-by-item or paragraph-by-paragraph refutation of such a target, taking on his or her poorly reasoned claims, inadequate evidence, emotional excesses, or lack of credibility. If possible, locate a transcript or reproduction of the text you want to refute so that you can work from the facts just as they have been offered. If you are examining a visual text you can reproduce electronically, experiment with using callouts to annotate the problems as you find them.

Special Assignments

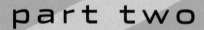

part two

Need a form you don't see here? Try "Genres," p. 2.

How to start

● **Got a test tomorrow?**
Read exam questions carefully. See page 253.

9

require answers written within a time limit

Essay Examinations

Essay examinations test not only your knowledge of a subject but also your ability to write about it coherently and professionally.

- For a class in nursing, you must write a short essay about the role health-care providers play in dealing with patients who have been victims of domestic abuse.

- For an examination in a literature course, you must do a close reading of a sonnet, explicating its argument and poetic images line by line.

- For a standardized test, you must read a passage by a critic of globalization and respond to the claim made and evidence presented.

- For a psychology exam, you must explore the ethical issues raised by two research articles on brain research and the nature of consciousness.

UNDERSTANDING ESSAY EXAMS. You've probably taken enough essay exams to know that there are no magic bullets to slay this dragon and that the best approach is to know the material well enough to make credible points within the time limit. You must also write—*under pressure*—coherent sentences and paragraphs. ○ Here are some strategies to increase your odds of success.

got a test ◀ tomorrow?

Anticipate the types of questions to be asked. What occurs in class— the concepts presented, issues raised, assignments given—is like a coming-attractions trailer for an exam. Attend class regularly and do the required readings, and you'll figure out many of an instructor's habitual moves and learn something to boot. Read over your notes, attend any review sessions, and look over sample essay exams—they may even be available on a course Web site.

Read exam questions carefully. Underscore key words such as *divide*, *classify*, *evaluate*, *compare*, *compare* and *contrast*, and *analyze* and then respect the differences between these strategies. ○ Exam questions may be like short essays themselves, furnishing contextual information or offering materials to read before the actual query appears. Respond to that specific question and not to your own take on the introductory materials.

Sketch out a plan for your essay(s). The first part of the plan should deal with *time*. Read all the exam questions carefully and then estimate how many minutes to spend on each— understanding that some will need more work than others. (Pay attention to point totals too: Focus on essay questions that count more, but don't ignore any. Five points is five points.) Allow time for planning, writing, and briefly editing each answer. Then stick to your time limits.

Organize your answers strategically. As quickly as possible, create a scratch outline and thesis for longer answers. ○ In the first paragraph, state this main point and then preview the structure of the whole essay. That way, even if you cannot finish, a reader will know where you were heading and possibly give you partial credit for incomplete work.

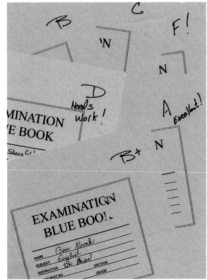

© Bill Aron/PhotoEdit.

improve your sentences p. 412

develop a draft p. 367

develop a statement p. 362

Offer strong evidence for your claims.   The overall pattern of your re-sponses to exam questions should convey your grasp of ideas—your ability to see the big picture. Within that structure, provide details and evidence to prove your command of the subject. Use memorable examples culled from class read-ing to make key points: Mention important names, concepts, and dates; touch on all critical issues and terms; rattle off the accurate titles of books and articles.

Come to a conclusion.   Even if you run short on time, find a moment to write a paragraph (or even a sentence) that brings your ideas together. Don't just repeat the topic sentences of your paragraphs. A reader will already have those ideas firmly in mind. So add something new at the end—an implication or extrapolation. O

Keep the tone serious.   Write essay examinations in a high or middle style. O Avoid a personal point of view unless the question invites your opinions. Given the time constraints, you can probably get away with contractions and standard abbreviations. But make sure the essay reads like prose, not a text message.

Keep your eye on the clock.   But *don't panic*. Everyone is working under the same constraints and will produce only so much prose in an hour or two. If you have prepared for the exam and start with a plan, ideas will come. Even if they don't, keep writing. You'll get no credit for blank pages.

Your Turn   Preparing for an examination now? Take a moment to list *from memory* as many as you can of the key names, titles, and concepts likely to appear on that exam—terms you are certain to need when you compose your essays. Then check these terms as you have written them down against the way they appear in your notes or textbooks, or on the course Web site. Have you gotten the names and titles right? Have you phrased the concepts cor-rectly, and can you explain what they mean? Just as important, as you review your course materials, do you notice any important ideas that should have made your list but didn't?

---

shape an
ending p. 391

refine your
tone p. 400

Getting the details right

Save a few minutes near the end of the exam period to reread your essays and insert corrections and emendations. You won't have time to fix large-scale problems: If you've confused the Spanish Armada with Torquemada, you're toast. But a quick edit may catch embarrassing gaffes or omissions. When you write quickly, you may leave out or transpose some words or simply use the wrong expressions (*it's* for *its* or *there* for *their*). Edit these fixable errors. In the process, you may also amplify or repair an idea or two. Here are some other useful strategies.

Use transitional words and phrases. Essay examinations are the perfect place to deploy conspicuous transitions such as *first, second,* and *third,* or *next, nonetheless, even more important, in contrast, in conclusion,* and so on. Don't be subtle: Transitions keep you on track as you compose and they help your instructor follow what you have to say. ○ You will seem in charge of the material.

Do a quick check of grammar, mechanics, and spelling. Some instructors take great offense at mechanical slips, even minor ones. At a minimum, avoid the common errors covered in Part 9 of this book. ○ Also be sure to spell correctly any names and concepts you've been reviewing in preparation for the examination. It's Macbeth, not McBeth.

Write legibly or print. Few people do much writing by hand anymore. But paper or blue books are still used sometimes for essay examinations. If your handwriting is flat-out illegible, then print and use a pen, as pencil can be faint and hard to read. Printing takes more time, but instructors appreciate the clarity. Also consider double-spacing your essays to allow room for corrections and additions. But don't spread your words too far apart. A blue book with just a few sentences per page undermines your ethos: It looks juvenile.

transitions
p. 416

help with common
errors p. 566

Examining a model

Wade Lamb offered the following response to this essay question on a midterm essay examination in a course titled Classical to Modern Rhetoric:

> The structure of Plato's *Phaedrus* is dominated by three speeches about the lover and non-lover—one by Lysias and two by Socrates. How do these speeches differ in their themes and strategies, and what point do they make about rhetoric and truth?

Lamb 1

Wade Lamb

Professor Karishky

Rhetoric 101

September 19, 20--

Plato's *Phaedrus* is unique among Platonic dialogues because it takes place in a rural setting between only two characters—Socrates and the youth Phaedrus. It is, however, like Plato's *Gorgias* in that it is "based on a distinction between knowledge and belief" and focuses on some of the ways we can use rhetoric to seek the truth.

The first speech presented in *Phaedrus*, written by Lysias and read aloud by Phaedrus, is the simplest of the three. Composed by Lysias to demonstrate the power of rhetoric to persuade an audience, it claims perversely that it is better to have a sexual relationship with someone who doesn't love you than someone who does.

Socrates responds with a speech of his own making the same point, which he composes on the spot, but which he describes as

[margin notes:]

Opening focuses directly on issues posed in question.

Short quotation functions as piece of evidence.

Sensibly organized around three speeches to be examined: one paragraph per speech.

Lamb 2

"a greater lie than Lysias's." Unlike Lysias, however, Socrates begins by carefully defining his terms and organizes his speech more effectively. He does so to teach Phaedrus that in order to persuade an audience, an orator must first understand the subject and divide it into its appropriate parts. However, Socrates delivers this speech with a veil over his head because he knows that what he and Lysias have claimed about love is false.

The third speech—again composed by Socrates—is the most important. In it, Socrates demonstrates that persuasion that leads merely to belief (not truth) damages both the orator and the audience. He compares rhetoric such as that used by Lysias to the unconcerned and harmful lust of a non-lover. Good rhetoric, on the other hand—which Socrates says is persuasion that leads to knowledge—is like the true lover who seeks to lead his beloved to transcendent truth. Socrates shows that he believes good rhetoric should ultimately be concerned with finding and teaching truth, not just with making a clever argument someone might falsely believe, as Lysias's speech does.

> Most important speech gets lengthiest and most detailed treatment.

By comparing the three speeches in *Phaedrus*, Plato shows that he gives some value to rhetoric, but not in the form practiced by orators such as Lysias. Plato emphasizes the importance of the distinction between belief and knowledge and argues that rhetoric should search for and communicate the truth.

> Conclusion states Lamb's thesis, describing the point he believes Plato wished to make about rhetoric in *Phaedrus*.

Confused?
Read the assignment carefully. See page 260.

10 Position Papers

require a brief critical response

A course instructor may ask you to respond to an assigned reading, lecture, film, or other activity with a position paper in which you record your reactions to the material, such as your impressions or observations. Such a paper is usually brief—often not much longer than a page or two—and due the next class session. Typically, you won't have time for more than a draft and quick revision.

- You summarize and assess the findings of a journal article studying the relationship between a full night's sleep and student success on college exams.

- You speculate about how a feminist philosopher of science, whose work you have read for a class, might react to recent developments in genetics.

- You respond to ideas raised by a panel of your classmates discussing a proposition to restore the military draft or require an alternative form of national service.

- You offer a gut reaction to your first-ever viewing of *Triumph of the Will*, a notorious propaganda film made by director Leni Riefenstahl for Germany's National Socialist (Nazi) Party in 1935.

UNDERSTANDING POSITION PAPERS.   Instructors have various reasons for assigning position or response papers: to focus attention on particular readings or class presentations; to measure how well you've understood course materials; to push you to connect course concepts or readings. Instructors may mark position papers less completely than full essays and grade them by different standards because they want to encourage you to take risks.

But don't blow off these quick, low-stakes assignments. Position papers give you practice in writing about a subject and thus prepare you for other papers and exams. These assignments *may* even preview the style of essay questions an instructor favors. Just as important, position papers establish your ethos in a course, marking you as a conscientious reader and thinker or, alternatively, someone just along for the ride.

Use a few simple strategies to write a strong position paper.

Protesters Taking a Position   While some feel that security cameras ensure safety, others believe them to be an invasion of privacy. © George Steinmetz/Corbis.

▶ confused?

Read the assignment carefully.   Understand exactly what your instructor wants: Look for key words such as *summarize, describe, classify, evaluate, compare, compare and contrast,* and *analyze* and then respect the differences between them. ○

Review the assigned material.   Consider printing or photocopying readings so that you can annotate their margins or underscore key claims and evidence. Look for conflicts, points of difference, or issues raised in class or in the public arena—what some writers call *hooks.* Then use the most provocative material to jump-start your thinking, using whatever brainstorming techniques work best for you. ○

Mine the texts for evidence.   Look for key sentences worth quoting or ideas worth describing in detail. ○ Anchor your position paper around such strong materials. Quote a brief passage you admire for how well it explains a key concept or highlight a paragraph full of claims that you resist. Then talk about these passages. Be sure you merge any quoted materials smoothly with your own writing.

Organize the paper sensibly.   Unless the assignment specifically states otherwise, don't write the position paper off the top of your head. Take the time to offer a thesis or to set up a comparison, an evaluation, or another pattern of organization. Give a position paper the same structural integrity you would a longer and more consequential assignment.

develop a
draft p. 367

get an
idea p. 331

use quotations
p. 466

Getting the details right

Though the assignment may seem minor, edit and proofread a position paper carefully. ○ Think of a position paper as a trial run for a longer paper. As such, it should follow the conventions of any given field or major.

Identify key terms and concepts and use them correctly and often. The instructor may be checking to see how carefully you read. So, in your paper, make a point of referring to the new concepts or terms you've found in your reading, as Heidi Rogers does with *ethos*, *pathos*, and *logos* in the model essay on page 262.

Treat your sources appropriately. Either identify them by author and title within the paper or list them at the end in the correct documentation form (e.g., MLA or APA). Make sure quotations are set up accurately, properly introduced, and documented. Offer page numbers for any direct quotations. ○

Spell names and concepts correctly. You lose credibility *very* quickly if you misspell technical terms or proper nouns that appear throughout the course readings. In literary papers especially, get characters' names and book titles right.

Respond to your classmates' work. Position papers are often posted to electronic discussion boards to jump-start conversations. So take the opportunity to reply substantively to what your classmates have written. Don't just say "I agree" or "You're kidding!" Add good reasons and evidence to your remarks. Remember, too, that your instructor might review these comments, looking for evidence of engagement with the course material. ○

revise and edit
p. 422

understand citation
styles p. 470

comment
p. 428

261

Examining a model

Here's a position paper written by Heidi Rogers as an early assignment in a lower-level course on visual rhetoric. Rogers's assignment was to offer an honest response to director Leni Riefenstahl's infamous documentary, *Triumph of the Will*, which showcases the National Socialist Party rallies in Munich in 1934. In the film, we see the German people embracing Hitler and his Nazi regime as they consolidate their power.

Rogers 1

Heidi Rogers

Professor Wachtel

Writing 203

September 22, 20--

Triumph of the Lens

The 1935 film *Triumph of the Will*, directed by Leni Riefenstahl, masterfully shows how visuals can be a powerful form of rhetoric. In the documentary we see Adolf Hitler, one of the greatest mass murderers in history, portrayed as an inspirational leader who could be the savior of Germany. Watching the film, I was taken aback. I am supposed to detest Hitler for his brutal crimes against humanity, and yet I found myself liking him, even smiling as he greets his fellow Germans on the streets of Munich. How did Riefenstahl accomplish this, drawing viewers into her film and giving Germans such pride in their leader?

Riefenstahl's technique is to layer selected visuals so as to evoke the emotions she wants her audience to feel toward Hitler and his regime. Her first step is to introduce images of nature and locations that are peaceful and soothing. Next, she

> Offers a thesis to explain how the film makes Hitler attractive.

> Rogers describes pattern she sees in Riefenstahl's editing technique.

Rogers 2

inserts images of the German people themselves: children playing, women blowing kisses to Hitler, men in uniform proudly united under the Nazi flag. The next step is to weave images of Hitler himself among these German people, so that even when he isn't smiling or showing any emotions, it seems as if he is conveying the happiness, pride, or strength evoked by the images edited around him. The final piece of the puzzle is always to put Hitler front and center, usually giving a rousing speech, which makes him seem larger than life.

A good example of this technique comes during the youth rally sequence. First, Riefenstahl presents peaceful images of the area around the Munich stadium, including beautiful trees with the sun streaming between the branches. We then see the vastness of the city stadium, designed by Hitler himself. Then we watch thousands of young boys and girls smiling and cheering in the stands. These masses erupt when Hitler enters the arena and Riefenstahl artfully juxtaposes images of him, usually with a cold, emotionless face, with enthusiastic youth looking up to him as if he were a god. Hitler then delivers an intoxicating speech about the future of Germany and the greatness that the people will achieve under his leadership. The crowd goes wild as he leaves the stage and we see an audience filled with awe and purpose.

Provides extended example to support claim about how *Triumph of the Will* was edited.

Rogers 3

Explores implications of claim — that clever editing enabled Riefenstahl to reach many audiences.

What Riefenstahl did in *Triumph of the Will* is a common technique in film editing. When you have to reach a massive audience, you want to cover all of your bases and appeal to all of them at once. Therefore, the more kinds of *ethos*, *pathos*, and *logos* you can layer onto a piece of film, the better your chances will be of convincing the greatest number of people of your cause. As hard as this is to admit, if I had lived in a devastated 1935 Germany and I had seen this film, I might have wanted this guy to lead my country too.

Triumph of the Will features numerous imposing shots of crowds cheering for Hitler. NSDAP/The Kobal Collection at Art Resource, NY.

Your Turn Many blogs and online publications (such as *Slate.com*, *Salon .com*, or national newspapers) encourage readers to comment on their postings. Use such sites to practice your skill at responding to what you read. On a news blog or another serious blog you scan regularly, locate a thought-provoking article to which some readers have already offered substantive responses (more than a line or two). First, read the article, thinking about what you might post in response. Then read through the actual postings. How does your brief response compare with what others have said? What strategies have they used that you admire? How did the best responders establish their credibility? And which responders did you take less seriously, *and why?*

Chances are you'll be disappointed in much of what you read in online commentary. People may respond from prejudiced positions, focus on irrelevant points, or take personal potshots at the original author. But from such respondents, you may learn what *not* to do in a serious academic paper.

How to start ● **Need to write a summary?**
Check Chapter 42 for more details. See page 460.

Annotated Bibliographies

summarize and assess sources

When you are preparing a term paper, senior thesis, or other lengthy research project, an instructor may expect you to submit an annotated bibliography. The bibliography may be due weeks before you turn in the paper, or it may be turned in with the finished project.

● A sociology instructor asks that your topic proposal for a mid-term paper on rural poverty include an annotated bibliography that demonstrates a range of perspectives in your reading.

● Your senior history thesis is based upon letters and archival materials found only in a local museum. So you attach an annotated bibliography to your completed project to give readers a clearer sense of what some of the handwritten documents cover.

● In writing a term paper on the cultural roots and connections of gangsta/reality rap, you decide to annotate your works cited items to let readers know what sources you found most authoritative and useful for future research.

UNDERSTANDING ANNOTATED BIBLIOGRAPHIES. An annotated bibliography is an alphabetical list of the sources and documents you have used in developing a research project, with each item in the list summarized and, very often, evaluated.

Instructors usually ask you to attach an annotated bibliography to the final version of a project so that they can determine at a glance how well you've researched your subject. But some may ask you to submit an annotated bibliography earlier in the writing process—sometimes even as part of the topic proposal—to be sure you're staying on track, poring over good materials, and getting the most out of them. O

Begin with an accurate record of research materials. Items recorded in the alphabetical list should follow the guidelines of some documentation system, typically MLA or APA. In a paper using MLA documentation, the list is labeled "Works Cited" and includes only books, articles, and other source materials actually mentioned in the project; it is labeled "Works Consulted" if you also want to include works you've read but not actually cited. In a project using APA style, the list is called "References." O

need to write a ◄
summary?

Describe or summarize the content of each item in the bibliography. These summaries should be *very* brief, often just one or two sentences. Begin with a concise description of the work if it isn't self-evident (*a review of; an interview with; a CIA report on*). Then, in your own words, describe its contents, scope, audience, perspective, or other features relevant to your project. Your language should be descriptive and impartial. Be sure to follow any special guidelines offered by your instructor. For more about summarizing, see Chapter 42, "Summarizing Sources." O

Lauren Nicole/Getty Images.

plan a project
p. 436

cite in APA
p. 512

understand citation
styles p. 470

Assess the significance or quality of the work.   Immediately following the summary, offer a brief appraisal of the item, responding to its authority, thoroughness, length, relevance, usefulness, age (e.g., *up-to-date/dated*), reputation in field (if known), and so on. Your remarks should be professional and academic: You aren't writing a movie review.

Explain the role the work plays in your research.   When an annotated bibliography is part of a topic proposal, size up the materials you have found so far and describe how you expect to use them in your project. Highlight the works that provide creative or fresh ideas, authoritative coverage, up-to-date research, diverse perspectives, or ample bibliographies.

Getting the details right

You will grasp the value of annotated bibliographies the moment you find a trustworthy one covering a subject you are researching. As you prepare such a list of your own, think how your work might help other readers and researchers.

Record the information on your sources accurately. As you format the items in your list, be sure that the titles, authors, page numbers, and dates are error-free so that users can quickly locate the materials you have used.

Follow a single documentation style. Documentation systems like MLA and APA can seem fussy, but they make life easier for researchers by standardizing the way all the identifying features of a source are treated. So when you get an entry right in your annotated bibliography, you make life easier for the next person who needs to cite that source. ○

Keep summaries and assessments brief. Don't get carried away. In most cases, instructors and other readers will want an annotated bibliography that they can scan. They'll appreciate writing that is both precise and succinct.

Follow directions carefully. Some instructors may provide specific directions for annotated bibliographies, depending on the field or subject of your research. For example, they may ask you to supply the volume numbers, locations, and physical dimensions of books; describe illustrations; provide URLs; and so on.

understand citation
styles p. 470

Examining a model

The following three items are from an annotated bibliography offered as part of a topic proposal on the cultural impact of the iPod.

Full bibliographical citation in MLA style.

Summary of Stephenson's argument.

Potential role source might play in paper.

Stephenson, Seth. "You and Your Shadow." *Slate.com*. Slate Group, 2 Mar. 2004. Web. 3 Mar. 2014. This article from *Slate.com*'s "Ad Report Card" series argues that the original iPod ads featuring silhouetted dancers may alienate viewers by suggesting that the product is cooler than the people who buy it. Stephenson explains why some people may resent the advertisements. The piece may be useful for explaining early reactions to the iPod as a cultural phenomenon.

Evaluation of Sullivan's opinion piece.

Sullivan, Andrew. "Society Is Dead: We Have Retreated into the iWorld." *Sunday Times*. Times Newspapers, 20 Feb. 2005. Web. 27 Feb. 2014. In this opinion piece, Sullivan examines how people in cities use iPods to isolate themselves from their surroundings. The author makes a highly personal but plausible case for turning off the machines. The column demonstrates how quickly the iPod has changed society and culture.

Citation demonstrates how to cite an article from a database — in this case, *Academic OneFile*.

Walker, Rob. "The Guts of a New Machine." *New York Times Magazine*, 30 Nov. 2003. *Academic OneFile*. Web. 1 Mar. 2014. This lengthy report describes in detail how Apple developed the concept and technology of the iPod. Walker not only provides a detailed early look at the product but also shows how badly Apple's competitors underestimated its market strength. May help explain Apple's later dominance in smartphones as well.

Your Turn   For a quick exercise in preparing an annotated bibliography, choose a film that has opened very recently, locate five or six reviews or news articles about it, and then prepare an annotated bibliography using these items. Imagine that you'll be writing a research paper about the public and critical reception the film received when it debuted. (Public and critical reaction may be quite different.) Be sure to choose a documentation system for your bibliography and to use it appropriately.

How to start ▶ ● **Need to write a synthesis paper?**
Summarize and paraphrase what you have read.
See page 273.

12 Synthesis Papers

require a
response
to multiple
sources

In some classes, you may be asked to write a synthesis paper, in which you summarize, compare, or assess the views of a variety of authors on a specific topic. The assignment might also require you to come up with a thesis of your own on that subject, based on your research. A synthesis paper (also sometimes described as a "review of literature") gives you practice in using sources in academic papers.

● For a first-year writing course, you write a detailed synthesis examining the positions of authors who both support and challenge your view that we have no choice but to adapt to new media and technology.

● For an engineering course, you prepare a literature review covering the most recently published research on lithium-ion polymer batteries.

● In preparing a prospectus for an end-of-semester research paper, you include a section in which you summarize the sources you expect to use and explain the different positions they represent.

UNDERSTANDING SYNTHESIS PAPERS.   In a synthesis, you typically survey a range of opinions on a topic, often a controversial one, summarizing and assessing a selection of reputable authorities. But pay close attention to the actual assignment: Note what types of sources you must review, whether you may quote from them, how to document them, ○ and whether you are, in fact, expected to develop a thesis of your own after reviewing all the material.

need to write ◀
a synthesis
paper?

   If your assignment is to prepare a review of literature, you will identify and report on the most important books and articles on a subject, usually over a specified period of time: *currently, from the last five years, over the past three decades.* The topic of the review may be assigned to you or it may be one you must prepare as part of a thesis, term paper, or capstone project. In either case, check whether your summary must follow a specific pattern of organization: Most literature reviews are chronological, though some are thematic, and still others are arranged by comparison and contrast. ○

Identify reputable sources on your subject.   Expect to find multiple articles, books, and research studies on any significant topic. You can locate relevant material using library catalogs, research guides, or online tools (see Chapter 38). Work with your instructor or a research librarian to separate mainstream and essential works from outliers, which may or may not deserve a closer look.

Summarize and paraphrase the works you have identified.   Take these notes carefully. Summaries capture the gist of every source you read, even those that don't pan out. Paraphrases are lengthier notes you take when you expect to refer to sources extensively or quote from them directly. (Review these skills, as necessary, in Chapters 42–43.)

In 1993, artists Tibor Kalman and Scott Stowell erected this yellow billboard in New York City's heavily trafficked Times Square perhaps to suggest a world of limitless choices. Exploring a new topic, you face similar possibilities and need to sort them out. © 1993, Maggie Hopp, photographer, Courtesy of Maira Kalman.

understand
citation styles p. 470

develop a
draft p. 367

Look for connections between your sources.   Once you have summarized and paraphrased a range of sources, examine them *in relationship to each other* to determine where they come down on your issue. Think about categories to describe their stances: *similarity/difference, congruence/divergence, consistency/inconsistency, conventional/radical,* and so on. Look for sources, too, that explain how a controversy has evolved and where it stands now. Introduce such materials with verbs of attribution such as *describes, reports, points out, asserts, argues, claims, agrees, concurs.*

Acknowledge disagreements and rebuttals.   Describe all the opinions you encounter accurately, introducing them with verbs of attribution such as *questions, denies, disagrees, contradicts, undermines, disputes, calls into question, takes issue with.* Your synthesis should represent a full range of opinions; be sure to present reputable sources that challenge any thesis you intend to develop.

Don't rush to judgment.   In synthesizing, writers sometimes divide their sources too conveniently between those that merely support a claim and those that oppose it, ignoring complications and subtleties. Quite often, the most interesting relationships are to be found in places where belligerent authors unexpectedly agree or orthodox research generates unexpected results. Don't precook the results or try to fit your materials into an existing framework.

Cite materials that both support and challenge your own thesis.   Any thesis you develop yourself as a result of your synthesis (as seen in the sample essay on p. 279) should reflect the inclusiveness of your research. Of course, you will draw on, quote from, and amplify the materials that help define you position. But be sure to acknowledge materials that run counter to your thesis too. In academic and professional writing, you must not only acknowledge these dissenters but also outline their ideas objectively and introduce any quotations from them fairly (Rosen *says*, not Rosen *whines*). O

use quotations
p. 466

Getting the details right

Although synthesis assignments vary enormously, certain organizational strategies and conventions are worth noting.

Provide a context for your topic. Open a synthesis paper by identifying your subject and placing it in historical or cultural context. Identify writers or sources that have defined the topic, and explain the rationale for your project. Help readers appreciate why an issue is important.

Tell a story. Whether your synthesis merely summarizes varying points of view or defends a thesis statement, it's often a good strategy to create a narrative readers can follow. ⭘ Help them understand the issues as you have come to appreciate them yourself. Separate major issues from minor ones, and use transitions as necessary to establish connections (*consequently*), highlight contrasts (*on the other hand*), show parallels (*similarly*), and so on.

Pay attention to language. Keep the style of your synthesis objective, neutral, and fairly formal. In most cases, avoid *I* when summarizing and paraphrasing. ⭘ Remember that the summaries of materials you cite should be in your own words; some synthesis assignments may even prohibit direct quotations. If you do quote from sources, choose statements that cogently represent the positions of your sources.

Be sure to document your sources. Record full bibliographic information for all the materials you read. You'll need it for the works cited or references page required at the end of most synthesis papers.

> **Your Turn**   On pages 276–78, you'll find paragraphs from sources used in the model synthesis paper on page 279. All these articles are available online. Choose two or three, find and read them, and then write a detailed synthesis of their authors' full positions, being sure to highlight the similarities and/or differences. Keep your analysis as neutral and objective as you can, *especially* if you find yourself taking sides. When you are done, a reader should have some sense of the overall media controversy that these pieces address, but have no idea where you might stand.

understand
narratives p. 4

refine your
tone p. 400

Examining a model

To give you an idea of how to bring sources together, we'll build a brief synthesis paper from selections drawn from essays that focus on one topic: whether new media technologies like the Web pose a threat to literacy and culture. Ideas that play a role in the synthesis essay are highlighted. Here are the sources, presented alphabetically by author:

I ask my students about their reading habits, and though I'm not surprised to find that few read newspapers or print magazines, many check in with online news sources, aggregate sites, incessantly. They are seldom away from their screens for long, but that's true of us, their parents, as well.

— Sven Birkerts, "Reading in a Digital Age"

The picture emerging from the research is deeply troubling, at least to anyone who values the depth, rather than just the velocity, of human thought. People who read text studded with links, the studies show, comprehend less than those who read traditional linear text. People who watch busy multimedia presentations remember less than those who take in information in a more sedate and focused manner. People who are continually distracted by e-mails, alerts, and other messages understand less than those who are able to concentrate. And people who juggle many tasks are less creative and less productive than those who do one thing at a time.

It is this control, this mental discipline, that we are at risk of losing as we spend ever more time scanning and skimming online. If the slow progression of words across printed pages damped our craving to be inundated by mental stimulation, the Internet indulges it. It returns us to our native state of distractedness, while presenting us with far more distractions than our ancestors ever had to contend with.

Top: Jackie Ricciardi/ *The Augusta Chronicle*/ZUMA PRESS. *Bottom:* Will Vragovis/ *St. Petersburg Times*/ZUMA PRESS.

— Nicholas Carr, "Does the Internet Make You Dumber?"

Today some 4.5 billion digital screens illuminate our lives. Words have migrated from wood pulp to pixels on computers, phones, laptops, game

consoles, televisions, billboards, and tablets. Letters are no longer fixed in black ink on paper, but flitter on a glass surface in a rainbow of colors as fast as our eyes can blink. Screens fill our pockets, briefcases, dashboards, living room walls, and the sides of buildings. They sit in front of us when we work — regardless of what we do. We are now people of the screen. And of course, these newly ubiquitous screens have changed how we read and write.

— Kevin Kelly, "Reading in a Whole New Way"

I have been reading a lot on my iPad recently, and I have some complaints — not about the iPad but about the state of digital reading generally. Reading is a subtle thing, and its subtleties are artifacts of a venerable medium: words printed in ink on paper. Glass and pixels aren't the same.

— Verlyn Klinkenborg, "Further Thoughts of a Novice E-reader"

Top: ZUMA PRESS. *Bottom:* Lannis Waters/*The Palm Beach Post*/ZUMA PRESS.

The new media have caught on for a reason. Knowledge is increasing exponentially; human brain-power and waking hours are not. Fortunately, the Internet and information technologies are helping us manage, search, and retrieve our collective intellectual output at different scales, from Twitter and previews to e-books and online encyclopedias. Far from making us stupid, these technologies are the only things that will keep us smart.

— Steven Pinker, "Mind over Mass Media"

No teenager that I know of regularly reads a newspaper, as most do not have the time and cannot be bothered to read pages and pages of text while they could watch the news summarized on the Internet or on TV.

— Matthew Robson, "How Teenagers Consume Media"

Then again, perhaps we will simply adjust and come to accept what James called "acquired inattention." E-mails pouring in, cell phones ringing, televisions blaring, podcasts streaming — all this may become background noise, like the "din of a foundry or factory" that James observed workers could scarcely avoid at first, but which eventually became just another part of their daily routine. For the younger generation of multitaskers, the great electronic din is an expected part of everyday life. And given what neuroscience and anecdotal evidence have shown us, this state of constant intentional self-distraction could well be of profound detriment to individual and cultural well-being. When people do their work only in the "interstices of their mind-wandering," with crumbs of attention rationed out among many competing tasks, their culture may gain in information, but it will surely weaken in wisdom.

— Christine Rosen, "The Myth of Multitasking"

The past was not as golden, nor is the present as tawdry, as the pessimists suggest, but the only thing really worth arguing about is the future. It is our misfortune, as a historical generation, to live through the largest expansion in expressive capability in human history, a misfortune because abundance breaks more things than scarcity. We are now witnessing the rapid stress of older institutions accompanied by the slow and fitful development of cultural alternatives. Just as required education was a response to print, using the Internet well will require new cultural institutions as well, not just new technologies.

— Clay Shirky, "Does the Internet Make You Smarter?"

Both Carr and Rosen are right about one thing: The changeover to digital reading brings challenges and changes, requiring a reconsideration of what books are and what they're supposed to do. That doesn't mean the shift won't be worth it. The change will also bring innovations impossible on Gutenberg's printed page, from text mixed with multimedia to components that allow readers to interact with the author and fellow consumers.

— Peter Suderman, "Don't Fear the E-reader"

Here is a brief paper that synthesizes the positions represented in the preceding materials, quoting extensively from them and leading up to a thesis. We have boldfaced the authors' names the first time they appear, to emphasize the number of sources used in this short example.

Chiu 1

Lauren Chiu

Professor Larondo

Writing 203

September 19, 2012

Time to Adapt?

There is considerable agreement that the Internet and other electronic media are changing the way people read, write, think, and behave. Scholars such as **Sven Birkerts** report that their students do not seem to read printed materials anymore, a fact confirmed by fifteen-year-old intern **Matthew Robson**, when asked by his employer Morgan Stanley to describe the media habits of teenagers in England: "No teenager that I know of regularly reads a newspaper, as most do not have the time and cannot be bothered to read pages and pages of text."

But the changes we are experiencing may be more significant than just students abandoning the printed word. Working with an iPad, for instance, makes **Verlyn Klinkenborg** wonder whether reading on a screen may actually be a different and less perceptive experience than reading on paper. More worrisome, **Nicholas Carr** points to a growing body of research suggesting that the cognitive abilities of those who use media frequently may actually be degraded, weakening their comprehension and concentration. Yet, according to **Clay Shirky**, the Internet is increasing our ability to communicate immeasurably,

Two sources are cited to support a general claim about the media.

Other authorities amplify and complicate the issue.

Carr and Shirky are well-known authors with opposing views of the Web.

Chiu 2

and so we simply have to deal with whatever consequences follow from such a major shift in technology. Thinkers like Shirky argue that we do not, in fact, have any choice but to adapt to such changes.

Even **Christine Rosen**, a critic of technology, acknowledges that people will probably have to adjust to their diminished attention spans (110). After all, are there really any alternatives to the speed, convenience, and power of the new technologies when we have become what **Kevin Kelly** describes as "people of the screen" and are no more likely to return to paper for reading than we are to vinyl for music recordings? Fears of the Internet may be overblown too. **Peter Suderman** observes that changes in media allow us to do vastly more than we can with print alone. Moreover, because the sheer amount of knowledge is increasing so quickly, **Steven Pinker** argues that we absolutely need the new ways of communicating: "[T]hese technologies are the only things that will keep us smart."

We cannot, however, ignore voices of caution. The differences Carr describes between habits of deep reading and skimming are especially troubling because so many users of the Web have experienced them. And who can doubt the loss of seriousness in our public and political discussions these days? Maybe Rosen *is* right when she worries that our culture is trading wisdom for a glut of information. But it seems more likely that society will be better off trying to fix the problems electronic media are causing than imagining that we can return to simpler technologies that have already just about vanished.

In a full-length essay, this section would be much longer and quote more sources.

Concerns about the Web are portrayed as reasonable.

The writer states a thesis that might guide a longer analysis.

Chiu 3

Works Cited

Birkerts, Sven. "Reading in a Digital Age." *The American Scholar*. Phi Beta Kappa, Spring 2010. Web. 10 Sept. 2012.

Carr, Nicholas. "Does the Internet Make You Dumber?" *Wall Street Journal*. Wall Street Journal, 5 June 2010. Web. 9 Sept. 2012.

Kelly, Kevin. "Reading in a Whole New Way." *Smithsonian.com*. Smithsonian, Aug. 2010. Web. 13 Sept. 2012.

Klinkenborg, Verlyn. "Further Thoughts of a Novice E-reader." *New York Times*. New York Times, 28 May 2010. Web. 12 Sept. 2012.

Pinker, Steven. "Mind over Mass Media." *New York Times*. New York Times, 10 June 2010. Web. 12 Sept. 2012.

Robson, Matthew. "How Teenagers Consume Media." *Guardian*. Guardian News and Media, 13 July 2009. Web. 14 Sept. 2012.

Rosen, Christine. "The Myth of Multitasking." *The New Atlantis* 20 (Spring 2008): 105-10. Print.

Shirky, Clay. "Does the Internet Make You Smarter?" *Wall Street Journal*. Wall Street Journal, 4 June 2010. Web. 9 Sept. 2012.

Suderman, Peter. "Don't Fear the E-reader." *Reason.com*. Reason Magazine, 23 Mar. 2010. Web. 11 Sept. 2012.

13 E-mails

communicate electronically

E-mail is the preferred method for most business (and personal) communication because it is quick, efficient, easy to archive, and easy to search.

- You write to the coordinator of the writing center to apply for a job as a tutor, courtesy copying the message to a professor who has agreed to serve as a reference.

- You send an e-mail to classmates in a writing class, looking for someone to collaborate on a Web project.

- You e-mail the entire College of Liberal Arts faculty to invite them to attend a student production of Chekhov's *Uncle Vanya*.

- You e-mail a complaint to your cable supplier because a premium sports channel you subscribe to has been unavailable for a week.

UNDERSTANDING E-MAIL.   E-mail is so common and informal that writers sometimes forget its professional side. Though usually composed quickly, e-mails have a long shelf life once they're archived. They can also spread well beyond their original audiences. So you need to take care with messages sent to organizations, businesses, professors, groups of classmates, and so on. The following strategies will help.

Explain your purpose clearly and logically.   Use both the subject line and first paragraph of an e-mail to explain your reason for writing. Be specific about names, titles, dates, places, expectations, requirements, and so on, especially when your message announces an event, explains a policy, invites a discussion, or makes an inquiry. Write your message so that it will still make sense a year or more later.

Tell readers what you want them to do.   In a professional e-mail, lay out a clear agenda for accomplishing one major task: Ask for a document, a response, or a reply by a specific date. If you have multiple requests to make of a single person or group, consider writing separate e-mails. It's easier to track short, single-purpose e-mails than to deal with complex documents requiring several different actions.

Write for intended and unintended audiences.   The specific audience in the "To" line is usually the only audience for your message. But e-mail is more public than traditional surface mail, easily duplicated and sent to whole net-works of recipients with just a click. So compose your business e-mails as if they *might* be read by everyone in a unit or even published in a local paper. Assume that nothing in business e-mail is private.

Keep your messages brief.   Lengthy blocks of e-mail prose without para-graph breaks irritate readers. Indeed, meandering or chatty e-mails in business situations can make a writer seem disorganized and out of control. Try to limit your e-mail messages to what fits on a single screen. Remember that people routinely view e-mail on mobile devices. Keep messages simple. O

think visually
p. 557

Distribute your messages sensibly.   Send a copy of an e-mail to anyone directly involved in the message, as well as to those who might need to be informed. For example, if you were filing a grade complaint with an instructor, you might also copy the chair of his or her academic department or the dean of students. But don't let the copy (CC) and blind copy (BCC) lines in the e-mail header tempt you to send messages beyond the essential audience.

"You invented a time machine to come back and hit Reply instead of Reply All?"
© Tom Toro/New Yorker Magazine/Condé Nast.

Getting the details right

Because most people receive e-mail messages frequently, make any you send easy to follow.

want to get ◄ the reader's attention?

Choose a sensible subject line.   The subject line should clearly identify the topic and include helpful keywords that might later be searched. If your e-mail is specifically about a grading policy, your student loan, or mold in your gym locker, make sure a word you'll recall afterward—like *policy, loan,* or *mold*—gets in the subject line. In professional e-mails, subjects such as *A question, Hi!* or *Meeting* are useless.

Arrange your text sensibly.   You can do almost as much visually in e-mail as you can in a word-processing program, including choosing fonts, inserting lines, and adding color, images, and videos. But because so many people read messages on mobile devices, a simple block style with spaces between single-spaced paragraphs works best. Keep the paragraphs brief.

Check the recipient list before you hit send.   Routinely double-check all the recipient fields—especially when you're replying to a message. The original writer may have copied the message widely: Do you want to send your reply to that entire group or just to the original writer?

Include an appropriate signature.   Professional e-mail of any kind should include a signature that identifies you and provides contact information readers need. Your e-mail address alone may not be clear enough to identify who you are, especially when you are writing to an instructor. Be sure to set up a signature for your laptop, desktop, or mobile device.

But be careful: Don't provide readers with a *home* phone number or address since you won't know who might see your e-mail message. When you send e-mail, the recipient can reach you simply by replying.

Consider, too, that a list of incoming e-mails on a cell phone typically previews just the first few lines of a message. If you want a reader's attention, make your point quickly.

Use standard grammar. Professional e-mails should be almost as polished as business letters: At least give readers the courtesy of a quick review to catch humiliating gaffes or misspellings. ○ Emoticons and smiley faces have also disappeared from most professional communications.

Have a sensible e-mail address. You might enjoy communicating with friends as HorribleHagar or DaisyGirl, but an e-mail signature like that will undermine your credibility with a professor or potential employer. Save the oddball name for a private e-mail account.

Don't be a pain. You just add to the daily clutter if you send unnecessary replies to e-mails—a pointless *thanks* or *Yes!* or *WooHoo!* Just as bad is CCing everyone on a list when you've received a query that needs to go to one person only.

> **Your Turn**   Take a quick look at the formatting of the e-mails that appear on a mobile device. Most phones now display images, complex page formats, or other textual features within e-mail. But note the limitations too. Images can clutter a message on a small screen, so place them after your text. And you might not want to put links you include too close together because they can be hard to select.

revise and
edit p. 422

Examining a model

Here's a fairly typical e-mail from a student to a professor. The e-mail provides clear and direct information (note that the student's majors are identified in the signature) and poses one clear question. It gets to the point quickly and politely asks for a response.

To: John Ruszkiewicz 📎

From: Kori Strickland
Sent: October 3, 2015 11:56 AM

Specific subject line

Re: Writing Center Course Eligibility
CC: Davida Charney

Dear Professor Ruszkiewicz,

Opening paragraph explains point of e-mail.

I'm currently a junior at the University of Texas at Austin applying for your Rhetoric 368C Writing Center Internship course in spring 2016. I have a question about my eligibility.

Business letters use a colon after greeting, but e-mails are often less formal.

The course description online says preference is given to students who can work two or more semesters in the writing center after they take the class. Do I still stand a reasonable chance at being admitted to RHE 368C if I will be able to work only one semester because of a study-abroad opportunity my senior year?

Second paragraph poses one specific question.

Tone is professional and correct.

Please let me know. In any case, I am attaching the required writing sample and have asked Professor Charney to write the brief recommendation requested for RHE 368C candidates.

Final paragraph asks for a reply and spells out other actions the writer has taken.

Sincerely,
Kori Strickland
University of Texas | Political Communication and Rhetoric
Fine Arts Council | Co-president

Signature is simple, informative, and professional.

📄
RHE 368C W...ple (22 KB)

Attachment included as indicated in the letter.

How to start

● **Want to get a response?**
Explain your purpose clearly and logically.
See page 289.

14 Business Letters

**communicate
formally**

The formal business letter remains an important instrument for sending information in professional situations. Though business letters can be transmitted electronically these days, legal letters or decisions about admissions to schools or programs often still arrive on paper, complete with a real signature.

- Responding to a summer internship opportunity, you outline your credentials for the position in a cover letter and attach your résumé.

- You send a brief letter to the director of admissions of a law school, graciously declining your acceptance into the program.

- You send a letter of complaint to an auto company, documenting the list of problems you've had with your SUV and indicating your intention to seek redress under your state's "lemon law."

- You write to a management company to accept the terms of a lease, enclosing a check for the security deposit on your future apartment.

UNDERSTANDING BUSINESS LETTERS.   Business letters are generally formal in tone and follow conventions designed to make the document a suitable record and to support additional communication. The principles for composing a business or job letter do not differ much from those for business e-mails. ○

want to get a ◀ response?

Explain your purpose clearly and logically.   Use the first paragraph to explain your purpose and announce any specific concerns. Anticipate familiar *who*, *what*, *where*, *when*, *how*, and *why* questions; be specific about names, titles, dates, and places. If you're applying for a job, scholarship, or admission to a program, name the exact position or program and mention that your résumé is attached. Remember that your letter may have a long life in a file cabinet: Write a document that will make sense months or years later.

Tell readers what you want them to do.   Don't leave them guessing about how to respond to your message. Lay out a clear agenda for accomplishing one task: Apply for a job, request information, or make an inquiry or complaint. Don't hesitate to ask for a reply, even by a specific date when that is necessary.

Write for your audience.   Quite often, you won't know the people to whom you are sending a business letter. So you have to construct a letter imagining how an executive, employer, admissions officer, or complaints manager might be most effectively persuaded. Courtesy and goodwill go a

Left: Tim Graham/Tim Graham Photo Library/Getty Images. *Right:* © Brigette M. Sullivan/PhotoEdit.

understand
e-mail p. 282

long way—though you may have to be firm and impersonal in many situations. Avoid phony emotions or tributes.

A job application or cover letter (with your résumé attached) poses special challenges. You want to present your credentials in the best possible light without seeming full of yourself. Be succinct and specific, letting achievements speak mostly for themselves—though you can fill in details that a reader might not appreciate. Focus on recent credentials and accomplishments and under-score the skills and strengths you bring to the job. Speak in your own voice, clipped slightly by a formal style. ⭘

Keep the letter focused and brief.   Like e-mails, business letters become hard to read when they extend much beyond one page. A busy administrator or employee prefers a concise message, handsomely laid out on good stationery. Even a job-application letter should be relatively short, highlighting just your strongest credentials: Leave it to the accompanying résumé or dossier to flesh out the details.

Follow a conventional form.   All business letters should include your address (called the *return address*), the date of the message, the address of the person to whom you are writing (called the *inside address*), a formal salutation or greeting, a closing, a signature in ink (when possible), and information about copies or enclosures.

Both block format and *modified-block format* are acceptable in business communication. In block forms, all elements are aligned against the left-hand margin (with the exception of the letterhead address at the top). In modified-block form, the return address, date, closing, and signature are aligned with the center of the page. In both cases, paragraphs in the body of the letter are set as single-spaced blocks of type, their first lines not indented, and with an extra line space between paragraphs.

In indented form (not shown), the elements of the letter are arranged as in modified-block form, but the first lines of body paragraphs are indented five spaces, with no line spaces between the single-spaced paragraphs.

define your
style p. 400

Getting the details right

Perhaps the most important detail in a business letter is keeping the format you use consistent and correct. Be sure to print your letter on good-quality paper or letterhead and to send it in a proper business envelope, one large enough to accommodate a page 8½ inches wide.

Use consistent margins and spacing.   Generally, 1-inch margins all around work well, but you can use larger margins (up to 1½ inches) when your message is short. The top margin can also be adjusted if you want to balance the letter on the page, though the body need not be centered.

Finesse the greeting.   Write to a particular person at a firm or institution. Address him or her as *Mr.* or *Ms.*—unless you actually know that a woman prefers *Mrs.* You may also address people by their full names: *Dear Margaret Hitchens.* When you don't have a name, you might use a person's title: *Dear Admissions Director* or *Dear Hiring Manager.* Or you can fall back on *Dear Sir or Madam* or *To Whom It May Concern*, though these forms of address (especially *madam*) are increasingly dated. When it doesn't sound absurd, you can even address the institution or entity: *Dear Exxon* or *Dear IRS*—again, this is not a preferred form.

Distribute copies of your letter sensibly.   Copy anyone involved in a message, as well as anyone who might have a legitimate interest in your action. For example, in filing a product complaint with a company, you may also want to send your letter to the state office of consumer affairs. Copies are noted and listed at the bottom of the letter, introduced by the abbreviation *CC* (for *courtesy copy*).

Spell everything right.   Be scrupulous about the grammar and mechanics too—especially in a job-application letter. Until you get an interview, that piece of paper represents you to a potential client or employer. Would you hire someone who misspelled your company's name or made noticeable errors? ○

© Gero Greloer/dpa/Corbis.

help with common
errors p. 566

Photocopy the letter as a record.   An important business letter needs a paper copy, even when you have an electronic version archived: The photocopied signature may mean something.

Don't forget the promised enclosures.   A résumé should routinely accompany a job-application letter. ○

Fold the letter correctly and send it in a suitable envelope.   Business letters always go on $8\frac{1}{2} \times 11$-inch paper and are sent in standard business envelopes, generally $4\frac{1}{8} \times 9\frac{1}{2}$ inches. Fold the letter in three sections, trying to put the creases through white space in the letter so that the body of the message remains readable.

John Humbert
95 Primrose Lane
Columbus, OH 43209

September 23, 2014

Home Design Magazine
3652 Delmar Drive
Prince, NY 10012

Dear *Home Design* Magazine:

I am a subscriber to your magazine, but I never received my July 2014 or August 2014 issues. When my subscription expires at the end of this year, please extend it two more months at no charge to make up for this error. Originally, my last issue would have been the December 2014 magazine. Since I have missed two issues and since my subscription was paid in full almost a year ago, please send me the January and February 2015 issues of *Home Design* at no additional charge.

Thank you for your attention.

Sincerely,
J. Humbert
John Humbert

understand
résumés p. 296

Examining models

The following are two business letters: The first is a concise letter of complaint; the second is a cover letter written by a student sending a résumé in a quest for a summer internship.

John Humbert
95 Primrose Lane
Columbus, OH 43209

September 23, 2014

Home Design Magazine
3652 Delmar Drive
Prince, NY 10012

Dear *Home Design* Magazine:

I am a subscriber to your magazine, but I never received my July 2014 or August 2014 issues. When my subscription expires at the end of this year, please extend it two more months at no charge to make up for this error. Originally, my last issue would have been the December 2014 magazine. Since I have missed two issues and since my subscription was paid in full almost a year ago, please send me the January and February 2015 issues of *Home Design* at no additional charge.

Thank you for your attention.

Sincerely,
J. Humbert
John Humbert

Letterhead is preprinted stationery carrying the return address of the writer or institution. It may also include a corporate logo.

Allow two or three spaces between the date and address.

Allow one line space above and below the salutation. A colon follows the greeting.

The letter is in block form, with all major elements aligned with the left margin.

COVER LETTER

In modified-block form, return address, date, closing, and signature are centered.

1001 Harold Circle #10
Austin, TX 78712
June 28, 20--

Mr. Josh Greenwood
ABC Corporate Advisers, Inc.
9034 Brae Rd., Suite 1111
Austin, TX 78731

Dear Mr. Greenwood:

Opening paragraph clearly states thesis of letter: Nancy Linn wants this job.

Rita Weeks, a prelaw adviser at the University of Texas at Austin, e-mailed me about an internship opportunity at your firm. Working at ABC Corporate Advisers sounds like an excellent chance for me to further my interests in finance and corporate law. I would like to apply for the position.

Letter highlights key accomplishments succinctly and specifically.

As my attached résumé demonstrates, I have already interned at an estate-planning law firm, where I learned to serve the needs of an office of professionals and clients. I also have a record of achievement on campus: I used my skills as a writer and speaker to obtain funding for the Honors Business Association at UT-Austin, for which I serve as vice president and financial director. By contacting corporate recruiters, I raised $5,500 from Microsoft, ExxonMobil, Deloitte, and other companies.

Candidate repeatedly explains how internship fits career goals.

I am ready for a job that more closely relates to my academic training and career goal: becoming a certified financial analyst and corporate lawyer. Please contact me at 210-555-0000 or NLINN@abcd.com to schedule an interview. Thank you for considering me as a potential intern. I look forward to meeting you.

Additional contact information provided.

Sincerely,

N. Linn

Nancy Linn

Courtesy copy of letter sent to adviser mentioned in first paragraph; can be contacted as reference.

Enclosure: Résumé
CC: Rita Weeks

Your Turn   Have you received a business letter recently? If so, pull it out
and take a moment to note the specific features described in this chapter.
They are easy to overlook: letterhead, date, inside address, greeting, closing,
attachments, spacing. Are their functions obvious and do they make sense?
Now take a look at a recent e-mail you may have received from an institution
or business (rather than a friend or classmate). What features does the business e-mail have in common with a business letter? In what ways are they
different?

Résumés

record professional achievements

A one-page résumé usually accompanies any letter of application you send for a position or job. The résumé gathers and organizes details about your experiences at school, on the job, and in the community. In some careers, you may recap years of work and achievements in a longer, but similarly organized, document called a CV (curriculum vitae).

- Applying for a part-time position at a local day-care center, you assemble a résumé that chronicles your relevant experience.

- For an application to graduate school, you prepare a résumé that gives first priority to your accomplishments as a dean's list dual major in government and English.

- You modify your résumé slightly to highlight your internships with several law firms because you are applying for a paralegal clerk position at Baker Botts LLP.

- For a campus service scholarship, you tweak your résumé to emphasize activities more likely to interest college administrators than potential employers.

UNDERSTANDING RÉSUMÉS. The point of a résumé is to provide a quick, easy-to-scan summary of your accomplishments to someone interested in hiring you. The document must be readable at a glance, meticulously accurate, and reasonably handsome. Think of it this way: A résumé is your one- or two-page chance to make a memorable first impression.

Résumés do vary enormously in design—though they often resemble outlines without the numbers or letters. You have to decide on everything from fonts and headings to alignments and paper. You can pay companies to craft your résumé or use widely available templates to design it and then post it online. But your word processor has all the power you need to create a competent résumé on your own. Here's some advice.

At a Walt Disney Company job fair for returning veterans, experts help vets polish their résumés. Associated Press/Reed Saxon.

For a tutorial on job searches, see **macmillanhighered.com/howtowrite3e.**
Tutorials > Digital Writing > Job Search/Personal Branding

Gather the necessary information. You'll have to collect this career data sooner or later. It's much simpler if you start in college and gradually build a full résumé. Don't guess or rely on memory for résumé information: Get the data right. Verify your job titles and your months or years of employment; give your major as it is identified in your college catalog; make an accurate list of your achievements and activities without embellishing them. Don't turn an afternoon at a sandlot into "coaching high school baseball." Focus on attainments during your college years and beyond. Grade school and high school achievements don't mean much, unless you're LeBron James.

Decide on appropriate categories. Contrary to what you may think, there's no standard form for résumés, but they do usually contain some mix of the following information:

- Basic contact data or heading: your name, address, phone number, and e-mail address
- Educational attainments (usually college and above, once you have a BA, BS, or other postsecondary credential): degrees earned, where, and when
- Work experience: job titles, companies, and dates of employment, with a brief list of skills you used in specific jobs (such as customer service, sales, software programs, language proficiencies, and so on)
- Other accomplishments: extracurricular activities, community service, volunteer work, honors, awards, and so on. These may be broken into subcategories.

Depending on the situation, you might also include the following elements:

- A brief statement of your career goals
- A list of people willing to serve as references (with their contact information)

You can add categories to a résumé too, whenever they might improve your chances for a position. As your career evolves, for instance, your résumé may eventually include items such as administrative appointments, committee service, awards, patents, publications, lectures, participation in business organizations, community service, and so on. But keep the document compact. Ordinarily, a first résumé shouldn't exceed one page—though it may have to run longer if you are asked to provide references.

Arrange the information within categories in reverse chronological order.   The most recent attainments come first in each of your categories. If such a list threatens to bury your most significant items, you have several options: Cut the lesser achievements from the list, break out special achievements in some consistent way, or highlight those special achievements in the cover letter that should always accompany a résumé. O

Design pages that are easy to read.   Basic design principles aren't rocket science: Headings and key information should stand out and individual items should be clearly separated. The pages should look substantive but not cluttered. White space makes any document friendly, but too much in a résumé can suggest a lack of achievement. O

    In general, treat the résumé as a conservative document. This is not the time to experiment with fonts and flash or curlicues. Don't include a photograph either, even a good one.

want to ◄
get a job?

Applying for a job need not be as dreary as it once was — or as sexist. © Hulton-Deutsch Collection/Corbis.

understand business letters p. 288

think visually p. 557

Getting the details right

With its fussy dates, headings, columns, and margins, a résumé is all about the details. Fortunately, it is brief enough to make a thorough going-over easy. Here are some important considerations.

Proofread every line in the résumé several times.   Careful editing isn't a minor "detail" when it comes to résumés: It can be the whole ball game. When employers have more job candidates than they can handle, they may look for reasons to dismiss weak cases. Misspelled words, poor design of headings and text, and incomplete or confusing chronology are the kinds of mistakes that can terminate your job quest. O

Don't leave unexplained gaps in your education or work career.   Readers will wonder about blanks in your history (Are you hiding something?) and so may dismiss your application in favor of candidates whose career paths raise no red flags. Simply account for any long periods (a year or so) you may have spent wandering the capitals of Europe or flipping burgers. Do so either in the résumé or in the job-application/cover letter—especially if the experiences contributed to your skills.

Be consistent.   Keep the headings and alignments the same throughout the document. Express all dates in the same form: For example, if you abbreviate months, do so everywhere. Use hyphens between dates.

Protect your personal data.   You don't have to volunteer information about your race, gender, age, or sexual orientation on a job application or résumé. Neither should you provide financial data, Social Security or credit card numbers, or other information you don't want in the public domain and that is not pertinent to your job search. However, you do need to be accurate and honest about the relevant job information: Any disparity about what you state on a résumé and your actual accomplishments may be a firing offense down the road.

Look for help.   Check whether your campus career center or writing center offers help with résumés. Online employment sites such as Headhunter.com and Monster also offer useful tips and tools for preparing and posting a résumé.

help with common
errors p. 566

Examining a model

The following résumé, by Andrea Palladino, is arranged in reverse chronological order. Palladino uses a simple design that aligns the major headings and dates in a column down the left-hand margin and indents the detailed accomplishments to separate them, making them highly readable.

Contact information centered at top of page for quick reference. If necessary, give both school and permanent addresses.

Andrea Palladino
600 Oak St.
Austin, TX 78705
(281) 555-1234

CAREER OBJECTIVE — Soon-to-be college graduate seeking full-time position that allows for regular interpersonal communication and continued professional growth.

Optional "career objective" functions like thesis.

EDUCATION
8/10-5/15 — University of Texas at Austin – Psychology, BA

EXPERIENCE
3/13-Present — Writing Consultant
University of Texas at Austin Undergraduate Writing Center – Austin, TX
Tutor students at various stages of the writing process. Work with a variety of assignments. Attend professional development workshops.

Alignments further emphasize headings and dates.

5/13-Present — Child Care Provider
CoCare Children's Services – Austin, TX
Care for infants through children aged ten, including children with physical and mental disabilities. Change diapers, give food and comfort, engage children in stimulating play, and clean/disinfect toys after child care. Work on standby and substitute for coworkers when needed.

Ample, but not excessive, white space enhances readability.

5/12-12/13 — Salesperson/Stockperson
Eloise's Collectibles – Katy, TX
Unpacked new shipments, prepared outgoing shipments, and kept inventory. Interacted with customers and performed the duties of a cashier.

ACCOMPLISHMENTS

2012-Present	College Scholar for three years—acknowledgment of in-residence GPA of at least 3.50
10/14-Present	Big Brothers Big Sisters of Central Texas
Fall 2012	University of Texas at Austin Children's Research Lab— Research Assistant

Your Turn   If you already have a résumé, open it up and check its features against the suggestions offered in this chapter. Consider how you might modify it for the different kinds of positions you may be applying for over the next several years. And if you don't yet have a résumé, now is an excellent time to draft one. You will more likely need it sooner than later.

16 Personal Statements

explain a person's experiences and goals

Preparing a short personal statement has become almost a ritual among people applying for admission to college, professional school, or graduate school, or for jobs, promotions, scholarships, internships, or even elective office.

- An application for an internship asks for an essay in which you explain how your career goals will contribute to a more tolerant and diverse society.

- All candidates for the student government offices you're interested in must file a personal statement explaining their positions. Your statement, limited to three hundred words, will be printed in the campus newspaper and posted online.

- You dust off the personal statement you wrote to apply to college to see what portions you can use in an essay required for admission to upper-division courses in the College of Communication.

UNDERSTANDING PERSONAL STATEMENTS. Institutions that ask for personal statements are rarely interested in who you are. Rather, they want to see whether you can *represent* yourself as a person with whom they might want to be affiliated. That may seem harsh, but consider the personal statements you have already written. At best, they are a slice of your life—the verbal equivalent of you all dressed up for the prom.

If you want a sense of what a school, business, or other institution expects in the essays it requests from applicants, read whatever passes for that group's core values or mission statement, often available online. If the words sound a bit solemn, inflated, and unrealistic, you've got your answer—except that you shouldn't actually sound as pretentious as an institution. A little blood has to flow through the veins of your personal statement, just not so much that someone in an office gets nervous about your emotional shape.

Associated Press/Susan Walsh.

Hitting the right balance between displaying overwhelming competence and admitting human foibles in a personal statement is tough. Here's some advice for composing a successful essay.

Read the essay prompt carefully.   Essay topics are often deliberately open-ended to give you some freedom in pursuing a topic, but only answer the question actually posed, not one you'd prefer to deal with. Ideally, the question will focus on a specific aspect of your work or education; try to write about this even if the question is more general.

Don't repeat in your personal statement what's already on record in an application letter or résumé. Instead, look for incidents that will bring your résumé lines to life. If the prompt encourages personal reminiscences (e.g., *the person who influenced you the most*), think hard about how to give your story a clear direction.

▶ feeling lost?

Decide on a focus or theme.   Personal statements are short, so make the best use of a reader's time. Don't ramble about summer jobs or vague educational opportunities. Instead, find a theme that focuses on the strongest aspects of your application. If you're driven by a passion for research, arrange the elements of your life to illustrate this. If your best work is extracurricular, explain in a scholarship application how your specific commitments to people and organizations make you a more well-rounded student. In other words, turn your life into a thesis statement and make a clear point about yourself. ○

Above all be honest and forthright. Here's good advice from a woman who worked with high school students who were composing college admission statements:

> In my years handling applications to elite schools, from Harvard to Haverford, Davidson to Dickinson and everything in between, I was often surprised by where students did gain acceptance. But in every case it was a student who wrote a fabulously independent essay. Not necessarily hyper-sophisticated. But true.
>
> My students always asked me, What should I write about?
>
> I'd answer: You are a student of the world. What is it that moves you? What incites you, enrages you? The first-person pronoun is a mighty tool. Use it.

develop a
statement p. 362

I have had successful students write about the virtues of napping (Middle-bury), failing a course (Harvard), and having to shoot a farm dog because it couldn't work stock (Princeton). Once a student came out to me in his fifth (and best) draft. His parents probably still don't know, but they got the Ivy Leaguer they wanted (Penn).

— Lacy Crawford, "Writing the Right College-Entrance Essay"

When you apply for professional programs, scholarships, and internships, your audiences will be different, but the basic principles outlined here still hold.

Be realistic about your audience.   Your personal statements are read by strangers. That's scary, but you can usually count on them to be reasonable people willing to give you a fair hearing. They measure you against other applicants—not unreachable standards of perfection. How might you overcome the initial anxiety? Experienced writing tutor Jacob Pietsch suggests that you address a statement to a real person in your life who doesn't know you very well: "Visualize them, and get ready to write them a letter."

Organize the piece strategically.   Many personal statements take a narrative form, though they may also borrow some elements of reports and even proposals. Malia Hamilton, a writing center consultant, offers a structure to consider: "Whenever I read a personal statement, I look to see if the writer has told me three things: (1) who they were, (2) who they are, and (3) who they want to be. If the writer has effectively incorporated these three stages of themselves into their personal statement, it's almost always an effective one." Whatever structures you adopt for your essay, pay attention to transitions: You cannot risk readers getting confused or lost. ○

Try a high or middle style.   You don't want to be breezy or casual in an essay for law school or medical school, but a *personal* statement does invite a human voice. So a style that marries the correctness and formal vocabulary of a high style with the occasional untailored feel of the middle style might be perfect for many personal statements. ○

connect ideas
p. 387

define your
style p. 400

Getting the details right

As with résumés, there's no room for errors or slips in personal statements. ○ They are a test of your writing skills, plain and simple, so you need to get the spelling, mechanics, and usage correct. In addition, consider the following advice.

Don't get too artsy.   A striking image or two may work well in the statement, as may the occasional metaphor or simile. But don't build your essay around a running theme, an extended analogy, or a pop-culture allusion that a reader might dismiss as hokey or simply not get. If a phrase or feature stands out too noticeably, change it, even though you may like it.

Use common sense.   You probably already have the good grace not to offend gender, racial, religious, and ethnic groups in your personal statement. You should also take the time to read your essay from the point of view of people from less protected groups who may take umbrage at your dismissal of *old folks, fundamentalists,* or even *Republicans.* You don't know who may be reading your essay.

Compose the statement yourself.   It's the ethical thing to do. If you don't and you're caught, you're toast. You might ask someone to review your essay or take a draft to a writing center for a consultation. ○ This review or any help from a parent or English-major roommate should not purge your voice from the essay. Remember, too, that when you arrive at a job or internship, you'll be expected to write at the level you display in the statement that got you there.

> **Your Turn**   Amused by the thought of your life as a thesis statement? Give it a try. Compose *three* thesis sentences that might be plausibly used to organize three different personal statements, emphasizing varying aspects of your life and career. Which statement do you think describes you best? Would it always be the best thesis for a personal statement? Why or why not?

help with common
errors p. 566

peer review
p. 428

Examining a model

The Academic Service Partnership Foundation asked candidates for an internship to prepare an essay addressing a series of questions. The prompt and one response to it follow.

ASPF NATIONAL INTERNSHIP PROGRAM

Please submit a 250- to 500-word typed essay answering the following three questions:

1. Why do you want an internship with the ASPF?
2. What do you hope to accomplish in your academic and professional career goals?
3. What are your strengths and skills, and how would you use these in your internship?

Specific questions limit reply, but also help organize it.

Michael Villaverde

April 14, 20--

Opening sentence states writer's thesis or intent; first two paragraphs address first question.

The opportunity to work within a health-related government agency alongside top-notch professionals initially attracted me to the Academic Service Partnership Foundation (ASPF) National Internship Program. Participating in the ASPF's internship program would enable me to augment the health-services research skills I've gained working at the VERDICT Research Center in San Antonio and the M. D. Anderson Cancer Center in Houston. This internship could also help me gain experience in health policy and administration.

I support the ASPF's mission to foster closer relations between formal education and public service and believe that I

Essay uses first person (*I*, *me*) but is fairly formal in tone and vocabulary, between high and middle style.

309

Personal note slips through in enthusiasm author shows for internship opportunity.

could contribute to this mission. If selected as an ASPF intern, I will become an active alumnus of the program. I would love to do my part by advising younger students and recruiting future ASPF interns. Most important, I make it a point to improve the operations of programs from which I benefit. Any opportunities provided to me by the ASPF will be repaid in kind.

This statement transitions smoothly into second issue raised in prompt.

Other strengths I bring to the ASPF's National Internship Program are my broad educational background and dedication. My undergraduate studies will culminate in two honors degrees (finance and liberal arts) with additional premed course work. Afterward, I wish to enroll in a combined MD/PhD program in health-services research. Following my formal education, I will devote my career to seeing patients in a primary-care setting, researching health-care issues as a university faculty member, teaching bioethics, and developing public policy at a health-related government agency.

Formidable and specific goals speak for themselves in straightforward language.

Another transition introduces third issue raised by the prompt.

The course work at my undergraduate institution has provided me with basic laboratory and computer experience, but my strengths lie in oral and written communication. Comparing digital and film-screen mammography equipment for a project at M. D. Anderson honed my technical-writing skills and comprehension of statistical analysis. The qualitative analysis methods I learned at VERDICT while evaluating strategies used by the Veterans Health Administration in implementing clinical practice guidelines will be a significant resource to any prospective employer. By the end of this

Qualifications offered are numerous and detailed.

semester, I will also possess basic knowledge of Statistical Package for the Social Sciences (SPSS) software.

During my internship I would like to research one of the following topics: health-care finance, health policy, or ethnic disparities in access to high-quality health care. I have read much about the Patient Protection and Affordable Care Act of 2010 and anticipate studying its implications. I would learn a great deal from working with officials responsible for the operation and strategic planning of a program like Medicare (or a nonprofit hospital system). The greater the prospects for multiple responsibilities, the more excited I will be to show up at work each day.

Special interest/ concern is noted and is likely to impress reviewers of statement.

Final sentence affirms enthusiasm for technical internship.

How to start ● **First time assembling a portfolio?**
Think about what you should include.
See page 313.

17 Writing Portfolios

gather samples of your work

Professionals in creative fields—art, architecture, photography, modeling—have long used portfolios to inventory their achievements or display their skills to potential clients or employers. The practice has spread to other fields because these careful collections of work provide an in-depth look at what people have actually accomplished over time. Not surprisingly, many schools now encourage (or require) students to assemble writing portfolios of various kinds to demonstrate what they have learned and to assist them in the job market.

● For a first-year writing course, you put together a portfolio that traces your composing process for two major assignments, from brainstorming, research, and topic proposal through draft and final versions.

● For an writing internship course that qualifies you to work at a writing center, you introduce your course portfolio with a "literacy narrative" and offer midterm and final self-assessments of your progress.

● For a portfolio that qualifies you to begin apprentice teaching, you compile a set of reflections on all the proficiencies of your training program.

UNDERSTANDING WRITING PORTFOLIOS.   As assignments, portfolios vary enormously in what they aim to do and how they achieve their goals. Some collections serve as learning tools for particular courses, supporting students as they develop sound writing habits; not incidentally, they also provide material for helpful assessments of writing skills. Portfolios in writing classes, which are now usually compiled online, typically include some of the following elements:

first time ◀
assembling
a portfolio?

- Literacy narratives or statements of goals
- Brainstorming/prewriting activities for individual assignments
- Research logs and maps or annotated bibliographies
- Topic proposals and comments
- First drafts and revisions, with the writer's reflections
- Peer and instructor comments
- Final drafts, with the writer's reflections
- Writer's midcourse and/or final assessments of learning goals
- Additional documents or media materials selected by the writer
- A holistic assessment of the portfolio by the teacher (rather than grading of individual items)

Instructors and classmates may play a role at every stage of the composing process, especially when the portfolio is developed online.

In other situations, materials collected in a portfolio provide evidence that a student has mastered specific writing, research, or even media proficiencies required for a job or professional advancement. Such career portfolios (for example, for prospective teachers) may stretch across a sequence of courses, whole degree programs, or college careers. Owners of the portfolio usually have some responsibility for shaping their collection, but certain elements may be recommended or mandated, such as the following:

- A personal statement or profile describing accomplishments and learning trajectory as well as career goals

- Work that illustrates mastery of a subject matter
- Evidence of proficiency in specific technical or research skills
- Written reflections on specific issues in a field, such as philosophy, diversity, or professional ethics
- Assessments, evaluations, and outsider comments
- Documents that illustrate skills in writing, media, technology, or other areas

This list is partial. College programs that require career or degree portfolios typically offer detailed specifications, criteria of evaluation, templates, and lots of support.

Take charge of the portfolio assignment.   Many students are intimidated by the prospect of assembling a writing portfolio. But you won't have a problem if, right from the start, you study the instructions for the assignment, ask any nagging questions, figure out your responsibilities, and get hands-on experience with the required technology. Since most writing portfolios now

Here's where you can start: the dashboard screen of a typical online portfolio program. Clippings.me.

clippings.me   For PRs   Sign in   Join now   More ▾

Stefan Casso

Writing Student

Professor Ruszkiewicz
RHE 325M

⚲ University of Texas at Austin

Stefan Casso's portfolio

Essay 1

Worth the Lie
Thesis

Worth the Lie
Rough Draft

Worth the Lie
Final Draft

Essay 2

Essay 3

Reflection
RHE 325M

All copyrights belong to their respective owners   Writing portfolio powered by clippings.me come together online, sit down with the platform and learn how it works. In many cases, you'll be expected not only to post your own work and reflections but also to respond regularly to your classmates' materials.

If you are submitting a portfolio in paper form, study the specifications carefully. Then, right from the start, settle on a template for all your submissions: consistent margins, fonts, headings, headers, pagination, captions, and so on. (You might simply adhere to MLA or APA guidelines.) Your work will be more impressive if you give careful attention to design.

Appreciate the audiences for a portfolio.   Portfolios are usually mandated by instructors or institutions, and the work you present is likely to influence a grade, certification, or even a job opportunity. Fortunately, such readers will typically offer clear-cut rubrics for measuring your performance. Study those standards carefully to find out what exactly a teacher or program expects in a portfolio.

You'll often prepare a portfolio in the company of classmates and you should be grateful when that is the case. Since they are in the same boat, they can keep you grounded and you can usually count on them for timely feedback and even encouragement. Respond in kind. In the long run, you may learn as much from these rough-and-tumble peer interactions as from your instructor.

One important audience for a portfolio remains: yourself. Creating a portfolio will underscore what it takes to be a writer, highlighting all your moves and making you more conscious of these choices. By discovering strengths and confronting weaknesses, you'll really learn the craft. So treat the portfolio as an opportunity, not just another long assignment.

Present authentic materials.   A writing portfolio demonstrates a process of learning, not a glide path to perfection. So be honest about what you post there, from topic proposals that feel reckless to first drafts that flop grandly. Your instructor will probably be more interested in your development as a writer than in any particular texts you produce: It's your overall performance that will be assessed, not a single, isolated assignment. Think of your portfolio as a movie, not a snapshot.

When you are allowed to choose what to include, look for materials that tell an important or illustrative story, from topic proposal to first draft to final version. Remember, too, that you can control this narrative (somewhat) through your reflections on these pieces. Here's how one student takes up that self-evaluative challenge in the first paragraph of an end-of-term assessment:

> Honestly, on the first day of English 109, I was not a happy student; I had failed the University of Waterloo English Proficiency Exam. Although I told everyone it was not a big deal after it happened, deep down I was bitter. So, signing up for this class to avoid retaking the proficiency exam, I decided to use the course to prove I was not illiterate. The Writing Clinic was wrong to think I was incompetent — a fifty-minute test would not define my writing abilities.

Take reflections seriously.   Several times during a semester or at various stages in the writing process, an instructor may require you to comment on your own work. Here, for example, is a brief reflective paragraph that accompanied the first draft of Susan Wilcox's "Marathons for Women," a report that appears in Chapter 2 (see p. 39):

> I focused my paper on the evolution of women in marathoning and the struggle for sporting equality with men. I had problems in deciding which incidents to include and which to ignore. Additionally, I'm expecting to hear back from some marathoners so I can possibly include their experiences in my paper; however, none of them have gotten back to me yet. When they do return the interview questions, I'll have to decide what, if anything, to remove from the paper to make room for personal anecdotes. Finally, I need some work on my introduction and conclusion. What do the current versions lack?

Like Susan, you might use the reflection to ask classmates for specific advice or for editing suggestions.

Most reflections for a portfolio will be lengthier and more evaluative. An instructor might ask for an explanatory comment after the final version of a paper is submitted. You can talk about items such as the following:

- Your goals in writing a paper and how well you have met them
- How you have defined your audience/readers and how you've adjusted your paper for them
- The strategies behind your organization or style
- How you have addressed problems pointed out by your instructor or peer editors

- What you believe succeeds and what you'd like to have handled better
- What specifically you learned from composing the paper

Don't try to answer all these questions. Give your reflection a point or focus. But your comments should be candid: An instructor will want to know both what you have learned and what you intend to work on more in subsequent assignments.

If asked to compose a midcourse evaluation or a final reflection, broaden your scope and think about the trajectory of your learning across a series of activities and assignments. Again, your instructor may specify what form this comprehensive reflection should take. Some instructors will ask focused questions, others may tie your responses to a specific learning rubric, and still others may even encourage you to write a letter. Here are some questions to think about on your own:

- What were your original goals for the writing course, and how well have you met them?
- What types of audiences do you expect to address in the future, and how prepared are you now to deal with them?
- What strategies of organization and style have you mastered?
- What did you gain from the responses and advice of classmates?
- What exactly did you learn during the term?
- What goals do you have for the writing you expect to do in the future?

If space permits, illustrate your points with examples from your papers or from comments you have received from classmates. For a sample midsemester course reflection, see "Examining a model" on page 320.

Getting the details right

Some parts of a writing portfolio may be more heavily edited than others: Midterm reflections might go through several drafts while topic proposals are often tentative and open-ended. And a writing portfolio might contain peer editing and other fairly off-the-cuff items. Yet the overall project should look competent, feel conscientious, and show attention to design.

With a career portfolio, plan on submitting nothing less than your best work—from cover to cover.

Polish your portfolio. If you complain that pop quizzes or one-shot finals don't reflect your true abilities, what can you say when you turn in a bungled course portfolio? This is not an assignment to do at the last minute. So keep up with all prompts and activities—and that includes giving timely feedback to the work of your classmates. Online portfolio platforms may help keep you on track, but you'll still need to meet due dates and submit important documents.

Understand the portfolio activities. You may be unfamiliar with some of the specific features of a writing portfolio. If you've never done a literacy narrative or a topic proposal, ask your instructor for models (or see p. 7 and p. 440). If your instructor suggests brainstorming activities, look to Chapter 19. If you have questions about peer editing, see Chapter 36. Other questions? Ask your instructor *and* talk with classmates.

Give honest feedback to classmates. Most students seriously underestimate the value of the comments they make on their classmates' work. Simply because you are an experienced reader, you will recognize when ideas are unclear, arguments are hard to follow, evidence seems unconvincing, sentences are confusing, and so on. You don't have to fix the problems you point to; writers just need to know where they are and how you are reacting to them. Be as clear as you can and focus on big issues: content, organization, audience, style. It's fine to point out problems in grammar and mechanics, but they shouldn't be your first priority when you are a peer editor. And don't forget to mention what in a paper strikes you as distinctive and successful. Writers need to know that as well. You'll be surprised how much you'll gain from peer editing.

Here's a screen from a portfolio program that allows students to highlight a passage and comment on it.

Take advantage of multimedia.   Portfolios routinely include examples of whatever genres of writing are important to a field or discipline (lesson plans, field reports, problem-solving logs, etc.). They may also display important kinds of media and can do so easily in electronic platforms. You can display and get feedback on digital images, podcasts, slide presentations, and videos you produce as part of your course work.

Your Turn   Search for the term "portfolio" on the Web sites for several post-secondary schools in your area. (You might exclude references to business and investment portfolios.) What kinds of portfolio programs or activities do you find described there? What do they have in common and how do they differ?

Examining a model

In the following brief midterm reflection, student Desiree Lopez describes her work in an internship class designed to train tutors for a campus writing center.

Describes initial course expectations.

When I first began the internship course, I was apprehensive and anxious about what was to come. To be honest, I had never been to the writing center and so I had little knowledge about the work the Undergraduate Writing Center (UWC) tutors did. My expectation was that writing tutors were people who helped polish student papers. I thought of the writing center as not so much a one-stop fix-it shop, but rather a center that anticipated what university professors were looking for in their students' papers and knew how to guide those students in the right direction.

Offers a revised point of view.

However, now that the semester is halfway completed and I have had the opportunity to observe tutors in action, my perception of the work done by campus writing centers has completely changed. I now see that, rather than polishing papers that are rough around the edges, the UWC helps students realize their potential while giving them the skills to polish their own papers.

I have learned how to help students identify what they are trying to do and organize their writing in ways appropriate to an assignment by asking simple questions such as "What are you trying to say here?" and "What do you want your readers to take from this?" I am happy to say that these tools have helped me hone my own skills as well. I have learned to ask myself those same questions while writing, and I now have a class of more than twenty peers to help me improve when I can't seem to figure out on my own what needs tweaking. Lastly, I have learned (mainly from the grammar quizzes) that my first instincts are generally right; if the sentence sounds correct, it probably is correct and I am just overthinking.

Lists specific techniques and skills already learned.

I know I still have more to learn about the writer-tutor relationship that can only be acquired through practice and hands-on experience. I am confident that I now have some of the tools I need and I know that, given the opportunity, I can tailor consultations to individual students and help them perceive their strengths and weaknesses. However, I am still nervous about the idea of conducting a consultation on my own. I worry that I have not yet perfected the art of nondirective/ nonevaluative tutoring and that I will slip up—telling students I believe that their papers are interesting or really good or better than something I might have written on the subject. But I'll resist that temptation and simply ask them, "What do *you* think you've done well?"

Explains concerns that still remain.

How to start ▸

● **Adapting material?**
Organize your presentation. See page 323.

18 Oral Reports

present information to a live audience

In an oral report, you present material you have researched to an audience listening and watching rather than reading. So you must organize information clearly and find ways to convey your points powerfully, memorably, and sometimes graphically.

- For a psychology course, you use presentation software to review the results of an experiment you and several classmates designed to test which types of music were most conducive to studying for examinations.

- In a Shakespeare class, you use slides to give an oral report on Elizabethan theaters that draws upon research you are doing for your end-of-semester term paper.

- Prepping a crowd for a protest march, you use a bullhorn and a little humor to review the very serious ground rules for staging a peaceful demonstration on the grounds of the state capitol.

UNDERSTANDING ORAL REPORTS. Oral reports can be deceptive. When watching someone give an effective five-minute talk, you may assume the speaker spent less time preparing it than he or she would a ten-page paper. But be warned: Oral presentations require all the research, analysis, and drafting of any other type of assignment, and then some. After all the background work is done, the material needs to be trimmed to its most important points and sold to an audience. Here is some advice for preparing effective oral reports.

Know your stuff. Having a firm grasp on your subject will make a presentation more effective—which is why you need to do serious research. Knowledge brings you confidence that will ease some anxieties about public speaking. You'll appear believable and persuasive to an audience. And you'll feel more comfortable when improvising or taking questions. When you are in command of a subject, you'll survive even if equipment fails or you misplace a note card.

Organize your presentation. If your report is based on material you've already written, reduce the text to an outline, memorize its key points (or put them on cards), and then practice speaking about each one. ○ If it helps, connect the main ideas to one or two strong examples listeners might later remember. Make the report seem spontaneous, but plan every move.

adapting ◀ material?

The process is similar for an oral report built from scratch. First, study your subject. Then list the points you want to cover and arrange them to engage listeners, choosing a pattern of organization that fits your topic. Use note cards or the outlining tools in programs like Word or PowerPoint to explore options for structuring the talk.

Cover only a limited number of points. You want an audience to walk away thinking about two or three key ideas.

The best equipment can't save a poorly prepared report. © Hulton-Deutsch Collection/Corbis.

order ideas
p. 377

Keep your audience on track.   At the beginning of your report, tell your audience briefly what you intend to cover and in what order. Then, at critical transitions in the report, remind listeners where you are simply by stating what comes next: *The second issue I wish to discuss . . . ; Now that we've examined the phenomenon, let's look at its consequences.* Don't be shy about making your main points this directly and don't worry about repetition. In an oral report, strategic repetition is your friend.

Stay connected to your listeners.   For about thirty seconds, you'll have the spontaneous goodwill of most audiences. After that, you've got to earn every minute of their attention. Begin by introducing yourself and your subject, if no one else performs that task. For longer reports, consider easing into your material with an anecdote that connects you, your subject, and your listeners. Self-deprecating humor usually works. (Short, in-class presentations won't need much, if any, warm-up.)

Establish eye contact with individual members of the group right from the start. Watch their reactions. When it's clear you've made a point, move on. If you see puzzled looks, explain more. No speaker charms everyone, so don't let a random yawn throw you. But if the whole crowd starts to snooze, you *are* the problem. Connect or lose 'em: Pick up your pace; move on to the next point; skip to your best material. ◯

Be sure to speak *to* your listeners, not to your notes or text. Arrange your materials and print them large enough so that you can read them easily from a distance and not lose your place. If you look downward too often or gaze at your own slides, you'll lose eye contact and your voice will be muffled, even with a microphone.

Use your voice and body.   Speak clearly and deliberately, and be sure people in the back of the room can hear you. Nervous speakers unconsciously speed up until they're racing to their conclusions. If you get skittish, calm yourself by taking a deep breath and smiling.

If the room is large and you're not confined by a fixed microphone, move around on the stage to address more of the audience. Use gestures too. They are a natural part of public speaking, especially for arguments and personal

connect ideas
p. 387

narratives. If you get stuck behind a podium, be sure to scan the entire audience (not just speak to the middle of the room) and modulate your voice. Keep your body steady too: Don't rock or sway as you speak.

Adapt your material to the time available.   If you know your subject well, don't worry about running out of things to say. Most speakers have the opposite problem: They talk too much. So be realistic about how much you can cover within an assigned time limit, especially if you have to take questions at the end. Tie your key ideas to fixed points on a clock. Know where you need to be at a quarter, half, and three-quarters of the way through the available time. If you're taking questions after your presentation, follow up with *Any questions?*

Practice your talk.   With any oral report, you need several dry runs to increase your confidence and identify potential problems. Speak your material aloud *exactly* as you intend to deliver it and go through all the motions, especially if you will use media such as slides or video clips. Have one or more friends or classmates observe you and offer feedback.

If your presentation is collaborative, choreograph the report with the full group in attendance, agreeing on the introductions, transitions, and interactions with the audience. Who manages the laptop? Who distributes the handouts and when? Who takes the questions? Handoffs like these seem minor until they are fumbled on game day.

Go through all your materials when you time the talk, including any audio and video clips. If you review the presentation only in your head, you will greatly underestimate its length.

Prepare for the occasion.   Before the report, check out the physical location if possible, as well as any equipment you will use. Be sure your laptop will connect to the multimedia projector in the room; know how to dim the lights; be sure a screen or electrical outlets are available.

Then dress up. A little spit and polish earns the goodwill of most audiences. Your classmates may razz you about the tie or skirt, but it just proves they're paying attention. And that's a good thing.

Viorika/E+ Collection/Getty Images.

Your Turn   Given the number of oral presentations and lectures you've sat through, most of them using PowerPoint, you could probably write your own chapter on this special assignment. Working with a small group, list five hallmarks of an effective oral report and five characteristics of a dismal one. Annotate the list with examples that you may recall from particular reports. Then compare the features your group has come up with to those generated by other groups.

Getting the details right

There's nothing wrong with a report that relies on the spoken word alone. Still, audiences do appreciate supporting material, including flip charts, handouts, slides, and visual or audio samplings. All such materials, clearly labeled and handsomely reproduced, should also be genuinely relevant to the report. Resist the temptation to show something just because it's cool.

Most oral reports use presentation software of some kind such as the dominant player in this field, PowerPoint. With presentation software, you build the report upon a sequence of slides, designing them yourself or picking them from a gallery of ready-made items. You can choose slide layouts to accommodate text-only presentations, text and photos, text and charts, images only, and so on.

Presentation software offers so many bells and whistles that novices tend to overdo it, allowing the software to dominate their reports. Here's how to make PowerPoint, Keynote, or Prezi work for you.

Be certain you need presentation software.   A short talk that makes only one or two points probably works better if viewers focus on you, not on a screen. Use presentation software to keep audiences on track through more complicated material, to highlight major issues or points, or to display images viewers really need to see. A little humor or eye candy is fine once in a while, but don't expect audiences to be impressed by glitz. What matters is the content of the report. O

Use slides to introduce points, not cover them.   If you find yourself reading your slides, you've put too many words on-screen. Offer the minimum that viewers need: main points, important evidence, clear charts, and essential images (see the "Edenlawn Estates" slides on p. 329). It's fine, too, for a slide to outline your presentation at the beginning and to summarize key points at the end. In fact, it's helpful to have a slide that signals your conclusion.

Use a simple and consistent design.   Select one of the design templates provided by your presentation software or create a design of your own that fits your subject. A consistent design scheme will unify your report and minimize distractions. O

For academic presentations, choose legible fonts in a size large enough for viewers at the back of the room to read easily. For reasons of legibility, avoid elegant, playful, or eccentric fonts, including Old English styles or those that

understand
reports p. 36

think visually
p. 557

For presentations, Prezi offers a range of design templates, as shown here. Courtesy of Prezi, Inc.

resemble handwriting. Some experts prefer sans serif fonts for headlines and serif fonts for supporting text. But don't use more than two or, more rarely, three fonts within a presentation. Use boldface very selectively for emphasis. If you have to boldface a font to make it visible at a distance, simply find a thicker font. Italics are fine for occasional use, but in some fonts they are hard to read at a distance.

Consider alternatives to slide-based presentations.   Anything you build on a laptop can be projected on-screen. So you need not use conventional slide-based presentation software for your oral report if you can create materials on your own. For example, various interactive Web 2.0 applications, from social-network software to blogs and wikis, can be configured for oral presentations, as can mind-mapping software and PowerPoint alternatives such as Prezi. In Prezi, for example, sequential slides are replaced by words, images, and media presented on an unending canvas; images move, rotate, and zoom in and out to provide different perspectives on a subject.

Examining a model

The following PowerPoint presentation was created by Terri Sagastume, a resident of a small Florida town who opposes a proposed real-estate development, Edenlawn Estates, on property near his home. J&M Investments, the real-estate developer that recently purchased the property, hopes to create a new multi-story condominium complex in place of the property's existing single-family homes. Sagastume's goal is to inform the public of the damage such a development would do to the surrounding area, and he is trying to convince his audience to sign a petition, which he will present to the local government in an effort to shut the project down.

The slides themselves are extremely simple and brief: They are merely the bullet points that Sagastume uses to anchor his presentation.

Edenlawn Estates

- What the developers want
- Why we should fight
- How we can win

What Developers Want

- Zoning variance
- Concrete seawall
- Four new traffic lights
- Height restriction exemption

Why We Should Fight

- Will cost taxpayers money
- Will harm environment
- Will increase traffic
- Will detract from quality of life

Stop Edenlawn Estates

Sign the petition today!

With the first slide as his backdrop, Sagastume provides a preview of his speech in three broad sections. First, he explains to his audience that the real-estate developer — a Miami-based conglomerate with no personal ties to the area — wants to change the existing building codes and zoning laws in order to maximize profits. Second, he reminds his audience of the reason those codes and laws are there and explains that much could be lost if exceptions are made. And finally, he convinces his audience that, together, they can fight the big developer and win.

Map your own writing process.

reference

Ideas

part three

3

Need help organizing or drafting? See p. 360.

19 Brainstorming

find a topic/
get an idea

What do you do when you find yourself clueless, stuck, or just overwhelmed by the topic possibilities at the start of a writing project? Simple answer: Brainstorm. Put a notion on the table and see where it goes. Toy with an idea like a kitten with a catnip mouse. Push yourself to think through, around, over, and under a proposition. Dare to be politically incorrect or, alternatively, so conventional that your good behavior might scare your elders.

Naturally, you'll match brainstorming techniques to the type of writing you hope to produce. Beginning a personal tale about a trip to Wrigley Field, you might make a list of sensory details to jog your memory—the smell of hot dogs, the catcalls of fans, the green grass of the outfield. ○ But for an assigned report on DNA fingerprinting, your brainstorming might itemize things you still must learn about the subject: what DNA fingerprinting is, how it is done, when it can be used, how reliable it is, and so on. ○

Find routines that support thinking. Use whatever brainstorming techniques get you interested in a project. Jogging, swimming, knitting, or sipping brew at the coffeehouse may be your stimulus of choice. Such routine activities keep the body occupied, allowing insights to emerge. Be sure to capture and record those ideas in notes or, perhaps, voice memos.

understand
narratives p. 4

understand
reports p. 36

Whiteboards, flip charts, and even sticky notes can help you rapidly record your ideas. Image Source/Getty Images.

One warning: Passive brainstorming routines can easily slip into procrastination. That comfortable corner at Starbucks might become a spot too social for much thinking or writing. When your productivity drops, change tactics.

Build from lists.   Write down every plausible topic or, if you already have a subject, the major points you might cover. Don't be picky at this stage: List everything that comes to mind. One idea will lead to another, then another. Even grocery lists work this way.

For instance, preparing a letter to the editor in defense of collegiate sports, you can first itemize arguments you've heard from friends or have made yourself. List the counterarguments you come up with too—as well as any relevant examples, news events, or people. Then pick out the more intriguing or plausible items, and arrange them tentatively, perhaps sequencing them by time or pairing arguments and counterarguments.

Map your ideas.   If you find a list too static as a prompt for writing, another way may be to explore the relationships between your ideas *visually*. Some writers use logic trees to represent their thinking, starting with a single general concept and breaking it into smaller and smaller parts. Others begin with a key concept (just a word or two), circle it, and then begin to free-associate, quickly

> Ideas won't keep; something must be done about them.

—Alfred North Whitehead

© Hulton-Deutsch Collection/Corbis.

writing down more circled concepts and linking them by lines of relationship. When a page is full, writers look for interesting patterns, connections, and ideas.

Try freewriting.   This is a technique of nonstop composing designed to loosen restraints we sometimes impose on our own thinking. Typically, free-writing sessions begin slowly, with a few disconnected phrases and words. But, suddenly, there's a spark and words stream onto the paper. Although freewriting comes in many forms, the basic formula is simple.

STAGE ONE

- Start with a blank screen or sheet of paper.
- Put your subject or title at the top of the page.
- Write on that subject nonstop for ten minutes.
- Don't stop typing or lift your pen from the paper during that time.
- Write nonsense if you must, but keep writing.

STAGE TWO

- Stop at ten minutes and review what you have written.
- Underscore or highlight the most intriguing idea, phrase, or sentence.
- Put the highlighted idea at the top of a new screen or sheet.
- Freewrite for another ten minutes on the new, more focused topic.

Like other brainstorming techniques, freewriting works best when you already know something about a subject. You might freewrite successfully about standardized testing or working at fast-food restaurants if you've experienced both; you'll stumble trying to compose freely on subjects you know next to nothing about, such as, perhaps, thermodynamics or the career of Maria Callas. Freewriting tends to work best for personal narratives, personal statements, arguments, ○ and proposals, ○ and less well for reports and technical projects.

Use memory prompts.   When writing personal narratives, institutional histories, or even résumés, you might trigger ideas with photographs, yearbooks, Facebook pages, or perhaps a Twitter feed. An image from a vacation may bring

understand
arguments p. 66

understand
proposals p. 160

events worth writing about flooding back to you. Even checkbooks or credit card statements may help you reconstruct past events or see patterns in your life worth exploring in writing.

Search online for your ideas.   You can get lots of ideas by simply exploring most topics online (or in a library catalog) through keywords. Indeed, determining those initial keywords and then following up with new terms you discover while browsing is in itself a potent form of brainstorming.

A photo album is a great place to look for writing ideas because we tend to document meaningful moments. *Left:* Allie Goldstein. *Center:* Courtesy of Ellen Darion. *Right:* Courtesy of Sid Darion.

> **Your Turn**   If you have never used freewriting as a brainstorming activity, give it a try. Pick a general topic from among courses you are currently studying, news events that interest you, or activities you are deeply involved in: for example, the Japanese concept of Bushido, immigration reform, or unpaid internships. (You want a topic about which you have *some* knowledge or opinions.) Then follow the preceding directions. See what happens.

Uncle Bob, who's a cop, complains about the "*CSI* effect." What is that?

I found a study by professors of law and psychology. What do they think?

1

Find reliable sources.

Wikipedia isn't an academic source, but it will help me get a sense of the big picture.

This article comes from a government publication—does that automatically mean it's not biased?

WIKIPEDIA
The Free Encyclopedia

Article | Discussion

CSI effect

From Wikipedia, the free encyclopedia

The **CSI effect**, also known as the **CSI syndrome**[1] and the CSI public perception. The term most often refers to the belief that jur American legal professionals, several studies have shown that cr

There are several other manifestations of the CSI effect. Greater and popularity of forensic science programs at the university leve forensic science shows teach criminals how to conceal evidence

Contents [hide]
1 Background
2 Manifestations
2.1 Trials
2.2 Academia
2.3 Crimes
2.4 Police investigations
3 References

Background

The CSI effect is named for *CSI: Crime Scene Investigation*, a te discovery of a dead body leads to a criminal investigation by mer which debuted in 2002, and *CSI: NY*, first aired in 2004. The *CSI Bones, Cold Case, Cold Case Files, Cold Squad, Criminal Minds*

Main page
Contents
Featured content
Current events
Random article
Donate to Wikipedia
▼ Interaction
  Help
  About Wikipedia
  Community portal
  Recent changes
  Contact Wikipedia
▶ Toolbox
▶ Print/export
▼ Languages
  Česky
  Deutsch
  Español
  Français
  Italiano

Wikipedia ® is a registered trademark of the Wikipedia Foundation.

OFFICE OF JUSTICE PROGRAMS

NATIONAL INSTITUTE OF JUSTICE
Research • Development • Evaluation

HOME | FUNDING | PUBLICATIONS & MULTIMEDIA | EVENTS | TRAINING |

NIJ Home Page > NIJ Journal > NIJ Journal No. 259

NIJ JOURNAL NO. 259

Director's Message

The 'CSI Effect': Does It Really Exist?

Voice Stress Analysis: Only 15 Percent of Lies About Drug Use Detected in Field Test

Shopping Malls: Are They Prepared to Prevent and Respond to Attack?

Software Defined Radios Help Agencies Communicate

The 'CSI Effect': Does It Really Exist?

by Honorable Donald E. Shelton

Crime and courtroom proceedings have long been fodder f scriptwriters. In recent years, however, the media's use of for drama has not only proliferated, it has changed focus. our criminal justice process, many of today's courtroom dr cases. *Court TV* offers live gavel-to-gavel coverage of trial month. Now, that's "reality television"!

Reality and fiction have begun to blur with crime magazine *Hours Mystery, American Justice,* and even, on occasion, portray actual cases, but only after extensively editing the narration for dramatic effect. Presenting one 35-year-old *Hours Mystery* filmed for months to capture all pretrial he trial; the program, however, was ultimately edited to a 1- the crime remained a "mystery" . . . notwithstanding the j

National Institute of Justice.

2 Stay alert to differing perspectives.

3 Question claims.

20 Smart Reading

read closely

There's probably no better strategy for generating ideas than reading. Reading can deepen your impressions of any subject you are exploring, provide necessary background information, sharpen your critical acumen, and introduce you to alternative views. Reading also places you within a community of writers who have already thought about a subject.

Of course, not all reading serves the same purposes.

- You check out a dozen scholarly books to do research for a paper and then look for journal articles online.
- You consult stock market quotes and baseball box scores because you want numbers *now*.
- You interpret an organization chart to figure out who actually controls the student government budget.
- You read an old diary to discover what life was like before photocopiers, air-conditioning, and (*gulp!*) smartphones.
- You pack a *Divergent* series novel for pleasure reading on the Jersey Shore.

Yet any of these reading experiences, as well as thousands of others, might lead to ideas for projects.

You've probably been thoroughly schooled in basic techniques of academic reading: Survey the table of contents, preread to get a sense of the whole, look up terms or concepts you don't know, summarize what you've read, and so on. Such suggestions are practical, especially

READ is registered trademark of the American Library Association. Image courtesy of ALA Graphics, alastore.ala.org. Used with permission from the American Library Association, www.ala.org.

For a tutorial on active reading, see **macmillanhighered.com/howtowrite3e.**
Tutorials › Critical Reading › Active Reading Strategies

for difficult scholarly or professional texts. The following advice about reading can help you sharpen your college-level writing.

Read to deepen what you already know.   Whatever your interests or experiences in life, you're not alone. Others have explored similar paths and have probably written about them. Reading their work may give you the confidence to bring your own thoughts to public attention. Whether your passion is tintype photography, skateboarding, or film fashions of the 1930s, you'll find excellent books on the subject by browsing library catalogs or checking online bookstores.

For example, if you have worked at a fast-food franchise and know what goes on there, you might find a book like Eric Schlosser's classic *Fast Food Nation: The Dark Side of the All-American Meal* engrossing. You'll be drawn in because your experience makes you an informed critic. You can agree and disagree intelligently with Schlosser and, perhaps, see how to extend or amend his arguments. At a minimum, you'll walk away from the book knowing the titles of dozens of additional sources, should you want to learn more.

Read above your level of knowledge.   It's easy to connect with people online who share your interests, but they often don't know much more about a topic than you do. To find fresh ideas, push your reading to a more demanding level. Spend time with experts whose books and articles you can't blow right through. You'll know you are there when you find yourself looking up names, adding terms to your vocabulary, and feeling humbled by what you still need to learn about a subject. That's when invention occurs and ideas germinate.

Read what makes you uncomfortable.   Most of us today have access to devices that connect us to endless sources of information. But all those voices also mean that we can choose to read (or watch) only materials that confirm our existing beliefs and prejudices—and many people do. Such narrowness will be exposed, however, whenever you write on a controversial subject and find readers arguing back with facts you never considered before. Surprise! The world is more complicated than you thought. The solution is simple: Get out of the echo chamber and read more broadly, engaging with those who see the world differently.

Read against the grain.   Skeptics and naysayers may be no fun at parties, but their habits may be worth emulating whenever you are reading. It makes

> If you don't have the time to read, you don't have the time or tools to write.

—Stephen King

© Dick Dickinson.

For an activity on critical reading, see **macmillanhighered.com/howtowrite3e.**
Tutorials › LearningCurve Activities › Critical Reading

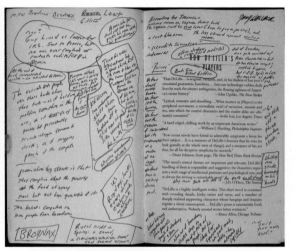

The late writer David Foster Wallace took copious notes when he read — in this case, the Don DeLillo novel *Players*. *PLAYERS* by Don DeLillo. Copyright © 1977 by Don DeLillo. Used by permission of the Wallace Literary Agency, Inc. David Foster Wallace notes used by permission of the David Foster Wallace Literary Trust and the Harry Ransom Center, The University of Texas at Austin.

sense to read with an open mind, giving reputable writers and their ideas a fair hearing. But you always want to raise questions about the assumptions writers make, the logic they use, the evidence they present, and the authorities and sources upon which they build their arguments.

Reading against the grain does not mean finding fault with everything, but rather letting nothing slip by without scrutiny. Treat the world around you as a text to be read and analyzed. O Ask questions. Why do so few men take liberal-arts courses? What topics does your campus paper avoid and why? How do friendships change when they are mostly online? Notice such phenomena, ponder their meaning, and write about them.

Read slowly.   Browsing online has made many of us superficial readers. For serious texts, forget speed-reading and your own Web habits. Settle in for the duration. Find the thesis; look up unfamiliar words and names; don't jump to another article until you've finished the one in hand.

Annotate what you read.   Find some way to record your reactions to whatever you read. If you own the text and don't mind marking it, use highlighting pens to flag key ideas. Then converse with them and leave a record. Electronic media and e-readers offer a range of built-in commenting tools. Even Post-it notes work in some circumstances.

> **Your Turn**   Working with a small group, make a list of the newspapers, Web sites, magazines, TV shows or networks, or other resources that you use to gather news and information about politics, society, and culture. Then try to locate these media resources along a ribbon that moves from the political far left to the political far right. Be prepared for considerable disagreement. When you are done, compare your placements with those of other groups working on the same project. What may account for your differences?
>
> Far left _____ Left _____ Center _____ Right _____ Far right

think critically
p. 343

Critical Thinking 21

think critically/ avoid fallacies

We all get edgy when our written work is criticized (or even edited) because the ideas we put on a page emerge from our own thinking—writing is *us*. Granted, our words rarely express *exactly* who we are or what we've been imagining, but such distinctions get lost when someone points to our work and says, "That's stupid" or "What crap!" The criticism cuts deep; it feels personal.

Fortunately, there's a way to avoid embarrassing gaffes in your work: *critical thinking*, a term that describes mental habits that reinforce logical reasoning and analysis. There are lots of ways to develop good sense, from following the strategies of smart reading described in Chapter 20 to using the rhetorical tactics presented throughout the "Guide" section of this book.

Here we focus on specific dimensions of critical thinking that you will find useful in college writing.

Think in terms of claims and reasons. Whenever you read reports, arguments, or analyses, chances are you begin by identifying the claims writers make and assessing the evidence that supports them. Logically, then, when you write in these genres, you should expect the same scrutiny.

Claims are the passages in a text where you make an assertion, offer an argument, or present a hypothesis for which you intend to provide evidence.

> Using a cell phone while driving is dangerous.
>
> Playing video games can improve intelligence.
>
> Worrying about childhood obesity is futile.

Claims may occur almost anywhere in a paper: in a thesis statement, in the topic sentences of paragraphs, in transitional passages, or in summaries or conclusions. (An exception may be formal scientific writing, in which the hypothesis, results, and discussion will occur in specific sections of an article.)

Make sure that all your major claims in a paper are accompanied by plausible supporting *reasons* either in the same sentence or in adjoining material. Such reasons are usually introduced by expressions as straightforward as *because*, *if*, *to*, and *so*. Once you attach reasons to a claim, you have made a deeper commitment to it. You must then do the hard work of providing readers with convincing evidence, logic, or conditions for accepting your claim. Seeing your ideas fully stated on paper early in a project may even persuade you to abandon an implausible claim—one you cannot or do not want to defend.

> Using a cell phone while driving is dangerous *since* distractions are a proven cause of auto accidents.
>
> Playing video games can improve intelligence *if* they teach young gamers to make logical decisions quickly.
>
> ~~Worrying about childhood obesity is futile because there's nothing we can do about it.~~

Think in terms of premises and assumptions.   Probe beneath the surface of key claims and reasons that writers offer, and you will discover their core principles, usually only implied but sometimes stated directly: These are called *premises* or *assumptions*. In oral arguments, when people say *I get where you're coming from*, they signal that they understand your assumptions. You want to achieve similar clarity, especially whenever the claims you make in a report or argument are likely to be controversial or argumentative. Your assumptions can be general or specific, conventional or highly controversial, as in the following examples.

> Improving human safety and well-being is a desirable goal. [general]
>
> We should discourage behaviors that contribute to traffic accidents. [specific]

Improving intelligence is desirable. [conventional]

Play should train children to think quickly. [controversial]

When writing for readers who mostly share your values, you usually don't have to explain where you're coming from. But be prepared to explain your values to more general or hostile readers: *This is what I believe and why.* Naturally—and here's where the critical thinking comes in—you yourself need to understand the assumptions upon which your claims rest. Are they logical? Are they consistent? Are you prepared to stand by them? Or is it time to rethink some of your principles?

Think in terms of evidence.   A claim without evidence attached is just that—a barefaced assertion no better than a child's "Oh, yeah?" So you should choose supporting material carefully, always weighing whether it is sufficient, complete, reliable, and unbiased. ○ Has an author you want to cite done solid research? Or does the evidence provided seem flimsy or anecdotal? Can you offer enough evidence yourself to make a convincing case—or are you cherry-picking only those facts that support your point of view? Do you even have the expertise to evaluate the evidence you present? These are questions to ask routinely and persistently.

Anticipate objections.   Critical thinkers understand that serious issues have many dimensions—and rarely just two sides. That's because they have done their homework, which means trying to understand even those positions with which they strongly disagree. When you start writing with this kind of inclusive perspective, you'll hear voices of the loyal opposition in your head and you'll be able to address objections even before potential readers make them. At a minimum, you will enhance your credibility. But more important, you'll have done the kind of thinking that makes you smarter.

Avoid logical fallacies.   Honest, fair-minded writers have nothing to hide. They name names, identify sources, and generate appropriate emotions. They acknowledge weaknesses in their arguments and concede graciously when the opposition scores a point. These are qualities you want to display in your serious academic and professional work.

refine your
search p. 442

One way to enhance your reputation as a writer and critical thinker is to avoid logical fallacies. *Fallacies* are rhetorical moves that corrupt solid reasoning—the verbal equivalent of sleight of hand. The following classic, but all too common, fallacies can undermine the integrity of your writing.

- **Appeals to false authority.** Be sure that any experts or authorities you cite on a topic have real credentials in the field and that their claims can be verified. Similarly, don't claim or imply knowledge, authority, or credentials yourself that you don't have. Be frank about your level of expertise. Framing yourself as an honest, if amateur, broker on a subject can even raise your credibility.

- *Ad hominem* **attacks.** In arguments of all kinds, you may be tempted to bolster your position by attacking the personal integrity of your opponents when character really isn't an issue. It's easy to resort to name-calling (*socialist*, *racist*) or character assassination, but it usually signals that your own case is weak.

- **Dogmatism.** Writers fall back on dogmatism whenever they want to give the impression, usually false, that they control the party line on an issue and have all the right answers. You are probably indulging in dogmatism when you begin a paragraph, *No serious person would disagree* or *How can anyone argue . . .*

- **Either/or choices.** A shortcut to winning arguments, which even Socrates abused, is to reduce complex situations to simplistic choices: good/bad, right/wrong, liberty/tyranny, smart/dumb, and so on. If you find yourself inclined to use some version of the *either/or* strategy, think again. Capable readers see right through this tactic and demolish it simply by pointing to alternatives that haven't been considered.

- **Scare tactics.** Avoid them. Arguments that make their appeals by preying on the fears of audiences are automatically suspect. Targets may be as vague as "unforeseen consequences" or as specific as particular organizations or groups of people who pose various threats. When such fears may be legitimate, make sure you provide evidence for the danger and don't overstate it.

- **Sentimental or emotional appeals.** Maybe it's fine for the Humane Society to decorate its pleas for cash with pictures of sad puppies, but you can see how the tactic might be abused. In your own work, be wary of

"Either you left the TV on downstairs or we have whales again."

using language that pushes buttons the same way, *oohing* and *aahing* readers out of their best judgment.

- **Hasty or sweeping generalizations.** Drawing conclusions from too little evidence or too few examples is a *hasty generalization* (*Climate change must be a fraud because we sure froze last winter*); making a claim apply too broadly is a *sweeping generalization* (*All Texans love pickups*). Competent writers avoid the temptation to draw conclusions that fit their preconceived notions—or pander to those of an intended audience. But the temptation is powerful, so you might find examples, even in college reading assignments.

- **Faulty causality.** Just because two events or phenomena occur close together in time doesn't mean that one caused the other. (The Red Sox didn't start winning *because* you put on the lucky boxers.) People are fond of leaping to such easy conclusions, and many pundits and politicians do routinely exploit this weakness, particularly in situations involving economics, science, health, crime, and culture. Causal relationships are almost always complicated, and you will get credit for dealing with them honestly. ○

- **Evasions, misstatements, and equivocations.** Evasions are utterances that avoid the truth, misstatements are untruths excused as mistakes, and equivocations are lies made to seem like truths. Skilled readers know when a writer is using these slippery devices, so avoid them.

- **Straw men.** *Straw men* are easy or habitual targets that writers aim at to win an argument. Often the issue in such an attack has long been defused or discredited: for example, middle-class families abusing food stamps, immigrants taking jobs from hardworking citizens, the rich not paying a fair share of taxes. When you resort to straw-man arguments, you signal to your readers that you may not have much else in your arsenal.

- **Slippery-slope arguments.** Take one wrong step off the righteous path and you'll slide all the way down the hill: That's the warning that slippery-slope arguments make. They aren't always inaccurate, but they are easy to overstate. Will using plastic bags really doom the planet? Maybe or maybe not. If you create a causal chain, be sure that you offer adequate support for every step and don't push beyond what's plausible.

© Ariel Molvig/The New Yorker/Condé Nast.

understand causal
analyses p. 128

Your Turn Working in a group, find an example of a short argument that impresses most of you. (Your instructor might suggest a particular article.) Carefully locate the claims within the piece that all of you regard as its most important, impressive, or controversial statements. Then see if you can formulate the premises or values upon which these claims rest. Try to state these premises as clearly as you can in a complete, declarative sentence. Are the assumptions you uncovered statements that you agree with? If the assumptions are controversial, does the piece explain or defend them? Be prepared to present your group's analysis and conclusions in class.

- **Bandwagon appeals.** You haven't made an argument when you simply tell people it's time to cease debate and get with popular opinion. Too many bad decisions and policies get enacted that way. If you order readers to jump aboard a bandwagon, expect them to resist.

- **Faulty analogies.** Similes and analogies are worth applauding when they illuminate ideas or make them comprehensible or memorable. But seriously analyze the implications of any analogies you use. Calling a military action either "another Vietnam" or a "crusade" might raise serious issues, as does comparing one's opponents to "Commies" or the KKK. Readers have a right to be skeptical of writers who use such ploys.

22 Experts

ask for help

Forget about *expert* as an intimidating word. When you need help with your writing, seek advice from authorities who either know more about your subject than you do or have more experience developing such a project. Advice may come from different sources, but that's not a problem: The more people you talk to, the better.

Talk with your instructor. Don't be timid. Instructors hold office hours to answer your questions, especially about assignments. Save yourself time and, perhaps, much grief by getting early feedback on your ideas and topic. It's better to learn that your thesis is unworkable before you compose a first draft.

Just as important, your instructor might help you see aspects of a topic you hadn't noticed or direct you to essential sources. Don't write a paper just to please instructors, but you'd be foolish to ignore their counsel.

Take your ideas to the writing center. Many student writers think the only time to use a campus writing center is when their instructor returns a draft on life support. Most writing-center tutors prefer not to be seen as EMTs. So they are eager to help at the start of a project, when you're still developing ideas. Tutors may not be experts on your subject, but they have reviewed enough papers to offer sensible advice for focusing a topic, shaping a thesis, or adapting a subject to an audience. ○ They also recognize when you're so clueless that you need to talk with your instructor pronto.

develop a statement p. 362

Find local experts.   Don't trouble an expert for information you could find easily yourself in the library or online: Save human contacts for when you need serious help on a major writing project—a senior thesis, an important story for a campus periodical, a public presentation on a controversial subject. But, then, do take advantage of the human resources around you. Campuses are teeming with knowledgeable people and that doesn't just include faculty in their various disciplines. Staff and administrative personnel at your school can advise you on everything from trends in college admissions to local crime statistics.

Look to the local community for expertise and advice as well. Is there a paper to be written about declining audiences for Hollywood blockbusters? You couldn't call J. J. Abrams and get through, but you could chat with a few local theater owners or managers to learn what they think about the business. Their insights might change the direction of your project.

Check with librarians.   Campus librarians have lots of experience helping writers find information, steering them toward feasible projects and away from ideas that may not have much intellectual standing. Librarians can't be as specific or directive as, for example, your instructor, but they know what sorts of topics the library's resources will and will not support.

Chat with peers.   Peers aren't really experts, but an honest classroom conversation with fellow students can be an eye-opening experience. You'll probably see a wide spectrum of opinions (if the discussion is frank) and even be surprised by objections you hadn't anticipated to your topic idea or first draft. Peers often have a surprising range of knowledge and, if the group is diverse, your classmates might bring enlightening life experiences to the conversation.

Departmental lists of academic faculty and staff often include information on their areas of special expertise. Women's Studies Department, Kansas State University.

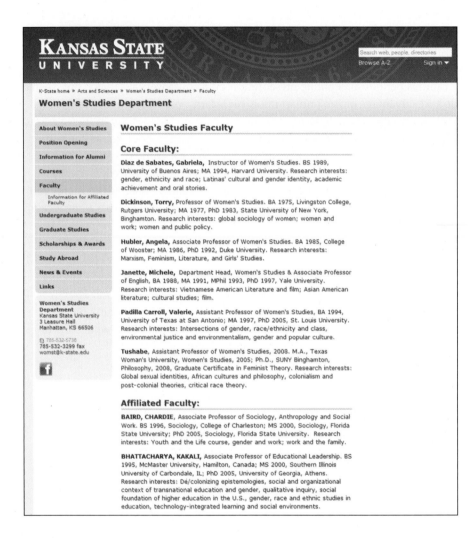

KANSAS STATE
UNIVERSITY

Search web, people, directories
Browse A-Z   Sign in ▼

K-State home » Arts and Sciences » Women's Studies Department » Faculty

Women's Studies Department

- About Women's Studies
- Position Opening
- Information for Alumni
- Courses
- Faculty
  - Information for Affiliated Faculty
- Undergraduate Studies
- Graduate Studies
- Scholarships & Awards
- Study Abroad
- News & Events
- Links

Women's Studies Department
Kansas State University
3 Leasure Hall
Manhattan, KS 66506

785-532-5738
785-532-3299 fax
womst@k-state.edu

Women's Studies Faculty

Core Faculty:

Diaz de Sabates, Gabriela, Instructor of Women's Studies. BS 1989, University of Buenos Aires; MA 1994, Harvard University. Research interests: gender, ethnicity and race; Latinas' cultural and gender identity, academic achievement and oral stories.

Dickinson, Torry, Professor of Women's Studies. BA 1975, Livingston College, Rutgers University; MA 1977, PhD 1983, State University of New York, Binghamton. Research interests: global sociology of women; women and work; women and public policy.

Hubler, Angela, Associate Professor of Women's Studies. BA 1985, College of Wooster; MA 1986, PhD 1992, Duke University. Research interests: Marxism, Feminism, Literature, and Girls' Studies.

Janette, Michele, Department Head, Women's Studies & Associate Professor of English, BA 1988, MA 1991, MPhil 1993, PhD 1997, Yale University. Research interests: Vietnamese American Literature and film; Asian American literature; cultural studies; film.

Padilla Carroll, Valerie, Assistant Professor of Women's Studies, BA 1994, University of Texas at San Antonio; MA 1997, PhD 2005, St. Louis University. Research interests: Intersections of gender, race/ethnicity and class, environmental justice and environmentalism, gender and popular culture.

Tushabe, Assistant Professor of Women's Studies, 2008. M.A., Texas Woman's University, Women's Studies, 2005; Ph.D., SUNY Binghamton, Philosophy, 2008, Graduate Certificate in Feminist Theory. Research interests: Global sexual identities, African cultures and philosophy, colonialism and post-colonial theories, critical race theory.

Affiliated Faculty:

BAIRD, CHARDIE, Associate Professor of Sociology, Anthropology and Social Work. BS 1996, Sociology, College of Charleston; MS 2000, Sociology, Florida State University; PhD 2005, Sociology, Florida State University. Research interests: Youth and the Life course, gender and work; work and the family.

BHATTACHARYA, KAKALI, Associate Professor of Educational Leadership. BS 1995, McMaster University, Hamilton, Canada; MS 2000, Southern Illinois University of Carbondale, IL; PhD 2005, University of Georgia, Athens. Research interests: Dé/colonizing epistemologies, social and organizational context of transnational education and gender, qualitative inquiry, social foundation of higher education in the U.S., gender, race and ethnic studies in education, technology-integrated learning and social environments.

Your Turn   If you were asked to identify yourself as an expert on a subject, what would it be? Don't consider academic subjects only. Think about any areas or activities about which you could confidently offer reliable advice. Make a list and share it with your classmates. Do their lists give you additional ideas about the kinds of expertise you may possess?

1 Bring materials with you, including the assignment, previous drafts or outlines, comments from your instructor if you have any, a pen, and a notebook.

2 Be actively involved during the session, and arrive with specific goals in mind. Your tutor may ask questions about your writing process and your paper. Be prepared to think about and respond to your tutor's suggestions.

3 Keep revising. While the tutor may be able to help you with some aspects of your writing, you are ultimately responsible for the finished paper — and your grade.

23

Writer's Block

tackle hard
stuff

Waiting until the last minute to write a paper hasn't been defined as a medical problem yet. But give it time. Already a condition called *executive dysfunction* describes the inability of some children and adults to plan, organize, pace, and complete tasks. No doubt we've all experienced some of its symptoms, describing the state as *procrastination* when it comes to doing the laundry and *writer's block* when it applies to finishing papers on time.

Getting writing done isn't hard because the process is painful, but rather because it is so fragile and vulnerable to ridiculous excuses and distractions. Who hasn't vacuumed a floor or washed a car rather than compose a paragraph? Writing also comes with no guarantees, no necessary connection between labor put in and satisfactory pages churned out.

Like baseball, writing is a game without time limits. When a paper isn't going well, you can stretch into fruitless twelfth and

© Peter Glass/age fotostock.

thirteenth innings with no end in sight. And if you do finish, readers may not like what you have done—even when you know your work is solid and is based on honest reading, observation, and research. Such concerns are enough to give anyone writer's block.

So what do you do when you'd rather crack walnuts with your teeth than write a term paper?

Break the project into parts.   Getting started is usually the hard part for writers simply because the project taken as a whole seems overwhelming. Even a simple one-page position paper can ruin a whole weekend, and a term paper—with its multiple drafts, abstract, notes, bibliography, tables, and graphs—stretches beyond the pale.

But what if, instead of stewing over how much time and energy the whole project will absorb, you divide it into manageable stages? Then you can do the work in chunks and enjoy the success that comes from completing each part. That position paper might be broken down into two, maybe three, less daunting steps: doing the assigned reading; brainstorming the paper; writing the page required. The same procedure makes a research paper less intimidating: You have more elements to manage, but you also have a strategy to finish them.

Set manageable goals.   Unless you are very disciplined, writing projects sop up all the time available for them. Worse, you'll probably expend more energy fretting than working. To gain control, set levelheaded goals for completing the project and stick to them. In other words, don't dedicate a whole Saturday to preparing your résumé or working up a lab report; instead, commit yourself to the full and uninterrupted two hours the task will really take if you sit down and concentrate.

If you have trouble estimating how much time a project may require, consider that it is better to set a goal than to face an open-ended commitment. That's one good reason both instructors and publishers set deadlines.

> Inspiration is wonderful when it happens, but the writer must develop an approach for the rest of the time. . . . The wait is simply too long.

—Leonard Bernstein

Photo by Marion S. Trikusko, *U.S. News & World Report* Magazine Photograph Collection/ Library of Congress, Prints and Photographs Division, LC-U9-24858- 17 (P & P).

Create a calendar.   For complicated assignments that extend over weeks or even months, create a calendar or timeline and stick with it. ○ First break the task into parts and estimate how much time each stage of the paper or other project will take. Knowing your own work habits, you can draw on past experiences with similar assignments to construct a feasible plan. You'll feel better once you've got a road map that leads to completion.

Don't draw up a schedule so elaborate that you build in failure by trying to manage too many events. Assume that some stages, especially research or drafting, may take more time than you originally expect. But do stick to your schedule, even if it means starting a draft with research still remaining or cutting off the drafting process to allow time for necessary revisions.

Limit distractions.   Put yourself in a place that encourages writing and minimizes any temptations that might pull you away from your work. Schedule a specific time for writing and give it priority over all other activities, from paying your bills to feeding the dog. (On second thought, feed that dog to stop the barking.) Log off your Facebook and Twitter accounts, turn off your cell phone, start writing, and don't stop for an hour. Really.

Do the parts you like first.   Movies aren't filmed in sequence and papers don't have to be written that way either. Compose those sections of a project that feel ready to go or interest you most. You can fix the transitions later to make the paper feel seamless, the way movie editors cut diverse scenes into coherent films. Once you have whole pages in hand, you'll be more inclined to keep working on a paper: The project suddenly seems manageable.

Write a zero draft.   When you are *really* blocked, try a zero draft—that is, a version of the paper composed in one sitting, virtually nonstop. The process may resemble freewriting, but this time you aren't trawling for topic ideas. You've already done the necessary background reading and research, and so you're primed to write. You might even have a thesis and an outline. All you lack is the confidence to turn all this preparation into coherent sentences. Repress your inhibitions by writing relentlessly, without pausing to reread and

plan a
project p. 436

review your stuff. Keep at it for several *hours* if need be. You can do it—just imagine you're writing a timed exam. ○

The draft you produce won't be elegant (though you might surprise yourself) and some spots will be rough indeed. But keep pushing until you've finished a full text, from introduction to conclusion. Set this version aside, delaying any revision for a few hours or even days. Then, instead of facing an empty tablet or screen, you will have full pages of prose to work with.

Reward yourself.   People respond remarkably well to incentives, so promise yourself some prize correlated to the writing task you face. Finishing a position paper is probably worth a pizza. A term paper might earn you dinner and a movie. A dissertation is worth a used Honda Civic.

Peter Dazeley/Getty Images.

> **Your Turn**   Do you have a good writer's block story to share? You might describe an odd thing you have done rather than start a paper—especially one that might seem far more arduous than putting words down on a page. Or maybe you have figured out an infallible method for overcoming procrastination. Or you have endured a roommate's endless excuses for failing to complete a writing assignment. Tell your story in a paragraph or two, which you will start writing *now*.

understand essay
exams p. 252

Shaping & Drafting

part four

Need help developing your ideas? See p. 329. / Need style help? See p. 398.

24 Thesis

make a claim

Offering a thesis is a move as necessary and, eventually, as instinctive to writers as stepping on a clutch before shifting used to be to drivers. No thesis, no forward motion.

A *thesis* is a statement in which a writer identifies or suggests the specific idea that will give focus to a paper. Typically, the thesis appears in an opening paragraph or section, but it may also emerge as the paper unfolds. In some cases, it may not be stated in classic form until the very conclusion. A thesis can be complex enough to require several sentences to explain, or a single sentence might suffice. But a thesis will be in the writing somewhere.

How do you write and frame a thesis? Consider the following advice.

Compose a complete sentence. Simple phrases might identify topic areas, even intriguing ones, but they don't make specific claims that provoke thinking and then require support. Sentences do. ⊙ Neither of the following phrases comes close to providing direction for a paper.

> Human trafficking in the United States
>
> Reasons for global warming

Make a significant claim or assertion. *Significant* here means that the statement stimulates discussion or inquiry. You want to give an audience a reason to spend time with your writing by making a point or raising an issue worth exploring.

help with common
errors p. 566

Until communities recognize that human trafficking persists in parts of the United States, immigrant communities will be exploited by the practice.

Global warming won't stop until industrial nations either lower their standards of living or admit the need for more nuclear power.

Write a declarative sentence, not a question.   Questions do focus attention, but they are often too broad to give direction to a paper. A humdrum question acting as a thesis can invite superficial or even sarcastic responses. So, while you might use a question to introduce a topic (or to launch your own research), don't rely on it to carry a well-developed and complex claim in a paper. There are exceptions to this guideline: Provocative questions often give direction to personal and exploratory writing.

Expect your thesis to mature.   Your initial thesis will usually expand and grow more complicated as you learn more about a subject. That's natural. But don't believe the myth that a satisfactory thesis must be a statement that breaks a subject into three parts. Theses that follow this pattern often read like shopping lists, with only vague connections between the ideas presented.

ORIGINAL THESIS

Crime in the United States has declined because more people are in prison, the population is growing older, and DNA testing has made it harder to get away with murder.

When you slip into an easy pattern like this, look for connections between the points you have identified and then explore the truth. The result can sometimes be a far more compelling thesis.

REVISED THESIS

It is **much more likely** that crime in the United States has declined because more people are in prison **than because** the population is growing older or DNA testing has made it harder to get away with murder.

Introduce a thesis early in a project.   This sound guideline applies especially to academic projects and term papers. Instructors usually want to know up front what the point of a report or argument will be. Whether phrased as a single sentence or several, a thesis typically needs one or more paragraphs to provide background and contexts for its claim. Here's the thesis (highlighted in yellow) of Andrew Kleinfeld and Judith Kleinfeld's essay "Go Ahead, Call Us Cowboys," following several sentences that offer the necessary lead-in.

> Everywhere, Americans are called *cowboys*. On foreign tongues, the reference to America's Western rural laborers is an insult. Cowboys, we are told, plundered the earth, arrogantly rode roughshod over neighbors, and were addicted to mindless violence. So some of us hang our heads in shame. We shouldn't. The cowboy is in fact our Homeric hero, an archetype that sticks because there's truth in it.

Or state a thesis late in a project.   In high school, you may have heard that the thesis statement is *always* the last sentence in the first paragraph. That may be so in conventional five-paragraph essays, but you'll rarely be asked to follow so predictable a pattern in college or elsewhere.

In fact, it is not unusual, especially in some arguments, for a paper to build toward a thesis—and that statement may not appear until the final paragraph or sentence. ○ Such a strategy makes sense when a claim might not be convincing or rhetorically effective if stated baldly at the opening of the piece. Bret Stephens uses this strategy in an essay titled "Just Like Stalingrad" to debunk frequent comparisons between former President George W. Bush and either Hitler or Stalin. Stephens's real concern turns out to be not these exaggerated comparisons themselves but rather what happens to language when it is abused by sloppy writers. The final two paragraphs of his essay summarize this case and, arguably, lead up to a thesis in the very last sentence of the piece—more rhetorically convincing there because it comes as something of a surprise.

> Care for language is more than a concern for purity. When one describes President Bush as a fascist, what words remain for real fascists? When one describes Fallujah as Stalingrad-like, how can we express, in the words that remain to the language, what Stalingrad was like?
>
> George Orwell wrote that the English language "becomes ugly and inaccurate because our thoughts are foolish, but the slovenliness of our language makes it easier for us to have foolish thoughts." In taking care with language, we take care of ourselves.
>
> — *Wall Street Journal*, June 23, 2004

understand
argument p. 66

Write a thesis to fit your audience and purpose.   Almost everything you write will have a purpose and a point (see the following table), but not every piece will have a formal thesis. In professional and scientific writing, readers want to know your claim immediately. For persuasive and exploratory writing, you might prefer to keep readers intrigued or have them track the path of your thinking, and delay the thesis until later.

Type of Assignment	Thesis or Point
Narratives	Thesis is usually implied, not stated.
Reports	Thesis usually previews material or explains its purpose. (See thesis example on p. 59.)
Arguments	Thesis makes an explicit and arguable claim. (See thesis example on p. 72.)
Evaluations	Thesis makes an explicit claim of value based on criteria of evaluation. (See thesis example on p. 123.)
Causal analyses	Thesis asserts or denies an explanatory or causal relationship, based on an analysis of evidence. (See thesis example on p. 147.)
Proposals	Thesis offers a proposal for action. (See thesis example on p. 165.)
Literary analyses	Thesis explains the point of the analysis. (See thesis example on p. 207.)
Rhetorical analyses	Thesis explains the point of the analysis. (See thesis example on p. 233.)
Essay examinations	Thesis previews the entire answer, like a mini-outline. (See thesis example on p. 257.)
Position papers	Thesis makes specific assertion about reading or issue raised in class. (See thesis example on p. 262.)
Annotated bibliographies	Each item may include a statement that describes or evaluates a source. (See example on p. 270.)
Synthesis papers	Thesis summarizes and paraphrases different sources on a specific topic. (See thesis example on p. 280.)
E-mails	Subject line may function as thesis or title. (See thesis example on p. 287.)
Business letters	Thesis states the intention for writing. (See thesis example on p. 293.)
Résumés	"Career objective" may function as a thesis. (See thesis example on p. 301.)
Personal statements	May state an explicit purpose or thesis or lead readers to inferences about qualifications. (See thesis example on p. 309.)
Portfolios	Various items may include a thesis, especially any summary reflections on work presented or done. (See thesis example on p. 320.)
Oral reports	Introduction or preview slide describes purpose. (See thesis example on p. 329.)

Your Turn   Transform two or three of the following song titles into full-blown thesis statements that might be suitable in an academic paper or newspaper op-ed piece. If these titles don't inspire you, start with several song, album, or movie titles of your own choosing. Be sure that your theses are full, declarative sentences that make a significant assertion.

"Taxman"	"Lost in the Supermarket"
"Stand by Your Man"	"Bleed American"
"Share the Ride"	"Especially in Michigan"
"Waiting on the World to Change"	"I Turn My Camera On"
"This Land Is Your Land"	"Someone Else's Problem"
"Concrete and Barbed Wire"	"Let the Idiot Speak"
"The Times They Are A-Changin'"	"Be True to Your School"

Strategies 25

develop a draft

Strategies are patterns of writing that you will use in many situations and across many genres. This chapter looks at some of these essential tools, such as description, division, classification, definition, and comparison/contrast. While you may sometimes write "descriptions" for their own sake, or you may "compare and contrast" movies, smartphones, or college majors just for the heck of it, mostly you will draw upon these modes of writing to serve some larger purpose: to tell a story, clarify a point, or move an argument forward.

Use description to set a scene. Descriptions, which use language to re-create physical scenes and impressions, can be impressive enough to stand on their own. But you'll often use them to support other kinds of writing—perhaps you'll write a descriptive sentence to set the scene in a narrative or you'll develop a cluster of paragraphs full of concrete details to enliven a historical event in a term paper. Writers adapt descriptions to particular situations. Your depiction of an apparatus in a lab report might be cold and technical, while a novelist might describe a scene just as factually yet suggest a whole lot more, as in the following paragraph.

> *Malpais,* translated literally from the Spanish, means "bad country." In New Mexico, it signifies specifically those great expanses of lava flow which make black patches on the map of the state. The malpais of the Checkerboard country lies just below Mount Taylor, having been produced by the same volcanic fault that, a millennium

earlier, had thrust the mountain fifteen thousand feet into the sky. Now the mountain has worn down to a less spectacular eleven thousand feet and relatively modern eruptions from cracks at its base have sent successive floods of melted basalt flowing southward for forty miles to fill the long valley between Cebolleta Mesa and the Zuni Mountains.

—Tony Hillerman, *People of Darkness*

Descriptions like this always involve selection. Just as a photographer carefully frames a subject, you have to decide which elements (visual, aural, tactile, and so on) in a scene will convey the situation most accurately, efficiently, or memorably and then turn them into words. Think nouns first, and only then modifiers: Adjectives and adverbs are essential, but it's easy to ruin a description by overdressing it. Be specific, tangible, and honest. ○

A smart procedure is to write down everything you want to include in a descriptive passage and then cut out any words or phrases not pulling their weight. Be sure to sketch a scene that a reader can imagine easily, providing directions for the eyes and mind. The following descriptive paragraphs are from the opening of a student's account of a trip she made to South Africa: Notice how lean and specific her sentences are, full of details that tell a story all on their own.

> In Soweto, I am seventeen, curious, and in the largest shantytown in the world, so many thousands of miles away from my home. Streets are dusty, houses are made of cinderblock, and their yards are pressed-flat dirt. If there is grass, there is no way to see the trails of a snake.
>
> Doors to homes are rare and inside I can see tired grandmothers with babies on their curved backs making spicy *potjieko* over smoky, single-burner stoves. Skinny cats stretch out in the sunshine. Every few homes has a flat-screen TV, shockingly out of place, wearing a veil of dust. They were stolen.
>
> Soweto spreads over forty miles and nearly one million people call it home. It is a striking sight to see so close to the upscale suburbs of Johannesburg. There are row upon row of homemade houses, punctuated by schools and churches with fresh coats of paint from well-meaning Westerners. Lean-to shacks on the corner sell cucumbers and *naartjes*. The ground is flat for as far as I can see.
>
> —Lily Parish, "Sala Kahle, South Africa"

improve your
sentences p. 412

Use division to divide a subject.   This strategy of writing is so common you might not notice it. A division involves no more than breaking a subject into its major components or enumerating its parts. In a report for an art history class, you might present a famous cathedral by listing and then describing its major architectural features, one by one: facade, nave, towers, windows, and so on. Or in a sports column on the Big Ten's NCAA football championship prospects, you could just run through its roster of twelve teams. That's a reasonable structure for a review, given the topic.

Division also puts ideas into coherent relationships that make them easier for readers to understand and use. The challenge comes when a subject doesn't break apart as neatly as a tangerine. Then you have to decide which parts are essential and which are subordinate. Divisions of this sort are more than mechanical exercises: They require your clear understanding of a subject. For example, in organizing a Web site for your school or student organization, you'd probably start by deciding which aspects of the institution merit top-tier placement on the home page. ○ Such a decision will then shape the entire project.

Left: Provided by Binghamton University. *Right:* Oklahoma State University.

learn media
conventions p. 542

Use classification to sort objects or ideas by consistent principles.
Classification divides subjects up not by separating their parts but by clustering their elements according to meaningful or consistent principles. Just think of all the ways by which people can be classified:

Body type: endomorph, ectomorph, mesomorph

Hair color: black, brown, blond, red, gray, other

Weight: underweight, normal, overweight, obese

Sexual orientation: straight, bisexual, gay/lesbian, transgender

Race: black, Asian, white, other

Religion: Hindu, Buddhist, Muslim, Christian, Jew, other, no religion

Ideally, a principle of classification should apply to every member of the general class studied (in this case, people), and there would be no overlap among the resulting groups. But almost all useful efforts to classify complex phenomena—whether people, things, or ideas—have holes, gaps, or overlaps. Classifying people by religious beliefs, for instance, usually means mentioning the major groups and then lumping tens of millions of other people in a convenient category called "other."

Even scientists who organize everything from natural elements to species of birds run into problems with creatures that cross boundaries (plant or animal?) or discoveries that upset familiar categories. You'll wrestle with such problems routinely when, for instance, you argue about social policy.

Use definition to clarify meaning.   Definitions don't appear only in dictionaries. Like other strategies in this chapter, they occur in many genres. A definition might become the subject of a scientific report (*What is a planet?*), the bone of contention in a legal argument (*How does the statute define* life?), or the framework for a cultural analysis (*Can a comic book be a serious novel?*). In all such cases, writers need to know how to construct valid definitions.

Though definitions come in various forms, the classic dictionary definition is based on principles of classification discussed in the previous section. Typically a term is defined first by placing it in a general class. Then its distinguishing features or characteristics are enumerated, separating it from other members of the larger class. You can see the principle operating in this comic paragraph, which first fits "dorks" into the general class of "somebody," that is to say, a *person*, and then claims two distinguishing characteristics.

> It's important to define what I truly mean by "dork," just so he or she doesn't get casually lumped in with "losers," "burnouts" and "lone psychopath bullies." To me, the dork is somebody **who didn't fit in at school** and who **therefore sought consolation in a particular field** — computers, *Star Trek*, theater, heavy metal, medieval war reenactments, fantasy, sports trivia, even isolation sports like cross-country and ice skating.
> —Ian R. Williams, "Twilight of the Dorks?" *Salon.com,* October 23, 2003

In much writing, definitions become crucial when a question is raised about whether a particular object does or does not fit into a particular group. You engage in this kind of debate when you argue about what is or isn't a sport, a hate crime, an act of terrorism, and so on. In outline form, the structure of such a discussion looks like this:

Defined group:
—General class
—Distinguishing characteristic 1
—Distinguishing characteristic 2 . . .

Controversial term
—**Is / is not in the general class**
—**Does / does not share characteristic 1**
—**Does / does not share characteristic 2** . . .

Controversial term is/is not in the defined group

Use comparison and contrast to show similarity and difference.   We seem to think better when we place ideas or objects side by side. So it's not surprising that comparisons and contrasts play a role in all sorts of writing, especially reports, arguments, and analyses. Paragraphs are routinely organized to show how things are alike or different.

Adam Zyglis, *The Buffalo News* (blogs.buffalonews/adam-zyglis).

> The late 1960s and early 1970s were a time of cultural conflict, a battle between what I have called the beautiful people and the dutiful people. While Manhattan glitterati thronged Leonard Bernstein's apartment to celebrate the murderous Black Panthers, ordinary people in the outer boroughs and the far-flung suburbs of New Jersey like Hamilton Township were going to work, raising their families, and teaching their children to obey lawful authority and work their way up in the world.
>
> — Michael Barone, "The Beautiful People vs. the Dutiful People,"
> *U.S. News & World Report*, January 16, 2006

Much larger projects can be built on similar structures of comparison and/or contrast.

To keep extended comparisons on track, the simplest structure is to evaluate one subject at a time, running through its features completely before moving on to the next. Let's say you decided to contrast economic conditions in France and Germany. Here's how such a paper might look in a scratch outline if you focused on the countries one at a time. ○

France and Germany: An Economic Report Card
I.   France
     A. Rate of growth
     B. Unemployment rate
     C. Productivity

order ideas
p. 377

D. Gross national product
E. Debt
II.   Germany
A. Rate of growth
B. Unemployment rate
C. Productivity
D. Gross national product
E. Debt

The disadvantage of evaluating subjects one at a time is that actual comparisons, for example, of rates of employment in the outline above, might appear pages apart. So in some cases, you might prefer a comparison/contrast structure that looks at features point by point. O

France and Germany: An Economic Report Card
I.   Rate of growth
A. France
B. Germany
II.   Unemployment rate
A. France
B. Germany
III. Productivity
A. France
B. Germany
IV.   Gross national product
A. France
B. Germany
V.   Debt
A. France
B. Germany

Your Turn   In a paper you have recently written (or an article you've been asked to read), point out all the examples you can find of the strategies described in this chapter: description, division, classification, definition, and comparison/contrast. Does the strategy dominate the piece — as comparison/contrast might in an essay evaluating different smartphones or describing law schools? Or is the use of the strategy incidental, for example, just a line or two of description or a quick definition offered to clarify a point?

understand
evaluations p. 100

26 Organization

shape your
work

To describe the structure of their projects, writers often use metaphors or other figures of speech. They visualize their work in terms of links, frames, templates, maps, or even skeletons. Such images help writers keep their emerging ideas on track. Just as important, familiar patterns of organization make life easier for readers who come to a project wondering how its ideas and elements will fit together.

In Parts 1 and 2, you'll find specific suggestions for structuring a wide variety of writing genres. The following advice on organization applies more generally.

Examine model documents. Many types of writing are highly conventional—which simply means that they follow predictable patterns and formulas. So when you are asked to compose in a new genre, study the arrangement of several examples. Some structural features are immediately obvious, such as headings or introductory and concluding sections. But look for more subtle moves too—for example, many editorials first describe a problem, then blame someone for it, and finally make a comment or offer a comparison. Good models will point you in the right direction.

Sketch out a plan or sequence. To give direction to a new project, try starting with a scratch (or informal) outline, even a rough one. You will probably discover relationships between your ideas (sequence, similarity, difference) or quickly note gaps or flaws in your thinking. Just as important, creating a structure makes a writing project suddenly seem more doable because you've broken a complex task into smaller, more manageable parts.

Technology can also make it easier to organize a project. Consider how effortlessly you can move the slides in a PowerPoint presentation until you find the most effective order. Yet pen and paper work almost as well, whether you use note cards to map out a senior thesis or draw an outline to clarify matters in a comparison/contrast piece. O

Provide cues or signals for readers.   Just because you understand how the parts of your project fit together, don't assume readers will. You have to give them cues—which come in various forms, including titles, headings, captions, and, especially, transitional words and phrases. For example, in a narrative you might include transitional words to mark the passage of time (*next, then, before, afterward*). Or, if you organize a project according to a principle of magnitude,

How many patterns of organization can you find in this storeroom of a hospital intensive care unit? © Justin Paget/ Corbis.

think
visually p. 557

you might give readers signals that clearly show a change from *best* to *worst*, *cheapest* to *most expensive*, *most common species* to *endangered species*. And if you are writing to inform or report, you might also rely heavily on visuals to help make your point. ○

Deliver on your commitments.   This is a basic principle of organization. If, for example, you promise in an introductory paragraph to offer two reasons in support of a claim, you need to offer two clearly identifiable reasons in that paper or readers will feel that they missed something. But commitments are broader than that: Narratives ordinarily lead somewhere, perhaps to a climax; editorials offer opinions; proposals offer and defend new ideas; evaluations make judgments. You can depart from these structural expectations, but you should do so knowing what readers expect and anticipating how they might react to your straying from the formula.

order
ideas p. 377

Outlines

Despite what you may believe, outlines are designed to make writing easier, not harder. You'll feel more confident when you begin a project with a plan. The trick is to start simple and let outlines evolve to fit your needs.

Start with scratch outlines. After researching a topic, many writers sketch out a quick, informal outline—the verbal equivalent of the clever mechanical idea hastily drawn on a cocktail napkin. Good ideas do often emerge from simple, sometimes crude, notions that suddenly make sense when seen on paper. Both the Internet and the structure of the DNA molecule can be traced to such visualizations.

order ideas

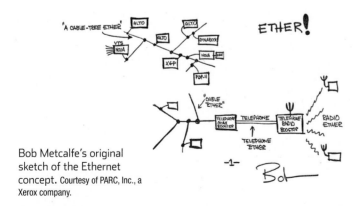

Bob Metcalfe's original sketch of the Ethernet concept. Courtesy of PARC, Inc., a Xerox company.

List key ideas.   Scratch outlines usually begin with ragged lists. You simply write down your preliminary thoughts and key ideas so you can see exactly how they relate, merging any that obviously overlap. Keep these notes brief but specific, using words and phrases rather than complete sentences. At this point, you might find yourself posing questions too. In fact, your initial scratch outline might resemble a mildly edited brainstorming list (see Chapter 19). Here's the first stage of a scratch outline addressing a topic much discussed in academia: the impact that massive open online courses (MOOCs) may have on higher education. (If you are unfamiliar with the term, you might do a quick Web search.)

Massive open online courses (MOOCs)

Taught by top-notch professors from prestigious schools

First-rate MOOCs are complex — expensive to produce

Rely on "superstar" professors

Can reach unlimited numbers of students across the country

How different from old-style correspondence or online courses?

Cheap: no classrooms; less administration; less "brick and mortar"

Less interaction with faculty

No face-to-face work with classmates

Available anytime and anywhere

Education through watching slick videos

Promise equal access to first-rate educational opportunities

Could replace large core courses at many schools

Use interactive online activities

Might drive down the high cost of postsecondary education

Differences between learning facts and gaining knowledge?

Very high attrition rate in early MOOCs

Depersonalized and dehumanizing: no real faculty-student interaction

A sprawling list like this could easily grow even longer, so you need to get it under control. To do that, you can apply the three principles that make outlining such a powerful tool of organization: *relationship*, *subordination*, and *sequence*.

Look for relationships.   Examine the initial items on your list and try grouping *like* with *like*—or look for opposites and contrasts. Experiment with various arrangements or clusters. In the scratch outline above, for example, you might decide that the items fall into three basic categories. A first cluster explains what MOOCs do, a second cluster focuses on their advantages, while a third and lengthier cluster considers their weaknesses.

> What MOOCs do
>
> Taught by top-notch professors from prestigious schools
>
> Use video lectures and interactive online activities
>
> Available anytime and anywhere
>
> Can reach unlimited numbers of students across the country
>
> Strengths of MOOCs
>
> Cheap: no classrooms; less administration; less "brick and mortar"
>
> Promise equal access to first-rate educational opportunities
>
> Could replace large core courses at many schools
>
> Might drive down the high cost of postsecondary education
>
> Weaknesses of MOOCs
>
> How different from old-style correspondence or online courses?
>
> Less interaction with faculty
>
> No face-to-face work with classmates
>
> First-rate MOOCs are complex—expensive to produce
>
> Rely on "superstar" professors
>
> Equate education to watching slick videos
>
> Differences between learning facts and gaining knowledge?
>
> Very high attrition rate in early MOOCs
>
> Depersonalized and dehumanizing: no real faculty-student interaction

Subordinate ideas. In outlines, you routinely divide subjects into topics and subtopics. This means that some ideas belong not only grouped with others but also grouped under them—which is to say, they become a subset within a larger group.

For instance, looking again at the lengthy group of "Weaknesses of MOOCs," you might notice that MOOCs seem to differ from old-style correspondence or online courses chiefly because more money is spent to develop them—an idea you connect to several supporting points, some of which you modify and amplify.

> MOOCs are high-class correspondence courses
>> Rely on well-paid "superstar" professors
>>
>> Require slick videos to keep students entertained
>>
>> Cost more to produce than most schools can afford
>>
>> Narrow the range of academic experiences

Then you notice a second cluster within the "Weaknesses of MOOCs" grouping, one related to your claim that MOOCs are "depersonalized and dehumanizing." Once again, you subordinate some initial points to a broader claim, enlarging and connecting them.

> MOOCs are depersonalized and dehumanizing
>> Support little interaction between online faculty and students
>>
>> Minimize face-to-face work with peers: no true classmates
>>
>> Equate learning facts with gaining knowledge
>>
>> [Consequently?] have a high attrition rate

At this point, you have pushed well beyond a list. You are using the outlining process to explore your ideas and turn them into, in this case, an argument.

Decide on a sequence. Once you have sorted out the patterns within an initial list of ideas, you are ready to arrange them to support a thesis. At this point, you have a great many options, depending on what type of project you are developing—a narrative, a report, an argument, or something else. You might sequence the items chronologically or by magnitude (for example, least to most important). Or you might determine your order rhetorically—by how you want readers to respond.

Continuing to pursue the MOOC project, you could, for example, do a detailed report on these new types of courses, focusing on what MOOCs do—the first cluster in your initial list of relationships. But, given the number of criticisms you generated of this technology, perhaps your heart is in writing an evaluation, one that weighs the strengths of MOOCs against the more numerous weaknesses you have identified. Your working outline, now considerably more formal than a scratch version, might look like the following:

A. What MOOCs are
   1. Highly evolved, technologically sophisticated online college courses
   2. Top professors from prestigious schools
B. What MOOCs aim to do
   1. Offer first-rate course material
   2. Lower the cost of college education
   3. Provide equal access to education for more students
C. What MOOCs really do
   1. Update old-style correspondence courses
      a. Rely on "superstar" model
      b. Use slick videos to keep students entertained
      c. Narrow the range of academic experiences
   2. Depersonalize and dehumanize learning
      a. Support little interaction between online faculty and students
      b. Minimize face-to-face encounters with classmates
      c. Equate learning facts with gaining knowledge

Needless to say, this is but one of many possible takes on this subject, as proponents of MOOCs would be quick to point out.

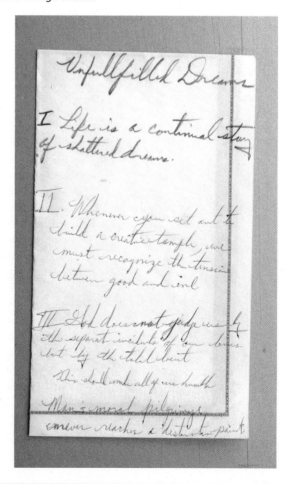

Here's an outline for a sermon titled "Unfulfilled Dreams" from a notebook of Rev. Martin Luther King, Jr.
Frances M. Roberts/Newscom.

Move up to a formal outline.   You may be required to submit a formal out-line with your final paper. When that's the case, be sure to follow the following guidelines—which may help you to detect even more relationships between your ideas:

- Carefully align the headings at every level (see example).

- Be sure to have at least two items at every heading level (I, A, and 1). If you can't find a second item to match the first in a new level of heads, perhaps the new level isn't needed.

- Express all items (except the thesis) as complete and parallel statements (not questions), properly punctuated.

- Position your thesis sentence above the outline, underlined or italicized. Seeing the thesis there may keep you from wandering off-subject.

Thesis: <u>Though massive open online courses (MOOCs) promise to solve the problems of higher education, they are just upgraded versions of older correspondence courses that will dehumanize learning</u>.

I. MOOCs represent the latest trend in higher education.
    A. They use advanced video and Web 2.0 technologies to make sophisti-cated online college courses widely available.
    B. They feature distinguished faculty from top-tier colleges and universities.
II. MOOCs aim to improve higher education.
    A. They make top-rated courses available to vastly more students.
    B. They claim to lower the cost of education.
       1. They reduce the number of faculty required.
       2. They eliminate many "brick and mortar" costs on campus.
    C. They equalize educational opportunity.
III. MOOCs depersonalize and dehumanize the process of education.
    A. Online lectures remove faculty from the lives of students.
       1. Professors in MOOCs become performers for students, not mentors.
       2. Students cannot personally question or challenge instructors.
    B. Students take MOOCs in isolation, without interaction with classmates.
    C. MOOCs encourage students to equate learning facts with becoming educated.

Paragraphs 28

Paragraphs are a practical invention, created to make long blocks of prose easier to read by dividing them up. Here are some helpful ways to think about them.

Make sure paragraphs lead somewhere.   Typically, you'll place a topic sentence at the beginning of a paragraph to introduce a claim that the rest of the paragraph will develop. Ron Rosenbaum's opener leaves little doubt about the direction his paragraph will take. ○

develop ideas

> The hysterical crusade against fat has become a veritable witch hunt. With New York City Mayor Michael Bloomberg's ban on supersize sodas (now temporarily thwarted) and the first lady's campaign to push leaves and twigs (i.e., salad) on reluctant school children — all in the name of stamping out obesity — it is fat-shaming time in America. Yes, there are countertrends, like the pro-fat TV shows of Paula Deen and Guy Fieri. But in the culture at large, eating that kind of fat has become a class-based badge of shame: redneck food (which I say as someone who likes rednecks and redneck food). It isn't food for someone who drives a Prius to Pilates class.
>
> — Ron Rosenbaum, "Let Them Eat Fat," *Wall Street Journal*, March 15, 2013

Sometimes, however, you may wait until the concluding sentences to divulge your point, or you may even weave a key idea into the fabric of the entire paragraph. Whatever your strategy, all

develop a
statement p. 362

paragraphs should do serious work: introduce a subject, move a narrative forward, offer a new argument or claim, provide support for a claim already made, contradict another point, amplify an idea, furnish more examples, even bring discussion to an end. A paragraph has to do something that readers see as purposeful and connected to what comes before and after.

Develop ideas adequately.   Instructors who insist that paragraphs run a minimum number of sentences (say 6–10) are usually just tired of students who don't back up claims with enough evidence. O In fact, experienced writers don't count sentences when they build paragraphs. Instead, they develop a sense for paragraph length, matching the swell of their ideas to the habits of their intended readers.

Consider the following paragraph, which describes the last moments of the final Apollo moon mission in December 1972. The paragraph might be reduced to a single sentence: *All that remained of the 363-foot* Apollo 17 *launch vehicle was a 9-foot capsule recovered in the ocean.* But what would be lost? The pleasure of the full paragraph resides in the details the writer musters to support the final sentence, which reveals his point.

> A powerful Sikorsky Sea King helicopter, already hovering nearby as they [the *Apollo 17* crew] hit the water, retrieved the astronauts and brought them to the carrier, where the spacecraft was recovered shortly later. The recovery crew saw not a gleaming instrument of exotic perfection, but a blasted, torn, and ragged survivor, its titanic strength utterly exhausted, a husk now, a shell. The capsule they hauled out of the ocean was all that remained of the *Apollo 17* Saturn V. The journey had spent, incinerated, smashed, or blistered into atoms every other part of the colossal, 363-foot white rocket, leaving only this burnt and brutalized 9-foot capsule. A great shining army had set out over the horizon, and a lone squadron had returned, savaged beyond recognition, collapsing into the arms of its rescuers, dead. Such was the price of reaching for another world.
>
> — David West Reynolds, *Apollo: The Epic Journey to the Moon*

Organize paragraphs logically.   It would be surprising if paragraphs didn't use the same structures found in full essays: thesis and support, division, classification, narrative. But it's ideas that drive the shape of paragraphs, not patterns

understand
arguments p. 66

of organization. Writers don't puzzle over whether their next paragraph should follow a comparison/contrast or cause/effect plan. They just write it, making sure it makes a point and appeals to readers.

In fact, individual paragraphs in any longer piece can be organized many different ways. And because paragraphs are relatively short, you usually see their patterns unfold right before your eyes. The following two passages are from an essay by Jon Katz titled "Do Dogs Think?" The paragraphs within them follow structures Katz needs at that given moment.

Blue, Heather's normally affectionate and obedient Rottweiler, began tearing up the house shortly after Heather went back to work as an accountant after several years at home. The contents of the trash cans were strewn all over the house. A favorite comforter was destroyed. Then Blue began peeing all over Heather's expensive new living-room carpet and systematically ripped through cables and electrical wires.

> *Narrative* paragraph describes changes in Blue's behavior.

Lots of dogs get nervous when they don't know what's expected of them, and when they get anxious, they can also grow restless. Blue hadn't had to occupy time alone before. Dogs can get unnerved by this. They bark, chew, scratch, destroy. Getting yelled at and punished later doesn't help: The dog probably knows it's doing something wrong, but it has no idea what. Since there's nobody around to correct behaviors when the dog is alone, how could the dog know which behavior is the problem? Which action was wrong?

> Katz uses *causal* pattern to explore Blue's behavioral problem.

I don't believe that dogs act out of spite or that they can plot retribution, though countless dog owners swear otherwise. To punish or deceive requires the perpetrator to understand that his victim or object has a particular point of view and to consciously work to manipulate or thwart it. That requires mental processes dogs don't have.

> A simple *statement/ proof* structure organizes this paragraph.

Why will Clementine come instantly if she's looking at me, but not if she's sniffing deer droppings? Is it because she's being stubborn or, as many people tell me, going through "adolescence"? Or because, when following her keen predatory instincts, she simply doesn't hear me? Should my response be to tug at her leash or yell? Maybe I should be sure we've established eye contact before I give her a command, or better yet, offer a liver treat as an alternative to whatever's distracting her. But how do I establish eye contact when her nose is buried? Can I cluck or bark? Use a whistle or hoot like an owl?

> Taken together, the two paragraphs in this passage follow a *problem/solution* structure common in proposal arguments.

I've found that coughing, of all things, fascinates her, catches her
attention, and makes her head swivel, after which she responds. If you walk
with us, you will hear me clearing my throat repeatedly. What can I say? It
works. She looks at me, comes to me, gets rewarded.

— *Slate.com*, October 6, 2005

Use paragraphs to manage transitions.   Paragraphs often give direction
to a paper. An opening paragraph, for example, can outline the content of a report or set the scene for a narrative. ○ In lengthy projects, you might need full
paragraphs at critical junctures to summarize what has been covered and then
send readers off in new directions.

You might even use very brief paragraphs—sometimes just a sentence or
two long—to punctuate a piece by drawing attention to a turn in your thinking
or offering a strong judgment. You've probably seen paragraphs that consist of
nothing more than an indignant "Nonsense!" or a sarcastic "Go figure." There's
a risk in penning paragraphs with so much attitude, but it's an option when the
subject calls for it.

Design paragraphs for readability.   It's common sense: Paragraph breaks
work best when they coincide with shifts of thought within the writing itself.
When they meet a new paragraph, readers assume that your ideas have moved
in some (sometimes small) way. But paragraphs are often at the mercy of a
text's physical environment as well. When you read a news items on the Web,
the short paragraphs used in those single-column stories look fine. But hit the
"print this article" button and the text suddenly sprawls across the screen,
becoming difficult to read.

The point? You should adjust the length and shape of paragraphs to the
space where your words will appear.

shape a
beginning p. 391

Transitions 29

What exactly makes words, sentences, and ideas flow from paragraph to paragraph as fluidly as Michael Phelps slipping through the water? *Transitional words and phrases*, many writers would reply—thinking of words such as *and, but, however, neither . . . nor, first . . . second . . . third*, and so on. Placed where readers need them, these connecting words make a paper read smoothly. But they are only part of the story.

Almost any successful piece of writing is held together by more devices than most writers can consciously juggle. A few of the ties—such as connections between pronouns and their referents—are almost invisible and seem to take care of themselves. Here are some guidelines for making smooth transitions between ideas in paragraphs and sections of your writing.

© Steve Terrill/Corbis.

Common Transitions

Connection or Consequence	Contrast	Correlation	Sequence or Time	Indication
and	but	if . . . then	first . . . second	this
or	yet	either . . . or	and then	that
so	however	from . . . to	initially	there
therefore	nevertheless		subsequently	for instance
moreover	on the contrary		before	for example
consequently	despite		after	in this case
hence	still		until	
	although		next	
			in conclusion	

Use appropriate transitional words and phrases.   There's nothing complicated or arcane about them: You'll recognize every word in any list of transitions. But be aware that they have different functions and uses, with subtle distinctions even between words as close in meaning as *but* and *yet*.

Transitional words are often found at the beginnings of sentences and paragraphs simply because that's the place where readers expect a little guidance. There are no rules, per se, for positioning transitions—though they can be set off from the rest of the sentence with commas.

Use the right word or phrase to show time or sequence.   Readers often need specific words or phrases to help keep events in order. Such expressions can simply mark off stages: *first, second, third.* Or they might help readers keep track of more complicated passages of time.

Use sentence structure to connect ideas.   When you build sentences with similar structures, readers will infer that the ideas in them are related. Devices you can use to make this kind of linkage include *parallelism* ○ and *repetition*.

In the following example, the first three paragraphs of James P. Gannon's "America's Quiet Anger," you can see both strategies at work, setting up an emotional argument that continues in this pattern for another three paragraphs. Parallel items are highlighted.

parallelism
p. 597

There is a quiet anger boiling in America.

It is the anger of millions of hardworking citizens who pay their bills, send in their income taxes, maintain their homes, and repay their mortgage loans — and see their government reward those who do not.

It is the anger of small town and Middle American folks who have never been to Manhattan, who put their savings in a community bank and borrow from a local credit union, who watch Washington lawmakers and presidents of both parties hand billions in taxpayer bailouts to the reckless Wall Street titans who brought down the economy in 2008.

—*American Spectator*, March 20, 2010

Pay attention to nouns and pronouns.   Understated transitions in a piece can occur between pronouns and their antecedents, but make sure the relationships between the nouns and pronouns are clear. ○ And, fortunately, readers usually don't mind encountering a pronoun over and over—except maybe *I*. Note how effortlessly Adam Nicolson moves between *George Abbot*, *he*, and *man* in the following paragraph from *God's Secretaries* (2003), in which he describes one of the men responsible for the King James translation of the Bible:

George Abbot was perhaps the ugliest of them all, a morose, intemperate man, whose portraits exude a sullen rage. Even in death, he was portrayed on his tomb in Holy Trinity, Guilford, as a man of immense weight, with heavy, wrinkled brow and coldly open, staring eyes. He looks like a bruiser, a man of such conviction and seriousness that anyone would think twice about crossing him. What was it that made George Abbot so angry?

Use synonyms.   Simply by repeating a noun from sentence to sentence, you make an obvious and logical connection within a paper—whether you are naming an object, an idea, or a person. To avoid monotony, vary terms you have to use frequently. But don't strain with archaic or inappropriate synonyms that will distract the reader.

Note the sensible variants on the word *trailer* in the following paragraph.

Hype and hysteria have always been a part of movie advertising, but the frenzy of film trailers today follows a visual style first introduced by music videos in the 1980s. The quick cut is everything, accompanied by a deafening soundtrack. Next time you go to a film, study the three

help with common
errors p. 566

or four previews that precede the main feature. How are these teasers constructed? What are their common features? What emotions or reactions do they raise in you? What might trailers say about the expectations of audiences today?

Use physical devices for transitions.   You know all the ways movies manage transitions between scenes, from quick cuts to various kinds of dissolves. Writing has fewer visual techniques to mark transitions, but they are important. Titles and headings in lab reports, for instance, let your reader know precisely when you are moving from "Methods" to "Results" to "Discussion." In books, you'll encounter chapter breaks as well as divisions within chapters, sometimes marked by asterisks or perhaps a blank space. Seeing these markers, readers expect that the narration is changing in some way. Even the numbers in a list or shaded boxes in a magazine can be effective transitional devices, moving readers from one place to another.

Read a draft aloud to locate weak transitions.   The best way to test your transitions in a paper or project may be to listen to yourself. As you read, mark every point in the paper where you pause, stumble, or find yourself adding a transitional word or phrase not in the original text. Record even the smallest bobble because tiny slips have a way of cascading into bigger problems.

Simone End/Getty Images.

Introductions and Conclusions

30

Introductions and conclusions are among the most important parts of a project. An introduction has to grab and hold a reader's attention while identifying topic and purpose and setting a context. A conclusion has to bring all the parts of a paper together and seal the deal with readers. None of these tasks—which vary according to genre—are easy.

shape a beginning and an ending

Shape an introduction. The opening of some projects must follow a template. Writing a story for a newspaper, you begin by providing essential facts, identifying *who*, *what*, *where*, and *when*. You'll also follow conventions with technical materials (lab reports, research articles, scholarly essays). To get such introductions right, study models of these genres and then imitate their structures.

When not constrained by a template, you have many options for an opening, the most straightforward being simply to announce your project. This blunt approach is common in academic papers where it makes sense to identify a subject and preview your plan for developing it. Quite often, the introductory material leads directly into a thesis or a hypothesis, as in the following student paper:

Paper opens by
identifying its general
topic or theme.

In her novel *Wuthering Heights* (1847), Emily Brontë presents the story of the families of Wuthering Heights and Thrushcross Grange through the seemingly impartial perspective of Nelly Dean, a servant who grows up with the families. Upon closer inspection, however, it becomes apparent that Nelly acts as much more than a bystander in the tragic events taking place around her. In her status as an outsider with influence over the families, Nelly strikingly resembles the Byronic hero Heathcliff and competes with him for power. Although the author depicts Heathcliff as the more overt gothic hero, Brontë allows the reader to infer from Nelly's story

Detailed thesis states
what paper will prove.

her true character and role in the family. The author draws a parallel between Nelly Dean and Heathcliff in their relationships to the Earnshaw family, in their similar roles as tortured heroes, and in their competition for power within their adoptive families.

— Manasi Deshpande, "Servant and Stranger: Nelly and Heathcliff in *Wuthering Heights*"

Reports and arguments may open more slowly, using an introductory section that helps readers appreciate why an issue deserves attention. You might, for example, present an anecdote, describe a trend, or point to some phenomenon readers may not have noticed. Then you can thrash out its significance or implications.

Opening paragraphs can also deliver necessary background information. The trick is always to decide what exactly readers need to know about a subject. Provide too little background information on a subject and readers may find the project confusing. Supply too much context and you lose fans quickly.

And yet, even when readers know a subject well, be sure to supply basic facts about the project. Name names in your introduction, provide accurate titles for works you are discussing, furnish dates, and explain what exactly your subject is. Imagine readers from just slightly outside your target audience who might not instantly recall, for instance, that it was Shakespeare who wrote a play titled *Henry V* or that Edwin "Buzz" Aldrin was the *second* person to walk on the surface of the moon. Don't leave readers guessing. But it's fair game to intrigue them.

So give them reasons to enter your text. Invite them with a compelling incident or provocative story, with a recitation of surprising or intriguing facts, with a dramatic question, with a memorable description or quotation. Naturally, any opening has to be in sync with the material that follows — not outrageously emotional if the argument is sober, not lighthearted and comic if the paper has a serious theme.

Typically, readers use an introduction to determine whether they belong to the audience of the piece. A paper that opens with highly technical language says "specialists only," while a more personal or colloquial style welcomes a broader group. Readers are also making judgments about you in those opening lines, so you can't afford errors of fact or even grammar and usage there. Such slips-ups cloud their impression of all that follows.

One last bit of advice: Don't write an introduction until you're ready. The opening of a project can be notoriously difficult to frame because it does so much work. If you are blocked at the beginning of a project, plunge directly into the body of the paper and see what happens. You can even write the opening section last, after you know precisely where the paper goes. No one will know.

Draw a conclusion.   Like introductions, conclusions serve different purposes and audiences. An e-mail to a professor may need no more of a sign-off than a signature, while a senior thesis could require a whole chapter to wrap things up. In reports and arguments, you typically use the concluding section to summarize what you've covered and draw out the implications. The following is the no-nonsense conclusion of a college report on a childhood developmental disorder, cri du chat syndrome (CDCS). Note that this summary paragraph also leads where many other scientific and scholarly articles do: to a call for additional research.

Even towns sometimes need introductions. Yee haw! Andre Jenny/Newscom.

<table>
<tr><td>

Major point

Major point

Conclusion ties together
main points made in
paper, using transitional
words and phrases.

</td><td>

Though research on CDCS remains far from abundant, existing studies prescribe early and ongoing intervention by a team of specialists, including speech-language pathologists, physical and occupational therapists, various medical and educational professionals, and parents. Such intervention has been shown to allow individuals with CDCS to live happy, long, and full lives. The research, however, indicates that the syndrome affects all aspects of a child's development and should therefore be taken quite seriously. Most children require numerous medical interventions, including surgery (especially to correct heart defects), feeding tubes, body braces, and repeated treatment of infections. Currently, the best attempts are being made to help young children with CDCS reach developmental milestones earlier, communicate effectively, and function as independently as possible. However, as the authors of the aforementioned studies suggest, much more research is needed to clarify the causes of varying degrees of disability, to identify effective and innovative treatments/interventions (especially in the area of education), and to individualize intervention plans.

— Marissa Dahlstrom, "Developmental Disorders: Cri du Chat Syndrome"

</td></tr>
</table>

On other occasions, you will want to finish dramatically and memorably, especially in arguments and personal narratives that seek to influence readers and change opinions. Since final paragraphs are what readers remember, it makes sense to use powerful language. Here's the conclusion of a lengthy personal essay by Shane McNamee on gay marriage that leads up to a poignant political appeal.

<table>
<tr><td>

Deliberate repetition
focuses readers on
serious point.

Conclusion makes direct
appeal to readers,
addressed as *you*.

Final sentence appeals
emotionally through
both images and
language.

</td><td>

Forget for the moment the rainbow flags and pink triangles. Gay pride is not about being homosexual; it's about the integrity and courage it takes to be honest with yourself and your loved ones. It's about spending life with whomever you want and not worrying what the government or the neighbors think. Let's protect that truth, not some rigid view of sexual orientation or marriage. Keep gay marriage out of your church if you like, but if you value monogamy as I do, give me an alternative that doesn't involve dishonesty or a life of loneliness. Many upstanding gay citizens yearn for recognition of their loving, committed relationships. Unless you enjoy being lied to and are ready to send your gay friends and family on a Trail of Queers to a state where gay marriage is legal then consider letting them live as they wish.

—"Protecting What Really Matters"

</td></tr>
</table>

Titles

31

Titles may not strike you as an important aspect of writing, but they can be. Sometimes the struggle to find a good title helps a writer shape a piece or define its main point. Of course, a proper title tells readers what a paper is about and makes searching for the document easier.

Use titles to focus documents. A title that is too broad early on in a project is a sure sign that you have yet to find a manageable topic. If all you have is "Sea Battles in World War II" or "Children in America," you need to do more reading and research. If no title comes to mind at all, it means you don't have a subject. ○ You're still exploring ideas.

For academic papers, titles need be descriptive. Consider these items culled at random from one issue of the *Stanford Undergraduate Research Journal*. As you might guess, scientific papers aimed at knowledgeable specialists have highly technical titles. Titles in the social sciences and humanities are less intimidating but just as focused on providing information about their subjects.

> "Molecular and Morphological Characterization of Two Species of Sea Cucumber, *Parastichopus parvimensis* and *Parastichopus californicus*, in Monterey, CA"
>
> —Christine O'Connell, Alison J. Haupt, Stephen R. Palumbi

name your work

develop a statement p. 362

"Justifiers of the British Opium Trade: Arguments by Parliament, Traders, and the *Times* Leading Up to the Opium War"

—Christine Su

"The Incongruence of the Schopenhauerian Ending in Wagner's *Götterdämmerung*"

—James Locus

Create searchable titles.   For academic or professional papers, a thoughtful title makes sense standing on its own and out of context. It should also include keywords by which it might be searched for in a database or online. For example, an essay titled "Smile!" wouldn't offer many clues about its content or purpose; far more useful is the title of a real journal article by Christina Kotchemidova, "From Good Cheer to 'Drive-By Smiling': A Social History of Cheerfulness." When Professor Kotchemidova's paper winds up in someone's bibliography or in an online database, readers know what its subject is.

If you must be clever or allusive, follow the cute title with a colon and an explanatory subtitle.

"'Out, Damn'd Spot!': Images of Conscience and Remorse in Shakespeare's *Macbeth*"

"Out, Damn'd Spot: Housebreaking Your Puppy"

Avoid whimsical or suggestive titles.   A bad title will haunt you like a silly screen name. At this point, you may not worry about publication, but documents take on a life of their own when uploaded to the Web or listed on a résumé. Any document posted where the public can search for it online needs a levelheaded title, especially when you enter the job market.

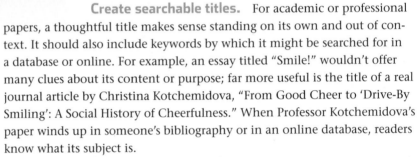

Titles tell readers what to expect. *Top:* Columbia Pictures/Photofest. *Center:* Federal Emergency Management Agency/Ready Campaign. *Bottom:* By permission. From *Merriam-Webster's Collegiate Dictionary* © 2014 by Merriam-Webster, Inc. (www.Merriam-Webster.com).

Capitalize and punctuate titles carefully.   The guidelines for capitalizing titles vary between disciplines. See Chapters 46 and 47 for the MLA and APA guidelines, or consult the style manual for your discipline.

Your titles should avoid all caps, boldface, underscoring, and, with some exceptions, italics (titles within titles and foreign terms may be italicized; see examples above). For Web sites, newsletters, PowerPoint presentations, and so on, you can be bolder graphically. ○

think visually
p. 557

Style

Need help revising and editing? See p. 420. / Need help with common errors? See p. 566.

32

High, Middle, and Low Style

define your
style/refine
your tone

We all have an ear for the way words work in sentences and paragraphs, for the distinctive melding of voice, tone, rhythm, and texture some call *style*. You might not be able to explain exactly why one paragraph sparkles and another is as flat as day-old soda, but you know when writing feels energetic, precise, and clear or stodgy, lifeless, and plodding. Choices you make about sentence type, sentence length, vocabulary, pronouns, and punctuation *do* create distinctive verbal styles—which may or may not fit particular types of writing. ○

In fact, there are as many styles of writing as of dress. In most cases, language that is clear, active, and economical will do the job. But even such a bedrock style has variations. Since the time of the ancient Greeks, writers have imagined a "high" or formal style at one end of a scale and a "low" or colloquial style at the other, bracketing a just-right porridge in the middle. Style is more complex than that, but keeping the full range in mind reveals some of your options.

Even dining has distinct levels of style and formality you grasp immediately. *Top:* Anna Brykhanova/Getty Images. *Center:* Steve Debenport/E+ Collection/ Getty Images. *Bottom:* Mary Altaffer/ Associated Press.

400

improve your
sentences p. 412

Use high style for formal, scientific, and scholarly writing.   You will find high style in professional journals, scholarly books, legal briefs, formal addresses, many newspaper editorials, some types of technical writing, and even traditional wedding invitations. Use it yourself when a lot is at stake—in a scholarship application, for example, or a job letter, term paper, or thesis. High style is signaled by some combination of the following features—all of which can vary.

John Cole, courtesy Cagle Cartoons.

- Serious or professional subjects
- Knowledgeable or professional audiences
- Impersonal point of view signaled by dominant, though not exclusive, third-person (*he, she, it, they*) pronouns
- Relatively complex and self-consciously patterned sentences (that display *parallelism, balance, repetition*)
- Sophisticated or professional vocabulary, often abstract and technical
- Few contractions or colloquial expressions
- Conventional grammar and punctuation; standard document design
- Formal documentation, when required, often with notes and a bibliography

The following example is from a scholarly journal. The article uses a formal scientific style, appropriate when an expert in a field is writing for an audience of his or her peers.

Temperament is a construct closely related to personality. In human research, temperament has been defined by some researchers as the inherited, early appearing tendencies that continue throughout life and serve as the foundation for personality (A. H. Buss, 1995; Goldsmith et al., 1987). Although this definition is not adopted uniformly by human researchers (McCrae et al., 2000), animal researchers agree even less about how to define temperament (Budaev, 2000). In some cases, the word *temperament* appears to be used purely to avoid using the word *personality*, which some animal researchers associate with anthropomorphism. Thus, to ensure that my review captured all potentially relevant reports, I searched for studies that examined either personality or temperament.

— Sam D. Gosling, "From Mice to Men: What Can We Learn About Personality from Animal Research?" *Psychological Bulletin*

Technical terms introduced and defined.

Sources documented.

Perspective generally impersonal—though *I* is used.

For an activity on appropriate language, see **macmillanhighered.com/howtowrite3e**.
Tutorials > LearningCurve Activities > Appropriate Language

The following excerpt from a 2013 Presidential Proclamation marking National Arts and Humanities Month also uses a formal style. The occasion calls for an expressive reflection on a consequential subject.

Opening is general and serious—with carefully balanced sentences.

Throughout our history, America has advanced not only because of our people's will or our leaders' vision, but also because of paintings and poems, stories and songs, dramas and dances. These works open our minds and nourish our souls, helping us understand what it means to be human and what it means to be American. . . .

Vocabulary is learned and dignified.

Our history is a testament to the boundless capacity of the arts and humanities to shape our views of democracy, freedom, and tolerance. Each of us knows what it is like to have our beliefs changed by a writer's perspective, our understanding deepened by a historian's insight, or our waning spirit lifted by a singer's voice. These are some of the most striking and memorable moments in our lives, and they reflect lasting truths — that

Ideas expressed are abstract and uplifting.

the arts and humanities speak to everyone and that in the great arsenal of progress, the human imagination is our most powerful tool.

Ensuring our children and our grandchildren can share these same experiences and hone their own talents is essential to our Nation's future. Somewhere in America, the next great author is wrestling with a sentence in her first short story, and the next great artist is doodling in the pages of

Voice is "presidential," speaking for the nation.

his notebook. We need these young people to succeed as much as we need our next generation of engineers and scientists to succeed. And that is why my Administration remains dedicated to strengthening initiatives that not only provide young people with the nurturing that will help their talents grow, but also the skills to think critically and creatively throughout their lives.

Final paragraph evokes well-calibrated emotions.

This month, we pay tribute to the indelible ways the arts and humanities have shaped our Union. Let us encourage future generations to carry this tradition forward. And as we do so, let us celebrate the power of artistic expression to bridge our differences and reveal our common heritage.

— Presidential Proclamation, National Arts and Humanities Month, September 20, 2013

Use middle style for personal, argumentative, and some academic writing.   This style, perhaps the most common, falls between the extremes and, like the other styles, varies enormously. It is the language of journalism, popular books and magazines, professional memos and nonscientific reports, instructional guides and manuals, and most commercial Web sites. Use this style in position papers, letters to the editor, personal statements, and business e-mails and memos—even in some business and professional work, once you are comfortable with the people to whom you are writing. Middle style doesn't so much claim features of its own as walk a path between formal and everyday language. It may combine some of the following characteristics:

- Full range of topics, from serious to humorous
- General audiences
- Range of perspectives, including first-person (*I*) and second-person (*you*) points of view
- Typically, a personal rather than an institutional voice
- Sentences in active voice that vary in complexity and length
- General vocabulary, more specific than abstract, with concrete nouns and action verbs and with unfamiliar terms or concepts defined
- Informal expressions, occasional dialogue, slang, and contractions, when appropriate to the subject or audience
- Conventional grammar and reasonably correct formats
- Informal documentation, usually without notes

In the following excerpt from an article that appeared in the popular magazine *Psychology Today*, Ellen McGrath uses a conversational but serious middle style to present scientific information to a general audience.

Families often inherit a negative thinking style that carries the germ of depression. Typically it is a legacy passed from one generation to the next, a pattern of pessimism invoked to protect loved ones from disappointment or stress. But in fact, negative thinking patterns do just the opposite, eroding the mental health of all exposed.

> Vocabulary is sophisticated but not technical.

When Dad consistently expresses his disappointment in Josh for bringing home a B minus in chemistry although all the other grades are A's, he is exhibiting a kind of cognitive distortion that children learn to deploy

> Familiar example (fictional son is even named) illustrates technical term: *cognitive distortion*.

Phrase following dash offers further clarification helpful to educated, but nonexpert, readers.

on themselves — a mental filtering that screens out positive experience from consideration.

Or perhaps the father envisions catastrophe, seeing such grades as foreclosing the possibility of a top college, thus dooming his son's future. It is their repetition over time that gives these events power to shape a person's belief system.

—"Is Depression Contagious?," July 1, 2003

The middle style works especially well for speakers addressing actual audiences. Compare the informal and personal style of Michelle Obama, in her role as first lady, advocating for arts education at an awards luncheon to the more stately language her husband uses in his presidential proclamation, also on the subject of the arts (p. 402):

Style is personal, with feelings close to the surface.

So for every Janelle Monae [an artist recognized at the luncheon], there are so many young people with so much promise [that] they never have the chance to develop. And think about how that must feel for a kid to have so much talent, so much that they want to express, but it's all bottled up inside because no one ever puts a paintbrush or an instrument or a script into their hand.

Sentences and clauses are parallel, rhythmic, and evocatively short.

Think about what that means for our communities, that frustration bottled up. Think about the neighborhoods where so many of our kids live — neighborhoods torn apart by poverty and violence. Those kids have no good outlets or opportunities, so for them everything that's bottled up — all that despair and anger and fear — it comes out in all the wrong places. It comes out through guns and gangs and drugs, and the cycle just continues.

Vocabulary choices are crisp and varied. Note the use of "kids" throughout.

But the arts are a way to channel that pain and frustration into something meaningful and productive and beautiful. And every human being needs that, particularly our kids. And when they don't have that outlet, that is such a tremendous loss, not just for our kids, but for our nation. And that's why the work you all are doing is so important.

—Remarks by the First Lady at the Grammy Museum's Jane Ortner Education Award Luncheon, July 14, 2014

Use a low style for personal, informal, and even playful writing.
Don't think of "low" here in a negative sense: A colloquial or informal style is
perfect when you want or need to sound more open and at ease. Low style can
be right for your personal e-mails and instant messaging, of course, as well as in
advertisements, magazines trying to be hip, personal narratives, humor writing,
and many blogs. Low style has many of the following features:

- Everyday or off-the-wall subjects, often humorous or parodic
- In-group or specialized readers
- Highly personal and idiosyncratic points of view; lots of *I, me, you, us,* and
  dialogue
- Shorter sentences and irregular constructions, especially fragments
- Vocabulary from pop culture and the street—idiomatic, allusive, and
  obscure to outsiders
- Colloquial expressions resembling speech
- Unconventional grammar and mechanics and alternative formats
- No systematic acknowledgment of sources

Here's a movie review from *Rolling Stone* written in the easy, informal style
expected by (and probably used by) its readers.

JOBS

PETER TRAVERS

AUGUST 15, 2013

Casting Ashton Kutcher as Apple's mercurial trailblazer, Steve Jobs, could have
backfired big-time. It's one thing being the highest-paid sitcom star on TV,
another for Charlie Sheen's replacement on *Two and a Half Men* to find the
gravitas to play a computer-and-marketing visionary pursued by personal and
professional demons. Kutcher nails the genius and narcissism. It's a quietly
dazzling performance.

> Opening paragraph flirts with middle-style vocabulary: *mercurial, gravitas, narcissism.*

As a movie, *Jobs* is a decidedly mixed bag. Director Joshua Michael Stern
(*Swing Vote*) and newbie screenwriter Matt Whiteley check off boxes in Jobs's
life like they're connecting the dots. Oddly, the film doesn't include Jobs's 2011
death from pancreatic cancer at fifty-six. The film kicks off in 2001 (Jobs intro'ing
the iPod) and works back to his career start. It's as if Kutcher were starring in the
thinking man's version of *That '70s Show.*

> Tone shifts in a more colloquial second paragraph: *mixed bag, newbie, connecting the dots.*

Sentence structures
imitate informal talk.

Jobs, the barefoot hippie and Reed College dropout, sets up shop with his geek buds in the California garage of his adoptive parents. That's where he and Steve "The Woz" Wozniak (Josh Gad) create Apple and start a revolution. Jobs loses the business. Then he wins it back. It plays like a Jobs Wiki page, including young Steve kicking his girlfriend Chrisann (Ahna O'Reilly) to the curb and initially disowning their daughter.

Travers renders a verdict
in the final sentence.

The kick comes in watching the man at work, where his blunt style wins few friends but real respect. Kutcher, rising to the occasion, makes every moment count. The skilled Gad looks eager to take him on, but the Woz is a painfully underwritten role. *Jobs* is a one-man show that needed to go for broke and doesn't. My guess is that Jobs would give it a swat.

Your Turn   Over the next day, look for three pieces of writing that seem to you to represent examples of high, middle, and low style. Then study several paragraphs or a section of each in detail, paying attention to the features listed in the checklists for the three styles. How well do the pieces actually conform to the descriptions of high, middle, and low style? Where would you place your three examples on a continuum that moves from high to low? Do the pieces share some stylistic features? Do you find any variations of style within the individual passages you examined?

The very serious story told in the *9/11 Commission Report* was retold in *The 9/11 Report: A Graphic Adaptation* (p. 407). Creators Sid Jacobson and Ernie Colón use the colloquial visual style of a comic book to make the formidable data and conclusions of a government report accessible to a wider audience. For more on choosing a genre, see the Introduction.

The Port Authority, at its own expense, installed a repeater system in 1994 to enhance the FDNY's radio communications in the tower.

In 1996, Mayor Giuliani created the Office of Emergency Management (OEM) to monitor the city's key communications channels, to improve the city's response to major incidents, and to play a crucial role in managing the city's overall response to an incident.

However, as of 9/11, the city was not prepared to comprehensively coordinate efforts in responding to a major incident. The OEM had not overcome this problem.

At 8:46:40, hijacked American Airlines Flight 11 flew into the upper portion of the North Tower, cutting through floors 93 to 99.

A jet fuel fireball erupted upon impact and shot down at least one bank of elevators.

The fireball exploded onto numerous floors, including the 77th, the 22nd, the lobby level, and four stories below.

SHOOM!

Evidence suggests that all three of the building's stairwells became impassable from the 92nd floor up.

Hundreds were killed instantly by the impact.

Hundreds more remained alive but trapped.

The burning jet fuel immediately created thick black smoke that enveloped the upper floors of the North Tower.
The roof of the South Tower was also engulfed in smoke because of the prevailing winds.

Hundreds of civilians trapped on or above the 92nd floor gathered in large and small groups between the 103rd and 106th floors.

Civilians were trapped in elevators, while others below the impact zone were trapped or waiting for assistance.

Panels combine verbal and visual elements to tell a story.

Political figures become characters in a real-life drama.

Sounds (*Shoom!*) are represented visually — as in superhero tales.

Real images (the photograph on the left) are sometimes juxtaposed with cartoon panels as part of the collage.

Excerpt from "Heroism and Horror" from *THE 9/11 REPORT: A GRAPHIC ADAPTATION* by Sid Jacobson and Ernie Colón. Copyright © 2006 by Castlebridge Enterprises, Inc. Reprinted by permission of Hill and Wang, a division of Farrar, Straus and Giroux LLC.

33

Inclusive and Culturally Sensitive Style

Remember Polish jokes? Let's hope not, and that's a good thing. Slowly, we're all learning to avoid offensive racial, ethnic, and gender stereotypes in our public lives and the bigoted language that propagated them. Thanks to electronic media, the world is smaller and more diverse today: When you compose any document electronically, it may sail quickly around the Web, conveying not only ideas but also your attitudes and prejudices. You can't please every reader in this vast potential audience, but you can at least write respectfully, accurately, and, yes, honestly. Language that is both inclusive and culturally sensitive can and should have the qualities described in the following guidelines.

Avoid expressions that stereotype genders or sexual orientation. Largely purged from contemporary English usage are job titles that suggest that they are occupied exclusively by men or women. Gone are *stewardess* and *poetess*, *policeman* and *chairman*, *male nurse* and *woman scientist*. When referring to professions, even those still dominated by one gender or another, avoid using a gendered pronoun.

Don't strain sense to be politically correct. *Nun* and *NFL quarterback* are still gendered, as are *witch* and *warlock*—and *surrogate mother*. Here are some easy solutions.

STEREOTYPED	The postman came up the walk.
INCLUSIVE	The letter carrier came up the walk.
STEREOTYPED	Among all her other tasks, a nurse must also stay up-to-date on her medical education.
INCLUSIVE	Among all their other tasks, nurses must also stay up-to-date on their medical education.

Outdated Terms	Alternatives
fireman	firefighter
mankind	humankind, people, humans
congressman	congressional representative
chairman	chair
policewoman	police officer
stewardess	flight attendant
actress, poetess	actor, poet

Avoid expressions that stereotype races, ethnic groups, or religious groups.   Deliberate racial slurs these days tend to be rare in professional writing. But it is still not unusual to find clueless writers (and politicians) noting how "hardworking," "articulate," "athletic," "well-groomed," or "ambitious" members of minority and religious groups are. The praise rings hollow because it draws on old and brutal stereotypes. You have an obligation to learn the history and nature of such ethnic caricatures and grow beyond them. It's part of your education, no matter what group or groups you belong to.

Refer to people and groups by the expressions used in serious publications, understanding that almost all racial and ethnic terms are contested: *African American, black* (or *Black*), *Negro, people of color, Asian American, Hispanic, Mexican American, Cuban American, Native American, Indian, Inuit, Anglo, white* (or *White*). Even the ancient group of American Indians once called Anasazi now goes by the more culturally and historically accurate Native Puebloans. While shifts of this sort may seem fussy or politically correct to some, it costs little to address people as they prefer, acknowledging both their humanity and our differences.

Be aware, too, that being part of an ethnic or racial group usually gives you license to say things about the group not open to outsiders. Anjelah Johnson and Hari Kondabolu can joke about topics that Jimmy Fallon can't touch, using epithets that would cost the *Tonight Show* host his job. In academic and professional settings, show similar discretion in your language—though not in your treatment of serious subjects. Sensitivities of language should not become an excuse for avoiding open debate, nor a weapon to chill it. In the following table are suggestions for inclusive, culturally sensitive terms.

Outdated Terms	Alternatives
Eskimo	Inuit
Oriental	Asian (better to specify country of origin)
Hispanic	Specify: Mexican, Cuban, Nicaraguan, and so on
Negro (acceptable to some)	African American, black
colored	people of color
a gay, the gays	gay, lesbian, gays and lesbians, the LGBT community
cancer victim	cancer survivor
boys, girls (to refer to adults)	men, women

Treat all people with respect.   This policy makes sense in all writing. Some slights may not be intended—against the elderly, for example. But writing that someone drives *like an old woman* manages to offend two groups. In other cases—such as when you are describing members of campus groups, religious groups, the military, gays and lesbians, athletes, and so on—you might mistakenly use language that implies most readers share your own prejudices or narrow vision. You know the derogatory terms and references well enough, and you should avoid them if for no other reason than the Golden Rule. Everyone is a member of some group that has at one time or another been mocked or stereotyped. So writing that is respectful will itself be treated with respect.

Avoid sensational language.   It happens every semester. One or more students ask the instructor whether it's okay to use four-letter words in their papers. Some instructors tolerate expletives in personal narratives, but it is difficult to make a case for them in academic reports, research papers, or position papers unless they are part of quoted material—as they may be in writing about contemporary literature or song lyrics.

Your Turn   Write a paragraph or two about any pet peeve you may have with language use. Your problem may address a serious issue like insensitivities in naming your ethnicity, community, or beliefs. Or you may just be tired of a friend insisting that you describe Sweetie Pie as your "animal companion" rather than use that demeaning and hegemonic term "pet." You'll want to share your paragraph and also read what others have written.

34

Vigorous, Clear, Economical Style

improve your
sentences

Ordinarily, tips and tricks don't do much to enhance your skills as a writer. But a few guidelines, applied sensibly, can improve your sentences and paragraphs noticeably—and upgrade your credibility as a writer. You sound more professional and confident when every word and phrase pulls its weight.

Always consider the big picture in applying the following tips: Work with whole pages and paragraphs, not just individual sentences. Remember, too, that these are guidelines, not rules. Ignore them when your good sense suggests a better alternative.

Build sentences around specific and tangible subjects and objects. Scholar Richard Lanham famously advised writers troubled by tangled sentences to ask, "Who is kicking who?" This question expresses the principle that readers shouldn't have to puzzle over what they read. They are less likely to be confused when they can identify the people or things in a sentence that act upon other people and things. Answering Professor Lanham's question often leads to stronger verbs and tighter sentences too.

CONFUSING	Current tax policies necessitate congressional reform if the reoccurrence of a recession is to be avoided.
BETTER	Congress needs to reform current tax policies to avoid another recession.
CONFUSING	In the Prohibition era, tuning cars enabled the bootleggers to turn ordinary automobiles into speed machines

for the transportation of illegal alcohol by simply altering certain components of the cars.

BETTER   In the Prohibition era, bootleggers modified their cars to turn them into speed machines for transporting illegal alcohol.

Both of the confusing sentences here work better with subjects capable of action: *Congress* and *bootleggers*. Once identified, these subjects make it easy to simplify the sentences, giving them more power.

Look for opportunities to use specific nouns and noun phrases rather than general ones.   This advice depends very much on context. Academic reports and arguments often require broad statements and general terms. But don't ignore the power and energy of specific words and phrases; they create more memorable images for readers, so they may have more impact.

GENERAL	SPECIFIC
bird	roadrunner
cactus	prickly pear
lawbreaker	mugger
business	pizzeria
jeans	501s

Many writers are fond of generic terms and the impenetrable phrases they inspire because they sound serious and sophisticated. But such language can be hard to figure out or even suggest a cover-up. What better way to hide an inconvenient truth than to bury it in words? So revise those ugly, unreadable, inhuman sentences:

ABSTRACT   All of the separate constituencies at this academic institution must be invited to participate in the decision-making process under the current fiscal pressures we face.

BETTER   Faculty, students, and staff at this school must all have a say during this current budget crunch.

Avoid sprawling phrases.   These constructions give readers fits, especially when they thicken, sentence after sentence, like limescale or sludge. Be alert whenever your prose shows any combination of the following features:

Don't use words too big for the subject. Don't say "infinitely" when you mean "very"; otherwise you'll have no word left when you want to talk about something really infinite.

—C. S. Lewis

Wolf Suschitzky/Time and Life Pictures/Getty Images.

- Strings of prepositional phrases
- Verbs turned into nouns via endings such as *-ation* (*implement* becomes *implementation*)
- Lots of articles (*the*, *a*)
- Lots of heavily modified verbals

Such expressions are not inaccurate or wrong, just tedious. They make readers work hard for no good reason. Fortunately, they are also easy to clean up once you notice the accumulation.

WORDY	members of the student body at Arizona State
BETTER	students at Arizona State
WORDY	the producing of products made up of steel
BETTER	steel production
WORDY	the prioritization of decisions for policies of the student government
BETTER	the student government's priorities

Avoid sentences with long windups.   The more stuff you pile up ahead of the main verb, the more readers have to remember. Very skillful writers can pull off complex sentences of this kind because they know how to build interest and manage clauses. But a safer strategy in academic and professional writing is to get to the point of your sentences quickly. Here's a sentence from the Internal Revenue Service Web site that keeps readers waiting far too long for a verb. Yet it's simple to fix once its problem is diagnosed:

ORIGINAL	A new scam e-mail that appears to be a solicitation from the IRS and the U.S. government for charitable contributions to victims of the recent Southern California wildfires has been making the rounds.
REVISED	A new scam e-mail making the rounds asks for charitable contributions to victims of the recent Southern California wildfires. Though it appears to be from the IRS and the U.S. government, it is a fake.

Favor simple, active verbs.   When a sentence, even a short one, goes off track, consider whether the problem might be a nebulous, strung-out, or un-imaginative verb. Replace it with a verb that does something:

For an activity on active and passive voice, see **macmillanhighered.com/howtowrite3e.** **Tutorials** > LearningCurve Activities > Active and Passive Voice

WORDY VERB PHRASE	We must make a decision soon.
BETTER	We must decide soon.
WORDY VERB PHRASE	Students are absolutely reliant on federal loans.
BETTER	Students need federal loans.
WORDY VERB PHRASE	Engineers proceeded to reinforce the levee.
BETTER	Engineers reinforced the levee.

You'll be a better writer the instant you apply this guideline.

Avoid strings of prepositional phrases. Prepositional phrases are simple structures, consisting of prepositions and their objects and an occasional modifier: *from the beginning; under the spreading chestnut tree; between you and me; in the line of duty; over the rainbow.* You can't write much without prepositional phrases. But use more than two or, rarely, three in a row and they drain the energy from a sentence. When that's the case, try turning the prepositions into more compact modifiers or moving them into different positions within the sentence. Sometimes you may need to revise the sentence even more substantially.

TOO MANY PHRASES	We stood in line at the observatory on the top of a hill in the mountains to look in a huge telescope at the moons of Saturn.
BETTER	We lined up at the mountaintop observatory to view Saturn's moons through a huge telescope.
TOO MANY PHRASES	To help first-year students in their adjustment to the rigors of college life, the Faculty Council voted for the creation of a new midterm break during the third week of October.
BETTER	To help first-year students adjust better to college life, the Faculty Council endorsed a new break in mid-October.

Don't repeat key words close together. You can often improve the style of a passage just by making sure you haven't used a particular word or phrase too often—unless you repeat it deliberately for effect (*government of the people, by the people, for the people*). Your sentences will sound fresher after you have eliminated pointless repetition; they may also end up shorter.

| REPETITIVE | Students in writing courses are often assigned common readings, which they are expected to read to prepare for various student writing projects. |
| BETTER | Students in writing courses are often assigned common readings to prepare them for projects. |

This is a guideline to apply sensibly: Sometimes for clarity, you must repeat key expressions over and over—especially in technical writing.

The *New Horizons* payload is incredibly power efficient, with the instruments collectively drawing only about 28 watts. The payload consists of three optical instruments, two plasma instruments, a dust sensor, and a radio science receiver/radiometer.

—NASA, "*New Horizons* Spacecraft Ready for Flight"

Avoid doublings.   In speech, we tend to repeat ourselves or say things two or three different ways to be sure listeners get the point. Such repetitions are natural, even appreciated. But in writing, the habit of doubling may irritate readers. And it is very much a habit, backed by a long literary tradition comfortable with pairings such as *home and hearth, friend and colleague, tried and true, clean and sober, neat and tidy*, and so on.

Sometimes, writers will add an extra noun or two to be sure they have covered the bases: *colleges and universities, books and articles, ideas and opinions*. There may be good reasons for a second (or third) item. But the doubling is often just extra baggage that slows down the train. Leave it at the station.

The same goes for redundant expressions. For the most part, they go unnoticed, except by readers who crawl up walls when someone writes *young in age*, *bold in character*, **totally** *dead*, **basically** *unhappy*, **current** *fashion*, **empty** *hole*, **extremely** *outraged*, *later in time*, *mix together*, *reply back*, and so on. (In each case, the boldfaced words restate what is already obvious.) People precise enough to care about details deserve respect: They land rovers on Mars. Cut the dumb redundancies. (Is *dumb* unnecessary here?)

Turn clauses into more direct modifiers.   If you are fond of *that, which, and who* clauses, be sure you need them. You can sometimes save a word or two by pulling the modifiers out of the clause and moving them directly ahead of the words they explain. Or you may be able to tighten a sentence just by cutting *that*, *which*, or *who*.

WORDY	Our football coach, who is nationally renowned, expected a raise.
BETTER	Our nationally renowned football coach expected a raise.
WORDY	Our football coach, who is nationally renowned and already rich, still expected a raise.
BETTER	Our football coach, nationally renowned and already rich, still expected a raise.

Cut introductory expressions such as *it is* and *there is/are* when you can.   These slow-moving expressions, called *expletives*, are fine when they are conventional, as in the following sentences, which would be difficult to rephrase.

It's going to rain today.

It was her first Oscar.

There is a tide in the affairs of men.

But don't default to easy expletives at the beginning of every other sentence. Your prose will suffer. Fortunately, revision is easy.

WORDY	It is necessary that we reform the housing policies.
BETTER	We need to reform the housing policies.
WORDY	There were many incentives offered by the company to its sales force.
BETTER	The company offered its sales force many incentives.

Expletives in a sentence often attract other wordy and vague expressions. Then the language swells like a blister. Imagine having to read paragraph after paragraph of prose like the following sentence.

SLOW	It is quite evident that an argument sociologist Annette Lareau supports is that it is important to find the balance between authoritarian and indulgent styles of parenting because it contributes to successful child development.
BETTER	Clearly, sociologist Annette Lareau believes that balancing authoritarian and indulgent styles of parenting contributes to successful child development.

Vary your sentence lengths and structures.   Sentences, like music, have rhythm. If all your sentences run about the same length or rarely vary from a predictable subject-verb-object pattern, readers will grow bored without knowing why. Every so often, surprise them with a really short statement. Or begin with a longer-than-usual introductory phrase. Or try compound subjects or verbs, or attach a series of parallel modifiers to the verb or object. Or let a sentence roll toward a grand conclusion, as in the following example.

> [Carl] Newman is a singing encyclopedia of pop power. He has identified, cultured, and cloned the most buoyant elements of his favorite Squeeze, Raspberries, Supertramp, and Sparks records, and he's pretty pathological about making sure there's something unpredictable and catchy happening in a New Pornographers song every couple of seconds—a stereo flurry of *ooohs*, an extra beat or two bubbling up unexpectedly.
>
> —Douglas Wolk, "Something to Talk About," *Spin*, August 2005

Read what you have written aloud.   Then fix any words or phrases that cause you to pause or stumble, and rethink sentences that feel *awkward*—a notoriously vague reaction that should still be taken seriously. Reading drafts aloud is a great way to find problems. After all, if you can't move smoothly through your own writing, a reader won't be able to either. Better yet, persuade a friend or roommate to read your draft to you. Take notes.

Understand, though, that prose never sounds quite like spoken language—and thank goodness for that. Accurate transcripts of dialogue are almost unreadable, full of gaps, disconnected phrases, pauses, repetitions, and the occasional obscenity. And yet written language, especially in the middle style, should resemble the human voice, with all its cadences and rhythms pulling readers along, making them want to read more.

Cut a first draft by 25 percent—or more.   If you tend to be wordy, try to cut your first drafts by at least one-quarter. Put all your thoughts down on the page when drafting a paper. But when editing, cut every unnecessary expression. Think of it as a competition. However, don't eliminate any important ideas and facts. If possible, ask an honest friend to read your work and point out where you might tighten your language.

If you ~~are aware that you~~ tend to ~~say more than you need to in your writing,~~ *be wordy,*

~~then get in the habit of~~ trying to cut ~~the~~ first drafts ~~that you have written~~ by *your*

at least one-quarter. ~~There may be good reasons for you to~~ put all your

thoughts ~~and ideas~~ down on the page when ~~you are in the process of~~

drafting a paper ~~or project~~. But when ~~you are in the process of~~ editing, ~~you~~

~~should be sure to~~ cut every unnecessary ~~word that is not needed or~~ *expression.*

~~necessary. You may find it advantageous to t~~hink of it as a competition ~~or a~~ *T*   .

~~game. In making your cuts, it is important that you~~ don't eliminate any *However,*

important ideas ~~that may be essential or~~ facts ~~that may be important.~~ If ~~you~~ *and*   .

~~find it~~ possible, ~~you might consider~~ asking an honest friend ~~whom you trust~~

to read your ~~writing~~ and ~~ask them to~~ point out ~~those places in your writing~~ *work*

where you might ~~make~~ your language ~~tighter.~~ *tighten*

I believe more in the scissors than I do in the pencil.

— Truman Capote

Roger Higgins/New York World-Telegram and the Sun Newspapers Photograph Collection/ Library of Congress, Prints and Photographs Division, LC-USZ62-119336.

Your Turn   Even if you think your prose is as tight as Scrooge, take a first draft you have written and try the 25 percent challenge. Count the words in the original version (or let your software do it for you) and then pare away until you come in under quota. And, while you are at it, turn abstract nouns and strung-out verbs into livelier expressions and eliminate long windups and boring chains of prepositional phrases. When you are done, read the revised version aloud — and then revise one more time.

Revising & Editing

Need style help? See p. 398. / Need help to develop your ideas? See p. 360.

35 Revising Your Own Work

revise
and edit

How much time should you spend revising a draft? That depends on the importance of the document and the time available to complete it. A job-application letter, résumé, or term paper had better be impressive. But you shouldn't send even an e-mail without a quick review, if only to make certain you're directing it to the right people and that your tone is spot-on. Errors might not bother you, but don't assume that other readers are just as easygoing. A well-edited piece always trumps sloppy work.

How you revise your work is a different matter. Some people edit line by line, perfecting every sentence before moving on to the next. Others write whole drafts quickly and then revise, and others combine these methods.

In most cases, it makes sense to draft a project fairly quickly and then edit it. Why? Because revising is hierarchical: Some issues matter more to your success than others. You might spend hours on a draft, getting each comma right and deleting every unneeded word. But then you read the whole thing and get that sinking feeling: The paper doesn't meet the assignment or is aimed at the wrong audience. So you trash paragraph after carefully edited paragraph and reorganize many of your ideas. Maybe you even begin from scratch.

Wouldn't it have been better to discover those big problems early on, before you put in so many hours polishing the punctuation? With major projects, consider revising and editing sequentially, starting with the top-tier issues like content and organization. Think of *revising* as making sweeping changes, and *editing* as finessing the details.

Revise to see the big picture.   Be willing to overhaul a whole project, if necessary. Of course, you'll need a draft first and it should be a real one with actual words on the page, not just good intentions. Revisions at this top level may require heavy rewrites of the paper, even starting over. Whatever it takes.

- **Does the project meet the assignment?** You really can get so wrapped up in a paper that you forget the original assignment. If you received an assignment sheet, go back and measure your first draft against its specifications. If it asks for a report and you have offered an argument, prepare for a major overhaul. Review, too, any requirements set for length, format, or use of sources.

- **Does the project reach its intended audience?** Who will read your paper? Are its tone and level of vocabulary right for these people? Have you used the type of sources readers expect: scholarly articles and books for an academic audience? Adjustments to satisfy the assigned audience may ripple throughout the piece.

- **Does the project do justice to its subject?** This is a tough question and you may want to get another reader's input. It might also help to review successful models of the assignment before you revise your paper. Look for such work in magazines, newspapers, and textbooks. How well does yours compare?

Edit to make the paper flow.   There are different opinions as to exactly what *flow* means when applied to writing, but everyone agrees that it's a good thing. With the major requirements of an assignment met, check how well you have put the piece together.

- **Does the organization work for the reader?** You may understand the paper, but will its structure be obvious to readers? Is a thesis statement, when one is required, clearly in place? Do your paragraphs develop coherent points? Pay particular attention to the opening sentences in those paragraphs: They must both connect to what you just wrote and preview the upcoming material.

- **Does the paper have smooth and frequent transitions?** Transitional words and phrases are road signs to help keep readers on track. Make sure they appear not only at the beginning of paragraphs but also throughout the project.

- **Is the paper readable?** Tinker to your heart's content with the language, varying sentence structures, choosing words to match the level of style you want, and paring away clumsy verbiage (which almost rhymes with *garbage*). Review Part 5 on style and apply those suggestions to the paper at this stage.

Edit to get the details right.   When editing a paper, nothing clears your mind as much as putting a draft aside for a few days and then looking at it with fresh eyes. You will be amazed at all the changes you will want to make. But you have to plan ahead to take advantage of this unsurpassed editing technique. Wait until the last minute to complete a project and you lose that opportunity.

- **Is the format correct right down to the details?** Many academic and professional projects follow templates from which you cannot vary. In fact, you may be expected to learn these requirements as a condition for entering a profession or major. So if you are asked to prepare a paper in Modern Language Association (MLA) or American Psychological Association (APA) style, for instance, invest the few minutes it takes to get the titles, margins, headings, and page numbers right. ○ Give similar attention to the formats for lab reports, e-mails, Web sites, and so on. You'll look like a pro if you do.

- **Are the grammar and mechanics right?** Word-processing programs offer a surprising amount of help in these areas. But use this assistance only as a first line of defense, not as a replacement for carefully rereading every word yourself. Even then, you still have to pay close attention to errors you make habitually. You know what they are. ○

- **Is the spelling correct?** Spell-checkers pick up some obvious gaffes but may not be any help with proper nouns or other special items—such as your professor's last name. They also don't catch correctly spelled words that simply aren't the ones you meant to use: *the* instead of *then, rein* instead of *reign*, and so on.

understand citation styles p. 470   help with common errors p. 566

Your Turn   Advice about revising can sound abstract, but the process is a real one you engage in regularly — or should. In a discussion with your class-mates (or in a paragraph or two), describe your habits of revision. Explore questions such as the following:

- Do you revise as you write, or do you prefer to wait until you have a full draft?

- How willing are you to make big changes in a draft?

- Have you ever been embarrassed or hurt by what seemed like minor errors?

- Do you know your specific areas of weakness, and how do you address them?

- Do you allow yourself enough time to give your projects a close second look? Should you?

- Have you ever had a surprising success with a paper you wrote at the last minute and turned in almost unrevised?

1 Put the paper aside for a few days (or at least a few hours) before revising.

2 Print out the paper, clear space on your desk, and read with fresh eyes. Does the paper respond to the assignment? Will it make sense to readers?

3 Read your paper aloud to yourself, your roommate, your goldfish — anyone who will listen. Mark the parts that confuse you or your audience.

36 Peer Editing

comment/
peer review/
proofread

Many people get nervous when asked to play editor, though such requests come all the time: "Read this for me?" Either they don't want to offend a friend or classmate with their criticisms or they have doubts about their own abilities. These are predictable reactions, but you need to get beyond them.

Your job in peer editing drafts is not to criticize other writers but to help them. And you will accomplish that best by approaching a project honestly, from the perspective of a typical reader. You may not grasp all the finer points of grammar, but you will know if a paper is boring, confusing, or unconvincing. Writers need this response.

And yet most peer editors in college or professional situations focus on tiny matters, such as misspellings or commas, and ignore arguments that completely lack evidence or paragraphs dull enough to make accountants yawn. Of course, spelling and punctuation errors are easy to catch. It's much tougher to suggest that whole pages need to be redone or that a colleague should do better research. But there's nothing charitable about ignoring these deeper issues when a writer's grade or career may be on the line. So what should you do?

First, before you edit any project, agree on ground rules for making comments. It is painless to annotate electronic drafts since you don't have to touch or change the original file. But writers may be more protective of paper copies of their work. Always ask whether you may write comments on a paper and then make sure that your handwriting is legible and your remarks are identified.

Peer edit the same way you revise your own work.   As suggested in Chapter 35, pay attention to global issues first. ○ Examine the purpose, audience, and subject matter of the project before dealing with its sentence structure, grammar, or mechanics. Deal with these major issues in a thoughtful and supportive written comment at the end of the paper. Use marginal comments and proofreading symbols (see pp. 431–32) to highlight mechanical problems. But don't correct these items. Leave it to the writer to figure out what is wrong.

Be specific in identifying problems or opportunities.   For instance, it doesn't help a writer to read "organization is confusing." Instead, point to places in the draft that went off track. If one sentence or paragraph exemplifies a particular problem—or strength—highlight it in some fashion and mention it in the final comment. Nothing helps a writer less than vague complaints or cheerleading:

> *You did a real good job, though I'm not sure you supported your thesis.*

It's far better to write something like the following:

> *Your thesis on the opening page is clear and challenging, but by the second page, you have forgotten what you are trying to prove. The paragraphs there don't seem connected to the original claim, and I don't find strong evidence to support the points you do make. Restructure these opening pages?*

Too tough? Not at all. The editor takes the paper seriously enough to explain why it's not working.

Offer suggestions for improvement.   You soften criticism when you follow it up with reasonable suggestions or strategies for revision. It's fine, too, to direct writers to resources they might use, from better sources to more effective software. Avoid the tendency, however, to revise the paper for your classmate or to recast it to suit your own opinions.

> No passion in the world is equal to the passion to alter someone else's draft.

—H. G. Wells

revise and
edit p. 422

Praise what is genuinely good in the paper. An editor can easily overlook what's working well in a paper, yet a writer needs that information as much as any apt criticism. Find something good to say, too, even about a paper that mostly doesn't work. You'll encourage the writer, who may be facing some lengthy revisions. But don't make an issue of it. Writers will know immediately if you are scraping bottom to find something to praise. Here's a detailed comment at the end of a first draft that makes many helpful moves, from encouraging a writer to making quite specific criticisms.

> Whit,
>
> I liked your draft and the direction your paper is going. Your use of imagery throughout was spot-on. I've never seen the movie Mad Max, but I can see the post-apocalyptic setting in my head.
>
> Your thesis is clear and concise, but as we discussed, perhaps you can do away with the low-budget innovation portion? That way you can focus on the film's themes and social impact, both of which relate more to why Mad Max should be treated as a film classic. . . . Also, focus more of your energy on the movie's influence because I think that is the best argument to support your claim.
>
> I do think your paper could benefit from more personal ethos: Say you are an avid film watcher and a humble fan of the movie so that the reader can trust your opinion easily.
>
> In terms of style, I found some of your sentences to be long and overbearing. Switch up short and long sentences so the reader can move through the paper easily.
>
> I think that's it. I can't wait to read the final draft of this paper, because I know it's going to be good. Good luck.
>
> — Stefan

Use proofreading symbols. Proofreading marks may seem fussy or impersonal, but they can be a useful way of quickly highlighting some basic errors or omissions. Here are some you might want to remember and use when editing a paper draft.

sp   Word misspelled (not a standard mark, but useful)

✗   Check for error here (not a standard mark)

ɤ   Delete marked item

⌒   Close up space

∧   Insert word or phrase

⌃̦   Insert comma

⌄⌄   Insert quotation marks

≡   Capitalize

⌄̇   Insert period

∿   Transpose or reverse the items marked

¶   Begin new paragraph

Insert or open up space

(ital)   Italicize word or phrase

Keep comments tactful.   Treat another writer's work the way you'd like to have your own efforts treated. Slips in writing can be embarrassing enough without an editor tweeting about them.

> **Your Turn**   Anderson Cooper of CNN reported on a teacher in North Carolina suspended without pay for two weeks for writing "Loser" on a sixth-grader's papers. Apparently the student wasn't offended because the teacher was known to be a "jokester," but administrators were. Did they overreact with the suspension (without pay), or should teachers and editors show discretion when commenting on something as personal as writing? Is there any room for sarcasm when peer editing? Make the case, one way or the other, in an exploratory paragraph.

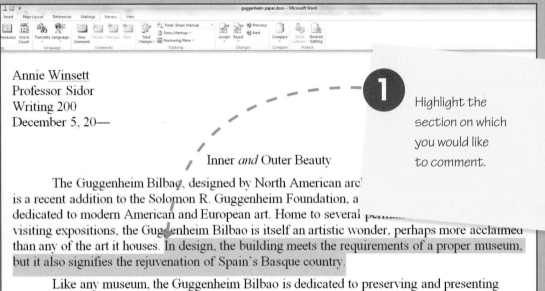

Annie Winsett
Professor Sidor
Writing 200
December 5, 20—

1 Highlight the section on which you would like to comment.

Inner *and* Outer Beauty

The Guggenheim Bilbao, designed by North American arch' is a recent addition to the Solomon R. Guggenheim Foundation, a dedicated to modern American and European art. Home to several pe... visiting expositions, the Guggenheim Bilbao is itself an artistic wonder, perhaps more acclaimed than any of the art it houses. In design, the building meets the requirements of a proper museum, but it also signifies the rejuvenation of Spain's Basque country.

Like any museum, the Guggenheim Bilbao is dedicated to preserving and presenting works of art. Paintings and sculptures are here to be protected. So the thick glass panes of the Bilbao serve not only to let in natural light, but also provide escape for the heat generated by the titanium outsides of the structure. The unconventional metal plating of the Guggenheim, guaranteed to last up to one hundred years, actually ensures its survival as well. Similarly, the floor material will be able to withstand the many visitors to come.

Even though the outside of the Guggenheim Bilbao appears to be composed of irregular

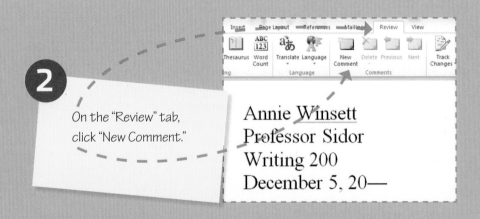

2 On the "Review" tab, click "New Comment."

Annie Winsett
Professor Sidor
Writing 200
December 5, 20—

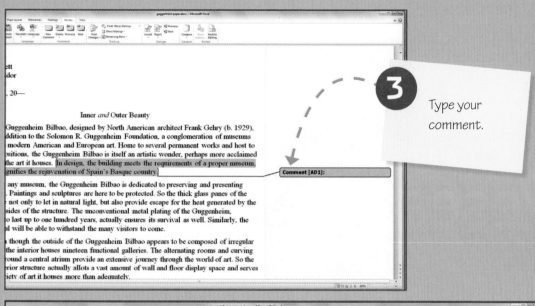

3 Type your comment.

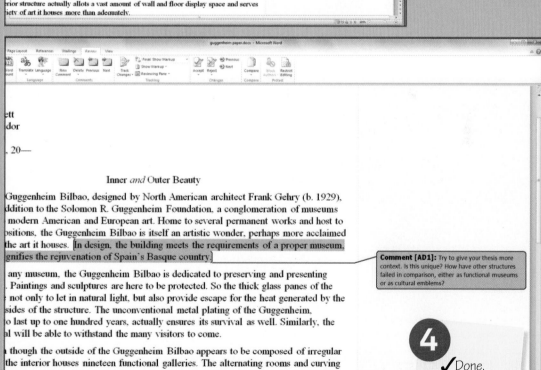

4 ✓ Done.

Research & Sources

part seven

37 Beginning Your Research

plan a project

Research can be part of any writing project. When doing research, you examine what is already known about a topic and then, sometimes, push the boundaries of knowledge forward. For humanities courses, this typically involves examining a wide range of books, articles, and Web sources. In the social and natural sciences, you might perform experiments or do field research and then share new data you have collected on a topic. For more on choosing a genre, see the Introduction.

So where do you begin your research project, and how do you keep from being swamped by the sheer quantity of information available? You need smart research strategies.

Know your assignment. When one is provided, review the assignment sheet for any project to establish exactly the kinds of research the paper requires. You may need to use only the reference section of the library for a one-page position paper related to a class discussion. An argument about current events will usually send you to newspapers, magazines, and Web sites, while a full-length term paper will need references drawn from academic books and journals. (For details and advice on a wide variety of assignments, refer to Parts 1 and 2.)

Come up with a plan. Research takes time because you have to find sources, read them, record your findings, and then write about them. Most research projects also require full documentation and some type of formal presentation, either as a research paper or, perhaps, an oral report. This stuff cannot be thrown together the night before. One way to avoid mayhem is to prepare a project calendar that ties specific tasks to specific dates. Simply creating the schedule (and you should keep it *simple*) might even jump-start your actual research. At a minimum, record important due dates in your phone or day planner. Here's a full schedule for a serious research paper with three key deadlines.

> Research is formalized curiosity. It is poking and prying with a purpose.

—**Zora Neale Hurston**

Photo by Carl Van Vechten/ Library of Congress, Prints and Photographs Division, LC-USZ62-79898.

Schedule: Research Paper

February 20: Topic proposal due
____ Explore and select a topic
____ Do preliminary library/Web research
____ Define a thesis or hypothesis
____ Prepare an annotated bibliography
March 26: First draft due
____ Read, summarize, paraphrase, and synthesize sources
____ Organize the paper
____ Draft the paper
April 16: Final draft due
____ Get peer feedback on draft
____ Revise the project
____ Check documentation
____ Edit the project

Find a manageable topic. For a research project, this often means defining a problem you can solve with available resources. (For advice on finding and developing topics, see Part 3.) Look for a question within the scope of the assignment that you can answer in the time available.

When asked to submit a ten- or twenty-page term paper, some writers panic, thinking they need a massive, general topic to fill up all those blank pages. But the opposite is true. You will have more success finding useful sources if you break off small but intriguing parts of much larger subjects.

not Military Aircraft, *but* The Development of Jet Fighters in World War II

not The History of Punk Rock, *but* The Influence of 1970s Punk Rock on Nirvana

not Developmental Disorders in Children, *but* Cri du Chat Syndrome

It's fine to read widely at first to find a general subject. But you have to narrow the project to a specific topic so that you can explore focused questions in your preliminary research. At this early stage in the research process, your goal is to turn a topic idea into a claim at least one full sentence long. ○

In the natural and social sciences, topics sometimes evolve from research problems already on the table in various fields. Presented with such a research agenda, do a "review of the literature" to find out what represents state-of-the-art thinking on the topic. You do this by reading what others have published on this subject in major journals. Then create an experiment in which your specific research question—offered as a claim called a *hypothesis*—either confirms the direction of ongoing work in the field or advances or changes it. In basic science courses, get plenty of advice from your instructor about formulating workable research questions and hypotheses.

Ask for help.   During preliminary research, you'll quickly learn that not all sources are equal. ○ They differ in purpose, method, media, audience, and authority. Until you get your legs as a researcher, never hesitate to ask questions about research tools and strategies: Get recommendations about the best available journals, books, and authors from instructors and reference librarians. Ask them which publishers, institutions, and experts carry the most intellectual weight in their fields. If your topic is highly specialized, expect to spend additional time tracking down sources from outside your own library.

Distinguish between primary and secondary sources.   A *primary source* is a document that provides an eyewitness account of an event or phenomenon; a *secondary source* is a step or two removed, an article or book that interprets or reports on events and phenomena described in primary sources. The famous Zapruder film of the John F. Kennedy assassination in Dallas (November 22, 1963) is a memorable primary historical document; the many books or articles that draw on the film to comment on the assassination are secondary sources. Both types of sources are useful to you as a researcher.

develop a
statement p. 362

find reliable
sources p. 451

Use primary sources when doing research that breaks new ground. Primary sources represent raw data—letters, journals, newspaper accounts, official documents, laws, court opinions, statistics, research reports, audio and video recordings, and so on. Working with primary materials, you generate your own ideas about a subject, free of anyone else's opinions or explanations. Or you can review the actual evidence others have used to make their claims and arguments, perhaps reinterpreting their findings, correcting them, or bringing a new perspective to the subject.

Use secondary sources to learn what others have discovered or claimed about a subject. In many fields, you spend most of your time reviewing secondary materials, especially when a subject is new to you. Secondary sources include scholarly books and articles, encyclopedias, magazine pieces, and many Web sites. In academic assignments, you may find yourself moving between different kinds of materials, first reading a primary text like *Hamlet* and then reading various commentaries on it.

Record every source you examine.   Whether you examine sources in libraries or look at them online, *you must* accurately list, right from the start, every research item you encounter, gathering the following information:

- Authors, editors, translators, sponsors (of Web sites), or other major contributors
- Titles, subtitles, edition numbers, and volumes

Web sites featuring government resources, such as Thomas or FedStats, and corporate annual reports provide primary material for analysis. *Left:* Thomas/Library of Congress, http://thomas.loc.gov. *Center:* FedStats, http://fedstats.gov. *Right:* Courtesy, General Motors.

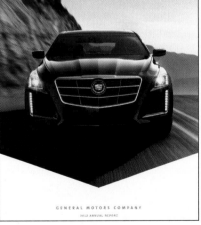

- Publication information, including places of publication and publishers (for books); titles of magazines and journals, as well as volume and page numbers; dates of publication and access (the latter for online materials)
- Page numbers, URLs, electronic pathways, keywords, DOI (digital object identifier), or other locators

You'll need this information later to document your sources.

It might seem obsessive to collect so much data on books and articles you may not even use. But when you spend weeks or months on an assignment, you don't want to have to backtrack, wondering at some point, "Did I read this source?" A log tells you whether you have.

Prepare a topic proposal.   Your instructor may request a topic proposal. Typically, this includes a topic idea, a draft thesis or hypothesis, potential sources, your intended approach, and a list of potential problems. It may also include an annotated bibliography of the books, articles, and other materials you anticipate using in your project—see Chapter 11 for more on annotated bibliographies.

Remember that such proposals are written to get feedback about your project's feasibility and that even a good idea raises questions. The following sample proposal for a short project is directed chiefly at classmates, who must respond via electronic discussion board as part of the assignment.

Books and magazines often provide secondary, not primary, information. *Top:* Book-cover from the book *Through the Language Glass: Why the World Looks Different In Other Languages* by Guy Deutscher. Book-cover design by Steve Attardo and Rodrigo Corral. Book-cover design copyright © 2011 by Steve Attardo and Rodrigo Corral. Used by permission of Henry Holt and Company, LLC. All rights reserved. *Bottom:* Reprinted by permission from Macmillan Publishers Ltd: *Nature*, copyright © 2008.

Eades 1

Micah Eades

Professor Kurtz

English 201

March 20, 20--

Causal Analysis Proposal: Awkward Atmospheres

People don't like going to the doctor's office. You wait in an office room decorated from the 1980s reading *Highlights* or last year's *Field & Stream* and listen to patients in the next room talking about the details of their proctology exam. Since I am planning a future as a primary care physician, I don't want people to dread coming to see me.

My paper will propose that patient dissatisfaction with visits to their physicians may be due not entirely to fear of upcoming medical examinations but rather to the unwelcoming atmosphere of most waiting and treatment rooms. More specifically, I will examine the negative effect that noise, poor interior design, and unsympathetic staff attitudes may have on patient comfort. I will propose that these factors have a much larger impact on patient well-being than previously expected. Additionally, I will propose possible remedies and ways to change these negative perceptions.

My biggest problem may be finding concrete evidence for my claims. For evidence, I do intend to cite the relatively few clinical studies that have been conducted on patient satisfaction and atmosphere. My audience will be a tough crowd: doctors who have neither an awareness of the problems I describe nor much desire to improve the ambience of their offices.

Title indicates that proposal responds to a specific assignment.

Opening paragraph offers a rationale for subject choice.

Describes planned content and structure of paper.

Has done enough research to know that literature on subject is not extensive.

Paper will be directed to a specific audience.

38

Finding Print and Online Sources

refine your
search

When writing an academic paper that requires facts, data, and reputable research or opinion, look to three resources in this order: local and school libraries, informational databases and indexes, and the Internet. Libraries remain your first resource because they have been set up specifically to steer you toward materials appropriate for academic projects. Informational databases and indexes are usually available to you only through libraries and their Web sites, so they are a natural follow-up. And the Internet places third on this list, an undeniably useful resource but still a rugged frontier when it comes to reliable information, particularly for a novice.

Search libraries strategically. At the library you'll find books, journals, newspapers, and other materials, both print and electronic, in a collection expertly overseen by librarians and information specialists, who are, perhaps, the most valuable resources in the building. They are specifically trained to help you find what you need. Get to know them.

Of course, the key to navigating a library is its catalog. All but the smallest or most specialized libraries now organize their collections electronically (rather than with printed cards), but there's still a learning curve. The temptation will be to plunge in and start searching. After all, you can locate most items by author, title, subject, keywords, and even call number. But spend a few minutes reading the available Help screens to discover the features and protocols of the catalog. Most searches tell you immediately if the library has a book or journal you need, where it is on the shelves or in data collections, and whether it is available.

Do not ignore, either, the advanced features of a catalog (such as searches by language, by date, by type of content); these options help you find just the items you need or can use. And since you will often use a library not to find specific materials but to choose and develop topics, pay attention to the keywords or search terms the catalog uses to index the subject you're exploring: You can use index terms for sources you find to look for other similar materials—an important way of generating leads on a subject.

Explore library reference tools.
In the age of Wikipedia, it's easy to forget that libraries still offer truly authoritative source materials in their reference rooms or online reference collections. Such standard works include encyclopedias, almanacs, historical records, maps, archived newspapers, and so on.

In addition to author, title, and publication information, the full entry for an item in a library catalog will also include subject headings. These terms may suggest additional avenues of research. Chicago Public Library.

Quite often, for instance, you will need reliable biographical facts about important people—dates of birth, countries of origin, schools attended, career paths, and so on. You *might* find enough data from a Web search or a Wikipedia entry for people currently in the news. But to get accurate and substantial materials on historical figures, consult library tools such as the *Oxford Dictionary of National Biography* (focusing on the United Kingdom) or the *Dictionary of American Biography*. The British work is available in an up-to-date online version. Libraries also have many more specialized biographical tools, both in print and online. Ask about them.

If you want information from old newspapers, you may need ingenuity. Libraries don't store newspapers, so local and a few national papers will be available only in clumsy (though usable) microfilm or microfiche form. Just as discouraging, very few older newspapers are indexed. So, unless you know the approximate date of an event, you may have a tough time finding a particular story in the microfilmed copies of newspapers. Fortunately, both the *New York*

Times and *Wall Street Journal* are indexed and available in most major libraries. You'll also find older magazines on microfilm. These may be indexed (up to 1982) in print bibliographies such as the *Readers' Guide to Periodical Literature*. Ask a librarian for assistance.

When your local library doesn't have resources you need, ask the people at the checkout or reference desks about interlibrary loan. If cooperating libraries have the books or materials you want, you can borrow them at minimal cost. But plan ahead. The loan process takes time.

Use professional databases.   Information databases and indexes—our second category of research materials—are also found at libraries, among their electronic resources. These tools give you access to professional journals, magazines, and newspaper archives, in either summary or full-text form. Your library or school purchases licenses to make these valuable, often password-protected, resources available—services such as *EBSCOhost*, *InfoTrac*, and *Lexis-Nexis*. And, once again, librarians can teach you how to navigate such complex databases efficiently.

Many academic research projects, for instance, begin with a search of multi-disciplinary databases such as *LexisNexis Academic*, *Academic OneFile*, or *Academic Search Premier*. These über-indexes cover a wide range of materials, including newspapers, reputable magazines, and many academic periodicals. Most libraries subscribe to one or more of these information services, which you can search online much like library catalogs, using basic and advanced search features.

For even more in-depth research, you need to learn to use databases within your specific field or major, tools such as *Ei* in engineering or the *MLA International Bibliography* in language and literature studies. There are, in fact, hundreds of such databases, far too many to list here, and some of them may be too specialized or technical for projects early in a college career. Librarians or instructors can direct you to the ones you can handle and, when necessary, explain how to use them. Such databases are sometimes less accessible than they seem at first glance.

Explore the Internet.   As you well know, you can find information simply by exploring the Web from your laptop or tablet, using search engines such as Google and Bing to locate data and generate ideas. The territory may seem familiar because you spend so much time there, but don't overestimate your ability to find what you need online. Browsing the Web daily to check sports scores and favorite blogs is completely different from using the Web for academic work.

For a tutorial on online research, see **macmillanhighered.com/howtowrite3e**.
Tutorials › Digital Writing › Online Research Tools

Research suggests that many students begin their projects by simply typing obvious terms into Web browsers, ignoring the advanced capabilities of search engines. To take more control of searches, follow the links on search engine screens that you now probably ignore: Learn to use the tools such as Advanced Search; Search Help; Help; Fix a Problem; Tips & Tricks; Useful Features; and More. You'll be amazed what you discover.

Then exercise care with Web sources. Always be sure you know who is responsible for the material you are reading (for instance, a government agency, a congressional office, a news service, a corporation), who is posting it, who is the author of the material or sponsor of the Web site, what the date of publication is, and so on. ○ A site's information is often skewed by those who pay its bills or run it; it can also be outdated if no one regularly updates the resource.

Keep current with Web developments too. Web companies such as Google are making more books and journal articles both searchable and available through their sites. Examine these resources as they come online. For instance, a tool such as Google Scholar will direct you to academic studies and scholarly papers on a given topic—exactly the kind of material you want to use in term papers or reports.

As an experiment, you might compare the hits you get on a topic with a regular Google search with those that turn up when you select the Scholar option. You'll quickly notice that the Scholar items are more serious and technical—and also more difficult to access. In some cases, you may see only an abstract of a journal article or the first page of the item. Yet the materials you locate may be worth a trip to the library to retrieve in their entirety.

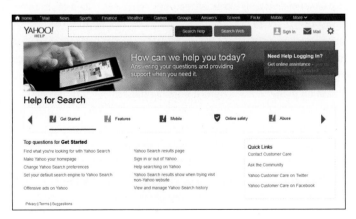

The Yahoo! Help screen provides tips on how to search the Internet. Reproduced with permission of Yahoo. © 2014 Yahoo. YAHOO! and the YAHOO! logo are registered trademarks of Yahoo.

find reliable
sources p. 451

Resources to Consult When Conducting Research			
Source	**What It Provides**	**Usefulness in Academic Research**	**Where to Find It**
Scholarly Books	Fully documented and detailed primary research and analyses by scholars	Highly useful if not too high-level or technical	Library, Google Scholar
Scholarly Journals	Carefully documented primary research by scientists and scholars	Highly useful if not too high-level or technical	Library, databases
Newspapers	Accounts of current events	Useful as starting point	Library, microfilm, databases (*LexisNexis*), Internet
Magazines	Wide topic range, usually based on secondary research; written for popular audience	Useful if magazine has serious reputation	Libraries, newsstands, databases (*EBSCOhost*, *InfoTrac*), Internet
Encyclopedias (General or Discipline-Specific)	Brief articles	Useful as starting point	Libraries, Internet
Wikipedia	Open-source encyclopedia: entries written/edited by online contributors	Not considered reliable for academic projects	Internet: www.wikipedia.org
Special Collections	Materials such as maps, paintings, artifacts, etc.	Highly useful for specialized projects	Libraries, museums; images available via Internet
Government, Academic, or Organization Web Sites	Vast data compilations of varying quality, some of it reviewed	Highly useful	Internet sites with URLs ending in *.gov*, *.edu*, or *.org*
Commercial Web Sites	Information on many subjects; quality varies	Useful if possible biases are known	Internet sites
Blogs	Controlled, often highly partisan discussions of specialized topics	Useful when affiliated with reputable sources such as newspapers	Internet
Personal Web Sites	Often idiosyncratic information	Rarely useful; content varies widely	Internet

Doing Field Research

39

While most writing you do will be built on the work of others—
that is, their books, articles, and fact-finding—you can do research
of your own in many situations. For instance, you might interview
people with experiences or information related to the subject you're
exploring. ○ Or you could support a claim for a psychology or
marketing paper by carefully observing and recording how people
actually think or behave.

interview
and observe

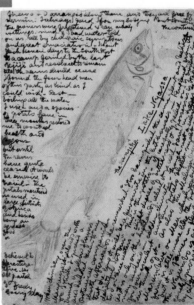

Field research is done
in many ways and with
different tools and media.
Left: TopFoto/The Image Works.
Center: TopFoto/The Image Works.
Right: PA Photos/Landov.

ask for
help p. 350

Interview people with unique knowledge of your subject.   When considering whether an interview makes sense for your project, ask yourself this important question: "What do I expect to learn from the interviewee?" If the information you seek is easily available online or in print, don't waste everyone's time going through with an interview. If, on the other hand, this person offers a fresh perspective on your topic, a personal interview could advance your research.

Interviews can be written or spoken. Written interviews, whether by e-mail or letter, instant messaging or online chat, allow you to keep questions and answers focused and provide a written record of the interviewee's responses. But spoken interviews, both in person and via Skype, allow in-depth discussion of a topic and may lead to more memorable reactions and deeper insights. Be flexible in setting up the type of interview most convenient for your subject. For oral interviews, keep the following suggestions in mind:

- Request an interview formally by phone, confirming it with a follow-up message.

- Give your subjects a compelling reason for meeting or corresponding with you; briefly explain your research project and why their knowledge or experience is important to your work.

- Let potential interviewees know how you chose them as subjects. If possible, identify a personal reference—that is, a professor or administrator who can vouch for you.

- Prepare a set of purposeful interview questions. Don't try to wing it.

- Think about how to phrase questions to open up the interview. Avoid queries that can be answered in one word. Don't ask, *Did you enjoy your years in Asia?* Instead, lead with, *What did you enjoy most about the decade you spent in Tokyo?*

- Start the interview by thanking the interviewee for his or her time and providing a very brief description of your research project.

- Keep a written record of material you intend to quote. If necessary, confirm the exact wording with your interviewee.

- End the interview by again expressing your thanks.

- Follow up with a thank-you note or e-mail and, if the interviewee's contributions were substantial, send him or her a copy of the final research paper.

- In your paper, give credit to any people interviewed by documenting the information they provided. ○

For an interview conducted in person, arrive at the predetermined meeting place on time and dressed professionally. If you wish to record the interview, be sure to ask permission first.

If you conduct your interview in writing, request a response by a certain date—one or two weeks is reasonable for ten questions. Refer to Chapter 13 for e-mail etiquette and Chapter 14 for guidelines on writing business letters.

For telephone interviews, call from a place with good reception, where you will not be interrupted. Your cell phone should be fully charged or plugged in.

> **Your Turn**   Prepare a full set of questions you would use to interview a classmate about some *academic* issue — for example, study habits, methods for writing papers, or career objectives. Think about how to sequence your questions, how to avoid one-word responses, and how to follow up on possible replies (if the interview is oral). Write your questions down and then pair up with a classmate for a set of mutual interviews.
>
> When you are done, write a one-page report based on what you learn and share the results with classmates.

Make careful and verifiable observations.   The point of systematic observation is to provide a reliable way of studying a narrowly defined activity or phenomenon. But in preparing reports or arguments that focus on small groups or local communities, you might find yourself without enough data to move your claims beyond mere opinion.

For example, an anecdote or two won't persuade administrators that community rooms in the student union are being scheduled inefficiently. But you could conduct a simple study of these facilities, showing exactly how many student groups use them and for what purposes, over a given period of time.

understand citation
styles p. 470

This kind of evidence usually carries more weight with readers, who can decide whether to accept or challenge your numbers.

Some situations can't be counted or measured as readily as the one described above. If you wanted, let's say, to compare the various community rooms to determine whether those with windows encouraged more productive discussions than rooms without, your observations would be "softer" and more qualitative. You might have to describe the tone of speakers' voices or the general mood of the room. But numbers might play a part; you could, for instance, track how many people participated in the discussion or the number of tasks accomplished during the meeting.

To avoid bias in their observations, many researchers use double-column notebooks. In the first column, they record the physical details of their observation as objectively as possible—descriptions, sounds, countable data, weather, time, circumstances, activity, and so on. In the second column, they record their interpretations and commentaries on the data.

In addition to careful and objective note-taking techniques, devices such as cameras, video recorders, and tape recorders provide reliable backup evidence about an event. Also, having more than one witness observe a situation can help verify your findings.

Learn more about fieldwork.   In those disciplines or college majors that use fieldwork, you will find guides or manuals to explain the details of such research procedures. You will also discover that fieldwork comes in many varieties, from naturalist observations and case studies to time studies and market research.

A double-column notebook entry.

OBSERVABLE DATA	COMMENTARY
9/12/11 2 P.M. Meeting of Entertainment Committee Room MUB210 (no windows) 91 degrees outside Air conditioning broken People appear quiet, tired, hot	Heat and lack of a/c probably making everyone miserable.

Evaluating Sources

40

In Chapter 38, you were directed to the best possible print and online sources for your research. But the fact is, all sources, no matter how prestigious, have strengths and weaknesses, biases and limitations. Even the most well-intentioned instructors, librarians, and experts have their preconceptions too. So evaluating the sources you've either found or been directed to is a necessary part of the research process. Here are some strategies for making those judgments.

find reliable sources

Preview source materials for their key features and strategies. Give any source a quick once-over, looking for clues to its aim, content, and structure. Begin with the title and subtitle, taking seriously its key terms and qualifiers. A good title tells what a piece is—and is not—about. For many scholarly articles, the subtitle (which typically follows a colon) describes the substance of the argument.

Then scan the introduction (in a book) or abstract (in an article). From these items, you should be able to quickly grasp what the source covers, what its methods are, and what the author hopes to prove or accomplish.

Inspect the table of contents in a book or the headings in an article methodically, using them to figure out the overall structure of the work or to find specific information. Briefly review charts, tables, and illustrations, too, to discover what they offer. If a book has an index—and a serious book should—look for the key terms or subjects you are researching to see how well they are covered.

If the work appears promising, read its final section or chapter. Knowing how the material concludes gives insight into its value for your research. Finally, look over the bibliography. The list of sources indicates how thorough the author has been and, not incidentally, points you to other materials you might want to examine.

Check who published or produced the source.   In general, books published by presses associated with colleges and universities (Harvard, Oxford, Stanford, etc.) are reputable sources for college papers. So are articles from professional journals described as *refereed* or *peer-reviewed*. These terms are used for journals in which the articles have been impartially evaluated by panels of experts prior to publication. Instructors and librarians can help you grasp these distinctions.

You can also usually rely on material from reputable commercial publishers and from established institutions and agencies. The *New York Times*; the *Wall Street Journal*; Random House; Farrar, Straus & Giroux; Simon & Schuster; and the U.S. Government Printing Office make their ample share of mistakes, of course, but are generally considered to be far more reliable than most blogs or personal Web sites. But you always need to be cautious.

Check who wrote a work.   Ordinarily, you should cite recognized authorities on your topic. Look for authors who are mentioned frequently and favorably within a field or whose works appear regularly in notes or bibliographies. Get familiar with them.

The Web makes it possible to examine the careers of other authors whom you might not recognize. Search for their names online to confirm that they are reputable journalists or recognized experts in their field. Avoid citing authors working too far beyond their areas of professional expertise. Celebrities especially like to cross boundaries, sometimes mistaking their passion for an issue (environmentalism, diet, public health) for genuine mastery of a subject.

Consider the audience for a source.   What passes for adequate information in the general marketplace of ideas may not cut it when you're doing academic research. Many widely read books and articles that popularize a subject—such as climate change or problems with education—may, in fact, be based on more technical scholarly books and articles. For academic projects, rely primarily on those scholarly works themselves, even if you were inspired to choose a subject by reading respectable nonfiction. Glossy magazines shouldn't play a role in your research either, though the lines can get blurry. *People*, *O*, *Rolling Stone*, or *Spin* might be important if you are writing about popular culture or music. Similarly, Wikipedia is invaluable for a quick introduction to a subject, but don't cite it as an authority in an academic paper.

Establish how current a source is.   Scholarly work doesn't come with an expiration date, but you should base your research on the latest information. For fields in which research builds on previous work, the date of publication may even be highlighted within its system of documentation. For books, you'll find the date of publication on the copyright page, which is the reverse side of the title page (see p. 487).

Check the source's documentation.   All serious scholarly and scientific research is documented. Claims are based on solid evidence backed up by formal notes, data are packed into charts and tables, and there is a bibliography at the end. All of this is done so that readers can verify the claims an author makes.

In a news story, journalists may establish the credibility of their information by simply naming their sources or, at a minimum, attributing their findings to reliable unnamed sources—and usually more than one. The authors of serious magazine pieces don't use footnotes and bibliographies either, but they, too, credit their major sources somewhere in the work. No serious claim should be left hanging. ○

For your own academic projects, avoid authors and sources with undocumented assertions. Sometimes you have to trust authors when they are writing about personal experiences or working as field reporters, but let readers know when your claims are based on uncorroborated personal accounts.

Entertainer Jenny McCarthy has disturbed many public health officials by her claims of a connection between childhood vaccination and autism. She has a personal connection to the issue but no medical or scientific credentials. Dennis Van Tine/Newscom.

think critically
p. 343

You can learn a lot about a
source by previewing a few
basic elements.

Available online at www.sciencedirect.com

SCIENCE @ DIRECT®

ACADEMIC
PRESS   Journal of Research in Personality 36 (2002) 607–614

JOURNAL OF
RESEARCH IN
PERSONALITY

www.academicpress.com

Brief report

Are we barking up the right tree? Evaluating a comparative approach to personality

Samuel D. Gosling [*] and Simine Vazire

Department of Psychology, University of Texas, Austin, TX, USA

- -
Playful title nonetheless
fits: Article is about
animals.

Abstract

Animal studies can enrich the field of human personality psychology by addressing questions that are difficult or impossible to address with human studies alone. However, the benefits of a comparative approach to personality cannot be reaped until the tenability of the personality construct has been established in animals. Using criteria established in the wake of the person–situation debate (Kenrick & Funder, 1988), the authors evaluate the status of personality traits in animals. The animal literature provides strong evidence that personality does exist in animals. That is, personality ratings of animals: (a) show strong levels of interobserver agreement, (b) show evidence of validity in terms of predicting behaviors and real-world outcomes, and (c) do not merely reflect the implicit theories of observers projected onto animals. Although much work remains to be done, the preliminary groundwork has been laid for a comparative approach to personality.

- -
Abstract previews entire
article.

Introduction

Personality characteristics have been examined in a broad range of nonhuman species including chimpanzees, rhesus monkeys, ferrets, hyenas, rats,

- -
Headings throughout
signal this is a research
article.

*Corresponding author. Fax: 1-512- 471-5935.
E-mail address: gosling@psy.utexas.edu (S.D. Gosling).

0092-6566/02/$ - see front matter © 2002 Elsevier Science (USA). All rights reserved.
PII: S0092-6566(02)00511-1

608   *Brief report / Journal of Research in Personality 36 (2002) 607 614*

sheep, rhinoceros, hedgehogs, zebra finches, garter snakes, guppies, and oc-
topuses (for a full review, see Gosling, 2001). Such research is important because animal studies can be used to tackle questions that are difficult or
impossible to address with human studies alone. By reaping the benefits
of animal research, a comparative approach to personality can enrich the
field of human personality psychology, providing unique opportunities to
examine the biological, genetic, and environmental bases of personality,
and to study personality development, personality-health links, and personality perception. However, all of these benefits hinge on the tenability of the
personality construct in non-human animals. Thus, the purpose of the present paper is to address a key question in the animal domain: is personality
real? That is, do personality traits reflect real properties of individuals or are
they fictions in the minds of perceivers?

    Thirty years ago, the question of the reality of personality occupied the
attention of human-personality researchers, so our evaluation of the comparative approach to personality draws on the lessons learned in the human domain. Mischel's (1968) influential critique of research on human
personality was the first of a series of direct challenges to the assumptions
that personality exists and predicts meaningful real-world behaviors. Based
on a review of the personality literature, Mischel (1968) pointed to the lack
of evidence that individuals' behaviors are consistent across situations (Mischel & Peake, 1982). Over the next two decades, personality researchers
garnered substantial empirical evidence to counter the critiques of personality. In an important article, Kenrick and Funder (1988) carefully analyzed the various arguments that had been leveled against personality
and summarized the theoretical and empirical work refuting these arguments.

    The recent appearance of studies of animal personality has elicited re-
newed debate about the status of personality traits. Gosling, Lilienfeld,
and Marino (in press) proposed that the conditions put forward by Kenrick
and Funder (1988) to evaluate the idea of human personality can be mobi-
lized in the service of evaluating the idea of animal personality. Gosling et
al. (in press) used these criteria to evaluate research on personality in non-
human primates. In the present paper, we extend their analysis to the broader field of comparative psychology, considering research on nonhuman
animals from several species and taxa. Kenrick and Funder's paper delin-
eates three major criteria that must be met to establish the existence of personality traits: (1) assessments by independent observers must agree with
one another; (2) these assessments must predict behaviors and real-world
outcomes; and (3) observer ratings must be shown to reflect genuine attri-
butes of the individuals rated, not merely the observers' implicit theories
about how personality traits covary. Drawing on evidence from the animal-
behavior literature, we evaluate whether these three criteria have been met
with respect to animal personality.

Point of this brief study is
defined at end of opening
paragraph.

This page reviews literature
on studies of animal
personality.

understand synthesis
papers p. 272

Annotating Sources

Once you locate trustworthy sources, review them to zero in on the best ideas and most convincing evidence for your project. During this process of critical reading, you annotate, summarize, ○ synthesize, ○ and paraphrase ○ your sources—in effect creating the notes you need to compose your paper.

Annotate sources to understand them. Examine important sources closely enough to figure out not only what they say but also how the authors reached their conclusions or gathered their data. Think of it as becoming an expert on the sources you cite. To preserve your ideas, mark up key texts with tools that work for you—notes in the margins, Post-it notes, electronic comments, and so forth. Simply writing these comments will draw you deeper into source materials and make you think more about them.

Read sources to identify claims. Begin by highlighting any specific claims, themes, or thesis statements a writer offers early in a text. Then pay attention to the way these ideas recur throughout the work, especially near the conclusion. At a minimum, decide whether a writer has made reasonable claims, developed them consistently, and delivered on promised evidence. In the example on pages 457–59, claims and reasons are highlighted in yellow.

Read sources to understand assumptions. Finding and annotating the assumptions in a source can be *much* trickier than

analyze claims and evidence/ take notes

sum up
ideas p. 460

understand
synthesis p. 272

restate
ideas p. 463

locating claims. Highlight any assumptions stated outright in the source; they will be rare. More often, you have to infer a writer's assumptions, put them into your own words, and perhaps record them in marginal notes. Identifying controversial or debatable assumptions is particularly important. For instance, if a writer makes the claim that *America needs tighter border security to prevent terrorist attacks*, you draw the inference that the writer believes that terrorism is caused by people crossing inadequately patrolled borders. Is that assumption accurate? Should the writer explain or defend it? Raise such questions. The one key assumption in the example that follows is highlighted in orange.

Read sources to find evidence.   Look for evidence that an author uses to support both the claims and assumptions in a text. Evidence can come in the form of data, examples, illustrations, or logical inferences. Since most academic materials you read will be thick with evidence, highlight only key items—especially any facts or materials you intend to mention in your own project. Make sure no crucial point goes unsupported; if you find one, make a note of it. In the following example, key evidence is highlighted in blue.

Record your personal reactions to source material.   When reading multiple sources, you'll want a record of what you favored or objected to in them. To be certain you don't later mistake your personal comments for observations *from* the source, use first person or pose questions as you respond. Use personal annotations, as well, to draw connections to other source materials you have read. In the following example, personal reactions appear on the left.

SANITY 101

Parents of adolescents usually strive for an aura of calm and reason. But just two words can trigger irrational behavior in parent and child alike: "college admissions."

It's not an unreasonable response, actually, given the list of exasperating questions facing parents seeking to maximize their children's prospects: Do I tutor my child to boost college admissions test scores? Do I

CLAIM AND REASON: Fear of college admissions procedures is key point in editorial.

rely on the school admissions counselor or hire a private adviser? Do I hire a professional editor to shape my child's college essay?

The price tags behind those decisions drive up the angst. A testing tutor "guaranteeing" a 200-point score boost on the SAT admissions test will charge roughly $2,400. Hiring a private college counselor can cost from $1,300 to $10,000. And hiring an essay editor can cost between $60 and $1,800. Wealthy suburbs are particularly lucrative for the college prep industry. Less affluent families are left with even greater reason to fret: Their children face an unfair disadvantage.

Now, private employers are stepping in to help out.

In a front-page article on Tuesday, *USA Today*'s education reporter Mary Beth Marklein revealed a range of counseling packages that companies are offering parents of college applicants, from brown-bag discussion lunches to Web-based programs that manage the entire admissions process.

It's thoughtful of the employers, but it shouldn't be necessary.

Thanks to overanxious parents, aggressive college admissions officials, and hustling college prep entrepreneurs, the admissions system has spun out of control. And the colleges have done little to restore sanity.

Take just one example, the "early decision" process in which seniors apply to a college by November 1 and promise to attend if admitted.

Early decision induces students to cram demanding courses into their junior year so they will appear on the application record. That makes an already stressful year for students and parents even more so. Plus, students must commit to a college long before they are ready. The real advantages of early decision go to colleges, which gain more control over their student mix and rise in national rankings by raising their acceptance rates.

Parents and students can combat the stress factor by keeping a few key facts in mind. While it's true that the very top colleges are ruthlessly selective — both Harvard and Yale accept slightly less than 10 percent of applicants — most colleges are barely selective. Of the 1,400 four-year colleges in the United States, only about 100 are very selective, and they aren't right for every student. Among the other 1,300, an acceptance rate of about 85 percent is more the norm.

CLAIM AND REASON:
Parents are worrying too much.

And the best part of all: Many of those 1,300 colleges are more interested in educating your child than burnishing their rankings on lists of the "top" institutions. So the next time you hear the words "college admissions," don't instantly open your wallet. First, take a deep breath.

—Editorial/Opinion, *USA Today*, January 19, 2006

EVIDENCE:
Statistics offer reasons not to fear college admissions procedures.

ASSUMPTION:
Change "are" to "should be" and you have the assumption underlying this entire argument.

Your Turn   Exchange a draft of a paper you are developing with that of a classmate. Then read your colleague's paper closely, as outlined in this chapter, imagining how you might use it as a source. First highlight its major claims and reasons; then identify any key assumptions in the paper. Bracket the sections of the project that primarily offer evidence. Finally, offer your personal reactions to various parts of the paper.

You might use highlighting pens of different colors to separate claims/reasons from assumptions and evidence, as in the sample essay.

Summarizing Sources

sum up ideas

Once you determine which materials deserve closer attention and you have read these articles, books, and other texts critically— with an eye toward using their insights and data in your research project—you're ready to summarize the individual items, putting ideas you've found into your own words. These brief summaries or fuller paraphrases can become the springboard for composing your paper. ○

Prepare a summary for every item you examine in a project. This advice seems self-evident, but it is not. A quick look may tell you that an article or book has no bearing on your project. Even so, describe it very briefly on a note card or in an electronic file (with complete bibliographic data). Such a record reminds you that you have, in fact, seen and reviewed that item—which can be no small comfort when working on projects that stretch over several weeks or months. After you've examined dozens and dozens of sources, it's easy to forget what exactly you've read.

Use a summary to recap what a writer has said. When a source is clearly relevant to your project, look carefully for its main point and build your summary on it, making sure that this state-ment *does* reflect the actual content of the source, not your opinion of it. Be certain that the summary is *entirely* in your own words. Include the author and title of the work, too, so you can easily cite

restate
ideas p. 463

it later. The following is one summary of the *USA Today* editorial reprinted on pages 457–59, with all the required citation information:

> In "Sanity 101," the editors of *USA Today* (January 19, 2006) criticize current college admission practices, which, they argue, make students and parents alike fear that getting into an appropriate school is harder than it really is.
>
> Source: "Sanity 101." Editorial. *USA Today* 19 Jan. 2006: 10A. Print.

Be sure your summary is accurate and complete. Even when a source makes several points, moves in contradictory directions, or offers a complex conclusion, your job is simply to describe what the material does. Don't embellish the material or blur the distinction between the source's words and yours. Include all bibliographical information (title, author, and date) from the source. The following summary of "Sanity 101" shows what can go wrong if you are not careful.

> According to *USA Today*, most students get into the colleges they want. But admission into most colleges is so tough that many parents blow a fortune on tutors and counselors so that their kids can win early admission. But the paper's advice to parents is don't instantly open your wallet. First, take a deep breath.

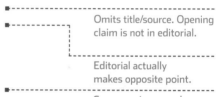

Omits title/source. Opening claim is not in editorial.

Editorial actually makes opposite point.

Summary improperly uses source's exact words. Might lead to inadvertent plagiarism later on.

Use a summary to record your take on a source. In addition to reporting the contents of the material accurately, note also how the source might (or might not) contribute to your paper. But make certain that your comments won't be confused with claims made in the summarized article itself. The following are two acceptable sample summaries for "Sanity 101."

> In "Sanity 101," *USA Today* (January 19, 2006) describes the efforts of college applicants and parents to deal with the progressively more competitive admissions policies of elite institutions. The editorial claims that most schools, however, are far less selective. The article includes a reference to another *USA Today* piece by Mary Beth Marklein on the support some companies offer employees to assist them with college admissions issues.
>
> Source: "Sanity 101." Editorial. *USA Today* 19 Jan. 2006: 10A. Print.

In an editorial (January 19, 2006) entitled "Sanity 101," *USA Today* counsels parents against worrying too much about hypercompetitive current college admission practices. In reality, only a small percentage of schools are highly selective about admissions. The editorial doesn't provide the schools' side of the issue.

Source: "Sanity 101." Editorial. *USA Today* 19 Jan. 2006: 10A. Print.

Use summaries to prepare an annotated bibliography.   In an annotated bibliography, brief summaries are provided for every item in an alphabetical list of sources. These summaries help readers understand the content and scope of materials. For more about annotated bibliographies, see Chapter 11. O

Your Turn   Practice writing summaries by pairing up with a classmate and finding (probably online) a newspaper or blog page with a variety of opinion-oriented articles. For instance, check out the "Opinion" page in the *New York Times* or the home page of *Arts & Letters Daily* or the *Huffington Post*.

Agree on one or two pieces that both of you will recap separately. Then write the paired summaries, being careful to identify the items, describe them accurately, and separate your recaps from any comments you make about the material you have read. When you are done, compare your summaries. Discuss their accuracy and make certain that neither of you has inadvertently borrowed language from the original articles.

understand annotated
bibliographies p. 266

Paraphrasing Sources

Paraphrases provide more complete records of the research materials you examine than do summaries. ○ Like a summary, a paraphrase records a book or article's main point, but it also recaps the reasons and key evidence supporting that conclusion. Paraphrase any materials you expect to use extensively in a project. Then consider how the research materials you have gathered stand in relationship to each other.

Identify the major claims and the structure of the source. Determine the main points made by the article, chapter, or text you are paraphrasing, and examine how the work organizes information to support its claims. ○ Then follow the same structure when you paraphrase the source. For example, your paraphrase will probably be arranged sequentially when a work has a story to tell, be arranged topic by topic when you're dealing with reported information, or be structured logically—by claims and evidence—when you take notes from arguments or editorials.

Track the source faithfully. A paraphrase should move through an article, chapter, or book succinctly while remaining faithful to its purpose, organization, tone, and, to some extent, style. In effect, you are preparing an abstract of the material, complete and readable on its own. Take concise and practical notes, adapting the paraphrase to your needs—understanding that materials especially valuable to your project will need to be described thoroughly. ○

restate
ideas

Record key pieces of evidence.   Thanks to photocopies and downloaded files, you don't usually have to copy data laboriously into your notes—and you probably shouldn't. (Chances of error greatly multiply whenever you transcribe information by hand.) Be certain, though, that your paraphrase sets down supporting reasons for all major claims in the source, as well as key evidence and facts. Key evidence is whatever proves a point or seals the deal in an argument. Keep track of page numbers for all the important data so you can cite this material in your paper without having to return to the original source.

Be certain your notes are entirely in your own words.   If you copy the language of sources as you paraphrase them, you risk plagiarism. Deliberately or not, you could transfer big chunks of someone else's writing into your project. But if you have paraphrased by the rules, setting all borrowed words between quotation marks, it's safe to import those notes directly into your project— giving the original writers due credit for their ideas, of course. When you write competent paraphrases, you've already started to compose your own paper. There is no lost motion.

The following is a possible paraphrase of "Sanity 101," the complete, fully annotated text of which appears in Chapter 41 (pp. 457–59). Compare the paraphrase here to the briefer summaries of the article that appear in Chapter 42 (pp. 461–62).

> In an editorial entitled "Sanity 101" (January 19, 2006), the editors of *USA Today* worry that many fearful parents are resorting to costly measures to help assure their child's college admission, some hiring private counselors and tutors that poorer families can't afford. Companies now even offer college admission assistance as part of employees' job packages. Colleges themselves are to blame for the hysteria, in part because of "early admission" practices that benefit them more than students. But parents and students should consider the facts. Only a handful of colleges are truly selective; most have acceptance rates near 85 percent. In addition, most schools care more about students than about their own rankings.

Avoid misleading or inaccurate paraphrasing.   Your notes won't be worth much if your paraphrases of sources distort the content of what you read. Don't rearrange the information, give it a spin you might prefer, or offer your own opinions on a subject. Make it clear, too, whenever your comments focus just on particular sections or chapters of a source, rather than on the entire piece. That way, you won't misread your notes days later and give readers a wrong impression about an article or book. The following is a paraphrase of "Sanity 101" that gets almost *everything* wrong.

> Parents of teens usually try to be reasonable, the editors of *USA Today* complained on January 19, 2006. But the words "college admission" can make both child and parent irrational. The response is not unreasonable, given all the irritating questions facing parents seeking to improve their children's prospects. But the fact is that just a few colleges are highly selective. Most of the four-year schools in the country have acceptance rates of 85 percent. So high school students and parents should just chill and not blow their wallets on extra expenses. Rely on the school admissions counselor; don't hire a private adviser or professional editor to shape your child's college essay. A testing tutor might charge $2,400; a private college counselor can cost from $1,300 to $10,000. This is unfair to poorer families too, especially when companies start offering special admissions services to their employees. As always, the colleges are to blame, with their pushy "early admissions" programs, which make them look good in rankings but just screw their students.

Opening sentences follow language of editorial too closely and also distort structure of editorial.

Paraphrase shifts tone, becoming much more colloquial than editorial.

Paraphrase borrows words and phrases too freely from original.

Opinion offered here distorts what is in the editorial.

Use your paraphrases to synthesize sources. If you are asked to prepare a literature review or synthesis paper on a subject, begin that work by carefully summarizing and paraphrasing a range of reputable sources. For more about synthesis and synthesis papers, see Chapter 12. ○

> **Your Turn** Practice writing paraphrases by pairing up with a classmate and choosing a full essay to paraphrase from Part 1 of this book.
>
> Write your paraphrases of the agreed-upon essay separately, just as if you intended to cite the piece later in a report, research paper, or argument yourself. When both of you are done, compare your paraphrases. What did you identify as the main point(s) or thesis of the piece? What kind of structure did the article follow: for example, narrative, report, comparison/contrast, argument, and so on? What evidence or details from the article did you include in your paraphrases? How do your paraphrases compare in length?
>
> Discuss the differences. How might you account for them?

understand synthesis
papers p. 272

Incorporating Sources into Your Work

avoid
plagiarism/
use
quotations

When you incorporate sources into your research projects cogently, you give readers information they need to appraise the thinking you've done. They discover what you've read and learned and how much purchase you have on ideas. Yet introducing borrowed ideas and quoted passages into papers is far from easy. You have to help readers identify paraphrased or quoted items, and you need to clearly identify any edits you made to quotations for accuracy or clarity.

Cue the reader in some way whenever you introduce borrowed material.   Readers *always* need to know what words and ideas are yours and what you have culled from other authors. So give them a verbal signal whenever you summarize, paraphrase, or quote directly from sources. Think of it as *framing* these borrowed materials to set them off from your own work. Such frames offer many options for introducing either ideas or direct quotes drawn from sources:

EXACT WORDS

Michelle Obama argued on *The View* that ". . . [quotation]."

"[Quotation] . . . ," says Jack Welch, former CEO of General Electric, pointing out that ". . . [more quotation]."

SUMMARIZED FACTS

According to a report in *Scientific American* (October 2012), the Mars rover *Curiosity* will soon . . . [your own words].

PARAPHRASED IDEA

Can a person talk intelligently about books even without reading them? Pierre Bayard, for one, **suggests that** . . . [your own words].

YOUR SUMMARY WITH QUOTATION

In *Encounters with the Archdruid*, author John McPhee **introduces** readers to conservationist David Brower, whom he **credits** with [your own words], **calling him** "... [quotation]."

As you see, a frame can introduce, interrupt, follow, or even surround the words or ideas taken from sources, but be sure that your signal phrases are grammatical and lead smoothly into the material.

Select an appropriate "verb of attribution" to frame borrowed material. These "signal verbs" influence what readers think of borrowed ideas or quoted material. Use neutral verbs of attribution in reports; save descriptive or even biased terms for arguments. Note that, by MLA convention, verbs of attribution are usually in the present tense when talking about current work or ideas. (In APA, these verbs are generally in the past or present perfect tense.)

Verbs of Attribution

Neutral	Descriptive	Biased
adds	acknowledges	admits
explains	argues	charges
finds	asserts	confesses
notes	believes	confuses
offers	claims	derides
observes	confirms	disputes
says	disagrees	evades
shows	responds	impugns
states	reveals	pretends
writes	suggests	smears

> **MLA and APA Style**
>
> The examples in this section follow MLA (Modern Language Association) style, covered in Chapter 46. For information on APA (American Psychological Association) style, see Chapter 47.

Use ellipsis marks [. . .] to shorten a lengthy quotation. When quoting a source in your paper, it's not necessary to use every word or sentence, as long as the cuts you make don't distort the meaning of the original material. An ellipsis mark, formed from three spaced periods, shows where words, phrases, full sentences, or more have been removed from a quotation. The mark doesn't replace punctuation within a sentence. Thus, you might see a period or a comma immediately followed by an ellipsis mark.

ORIGINAL PASSAGE

Although gift giving has been a pillar of Hopi society, trade has also flourished in Hopi towns since prehistory, with a network that extended from the Great Plains to the Pacific Coast, and from the Great Basin, centered on present-day Nevada and Utah, to the Valley of Mexico. Manufactured goods, raw materials, and gems drove the trade, supplemented by exotic items such as parrots. The Hopis were producers as well, manufacturing large quantities of cotton cloth and ceramics for the trade. To this day, interhousehold trade and barter, especially for items of traditional manufacture for ceremonial use (such as basketry, bows, cloth, moccasins, pottery, and rattles), remain vigorous.

—Peter M. Whiteley, "Ties That Bind: Hopi Gift Culture and Its First Encounter with the United States," *Natural History*, November 2004, p. 26

Highlighting shows words to be deleted when passage is quoted.

PASSAGE WITH ELLIPSES

Whiteley has characterized the practice this way:

> Although gift giving has been a pillar of Hopi society, trade has also flourished in Hopi towns since prehistory. . . . Manufactured goods, raw materials, and gems drove the trade, supplemented by exotic items such as parrots. The Hopis were producers as well, manufacturing large quantities of cotton cloth and ceramics for the trade. To this day, interhousehold trade and barter, especially for items of traditional manufacture for ceremonial use, . . . remain vigorous. (26)

Ellipses show where words have been deleted.

Use brackets [ ] to insert explanatory material into a quotation. By convention, readers understand that the bracketed words are not part of the original material.

Writing in the *London Review of Books* (January 26, 2006), John Lancaster describes the fears of publishers: "At the moment Google says they have no intention of providing access to this content [scanned books still under copyright]; but why should anybody believe them?"

Use ellipsis marks, brackets, and other devices to make quoted materials fit the grammar of your sentences.   Sometimes, the structure of sentences you want to quote won't quite match the grammar, tense, or perspectives of your own surrounding prose. If necessary, cut up a quoted passage to slip appropriate sections into your own sentences, adding bracketed changes or explanations to smooth the transition.

ORIGINAL PASSAGE

Among Chandler's most charming sights are the business-casual dads joining their wives and kids for lunch in the mall food court. The food isn't the point, let alone whether it's from Subway or Dairy Queen. The restaurants merely provide the props and setting for the family time. When those kids grow up, they'll remember the food court as happily as an older generation recalls the diners and motels of Route 66 — not because of the businesses' innate appeal but because of the memories they evoke.

— Virginia Postrel, "In Defense of Chain Stores," *The Atlantic*, December 2006

Words to be quoted are highlighted.

MATERIAL AS QUOTED

People who dislike chain stores should ponder the small-town America that cultural critic Virginia Postrel describes, one where "business-casual dads [join] their wives and kids for lunch in the mall food court," a place that future generations of kids will remember "as happily as an older generation recalls the diners and motels of Route 66. "

Words quoted from source are highlighted.

Use [sic] to signal an obvious error in quoted material.   You don't want readers to blame a mistake on you, and yet you are obligated to reproduce a quotation exactly—including blunders in the original. You can highlight an error by putting *sic* (the Latin word for "thus") in brackets immediately following the mistake. The device says, in effect, that this is the way you found it.

The late Senator Edward Kennedy once took Supreme Court nominee Samuel Alito to task for his record: "In an era when America is still too divided by race and riches, Judge Alioto [sic] has not written one single opinion on the merits in favor of a person of color alleging race discrimination on the job."

45 Documenting Sources

understand
citation
styles

Required to document your research paper? It seems simple in theory: List your sources and note where and how you use them. But the practice can be intimidating. For one thing, you have to follow rules for everything from capitalizing titles to captioning images. For another, documentation systems differ between fields. What worked for a Shakespeare paper won't transfer to your psychology research project. Bummer. What do you need to do?

Understand the point of documentation. Documentation systems differ to serve the writers and researchers who use them. Modern Language Association (MLA) documentation, which you probably know from composition and literature classes, highlights author names, books, and article titles and assumes that writers will be quoting a lot—as literature scholars do. American Psychological Association (APA) documentation, gospel in psychology and social sciences, focuses on publication dates because scholars in these fields value the latest research. Council of Science Editors (CSE) documentation, used in the hard sciences, provides predictably detailed advice for handling formulas and numbers.

So systems of documentation aren't arbitrary. Their rules simply reflect the specialized needs of writers in various fields.

Understand what you accomplish through documentation. First, you clearly identify the sources you have used. In a world awash with information, readers really do need to have reliable information about titles, authors, data, media of publication, and so on.

For a tutorial on documentation, see **macmillanhighered.com/howtowrite3e**.
Tutorials > Documentation and Working with Sources > Do I Need to Cite That?

In addition, by citing your sources, you certify the quality of your research and, in turn, receive credit for your labor. You also provide evidence for your claims. An appreciative reader or instructor can tell a lot from your bibliography alone.

Finally, when you document a paper, you encourage readers to follow up on your work. When you've done a good job, serious readers will want to know more about your subject. Both your citations and your bibliography enable them to take the next step in their research.

Style Guides Used in Various Disciplines

Field or Discipline	Documentation and Style Guides
Anthropology	*AAA Style Guide* (2009) and *Chicago Manual of Style* (16th ed., 2010)
Biology	*Scientific Style and Format: The CSE Manual for Authors, Editors, and Publishers* (8th ed., 2014)
Business and management	*The Business Style Handbook: An A-to-Z Guide for Writing on the Job* (2nd ed., 2012)
Chemistry	*The ACS Style Guide: Effective Communication of Scientific Information* (3rd ed., 2006)
Earth sciences	*Geowriting: A Guide to Writing, Editing, and Printing in Earth Science* (rev. ed., 2004)
Engineering	Varies by area; *IEEE Standards Style Manual* (online)
Federal government	*United States Government Printing Office Manual* (30th ed., 2008)
History	*Chicago Manual of Style* (16th ed., 2010)
Humanities	*MLA Handbook for Writers of Research Papers* (7th ed., 2009)
Journalism	*The Associated Press Stylebook and Briefing on Media Law* (2013); *UPI Stylebook and Guide to Newswriting* (4th ed., 2004)
Law	*The Bluebook: A Uniform System of Citation* (19th ed., 2010)
Mathematics	*A Manual for Authors of Mathematical Papers* (8th ed., 1990)
Music	*Writing about Music: An Introductory Guide* (4th ed., 2008)
Nursing	*Writing for Publication in Nursing* (2nd ed., 2010)
Political science	*The Style Manual for Political Science* (2006)
Psychology	*Publication Manual of the American Psychological Association* (6th ed., 2010)
Sociology	*American Sociological Association Style Guide* (4th ed., 2010)

46 MLA Documentation and Format

cite in MLA

The style of the Modern Language Association (MLA) is used in many humanities disciplines. For complete details about MLA style, consult the *MLA Handbook for Writers of Research Papers*, 7th ed. (2009). The basic details for documenting sources and formatting research papers in MLA style are presented below.

Document sources according to convention.   When you use sources in a research paper, you are required to cite the source, letting readers know that the information has been borrowed from somewhere else and showing them how to find the original material if they would like to study it further. An MLA-style citation includes two parts: a brief in-text citation and a more detailed works cited entry to be included in a list at of the end of your paper.

In-text citations must include the author's name as well as the number of the page where the borrowed material can be found. The author's name (shaded in orange) is generally included in the signal phrase that introduces the passage, and the page number (shaded in yellow) is included in parentheses after the borrowed text.

> Frazier points out that the Wetherill-sponsored expedition to explore Chaco Canyon was roundly criticized (43).

Alternatively, the author's name can be included in parentheses along with the page number.

> The Wetherill-sponsored expedition to explore Chaco Canyon was roundly criticized (Frazier 43).

At the end of the paper, in the works cited list, a more detailed citation includes the author's name as well as the title (shaded in green) and publication information about the source (shaded in blue).

Frazier, Kendrick. *People of Chaco: A Canyon and Its Culture*. Rev. ed. New York: Norton, 1999. Print.

Both in-text citations and works cited entries can vary greatly depending on the type of source cited (book, periodical, Web site, etc.). The following pages give specific examples of how to cite a wide range of sources in MLA style.

Directory of MLA In-Text Citations

1. Author named in signal phrase 474
2. Author named in parentheses 474
3. With block quotations 474
4. Two or three authors 475
5. Four or more authors 475
6. Group, corporate, or government author 475
7. Two or more works by the same author 475
8. Authors with same last name 476
9. Unidentified author 476
10. Multivolume work 476
11. Work in an anthology 476
12. Entry in a reference book 477
13. Literary work 477
14. Sacred work 478
15. Entire work 478
16. Secondary source 478
17. No page numbers 478
18. Multiple sources in the same citation 479

For an activity on MLA style, see **macmillanhighered.com/howtowrite3e.**
Tutorials > LearningCurve Activities > Working with Sources (MLA)

MLA in-text citation

1. Author Named in Signal Phrase

Include the author's name in the signal phrase that introduces the borrowed material. Follow the borrowed material with the page number of the source in parentheses. Note that the period comes after the parentheses. For a source without an author, see item 9; for a source without a page number, see item 17.

> According to Seabrook, "astronomy was a vital and practical form of knowledge" for the ancient Greeks (98).

2. Author Named in Parentheses

Follow the borrowed material with the author and page number of the source in parentheses, and end with a period. For a source without an author, see item 9; for a source without a page number, see item 17.

> For the ancient Greeks, "astronomy was a vital and practical form of knowledge" (Seabrook 98).

Note: Most of the examples below follow the style of item 1, but naming the author in parentheses (as shown in item 2) is also acceptable.

3. With Block Quotations

For quotations of four or more lines, MLA requires that you set off the borrowed material indented one inch from the left-hand margin. Include the author's name in the introductory text (or in the parentheses at the end). End the block quotation with the page number(s) in parentheses, *after* the end punctuation of the quoted material.

> Jake Page, writing in *American History*, underscores the significance of the well-organized Pueblo revolt:
>
> > Although their victory proved temporary, in the history of Indian-white relations in North America the Pueblo Indians were the only Native Americans to successfully oust European invaders from their territory. . . . Apart from the Pueblos, only the Seminoles were able to retain some of their homeland for any length of time, by waging war from the swamps of the Florida Everglades. (36)

4. Two or Three Authors

If your source has two or three authors, include all their names in either the signal phrase or parentheses.

Muhlheim and Heusser assert that the story "analyzes how crucially our actions are shaped by the society . . . in which we live" (29).

According to some experts, "Children fear adult attempts to fix their social lives" (Thompson, Grace, and Cohen 8).

5. Four or More Authors

If your source has four or more authors, list the first author's name followed by "et al." (meaning "and others") in the signal phrase or parentheses.

Hansen et al. estimate that the amount of fish caught and sold illegally worldwide is between 10 and 30 percent (974).

6. Group, Corporate, or Government Author

Treat the name of the group, corporation, or government agency just as you would any other author, including the name in either the signal phrase or the parentheses.

The United States Environmental Protection Agency states that if a public water supply contains dangerous amounts of lead, the municipality is required to educate the public about the problems associated with lead in drinking water (3).

7. Two or More Works by the Same Author

If your paper includes two or more works by the same author, add a brief version of the works' titles (shaded in green) in parentheses to help readers locate the right source.

Mills suggests that new assessments of older archaeological work, not new discoveries in the field, are revising the history of Chaco Canyon ("Recent Research" 66). She argues, for example, that new analysis of public spaces can teach us about the ritual of feasting in the Puebloan Southwest (Mills, "Performing the Feast" 211).

8. Authors with Same Last Name

If your paper includes two or more sources whose authors have the same last name, include a first initial with the last name in either the signal phrase or the parentheses.

> According to T. Smith, "[A]s much as 60 percent of the computers sold in India are unbranded and made by local assemblers at about a third of the price of overseas brands" (12).

9. Unidentified Author

If the author of your work is unknown, include a brief title of the work in parentheses.

> Though a single language, Spanish varies considerably, a fact that "befuddles advertisers who would aim to sell to the entire Spanish-speaking world, like the shampoo-maker who discovered that *cabello chino* ("Chinese hair") means curly hair in almost all Latin America save Ecuador, where it means straight hair" ("The Rise of Spanish" 1).

10. Multivolume Work

If you cite material from more than one volume of a multivolume work, include in the parentheses the volume number followed by a colon before the page number. (See also item 11, on p. 485, for including multivolume works in your works cited list.)

> Odekon defines *access-to-enterprise zones* as "geographic areas in which taxes and government regulations are lowered or eliminated as a way to stimulate business activity and create jobs" (1: 2).

11. Work in an Anthology

Include the author of the work in the signal phrase or parentheses. There is no need to refer to the editor of the anthology in the in-text citation; this and other details will be included in the works cited list at the end of your paper.

> Vonnegut suggests that *Hamlet* is considered such a masterpiece because "Shakespeare told us the truth, and [writers] so rarely tell us the truth" (354).

12. Entry in a Reference Book

In the signal phrase, include the author of the entry you are referring to, if there is an author. In the parentheses following the in-text citation, include the title of the entry and the page number(s) on which the entry appears.

> Willis points out that the Empire State Building, 1,250 feet tall and built in just over one year, was a record-breaking feat of engineering ("Empire State Building" 375-76).

For reference entries with no author (such as dictionaries), simply include the name of the article or entry in quotation marks along with the page reference in parentheses.

> Supersize—one of the newest pop culture terms added to the dictionary—is a verb meaning "to increase considerably the size, amount, or extent of" ("Supersize" 714).

13. Literary Work

Include as much information as possible to help readers locate your borrowed material. For classic novels, which are available in many editions, include the page number, followed by a semicolon, and additional information such as book ("bk."), volume ("vol."), or chapter ("ch.") numbers.

> At the climax of Brontë's *Jane Eyre,* Jane fears that her wedding is doomed, and her description of the chestnut tree that has been struck by lightning is ominous: "it stood up, black and riven: the trunk, split down the center, gaped ghastly" (274; vol. 2, ch. 25).

For classic poems and plays, include division numbers such as act, scene, and line numbers; do not include page numbers. Separate all numbers with periods. Use Arabic (1, 2, 3, etc.) numerals instead of Roman (I, II, III, etc.) unless your instructor prefers otherwise.

> In Homer's epic poem *The Iliad,* Agamemnon admits that he has been wrong to fight with Achilles, but he blames Zeus, whom he says "has given me bitterness, who drives me into unprofitable abuse and quarrels" (2.375-76).

14. Sacred Work

Instead of page numbers, include book, chapter, and verse numbers when citing material from sacred texts.

> Jesus's association with the sun is undeniable in this familiar passage from the Bible: "I am the light of the world. Whoever follows me will not walk in darkness, but will have the light of life" (John 8.12).

15. Entire Work

When referring to an entire work, there is no need to include page numbers in parentheses; simply include the author's name(s) in the signal phrase.

> Dobelli claims that cognitive errors tend to be ingrained in us, making it likely we'll stumble over the same mistakes again and again unless we alter our way of thinking.

16. Secondary Source

To cite a source you found within another source, include the name of the original author in the signal phrase. In the parentheses, include the term "qtd. in" and give the author of the source where you found the quote, along with the page number. Note that your works cited entry for this material will be listed under the secondary source name (Pollan) rather than the original writer (Howard).

> Writing in 1943, Howard asserted that "artificial manures lead inevitably to artificial nutrition, artificial food, artificial animals, and finally to artificial men and women" (qtd. in Pollan 148).

17. No Page Numbers

If the work you are citing has no page numbers, include only the author's name (or the brief title, if there is no author) for your in-text citation.

> According to Broder, the Federal Trade Commission has begun to police and crack down on false company claims of producing "environmentally friendly" or "green" merchandise.

18. Multiple Sources in the Same Citation

If one statement in your paper can be attributed to multiple sources, alphabetically list all the authors with page numbers, separated by semicolons.

> Two distinct Harlems coexisted in the late 1920s: one a cultural and artistic force—the birthplace of a renaissance of literature, music, and dance—and the other, a slum and profit center for organized crime (Giddins and DeVeaux 132; Gioia 89).

Directory of MLA Works Cited Entries

(Continued)

Directory of MLA Works Cited Entries (*Continued*)

General Guidelines for MLA Works Cited Entries

AUTHOR NAMES

- Authors listed at the start of an entry should be listed last name first and should end with a period.
- Subsequent author names, or the names of authors or editors listed in the middle of the entry, should be listed first name first.

DATES

- Format dates as day month year: 27 May 2014.
- Use abbreviations for all months except for May, June, and July, which are short enough to spell out: Jan., Feb., Mar., Apr., Aug., Sept., Oct., Nov., Dec. (Months should always be spelled out in the text of your paper.)

TITLES

- Italicize the titles of long works—such as books, plays, periodicals, entire Web sites, and films. (Underlining is an acceptable alternative to italics, but note that whichever format you choose, you should be consistent throughout your paper.)
- Titles of short works—such as essays, articles, poems, and songs—should be placed in quotation marks.

PUBLICATION INFORMATION

- Include only the city .name.
- Abbreviate familiar words such as "University" ("U") and "Press" ("P") in the publisher's name. Leave out terms such as "Inc." and "Corp."
- Include the medium of publication for each entry ("Print," "Web," "DVD," "Radio," etc.).

MLA works cited entries

AUTHOR INFORMATION

1. Single Author

> Author's Last Name, First Name. *Book Title*. Publication City: Publisher, Year of Publication. Medium.

Bazelon, Emily. *Sticks and Stones: Defeating the Culture of Bullying and Rediscovering the Power of Character and Empathy*. New York: Random, 2013. Print.

2. Two or Three Authors

List the authors in the order shown on the title page.

> First Author's Last Name, First Name, and Second Author's First Name Last Name. *Book Title*. Publication City: Publisher, Year of Publication. Medium.

Power, Michael L., and Jay Schulkin. *The Evolution of Obesity*. Baltimore: Johns Hopkins UP, 2009. Print.

Michaels, Ed, Helen Handfield-Jones, and Beth Axelrod. *The War for Talent*. Boston: Harvard Business School, 2001. Print.

3. Four or More Authors

When a source has four or more authors, list only the name of the first author (last name first) followed by a comma and the Latin term "et al." (meaning "and others").

> First Author's Last Name, First Name, et al. *Book Title*. Publication City: Publisher, Year of Publication. Medium.

Roark, James L., et al. *The American Promise: A History of the United States*. 5th ed. Boston: Bedford, 2012. Print.

4. Corporate Author

If a group or corporation rather than a person appears to be the author, include that name as the work's author in your list of works cited.

Name of Corporation. *Book Title.* Publication City: Publisher, Year of Publication.
Medium.

World Health Organization. *Technical Report of the TDR Thematic Reference
Group on Environment, Agriculture, and Infectious Diseases of Poverty.*
Geneva: WHO, 2013. Print.

5. Unidentified Author

If the author of a work is unknown, begin the works cited entry with the title of
the work.

Note that in the example given, "The New Yorker" is not italicized because
it is a title within a title (see item 19).

Book Title. Publication City: Publisher, Year of Publication. Medium.

The New Yorker *Top 100 Cartoons.* New York: Cartoon Bank, 2004. Print.

6. Multiple Works by the Same Author

To cite two or more works by the same author in your list of works cited,
organize the works alphabetically by title (ignoring introductory articles such as
The and *A*). Include the author's name only for the first entry; for subsequent
entries by this same author, type three hyphens followed by a period in place of
the author's name.

Author's Last Name, First Name. *Title of Work.* Publication City: Publisher, Year of
Publication. Medium.

---. *Title of Work.* Publication City: Publisher, Year of Publication. Medium.

Krakauer, Jon. *Under the Banner of Heaven: A Story of Violent Faith.*
Harpswell: Anchor, 2004. Print.

---. *Three Cups of Deceit: How Greg Mortenson, Humanitarian Hero, Lost
His Way.* Harpswell: Anchor, 2011. Print.

BOOKS

7. Book: Basic Format

The example here is the basic format for a book with one author. For author variations, see items 1–6. For more information on the treatment of authors, dates, titles, and publication information, see the box on page 481. After listing the author's name, include the title (and subtitle, if any) of the book, italicized. Next give the publication city, publisher's name, and year. End with the medium of publication.

Author's Last Name, First Name. *Book Title: Book Subtitle.* Publication City: Publisher, Publication Year. Medium.

Seeling, Charlotte. *Fashion: 150 Years of Couturiers, Designers, Labels.* Potsdam: Ullmann, 2012. Print.

8. Author and Editor

Include the author's name first if you are referring to the text itself. If, however, you are citing material written by the editor, include the editor's name first, followed by a comma and "ed."

Author's Last Name, First Name. *Book Title.* Year of Original Publication. Ed. Editor's First Name Last Name. Publication City: Publisher, Year of Publication. Medium.

Editor's Last Name, First Name, ed. *Book Title.* Year of Original Publication. By Author's First Name Last Name. Publication City: Publisher, Year of Publication. Medium.

Dickens, Charles. *Great Expectations.* 1861. Ed. Janice Carlisle. Boston: Bedford, 1996. Print.

Carlisle, Janice, ed. *Great Expectations.* 1861. By Charles Dickens. Boston: Bedford, 1996. Print.

9. Edited Collection

Editor's Last Name, First Name, ed. *Book Title.* Publication City: Publisher, Year of Publication. Medium.

Abbott, Megan, ed. *A Hell of a Woman: An Anthology of Female Noir.* Houston: Busted Flush, 2007. Print.

10. Work in an Anthology or a Collection

> Author's Last Name, First Name. "Title of Work." *Book Title.* Ed. Editor's First Name
> Last Name. Publication City: Publisher, Year of Publication. Page Numbers
> of Work. Medium.

Okpewho, Isidore. "The Cousins of Uncle Remus." *The Black Columbiad:
Defining Moments in African American Literature and Culture.* Ed.
Werner Sollors and Maria Diedrich. Cambridge: Harvard UP, 1994.
15-27. Print.

11. Multivolume Work

To cite one volume of a multivolume work, include the volume number after
the title. Including the volume number in your list of works cited means that
you do not need to list it in your in-text citation. To cite two or more volumes,
include the number of volumes after the title. In this case, you would need to
include the specific volume number in each of your in-text citations for this
source.

> Author or Editor's Last Name, First Name. *Title of Work.* Vol. Number.
> Publication City: Publisher, Year of Publication. Medium.

Odekon, Mehmet, ed. *Encyclopedia of World Poverty.* Vol. 2. Thousand
Oaks: Sage, 2006. Print.

> Author or Editor's Last Name, First Name. *Title of Work.* Number of vols.
> Publication City: Publisher, Year of Publication. Medium.

Odekon, Mehmet, ed. *Encyclopedia of World Poverty.* 3 vols. Thousand
Oaks: Sage, 2006. Print.

12. Part of a Series

After the title of the book, include the series title and number (if any) from the
title page.

> Author or Editor's Last Name, First Name. *Title of Work.* Title and Number of
> Series. Publication City: Publisher, Year of Publication. Medium.

Haugen, David M. *Illegal Immigration.* Opposing Viewpoints Ser.
Farmington Hills: Greenhaven, 2011. Print.

How to...
Cite from a book (MLA)

BOOK COVER

TITLE PAGE

Andrews McMeel Publishing, LLC
Kansas City · Sydney · London

1 author

2 book title and subtitle

3 city of publication and publisher

> When a publisher lists more than one city, use the first one.

For a video tutorial, see **macmillanhighered.com/howtowrite3e**.
Tutorials > Documentation and Working with Sources > How to Cite a Book in MLA Style

COPYRIGHT PAGE

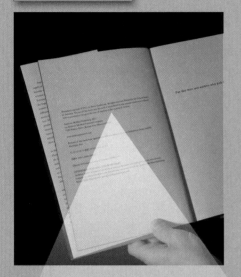

Tomatoland copyright © 2011 by Barry Estabrook.

QUOTED PAGE

145

4 year of publication

5 page number

6 medium

MLA in-text citation

Describing his vision for the new tomato breed, the seed company owner explained, "We were going to start with roadside growers and chefs. People who were interested in good flavor and good quality" (Estabrook 145).

 1 **5**

1 **2**

MLA works cited entry

Estabrook, Barry. *Tomatoland: How Modern Industrial Agriculture Destroyed*

3 **4**

Our Most Alluring Fruit. Kansas City: Andrews McMeel, 2011. Print.

13. Republished Book

If the book you are citing was previously published, include the original publication date after the title. If the new publication includes additional text, such as an introduction, include that, along with the name of its author, before the current publication information.

> Author's Last Name, First Name. *Title of Work.* Original Year of Publication. New Material Author's First Name Last Name. Publication City: Publisher, Year of Publication. Medium.

> Davidson, Bruce. *Subway.* 1986. Introd. Fred Brathwaite. New York: Aperture, 2011. Print.

14. Later Edition

Include the edition number as a numeral with letters ("2nd," "3rd," "4th," etc.) followed by "ed." after the book's title. If the edition is listed on the title page as "Revised," without a number, include "Rev. ed." after the title of the book.

> Author(s). *Title of Work.* Number ed. Publication City: Publisher, Year of Publication. Medium.

> Bodley, John H. *Anthropology and Contemporary Human Problems.* 6th ed. Lanham: AltaMira, 2012. Print.

15. Sacred Work

Include the title of the work as it is shown on the title page. If there is an editor or a translator listed, include the name after the title with either "Ed." or "Trans."

> *Title of Work.* Editor or Translator. Publication City: Publisher, Year of Publication. Medium.

> *The King James Bible: 400th Anniversary Edition.* New York: Oxford UP, 2010. Print.

> *The Qur'an.* Trans. M. A. S. Abdel Haleem. New York: Oxford UP, 2008. Print.

16. Translation

> Original Author's Last Name, First Name. *Title of Work.* Trans. Translator's First
> Name Last Name. Publication City: Publisher, Year of Publication. Medium.

Alighieri, Dante. *Inferno: A New Translation.* Trans. Mary Jo Bang.
Minneapolis: Graywolf, 2012. Print.

17. Article in a Reference Book

If there is no article author, begin with the title of the article.

> Article Author's Last Name, First Name. "Title of Article." *Book Title.*
> Publication City: Publisher, Year of Publication. Medium.

Dirr, Michael A. "Brunfelsia." *Dirr's Encyclopedia of Trees and Shrubs.*
Portland: Timber, 2011. Print.

"Supreme Court Decisions." *The World Almanac and Book of Facts 2013.*
New York: World Almanac, 2013. Print.

18. Introduction, Preface, Foreword, or Afterword

> Book Part Author's Last Name, First Name. Name of Book Part. *Book Title.* Ed. Book
> Author or Editor's First Name Last Name. Publication City: Publisher, Year of
> Publication. Page Numbers. Medium.

Gladwell, Malcolm. Foreword. *The Book of Basketball: The NBA According to
The Sports Guy.* Bill Simmons. New York: Ballantine, 2009. xi-xiii. Print.

19. Title within a Title

If a book's title includes the title of another long work (play, book, or periodical) within it, do not italicize the internal title.

> Author's Last Name, First Name. *Book Title* Title within Title. Publication City:
> Publisher, Year of Publication. Medium.

Mayhew, Robert, ed. *Essays on Ayn Rand's* Atlas Shrugged. Lanham:
Lexington, 2009. Print.

PERIODICALS

20. Article in a Scholarly Journal

List the author(s) first, and then include the article title, the journal title (in italics), the volume number, the issue number, the publication year, the page numbers, and the publication medium.

> Author's Last Name, First Name. "Title of Article." *Title of Journal* Volume
>   Number.Issue Number (Year of Publication): Page Numbers. Medium.

> Dorson, James. "Demystifying the Judge: Law and Mythical Violence in
>   Cormac McCarthy's *Blood Meridian.*" *Journal of Modern Literature*
>   36.2 (2013): 105-21. Print.

21. Article in a Scholarly Journal with No Volume Number

Follow the format for scholarly journals (as shown in item 20), but list only the issue number before the year of publication.

> Author's Last Name, First Name. "Title of Article." *Title of Journal* Issue
>   Number (Year of Publication): Page Numbers. Medium.

> Leow, Joanne. "Mis-mappings and Mis-duplications: Interdiscursivity
>   and the Poetry of Wayde Compton." *Canadian Literature* 214 (2012):
>   47-66. Print.

22. Magazine Article

Include the date of publication rather than volume and issue numbers. (See abbreviation rules in the box on p. 481.) If page numbers are not consecutive, add "+" after the initial page.

> Author's Last Name, First Name. "Title of Article." *Title of Magazine* Date of
>   Publication: Page Numbers. Medium.

> Wasik, Bill. "Welcome to the Programmable World." *Wired* June 2013:
>   202-9. Print.

23. Newspaper Article

If a specific edition is listed on the newspaper's masthead, such as "Late Edition" or "National Edition," include an abbreviation of this after the date. If page numbers are not consecutive, add "+" after the initial page.

Author's Last Name, First Name. "Title of Article." *Title of Newspaper* Date of
     Publication: Page Numbers. Medium.

Birnbaum, Michael. "Autobahn Speed Limit Proposal Revs Up Debate in
     Germany." *Washington Post* 20 May 2013: A1+. Print.

Author's Last Name, First Name. "Title of Article." *Title of Newspaper* Date of
     Publication, Spec. ed.: Page Numbers. Medium.

Kaminer, Ariel. "On a College Waiting List? Sending Cookies Isn't Going
     to Help." *New York Times* 11 May 2013, natl ed.: 2. Print.

If a newspaper numbers each section individually, without attaching letters to
the page numbers, include the section number in your citation.

Author's Last Name, First Name. "Title of Article." *Title of Newspaper* Date of
     Publication, sec. Section Number: Page Numbers. Medium.

Bowley, Graham. "Keeping Up with the Windsors." *New York Times* 15
     July 2007, sec. 3: 1+. Print.

24. Editorial

For a newspaper editorial, do not include an author, but do include the word
"Editorial," followed by a period, after the title of the article.

"Title of Article." Editorial. *Title of Newspaper* Date of Publication: Page Number(s).
     Medium.

"Do Teachers Really Discriminate against Boys?" Editorial. *Time* 6 Feb.
     2013: 37. Print.

25. Letter to the Editor

Letter Writer's Last Name, First Name. Letter. *Title of Newspaper* Date of
     Publication: Page Number. Medium.

Le Tellier, Alexandra. Letter. *Los Angeles Times* 18 Apr. 2013: 12. Print.

26. Unsigned Article

"Title of Article." *Title of Newspaper* Date of Publication: Page Number. Medium.

"An Ounce of Prevention." *The Economist* 20 Apr. 2013: 27. Print.

How to...
Cite from a magazine (MLA)

March 2010

By Marcus E. Raichle

1 magazine title

2 publication date

3 author

4 article title

48

5 page number of quoted passage

44 **49**

6 first and last page numbers of article

7 medium

MLA in-text citation

As early as 1929, Hans Berger proposed that "we have to assume that the central nervous system is always, and not only during wakefulness, in a state of considerable activity" (Raichle 48).

3 **5**

3 **4** **1** **2**

MLA works cited entry

Raichle, Marcus E. "The Brain's Dark Energy." *Scientific American* Mar.

6 **7**

2010: 44-49. Print.

27. Review

Add "Rev. of" before the title of the work being reviewed.

Review Author's Last Name, First Name. "Title of Review." Rev. of *Title of Work Being Reviewed,* by Author of Work Being Reviewed First Name Last Name. *Title of Publication in Which Review Appears* Date of Publication: Page Numbers. Medium.

Gogolak, Emily. "*The Unchangeable Spots of Leopards* Review: How to Become a Person." Rev. of *The Unchangeable Spots of Leopards,* by Kristopher Jansma. *Village Voice* 20 Mar. 2013: 9. Print.

ELECTRONIC SOURCES

28. Short Work from a Web Site

Short Work Author's Last Name, First Name. "Title of Short Work." *Title of Web Site.* Name of Sponsoring Organization, Date of Publication or Most Recent Update. Medium. Date of Access.

Frick, Kit. "On Heroism and The Oregon Trail." *Booth.* Butler University, 8 Feb. 2013. Web. 7 July 2014.

29. Entire Web Site

Web Site Author's Last Name, First Name. *Title of Web Site.* Name of Sponsoring Organization, Date of Publication or Most Recent Update. Medium. Date of Access.

Zaretsky, Staci. *Above the Law.* Breaking Media, 28 May 2013. Web. 2 Jan. 2014.

30. Entire Blog (Weblog)

Include any of the following elements that are available. If there is no publisher or sponsoring organization, use the abbreviation "N.p."

Blog Author's Last Name, First Name. *Title of Blog.* Name of Sponsoring Organization
    (if any), Date of Most Recent Post. Medium. Date of Access.

Asher, Levi. *Literary Kicks*. N.p., 18 May 2013. Web. 23 Sept. 2014.

31. Entry in a Blog (Weblog)

Entry Author's Last Name, First Name. "Title of Blog Entry." *Title of Blog.* Name
    of Sponsoring Organization (if any), Date of Entry. Medium.
    Date of Access.

Smith, Alisa. "How College Students Can Eat Locally When Held Captive
    to a Meal Plan." *The Daily Green*. Hearst Communications, 4 Sept.
    2007. Web. 5 Dec. 2014.

32. Online Book

Book Author's Last Name, First Name. *Title of Book.* Book Publication City:
    Book Publisher, Book Publication Year. *Title of Web Site.* Medium.
    Date of Access.

Wells, H. G. *A Short History of the World*. New York: MacMillan, 1922.
    Bartleby.com: Great Books Online. Web. 7 Aug. 2014.

33. Work from a Library Subscription Service (such as *InfoTrac* or *FirstSearch*)

Follow the format for periodical articles as shown in items 20–27, above. If page
numbers are not available, use the abbreviation "n. pag." End the citation with
the database name (in italics), the publication medium ("Web"), and the date of
access.

Article Author(s). "Title of Article." *Title of Periodical* Volume Number.Issue Number
    (Year of Publication): Page Numbers. *Name of Database*. Medium.
    Date of Access.

Waters, Mary C., et al., eds. "Coming of Age in America: The Transition to
    Adulthood in the Twenty-First Century." *American Journal of Sociology*
    118.2 (2012): 517-19. *InfoTrac*. Web. 7 Oct. 2014.

How to...
Cite from a Web site (MLA)

1 Web site title

2 article title

3 JAD ABUMRAD and ROBERT KRULWICH
author

4 August 17, 2010
update date

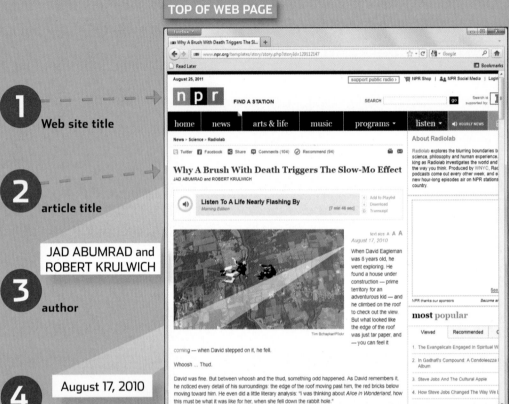

For a video tutorial, see **macmillanhighered.com/howtowrite3e.**
Tutorials › Documentation and Working with Sources › How to Cite a Web Site in MLA Style

BOTTOM OF WEB PAGE

7 medium

Copyright 2011 NPR

5 Web site sponsor

August 25, 2011

6 date of access

MLA in-text citation

Dr. Eagleman suggests that moments of near-death panic prompt the brain to form memories of otherwise-ignored stimuli, and "when you read that back out, the experience feels like it must have taken a very long time" (Abumrad and Krulwich).

3

3   **2**

MLA works cited entry

Abumrad, Jad, and Robert Krulwich. "Why a Brush with Death Triggers the

1 **5**   **4**   **7**   **6**

Slow-Mo Effect." *NPR*. NPR, 17 Aug. 2010. Web. 25 Aug. 2011.

How to...
Cite from a database (MLA)

5 volume and issue number

6 publication date

7 name of database

1 journal title

2 article title

3 author

4 page numbers

DATABASE SCREEN

Most databases have a way to download the journal article, often as a PDF.

For a video tutorial, see **macmillanhighered.com/howtowrite3e.**
Tutorials > Documentation and Working with Sources > How to Cite a Database in MLA Style

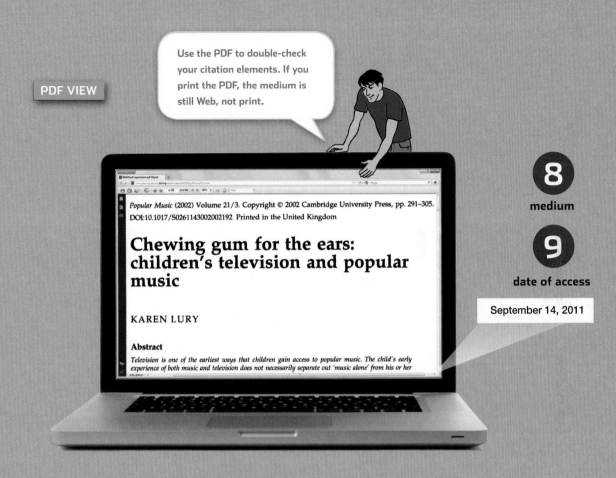

PDF VIEW

Use the PDF to double-check your citation elements. If you print the PDF, the medium is still Web, not print.

8 medium

9 date of access

September 14, 2011

MLA in-text citation

Children accept even nonsensical lyrics as legitimate musical expression, and one researcher calls their tolerance "a mode of engagement carried productively into the adult's experience of popular songs" (Lury 300).

3 4

3 Lury, Karen. **2** "Chewing Gum for the Ears: Children's Television and

MLA works cited entry

Popular Music." **1** *Popular Music* **5** 21.3 **6** (2002): **4** 291-305. **7** *JSTOR*.

8 Web. **9** 14 Sept. 2011.

34. Work from an Online Periodical

Follow the format for periodical articles as shown in items 20–27, above, listing the Web site name, in italics, as the periodical title. For articles in scholarly journals, include page numbers (or the abbreviation "n. pag." if page numbers are unavailable). End the citation with the publication medium ("Web") and the date of access.

Journal Article Author(s). "Title of Article." *Title of Online Journal* Volume Number.Issue Number (Year of Publication): Page Numbers (or "n. pag."). Medium. Date of Access.

Clarke, Laura Hurd, and Erica Bennett. "'You Learn to Live with All the Things That Are Wrong with You': Gender and the Experience of Multiple Chronic Conditions in Later Life." *Ageing and Society* 33.2 (2013): 342-60. Web. 27 Dec. 2014.

For articles appearing in online magazines and newspapers, list the publisher's name after the online periodical title. Page numbers are not required for nonscholarly articles published online.

Magazine or Newspaper Article Author(s). "Title of Article." *Title of Online Periodical.* Periodical Publisher, Publication Date. Medium. Date of Access.

Gogoi, Pallavi. "The Trouble with Business Ethics." *BusinessWeek.* McGraw, 25 June 2007. Web. 3 Oct. 2014.

35. Online Posting

Post Author's Last Name, First Name. "Title (or Subject) of Post." *Title of Message Board or Site Name.* Date of Post. Medium. Date of Access.

Cravens, Jayne. "Can a 6 Second Video Make a Difference?" *TechSoup Forum.* 5 May 2013. Web. 18 Nov. 2014.

36. E-mail

E-mail Author's Last Name, First Name. "Subject of E-mail." Message to the author (or Name of Recipient). Date Sent. Medium.

Jobs, Steve. "HarperCollins." Message to James Murdoch. 22 Jan. 2010. E-mail.

37. CD-ROM

CD-ROM Author's (if any) Last Name, First Name. *Title of CD-ROM.* Publication City: Publisher, Publication Year. Medium.

Car Talk: 25 Years of Lousy Car Advice. Minneapolis: HighBridge, 2013. CD-ROM.

38. Podcast

For downloaded podcasts, include the file type, such as "MP3 file," as the medium. If the file type is unknown, use the term "MP3 file."

"Title of Podcast." Names and Function of Pertinent Individual(s). *Title of Web Site.* Name of Sponsoring Organization, Date of Publication. Medium.

"Are Humans Meant for Monogamy?" Prod. Ben Valsler and Meera Senthilingam. *The Naked Scientists.* Cambridge University, 14 Feb. 2013. MP3 file.

For podcasts that were listened to directly from the host Web site, list "Web" as the medium and include an access date at the end.

39. Entry in a Wiki

Wiki content is continually edited by its users, so there is no author to cite.

"Title of Entry." *Title of Wiki.* Name of Sponsoring Organization, Date of Publication or Most Recent Update. Medium. Date of Access.

"Selfie." *Wikipedia.* Wikimedia Foundation, 24 May 2013. Web. 7 June 2013.

OTHER

40. Dissertation

For unpublished dissertations, put the title in quotation marks.

Author's Last Name, First Name. "Dissertation Title." Diss. Name of University, Year. Medium.

Yadav, Lekha. "The Effect of Ozone on the Growth and Development of Selected Food Spoilage Fungi." Diss. Newcastle Univ., 2009. Print.

If the dissertation is published as a book, italicize the title and include the publication information.

> Author's Last Name, First Name. *Dissertation Title.* Diss. Name of University, Year. Publication City: Publisher, Publication Year. Medium.

> Dugas, Kevin. "Can You Keep a Secret?": *The Effects of Coaching and Moral Stories on Children's Concealment of an Adult's Transgression.* Diss. McGill University, 2012. Montreal: McGill Univ., 2012. Print.

41. Published Conference Proceedings

List the name(s) of the editor(s), followed by "ed." or "eds.," and italicize the title of the proceedings. Before the conference information, add "Proc. of" and follow with the conference title, date, and location.

> Editor(s), ed(s). *Title of Proceedings.* Proc. of Conference Title, Conference Date, Conference Location. Publication City: Publisher, Year. Medium.

> Frischer, Bernard, Jane Webb Crawford, and David Koller, eds. *Making History Interactive: Computer Applications and Quantitative Methods in Archaeology.* Proc. of the Conference of Computer Applications and Quantitative Methods in Archaeology, March 2010, Williamsburg. Oxford: Archaeopress, 2010. Print.

42. Government Document

List the government (usually a country or state) that issued the document, and then list the department or agency. Most U.S. government documents are published by the Washington-based Government Printing Office (GPO).

> Government. Department or Agency. *Title of Document.* Publication City: Publisher, Date of Publication. Medium.

> United States. National Cancer Institute. *Clear Pathways: Winning the Fight against Tobacco.* Bethesda: National Institutes of Health, Jan. 2013. Print.

43. Pamphlet

> *Pamphlet Title.* Publication City: Publisher, Year of Publication. Medium.

> *Weathering the Storm: Financial Education Resources for Hurricane Recovery. Gulf Coast Edition: Alabama, Florida, Louisiana, Mississippi, Texas.* Washington: U.S. Dept. of the Treasury, 2012. Print.

44. Letter (Personal and Published)

For personal letters that you received, give the name of the letter writer, followed by the description "Letter to the author." For publication medium, list "TS" ("typescript") for typed letters or "MS" ("manuscript") for handwritten letters. For e-mail, see item 36.

> Letter Writer's Last Name, First Name. Letter to the author. Date of Letter. Medium.

> Warren, Elizabeth. Letter to the author. 10 Feb. 2013. TS.

For published letters, list the letter writer as well as the recipient.

> Letter Writer's Last Name, First Name. Letter to First Name Last Name. Date of Letter. *Title of Book.* Ed. Editor's First Name Last Name. Publication City: Publisher, Year. Medium.

> Lincoln, Abraham. Letter to T. J. Pickett. 16 Apr. 1859. *Wit & Wisdom of Abraham Lincoln: As Reflected in His Letters and Speeches.* Ed. H. Jack Lang. Mechanicsburg: Stackpole, 2006. Print.

45. Legal Source

List the names of laws or acts (with no underlining or quotation marks), followed by the Public Law number and the date. Also give the Statutes at Large cataloging number and the medium. For other legal sources, refer to *The Bluebook: A Uniform System of Citation*, 19th ed. (Cambridge: Harvard Law Review Assn., 2010).

> Title of Law. Pub. L. number. Stat. number. Date of Enactment. Medium.

> Violence against Women Reauthorization Act. Pub. L. 113-114. Stat. 47. 7 Mar. 2013. Print.

46. Lecture or Public Address

For the medium, describe the type of speech ("Reading," "Address," "Lecture," etc.).

> Speaker's Last Name, First Name. "Title of Speech." Name of Sponsoring Institution. Location of Speech. Date of Speech. Medium.

> Brooks, David. "What Not to Worry About." Indiana University. Bloomington. 3 May 2013. Address.

47. Interview

For published or broadcast interviews, give the title (if any), followed by the publication or broadcast information for the source that aired or published the interview. If there is no title, use "Interview" followed by a period.

> Interviewee's Last Name, First Name. "Title of Interview." *Book, Periodical, Web Site, or Program Title.* Publication or Broadcast Information (see specific entry for guidance). Medium.

> Biden, Joe. "Joe Biden: The *Rolling Stone* Interview." *Rolling Stone* 9 May 2013: 33-36. Print.

> Brooks, Mel. Interview. *Fresh Air.* Natl. Public Radio. WBEZ, Chicago. 20 May 2013. Radio.

For interviews that you conduct yourself, include the name of the interviewee, interview type ("Personal interview," "E-mail interview," "Telephone interview," etc.), and date.

> Dean, Howard. E-mail interview. 3 May 2011.

48. Television or Radio Program

If you access an archived show online, include the access date after the medium.

> "Episode Title." *Program Title. or Series Title.* Network. Local Channel's Call Letters, City (if any). Air Date. Medium. Date of Access.

> "Mr. Selfridge: Episode 2." *Masterpiece.* PBS. KCTS, Seattle. 13 Jan. 2014. Television.

> "The Future of Marriage." *On Being.* Amer. Public Media. 4 Apr. 2013. Web. 1 June 2014.

49. Film or Video Recording

If you accessed the film via videocassette or DVD, include the distributor name and release date.

> *Film Title.* Dir. Director's First Name Last Name. Original Release Date. Distributor, Release Date of Recording. Medium.

> *3:10 to Yuma.* Dir. Delmer Daves. 1957. Criterion, 2013. DVD.

To highlight a particular individual's performance or contribution, begin with that person's name, followed by a descriptive label (for example, "perf." or "chor.").

> Ford, Glenn, perf. *3:10 to Yuma*. Dir. Delmer Daves. 1957. Criterion, 2013. DVD.

50. Sound Recording

> Performer's Last Name, First Name or Band's Name. "Title of Song." *Title of Album*. Record Label, Year. Medium.

> Benson, George. "Unforgettable." *Inspiration: A Tribute to Nat King Cole*. Concord Jazz, 2013. CD

51. Musical Composition

Long works such as operas, ballets, and named symphonies should be italicized. Additional information, such as key or movement, may be added at the end.

> Composer's Last Name, First Name. *Title of Long Work*. Artists' names. Orchestra. Conductor. Manufacturer, Date. Medium.

> Bellini, Vincenzo. *I Capuleti e i Montecchi*. Perf. Beverly Sills, Janet Baker, Nicolai Gedda, Raimund Herincx, and Robert Lloyd. New Philharmonia Orchestra. Cond. Giuseppe Patanè. EMI Classics, 2005. CD.

> Mozart, Wolfgang Amadeus. *Sonata for 2 Pianos in D Major, K. 448*. Perf. Radu Lupu and Murray Perahia. Sony, 2003. CD.

52. Live Performance

> *Performance Title*. By Author Name. Dir. Director Name. Perf. Performer Name(s). Theater or Venue Name, City. Date of Performance. Medium.

> *Lucky Guy*. By Nora Ephron. Dir. George C. Wolfe. Perf. Tom Hanks and Peter Scolari. Broadhurst Theatre, New York. 3 Jul. 2013. Performance.

53. Work of Art

> Artist's Last Name, First Name. *Title of Artwork*. Date. Institution, City.

> Picasso, Pablo. *Les Demoiselles d'Avignon*. 1907. Museum of Modern Art, New York.

A publication medium is required only for reproduced works, such as in books or online. For works accessed on the Web, include an access date.

> Opie, Catherine. *Untitled #1 (Michigan Womyn's Music Festival)*. 2010.
> Institute of Contemporary Art, Boston. ICA Online. Web.
> 22 Mar. 2014.

54. Map or Chart

Title of Map. Map. Publication City: Publisher Name, Year. Medium.

> *West Coast Trail and Carmanah Valley*. Map. Vancouver: Intl. Travel Maps,
> 2010. Print.

If you accessed the map online, include an access date.

> *Cambodia*. Map. Google Maps. 2014. Web. 15 April 2014.

55. Cartoon or Comic Strip

Artist's Last Name, First Name. "Cartoon Title" (if given). Cartoon. *Title of Periodical* Date: Page Number. Medium.

> Crawford, Michael. "Effective Catcalls." Cartoon. *New Yorker* 11 Feb.
> 2013: 109. Print.

56. Advertisement

Product Name. Advertisement. *Title of Periodical* Date: Section Number: Page Number(s). Medium.

> Pictionary. Advertisement. *Reader's Digest* 23 Nov. 2011, 12-13. Print.

If you accessed the advertisement online, include an access date.

> iPhone 5. Advertisement. Apple YouTube Channel. Web. 18 Sept. 2014.

Format an MLA paper correctly.   You can now find software to format your academic papers in MLA style, but the key alignments for such documents are usually simple enough for you to manage on your own.

- Set up a header on the right-hand side of each page, one-half inch from the top. The header should include your last name and the page number.

- In the upper left on the first—or title—page, include your name, the instructor's name, the course title and/or number, and the date.

- Center the title above the first line of text.

- Use one-inch margins on all sides of the paper.

- Double-space the entire paper (including your name and course information, the title, and any block quotations).

- Indent paragraphs one-half inch.

- Use block quotations for quoted material of four or more lines. Indent block quotations one inch from the left margin.

- Do not include a separate title page unless your instructor requires one.

- When you document using MLA style, you'll need to create an alphabetically arranged works cited page at the end of the paper so that readers have a convenient list of all the books, articles, and other data you have used.

Wilcox 1

Susan Wilcox

Professor Longmire

Rhetoric 325M

March 7, 20--

Marathons for Women

Today in America, five women are running. Two of them live in Minnesota, one in Virginia, and two in Texas. Their careers are different, their political views are divergent, and their other hobbies are irrelevant, for it is running that draws these women together. They are marathoners. Between them, they are eighteen-time veterans of the 26.2-mile march of exhaustion and exhilaration.

These five women are not alone; over 205,000 women in the United States alone ran a marathon in 2010 (RunningUSA). They sacrifice sleeping late, watching TV, and sometimes even toenails (lost toenails are a common malady among marathon runners) for the sake of their sport. Why do these women do this to themselves? Karin Warren explains, "It started out being about losing weight and getting fit again. But I enjoyed running so much—not just how physically fit I felt afterward, but the actual act of running and how it cleared my mind and made me feel better about myself in all aspects of my life—that it became a part of who I am." The other women agree, using words like "conquer," "powerful," and "confident" to describe how running makes them feel.

However, these women know that only a generation ago, marathons weren't considered suitable for women. Tammy Moriearty and Wendy Anderson remember hearing that running could make a woman's uterus fall out; Tammy adds, "It floors me that medical professionals used to believe that." Michelle Gibson says that her friends cautioned her against running when she was pregnant (she ran anyway; it's safe). Naomi Olson has never heard a specific caution, but "lots of people think I am crazy," she says. Female runners, like their male counterparts, do have to maintain adequate nutrition during training (Third Age), but "there are no inherent health risks involved with marathon preparation and participation" (Dilworth). Unfortunately, scientists were not researching running health for women when the marathon was born, and most people thought women were too fragile to run that far. The myth that marathoning is dangerous for women was allowed to fester in the minds of race organizers around the world.

Legend holds that the original marathon runner, Pheidippides, ran from the Battle of Marathon to Athens to bring news of the Athenian victory over Persia. Pheidippides died of exhaustion after giving the news, and the marathon race today is held in honor of his final journey (Lovett x). Historians doubt all the details of this legend, including that a professional runner in Greece would die after what would have been a relatively short distance for him (x–xi) Nevertheless, the myth

Wilcox 8

Works Cited

Anderson, Wendy. Facebook interview. 25 Feb. 2012.

Associated Press. "Paula Radcliffe to Keep Marathon Record."
    ESPN Olympic Sports. ESPN, 9 Nov. 2011. Web. 19 Feb.
    2012.

Brown, Gwilym S. "A Game Girl in a Man's Game." *Sports
    Illustrated*. SI Vault, 2 May 1966. Web. 19 Feb. 2012.

Dilworth, Mark. "Women Running Marathons: Health Risks."
    EmpowHER. EmpowHER Media, 23 Apr. 2010. Web.
    19 Feb. 2012.

ESPN. "Paula Radcliffe to Keep Marathon Record." *ESPN
    Olympic Sports*. ESPN, n.d. Web. 9 Nov. 2012.

Gibb, Roberta. "A Run of One's Own." *Running Past*. Running
    Past, 2011. Web. 19 Feb. 2012.

Gibson, Michelle. Facebook interview. 20 Feb. 2012.

Longman, Jeré. "Still Playing Catch-Up." *New York Times*. New
    York Times, 5 Nov. 2011. Web. 19 Feb. 2012.

Lovett, Charles C. *Olympic Marathon: A Centennial History
    of the Games' Most Storied Race*. Westport: Praeger-Green-
    wood, 1997. Print.

Moriearty, Tammy. Facebook interview. 21 Feb. 2012.

Olson, Naomi. Facebook interview. 21 Feb. 2012.

Run Like a Girl. "History of Women's Distance Running." *Run
    Like a Girl Film*. Run Like a Girl, n.d. Web. 20 Feb. 2012.

"Works Cited" centered at top of page.

Begins on separate page.

Entries arranged alphabetically.

Entire page is double-spaced: no extra spaces between entries.

Second and subsequent lines of entries indent five spaces or one-half inch.

Wilcox 9

RunningUSA. "RunningUSA's Annual Marathon Report."

    RunningUSA. RunningUSA, 16 Mar. 2011. Web.

    19 Feb. 2012.

Switzer, Kathrine. *Marathon Woman: Running the Race*

    to Revolutionize Women's Sports. New York: Avalon,

    2007. Print.

Third Age. "Women Running Marathons: Do Benefits

    Outweigh Risks?" *Third Age*. Third Age Media,

    1 July 2008. Web. 19 Feb. 2012.

Warren, Karin. Facebook interview. 21 Feb. 2012.

47 APA Documentation and Format

APA (American Psychological Association) style is used in many social science disciplines. For full details about APA style and documentation, consult the *Publication Manual of the American Psychological Association*, 6th ed. (2010). The basic details for documenting sources and formatting research papers in APA style are presented below.

cite in APA

Document sources according to convention. When you use sources in a research paper, you are required to cite the source, letting readers know that the information has been borrowed from somewhere else and showing them how to find the original material if they would like to study it further. Like MLA style, APA includes two parts: a brief in-text citation and a more detailed reference entry.

In-text citations should include the author's name, the year the material was published, and the page number(s) that the borrowed material can be found on. The author's name and year of publication are generally included in a signal phrase that introduces the passage, and the page number is included in parentheses after the borrowed text. Note that for APA style, the verb in the signal phrase should be in the past tense (*reported*, as in the following example) or present perfect tense (*has reported*).

> Millman (2007) reported that college students around the country are participating in Harry Potter discussion groups, sports activities, and even courses for college credit (p. A4).

Alternatively, the author's name and year can be included in parentheses with the page number.

> College students around the country are participating in Harry Potter discussion groups, sports activities, and even courses for college credit (Millman, 2007, p. A4).

The list of references at the end of the paper contains a more detailed citation that repeats the author's name and publication year and includes the title and additional publication information about the source. Inclusive page numbers are included for periodical articles and parts of books.

> Millman, S. (2007). Generation hex. *The Chronicle of Higher Education, 53*(46), A4.

Both in-text citations and reference entries can vary greatly depending on the type of source cited (book, periodical, Web site, etc.). The following pages give specific examples of how to cite a wide range of sources in APA style.

Directory of APA In-Text Citations

General Guidelines for In-Text Citations in APA Style

AUTHOR NAMES

- Give last names only, unless two authors have the same last name (see item 9 on p. 517) or the source is a personal communication (see item 11 on p. 518). In these cases, include the first initial before the last name ("J. Smith").

DATES

- Give only the year in the in-text citation. The one exception to this rule is personal communications, which should include a full date (see item 11 on p. 518).
- Months and days for periodical publications should not be given with the year in in-text citations; this information will be provided as needed in the reference entry at the end of your paper.
- Add a small letter to the common date to differentiate between the items. See item 8 on page 517 and item 6 on p. 523.
- If you can't locate a date for your source, include the abbreviation "n.d." (for "no date") in place of the date in parentheses.

TITLES

- Titles of works generally do not need to be given in in-text citations. Exceptions include two or more works by the same author and works with no author. See items 8 and 10 on page 517 for details.

PAGE NUMBERS

- Include page numbers whenever possible in parentheses after borrowed material. Put "p." (or "pp.") before the page number(s).
- When you have a range of pages, list the full first and last page numbers (for example, "311-320"). If the borrowed material isn't printed on consecutive pages, list all the pages it appears on (for example, "A1, A4-A6").
- If page numbers are not available, use section names and/or paragraph (written as "para.") numbers when available to help a reader locate a specific quotation. See items 7 and 12 on pages 517 and 518 for examples.

APA in-text citation

1. Author Named in Signal Phrase

> While McWilliams (2010) acknowledged not only the growing popularity but also the ecological and cultural benefits of the locavore diet, he still maintained that "eating local is not, in and of itself, a viable answer to sustainable food production on a global level" (p. 2).

2. Author Named in Parentheses

For a source without an author, see item 10; for an electronic source without a page number, see item 12.

> "Eating local is not, in and of itself, a viable answer to sustainable food production on a global level" (McWilliams, 2010, p. 2).

3. With Block Quotations

For excerpts of forty or more words, indent the quoted material one-half inch and include the page number at the end of the quotation after the end punctuation.

> Pollan (2006) suggested that the prized marbled meat that results from feeding corn to cattle (ruminants) may not be good for us:
>> Yet this corn-fed meat is demonstrably less healthy for us, since it contains more saturated fat and less omega-3 fatty acids than the meat of animals fed grass. A growing body of research suggests that many of the health problems associated with eating beef are really problems with corn-fed beef. . . . In the same way ruminants are ill adapted to eating corn, humans in turn may be poorly adapted to eating ruminants that eat corn. (p. 75)

4. Two Authors

Note that if you name the authors in the parentheses, connect them with an ampersand (&).

> Sharpe and Young (2005) reported that new understandings about tooth development, along with advances in stem cell technology, have brought researchers closer to the possibility of producing replacement teeth from human tissue (p. 36).

New understandings about tooth development, along with advances in stem cell technology, have brought researchers closer to the possibility of producing replacement teeth from human tissue (Sharpe & Young, 2005, p. 36).

5. Three to Five Authors

The first time you cite a source with three to five authors, list all their names in either the signal phrase or parentheses. If you cite the same source again in your paper, use just the first author's name followed by "et al."

Frueh, Anouk, Elhai, and Ford (2010) identified the homecoming of Vietnam veterans as the advent for PTSD's eventual inclusion in the DSM, pointing out that "in the immediate, post-Vietnam era, compensation for significant functional impairment was difficult to obtain other than for observable physical injuries, and access to Veterans Administration (VA) medical services were possible only via a 'war-related' disorder" (p. 3).

Frueh et al. (2010) presented data to combat the assumption that although most people who endure a trauma will develop PTSD, "only a small minority of people will develop distress and functional impairment that rises to the level of a psychiatric disorder. Instead, long-term resilience is actually the norm rather than the exception for people after trauma" (p. 7).

6. Six or More Authors

List the first author's name only, followed by "et al."

While supportive parenting has not been found to decrease the incidence of depression in bullied adolescents, Bilsky et al. (2013) have insisted that parental support can still offset or counterbalance the negative effects of peer victimization (p. 417).

7. Group, Corporate, or Government Author

Treat the name just as you would any other author, and include the name in either the signal phrase or the parentheses.

The resolution called on the United States to ban all forms of torture in interrogation procedures (American Psychological Association

[APA], 2007, para. 1). It also reasserted "the organization's absolute opposition to all forms of torture and abuse, regardless of circumstance" (APA, 2007, para. 5).

8. Two or More Works by the Same Author

Two or more works by the same author will be differentiated by the publication year of the work being referenced, unless you're citing two works by the same author that were published in the same year. In this case, add a lowercase letter after the year to indicate which entry in the references list is being cited. To see reference list entries for these sources, see item 6 on page 523.

> Shermer (2005a) has reported that false acupuncture (in placebo experiments) is as effective as true acupuncture (p. 30).

> Shermer (2005b) has observed that psychics rely on vague and flattering statements, such as "You are wise in the ways of the world, a wisdom gained through hard experience rather than book learning," to earn the trust of their clients (p. 6).

9. Authors with the Same Last Name

Distinguish the authors in your in-text citations by including initials of their first names.

> S. Harris (2012) argued that free will is actually an illusion—a by-product of our past experiences, over which we believe we have more control than we actually do (p. 64).

10. Unknown Author

Identify the item by its title. However, if the author is actually listed as "Anonymous," treat this term as the author in your citation.

> Tilapia provides more protein when eaten than it consumes when alive, making it a sustainable fish ("Dream Fish," 2007, p. 26).

> The book *Go Ask Alice* (Anonymous, 1971) portrayed the fictional life of a teenager who was destroyed by her addiction to drugs.

11. Personal Communication

If you cite personal letters or e-mails or your own interviews for your research paper, cite these as personal communication in your in-text citation, including the author of the material (with first initial), the term "personal communication," and the date. Personal communications should not be included in your reference list.

> One instructor has argued that it is important to "make peer review a lot more than a proofreading/grammar/mechanics exercise" (J. Bone, personal communication, July 27, 2007).

To include the author of a personal communication in the signal phrase, use the following format:

> C. Garcia (personal communication, December 11, 2013) has argued that "while it's important to accept criticism of your writing, you should be able to distinguish between a valid suggestion and an opinion that your target audience does not share."

12. Electronic Source

If page numbers are not given, use section names or paragraph numbers to help your readers track down the source.

> Our natural feelings of disgust—for example, at the sight of rotten food or squirming maggots—are "evolutionary messages telling us to get as far away as possible from the source of our discomfort" ("How Our Brains Separate Empathy from Disgust," 2013, para. 15).

13. Musical Recording

> In an ironic twist, Mick Jagger sang backup on the song "You're So Vain" (Simon, 1972, track 3).

14. Secondary Source

Include the name of the original author in the signal phrase. In the parentheses, add "as cited in," and give the author of the quoted material along with the date and page number. Note that your end-of-paper reference entry for this material will be listed under the secondary source name (Pollan) rather than the original writer (Howard).

> Writing in 1943, Howard asserted that "artificial manures lead inevitably to artificial nutrition, artificial food, artificial animals, and finally to artificial men and women" (as cited in Pollan, 2006, p. 148).

15. Multiple Sources in Same Citation

If one statement in your paper can be attributed to multiple sources, alphabetically list all the authors with dates, separated by semicolons.

> Black Sabbath, considered the originators of heavy metal music, used their bleak upbringing in the failing industrial town of Birmingham, England, to power the darkness and passion in a sound that wowed the masses and disgusted the critics (Christe, 2004; Widerhorn & Turman, 2013).

Directory of APA Reference Entries

Directory of APA Reference Entries (*continued*)

General Guidelines for Reference Entries in APA Style

AUTHOR NAMES

- When an author's name appears *before* the title of the work, list it by last name followed by a comma and first initial followed by a period. (Middle initials may also be included.)
- If an author, editor, or other name is listed *after* the title, then the initial(s) precede the last name (see examples on pp. 523, 524–25, 527).
- When multiple authors are listed, their names should be separated by commas, and an ampersand (&) should precede the final author.

DATES

- For scholarly journals, include only the year (2014).
- For monthly magazines, include the year followed by a comma and the month (2014, May).
- For newspapers and weekly magazines, include the year followed by a comma and the month and the day (2014, May 27).
- Access dates for electronic documents use the month-day-year format: "Retrieved May 27, 2014."
- Months should not be abbreviated.
- If a date is not available, use "n.d." (for "no date") in parentheses.

TITLES

- Titles of periodicals should be italicized, and all major words capitalized (*Psychology Today*; *Journal of Archaeological Research*).
- Titles of books, Web sites, and other nonperiodical long works should be italicized. Capitalize the first word of the title (and subtitle, if any) and proper nouns only (*Legacy of ashes: The history of the CIA*).
- For short works such as essays, articles, and chapters, capitalize the first word of the title (and subtitle, if any) and proper nouns only (The black sites: A rare look inside the CIA's secret interrogation program).

PAGE NUMBERS

- Reference entries for periodical articles and sections of books should include the range of pages: "245-257." For material in parentheses, include the abbreviation "p." or "pp." before the page numbers ("pp. A4-A5").
- If the pages are not continuous, list all the pages separated by commas: "245, 249, 301-306."

APA reference entries

AUTHOR INFORMATION

1. One Author

Golden, E. (2013). *John Gilbert: The last of the silent film stars*. Lexington, KY: University Press of Kentucky.

2. Two Authors

Cox, B., & Cohen, A. (2011). *Wonders of the universe*. New York, NY: HarperCollins.

3. Three or More Authors

List every author up to and including seven; for a work with eight or more authors, give the first six names followed by three ellipsis dots and the last author's name.

Holstein, M. B., Parks, J., & Waymack, M. (2010). *Ethics, aging, and society: The critical turn*. New York, NY: Springer.

Barry, A. E., Stellefson, M. L., Piazza-Gardner, A. K., Chaney, B. H., & Dodd, V. (2013). The impact of pre-gaming on subsequent blood alcohol concentrations: An event-level analysis. *Addictive Behaviors, 38*(8), 2374-2377.

4. Group, Corporate, or Government Author

In many cases, the group name is the same as the publisher. Instead of repeating the group name, use the term "Author" for the publisher's name.

Scientific American Editors. (2012). *Storm warnings: Climate change and extreme weather*. New York, NY: Author.

5. Unidentified Author

If the author is listed on the work as "Anonymous," list that in your reference entry, alphabetizing accordingly. Otherwise, start with and alphabetize by title.

Anonymous. (1996). *Primary colors: A novel of politics*. New York, NY: Random House.

Quantum computing: Faster, slower—or both at once? (2013, May). *The Economist*, 57-58.

6. Multiple Works by the Same Author

Shermer, M. (2003). I knew you would say that [Review of the book *Intuition: Its powers and perils*]. *Skeptic, 10*(1), 92-94.

Shermer, M. (2005a, August). Full of holes: The curious case of acupuncture. *Scientific American, 293*(2). 30.

Shermer, M. (2005b). *Science friction*. New York, NY: Henry Holt, 6.

BOOKS

7. Book: Basic Format

Author. (Publication Year). *Book title: Book subtitle.* Publication City, State (abbreviated) or Country of Publication: Publisher.

O'Neil, S. K. (2013). *Two nations indivisible: Mexico, the United States, and the road ahead.* New York, NY: Oxford University Press.

8. Author and Editor

Author. (Publication Year). *Book title: Book subtitle* (Editor's Initial(s). Editor's Last Name, Ed.). Publication City, State (abbreviated) or Country of Publication: Publisher.

Faulkner, W. (2004). *Essays, speeches, and public letters* (J. B. Meriwether, Ed.). New York, NY: Modern Library.

9. Work in an Anthology or a Collection

Begin with the author and date of the short work and include the title as you would a periodical title (no quotations and minimal capitalization). Then list "In" and the editor's first initial and last name followed by "Ed." in parentheses. Next give the anthology title and page numbers in parentheses. End with the publication information. If an anthology has two editors, connect them with an ampersand (&) and use "Eds."

> Author. (Publication Year). Title of short work. In Editor's initials. Editor's Last Name (Ed.), *Title of anthology* (pp. Page Numbers). Publication City, State (abbreviated) or Country of Publication: Publisher.

Keller, H. (2008). I go adventuring. In P. Lopate (Ed.), *Writing New York: A literary anthology* (pp. 505-508). New York, NY: Library of America.

For more than two editors, connect them with commas and an ampersand. For large editorial boards, give the name of the lead editor followed by "et al."

J. Smith, L. Hoey, & R. Burns (Eds.)

N. Mallen et al. (Eds.)

10. Edited Collection

> Editor. (Ed.). (Publication Year). *Book title: Book subtitle.* Publication City, State (abbreviated) or Country of Publication: Publisher.

McKibben, B. (Ed.). (2008). *American Earth: Environmental writing since Thoreau.* New York, NY: Library of America.

11. Multivolume Work

> Author(s) or Editor(s) (Eds.). (Publication Year). *Book title: Book subtitle* (Vols. volume numbers). Publication City, State (abbreviated) or Country of Publication: Publisher.

Wright, W., Gardner, S., Graves, J., & Ruffin, P. (Eds.). (2011). *The southern poetry anthology* (Vols. 1-5). Huntsville, TX: Texas Review Press.

12. Later Edition

In parentheses include the edition type (such as "Rev." for "Revised" or "Abr." for "Abridged") or number ("2nd," "3rd," "4th," etc.) as shown on the title page, along with the abbreviation "ed." after the book title.

> Author. (Publication Year). *Book title* (Edition Type or Number ed.). Publication City, State (abbreviated) or Country of Publication: Publisher.

Akmajian, A., Demers, R. A., Farmer, A. K., & Harnish, R. M. (2010). *Linguistics: An introduction to language and communication* (6th ed.). Cambridge, MA: MIT Press.

13. Translation

List the translator's initial, last name, and "Trans." in parentheses after the title. After the publication information, list "Original work published" and year in parentheses. Note that the period is omitted after the final parenthesis.

Author. (Publication Year of Translation). *Book title* (Translator Initial(s). Last Name, Trans.). Publication City, State (abbreviated) or Country of Publication: Publisher. (Original work published Year)

Camus, A. (1988). *The stranger* (M. Ward, Trans.). New York, NY: Knopf. (Original work published 1942)

14. Article in a Reference Book

Article Author. (Publication Year). Article title. In Initial(s). Last Name of Editor (Ed.), *Reference book title* (pp. Page Numbers). Publication City, State (abbreviated) or Country of Publication: Publisher.

Stroud, S. (2013). Value theory. In H. LaFollette (Ed.), *The international encyclopedia of ethics* (pp. 789-790). Malden, MA: John Wiley & Sons.

If a reference book entry has no author, begin with the title of the article.

Article title. (Publication Year). In *Book title*. Publication City, State (abbreviated) or Country of Publication: Publisher.

Top 10 news topics of 2012. (2012). In *The world almanac and book of facts 2013*. New York, NY: World Almanac Books.

PERIODICALS

15. Article in a Journal Paginated by Volume

Article Author. (Publication Year). Title of article. *Title of Journal, Volume Number,* Page Numbers.

Mace, B. L., Corser, G. C., Zitting, L., & Denison, J. (2013). Effects of overflights on the national park experience. *Journal of Environmental Psychology, 35,* 30-39.

16. Article in a Journal Paginated by Issue

Article Author. (Publication Year). Title of article. *Title of Journal, Volume Number*(Issue Number), Page Numbers.

Clancy, S., & Simpson, L. (2002). Literacy learning for indigenous students: Setting a research agenda. *Australian Journal of Language and Literacy, 25*(2), 47-64.

17. Magazine Article

Article Author. (Publication Year, Month). Title of article. *Title of Magazine, Volume Number*(Issue Number), Page Number(s).

Doll, J. (2013, June). The evolution of hand gestures: Why do some die out and others endure? *The Atlantic, 200*(1167): 58-60.

18. Newspaper Article

Article Author. (Publication Year, Month Day). Title of article. *Title of Newspaper,* p. Page Number.

Tobar, H. (2013, May 28). Tech-savvy parents prefer print over e-books for kids, PEW reports. *Los Angeles Times,* p. 24.

19. Letter to the Editor

Include "Letter to the editor" in brackets after the letter title (if any) and before the period.

Author. (Publication Year, Month Day). Title of letter [Letter to the editor]. *Title of Newspaper,* p. Page Number.

Murray, M. (2013, April 24). Giving cash to panhandlers is the wrong way to help [Letter to the editor]. *Denver Post,* p. A17.

20. Review

After the review title (if any), include in brackets "Review of the" and the medium of the work being reviewed ("book," "film," "CD," etc.), followed by the title of the work in italics. If the reviewed work is a book, include the author's name after a comma; if it's a film or other media, include the year of release.

> Author Name. (Publication Year, Month Day). Title of review [Review of the book *Book title*, by Author Name]. *Title of Periodical, Volume Number,* Page Number.

> Abramson, J. (2012, November 11). Grand bargainer [Review of the book *Thomas Jefferson: The art of power*, by J. Meacham]. *The New York Times Book Review, 3,* 1.

ELECTRONIC SOURCES

21. Article with a DOI

A DOI (digital object identifier) is a unique number assigned to specific content, such as a journal article. Include the DOI but not the database name or URL. Note that there is no period after the DOI.

> DiGangi, J., Jason, L. A., Mendoza, L., Miller, S. A., & Contreras, R. (2013). The relationship between wisdom and abstinence behaviors in women in recovery from substance abuse. *The American Journal of Drug and Alcohol Abuse, 39*(1), 33-37. doi: 10.3109/00952990.2012.702172

22. Article without a DOI

Give the exact URL or the URL for the journal's home page if access requires a subscription. Do not give the database name. Note that there is no period after the URL.

> McDermott, L. A., & Pettijohn, T. F., II (2011). The influence of clothing fashion and race on the perceived socioeconomic status and person perception of college students. *Psychology & Society, 4*(2), 64-75. Retrieved from http://www.psychologyandsociety.org/__assets /__original/2012/01/McDermott_Pettijohn.pdf

23. Article in Internet-Only Periodical

An article published exclusively online is unlikely to have page numbers.

> Palmer, B. (2013, May 24). How accurate are AAA's travel forecasts? *Slate. com*. Retrieved from http://www.slate.com/articles/health_and
> _science/explainer/2013/05/aaa_memorial_day_travel_forecast_are
> _holiday_driving_predictions_accurate.html

24. Multipage Web Site

Include a retrieval date before the URL if the material is likely to be changed or updated or if it lacks a set publication date. Do not add a period at the end of the entry.

> Web Site Author or Sponsor. (Date of Most Recent Update). *Title of Web site.* Retrieved date, from URL

> Department of Homeland Security. (2013). *Disasters*. Retrieved January 14, 2014, from http://www.dhs.gov/topic/disasters

> Linder, D. O. (2013). *Famous trials*. Retrieved March 2, 2014, from http://law2.umkc.edu/faculty/projects/ftrials/ftrials.htm

25. Part of a Web Site

> Short Work Author. (Date of Most Recent Update). Title of short work. *Title of Web site.* Retrieved date, from URL

> Slate, M., & Sestan, N. (2012, September 18). The emerging biology of autism spectrum disorders. *Autism speaks*. Retrieved from http:// www.autismspeaks.org/blog/2012/09/18/emerging-biology-autism -spectrum-disorders

26. Online Posting

For detailed advice on citing social media, see http://blog.apastyle.org/apastyle /social-media.

> Post Author. (Year, Month Day of post). Title of post [Description of post]. Retrieved date, from URL

> Parkin, G. (2011, December 5). Mobile learning platforms and tools [Online forum comment]. Retrieved from http://community.astd.org/eve /forums/a/tpc/f/6401041/m/142107851

27. Computer Software or App

If the software or app has an author or editor listed, the reference begins with that.

Title of software [Computer software]. (Publication Year). Publication City, State (abbreviated) or Country of Publication: Publisher.

History: The French revolution [Computer software]. (2009). San Jose, CA: Innovative Knowledge.

When citing an app, look at the most recent update for the publication date.

Title of app. (Publication Year). Creator and version number [Mobile application software]. Retrieval information.

Medscape. (2014). WebMD Health (Version 4.4.1) [Mobile application software]. Retrieved from http://itunes.apple.com

28. Entry in a Blog (Weblog)

Hasselbrink, K. (2013, February 5). Chai [Web log post]. Retrieved from http://theyearinfood.com/2013/02/chai.html

29. Podcast

Fogarty, M. (Producer). (2013, May 10). How texting is changing English. [Audio podcast]. *Grammar Girl*. Retrieved from http://grammar .quickanddirtytips.com/how-texting-is-changingenglish.aspx

30. Entry in a Wiki

Article title. Posting date (if any). Retrieved date, from URL

Selfie. (n.d.). Retrieved July 27, 2013, from http://en.wikipedia.org/wiki /Selfie

How to...
Cite from a Web site (APA)

2 publisher of report (if not named as author)

3 report number

4 title of online report

5 author

1 publication date

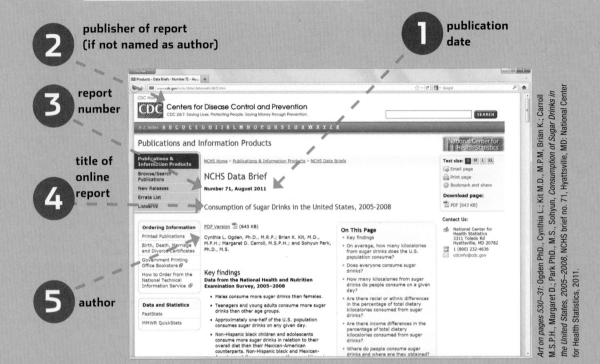

Art on pages 530–31: Ogden PhD., Cynthia L.; Kit M.D., M.P.M, Brian K.; Carroll M.S.P.H., Margaret D.; Park PhD., M.S., Sohyun, *Consumption of Sugar Drinks in the United States, 2005–2008*, NCHS brief no. 71, Hyattsville, MD: National Center for Health Statistics, 2011.

If you cite a source with three or more authors more than once in text, only list all of the authors the first time. Subsequent times only need the first author's last name, like this: (Ogden et al.).

For a video tutorial, see **macmillanhighered.com/howtowrite3e.**
Tutorials > Documentation and Working with Sources > How to Cite a Web Site in APA Style

SECTION BEING CITED

6 URL of section

7 section title

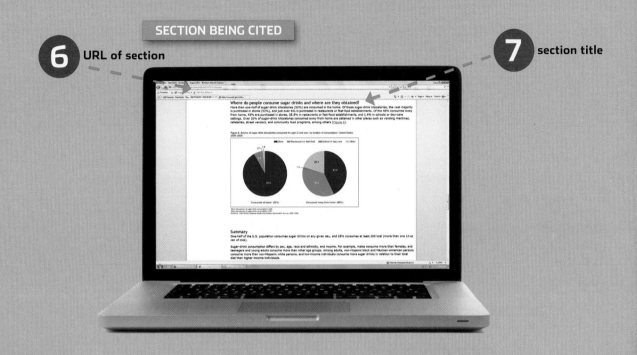

APA in-text citation

A nutrition survey of U.S. behavior between 2005 and 2008 found that an overwhelming 92% of sugar-drink kilocalories consumed outside the home were from drinks purchased in stores, not restaurants (Ogden, Kit, Carroll, & Park, 2011).

1   5

APA references list entry

1   5   1   7

Ogden, C. L., Kit, B. K., Carroll, M. D., & Park S. (2011, August). Where do

4

people consume sugar drinks and where are they obtained? In Consumption

3

of sugar drinks in the United States, 2005–2008 (NCHS Data Brief No. 71).

2

Retrieved from Centers for Disease Control and Prevention website:

6

http://www.cdc.gov/nchs/data/databriefs/db71.htm#people

How to...
Cite from a database (APA)

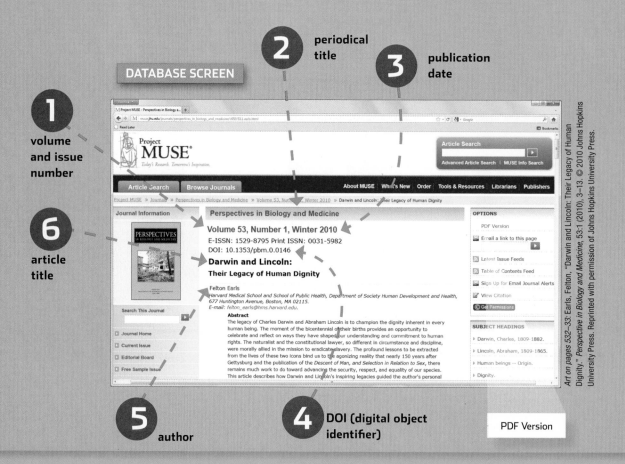

DATABASE SCREEN

2 periodical title

3 publication date

1 volume and issue number

6 article title

5 author

4 DOI (digital object identifier)

PDF Version

For a video tutorial, see **macmillanhighered.com/howtowrite3e.**
Tutorials › Documentation and Working with Sources › How to Cite a Database in APA Style

If you're reading an article in an Internet browser and aren't sure where to find the information you need, try viewing the article as a PDF, which usually shows what originally appeared in the print journal.

PDF VIEW (FIRST PAGE)

I T IS WITH A SENSE of intellectual excitement that this year we celebrate the bicentennial of two extraordinary men who just happened to be born on the same day, February 12, 1809. Charles Darwin was born into a learned and landed family in Shropshire, England. Quite a different social and economic setting prevailed in Abraham Lincoln's home in Kentucky. His father was a poor and une-

Harvard Medical School and School of Public Health , Department of Society Human Development and Health, 677 Huntington Avenue, Boston, MA 02115.
E-mail: felton_earls@hms.harvard.edu.

*Max Perutz Memorial Lecture, Ninth Biennial Meeting, International Human Rights Network of Academies and Scholarly Societies, Rabat, Morocco, May 21, 2009.

Perspectives in Biology and Medicine, volume 53, number 1 (winter 2010):3–15
© 2010 by The Johns Hopkins University Press

3

7 page range

APA in-text citation

It's important to note the contributions of Darwin and Lincoln to modern conceptions of human rights, "particularly the beliefs that scientists are free to pursue knowledge, no matter how different from or risky to the prevailing wisdom, and that one of the responsibilities of modern governments is to protect this right to rationality and critical inquiry" (Earls, 2011, 4).

5 **3** **7**

APA references list entry

5 **3** **6**
Earls, F. (2011, Winter). Darwin and Lincoln: Their legacy of human dignity.

2 **1** **7** **4**
Perspectives in Biology and Medicine, 53(1), 3-15. doi:10.1353/pbm.0.0146

OTHER

31. Group, Corporate, or Government Document

List the group or agency as the author, and include any identifying numbers. Many federal agencies' works are published by the U.S. Government Printing Office. If the group is also the publisher, use the word "Author" rather than repeating the group name at the end of the entry.

> Name of Group, Corporation, or Government Agency. (Publication Year). *Title of document* (Identifying number, if any). Publication City, State (abbreviated) or Country of Publication: Publisher.

> National Equal Pay Task Force. (2013). *Fifty years after the Equal Pay Act: Assessing the past, taking stock of the future* (PREX 1.2:EQ 2). Washington, DC: U.S. Government Printing Office.

> Maine Department of Health and Human Services. (2011). *Connections: A guide for family caregivers in Maine*. Augusta, ME: Author.

32. Published Conference Proceedings

> Editor(s). (Eds.). (Publication Year). *Proceedings of the Conference Name: Book title.* Publication City, State (abbreviated) or Country of Publication: Publisher.

> Contreras, F., Farjas, M., & Melero, F. J. (Eds.). (2013). *Proceedings of the 38th annual Conference on Computer Applications and Quantitative Methods in Archaeology: Fusion of cultures*. Oxford, United Kingdom: Archaeopress.

33. Dissertation Abstract

For dissertations abstracted in Dissertation Abstracts International, include the author's name, date, and dissertation title. Then include the volume, issue, and page number. If you access the dissertation from an electronic database, identify the type of work ("Doctoral dissertation") before giving the database name and any identifying number. If you retrieve the abstract from the Web, include the name of the institution in the parentheses, and then give the URL.

Author. (Year of Publication). *Title of dissertation. Dissertation Abstracts International, Volume Number*(Issue Number), Page Number.

Hand, J. A. (2011). *Making sense of change: Sexuality transformation at midlife. Dissertation Abstracts International, 72*(9), 8745B.

Hand, J. A. (2011). *Making sense of change: Sexuality transformation at midlife* (Doctoral dissertation). Available from ProQuest Dissertations and Theses database. (9347727101).

Hand, J. A. (2011). *Making sense of change: Sexuality transformation at midlife* (Doctoral dissertation. Temple University). Retrieved from http://cdm16002.contentdm.oclc.org/cdm/compoundobject/collection /p245801coll10/id/108810/rec/14

34. Film

Writer(s), Producer(s), Director(s). (Release year). *Film title* [Motion picture]. Country of Origin: Movie Studio.

Terrio, C. (Writer), Affleck, B. (Director/Producer), & Clooney, G., & Heslov, G. (Producers). (2012). *Argo* [Motion picture]. United States: GK Films.

35. Television Program

Writer(s), Producer(s), Director(s). (Year of Release). Title of episode [Television series episode]. In Producer Initials. Last Name (Producer), *Title of series*. City, State (abbreviated) or Country of Publication: Broadcast Company.

Zwonitzer, M. (Writer/Producer/Director). (2013). Jesse James [Television series episode]. In M. Samels (Producer), *American Experience*. Boston, MA: WGBH.

36. Musical Recording

Writer. (Copyright Year). Title of song [Recorded by Artist Name]. On *Album title* [Recording medium]. City of Recording, State (abbreviated) or Country of Publication: Record Label. (Recording Year).

Lennon, J., & McCartney, P. (1967). With a little help from my friends [Recorded by The Beatles]. On *Sgt. Pepper's Lonely Hearts Club Band: Remastered* [CD]. Los Angeles, CA: Capitol. (2009).

Format an APA paper correctly.   The following guidelines will help you prepare a manuscript using APA style.

- Set up a header on each page, one-half inch from the top. The header should include a brief title (shortened to no more than fifty characters) in all capital letters and should align left. Page numbers should appear in the upper right corner.

- Margins should be set at one inch on all sides of the paper.

- Check with your instructor to see if a title page is preferred. If so, at the top of the page, you need the short title you'll use in your header, in all capital letters, preceded by the words "Running head" and a colon. The page number appears on the far right. Next, the full title of your paper, your name, and your affiliation (or school) appear in the middle of the page, centered.

- If you include an abstract for your paper, put it on a separate page, immediately following the title page.

- All lines of text (including the title page, abstract, block quotations, and the list of references) should be double-spaced.

- Indent the first lines of paragraphs one-half inch or five spaces.

- Use block quotations for quoted material of four or more lines. Indent block quotations one inch from the left margin.

- When you document a paper using APA style, you'll need to create an alphabetically arranged references page at the end of the project so that readers have a convenient list of all the books, articles, and other data you have used in the paper or project.

Running head: CRI DU CHAT SYNDROME   1

Short title in all capitals is aligned left. Arabic numerals are used for page numbers.

Developmental Disorders:

Cri du Chat Syndrome

Marissa Dahlstrom

University of Texas at Austin

Full title, writer's name, and affiliation are all centered in middle of page.

CRI DU CHAT SYNDROME   2

This paper does not include an abstract; check with your instructor to find out whether an abstract is required.

Center the title.

Developmental Disorders: Cri du Chat Syndrome

Developmental disorders pose a serious threat to young children. However, early detection, treatment, and intervention often allow a child to lead a fulfilling life. To detect a problem at the beginning of life, medical professionals and caregivers must recognize normal development as well as potential warning signs. Research provides this knowledge. In most cases, research also allows for accurate diagnosis and effective intervention. Such is the case with cri du chat syndrome (CDCS), also commonly known as cat cry syndrome and 5p– (5p minus) syndrome.

Cri du chat syndrome, a fairly rare genetic disorder first identified in 1963 by Dr. Jerome Lejeune, affects between 1 in 15,000 to 1 in 50,000 live births (Campbell, Carlin, Justen, & Baird, 2004). The syndrome is caused by partial deletion of chromosome number 5, specifically the portion labeled as 5p; hence the alternative name for the disorder (5P– Society). While the exact cause of the deletion is unknown, it is likely that "the majority of cases are due to spontaneous loss . . . during development of an egg or sperm. A minority of cases result from one parent carrying a rearrangement of chromosome 5 called a translocation" (Sondheimer, 2005). The deletion leads to many different symptoms and outcomes. Perhaps the most noted characteristic of children affected by this syndrome—a high-pitched cry resembling the mewing of a cat—explains Lejeune's choice of the name cri du chat. Pediatric nurse Mary Kugler writes that the cry is caused by "problems with the

The authors' names and publication date appear in parentheses.

A signal phrase including author's name introduces quotation, so only the date appears in parentheses.

CRI DU CHAT SYNDROME   6

References

Campbell, D., Carlin M., Justen, J., III, & Baird, S. (2004).
     Cri-du-chat syndrome: A topical overview. *5P– Society*
     Retrieved from http://www.fivepminus.org/online.htm

Denny, M., Marchand-Martella, N., Martella, R., Reilly, J. R., &
     Reilly, J. F. (2000). Using parent-delivered graduated
     guidance to teach functional living skills to a child with
     cri du chat syndrome. *Education & Treatment of Children*,
     23(4), 441.

5P– Society. (n.d.). About 5P–syndrome. *5P– Society Web site*.
     Retrieved from http://www.fivepminus.org/about.htm

Kugler, M. (2006). Cri-du-chat syndrome: Distinctive kitten-
     like cry in infancy. *About.com Rare Diseases*. Retrieved
     from http://rarediseases.about.com/cs/criduchatsynd
     /a/010704.htm

McClean, P. (1997). Genomic analysis: *In situ* hybridization.
     Retrieved from http://www.ndsu.nodak.edu/instruct
     /mcclean/plsc431/genomic/genomic2.htm

Sarimski, K. (2003). Early play behavior in children with 5p–
     syndrome. *Journal of Intellectual Disability Research,*
     47(2), 113-120. doi: 10.1046/j.1365-2788.2003.00448.x

Sondheimer, N. (2005). Cri du chat syndrome. In *MedlinePlus*
     medical encyclopedia. Retrieved from http://www.nlm
     .nih.gov/medlineplus/ency/article/001593.htm

Media & Design

part eight

48

Understanding Digital Media

Schools, businesses, and professional organizations are finding innovative uses for new media tools and services such as blogs, wikis, digital video, Web-mapping software, social networks, and more. The resulting texts—often spun from Web 2.0 interactive media technologies—represent genres much in flux. And yet they already

Plotting Flickr and Twitter locations in Europe produces this luminous map of the continent, suggesting the sweep of new media activity. Eric Fischer.

play a role in many classrooms. You are employing new media if you contribute to a college service project hosted on a blog, schedule study sessions with classmates via Facebook, use slide software to spiff up a report to the student government, or find yourself enrolled in a MOOC (massive open online course).

Choose a media format based on what you hope to accomplish.   A decision to compose with digital tools or to work in environments such as Facebook, Twitter, or Instagram should be based on what these media offer you. An electronic tool may support your project in ways that conventional printed texts simply cannot—and that's the reason to select it. Various media writing options are described in the following table.

Format	Elements	Purpose	Software Technology/Tools
Social networks, blogs	Online discussion postings; interactive; text; images; video; links	Create communities (fan, political, academic); distribute news and information	Facebook; Twitter; Reddit; Blogger; Instagram; Tumblr; WordPress
Web sites	Web-based information site; text; images; video; links; interactive posts	Compile and distribute information; establish presence on Web; sell merchandise, etc.	Dreamweaver; Drupal; WordPress, Google Sites
Wikis	Collaboratively authored linked texts and posts; Web-based; information; text; images; data	Create and edit collaborative documents based on community expertise; distribute and share information	DokuWiki; MediaWiki; Tiki Wiki
Podcasts, music	Digital file-based audio or (sometimes) video recording; downloadable; voice; music; episodic	Distribute mainly audio texts; document or archive audio texts and performances	Audacity; GarageBand
Maps	Interactive image maps; text; data; images; mind maps	Give spatial or geographical dimension to data, texts, ideas; help users locate or visualize information	iMapBuilder; Google Earth; Google Maps; NovaMind
Video	Recorded images; live-action images; enhanced slides; animation; sound; music	Record events; provide visual documentation; create presentations; furnish instructions, etc.	Animoto; Camtasia; iMovie; Movie Maker; Blender; Soundslides

Use social networks and blogs to create communities. You know, of course, that Facebook and Twitter have transformed the way people share their lives and ideas. Social networks such as these are vastly more interactive versions of the online exchanges hosted by groups or individuals on blogs—which typically focus on topics such as politics, news, sports, technology, and entertainment. Social networks and blogs integrate comments, images, videos, and links in various ways; they are constantly updated, most are searchable, and some are archived.

College courses might use social networks and blogs to spur discussion of class materials, to distribute information, and to document research activities: Students in courses often set up their own social media groups. When networking or blogging is part of a course assignment, understand the ground rules. Instructors often require a defined number of postings/comments of a specific length. Participate regularly by reading and commenting on other students' posts; by making substantive comments of your own on the assigned topic; and by contributing relevant images, videos, and links.

Keep your academic postings focused, title them descriptively, and make sure they reflect the style of the course—most likely informal, but not quite as colloquial as public online groups. Pay attention to grammar and mechanics too. Avoid the vitriol you may encounter on national sites: Remember that anyone—from your mother to a future employer—might read your remarks.

This masthead appears on a Web site created by a college professor for his students and colleagues at McDaniel College in Maryland. Dr. Paul Muhlhauser, McDaniel College, English Department.

Create Web sites to share information. Not long ago, building Web sites was at the leading edge of technological savvy in the classroom. Today, social

networks, blogs, and wikis are far more efficient vehicles for academic communication. Still, Web sites remain useful because of their capacity to organize large amounts of text and information online. A Web site you create for a course might report research findings or provide a portal to information on a complex topic.

When creating a site with multiple pages, plan early on how to organize that information; the structure will depend on your purpose and audience. A simple site with sequential information (e.g., a photo-essay) might lead readers through items one by one. More complicated sites may require a complex, hierarchical structure, with materials organized around careful topic divisions. The more comprehensive the site, the more deliberately you will need to map out its structure, allowing for easy navigation and growth.

Use wikis to collaborate with others.   If you have ever looked at Wikipedia, you know what a wiki does: It enables a group to collaborate on the development of an ongoing online project—from a comprehensive encyclopedia to focused databases on just about any imaginable topic. Such an effort combines the knowledge of all its contributors, ideally making the whole greater than its parts.

In academic courses, instructors may ask class members to publish articles on an existing wiki—in which case you should read the site guidelines, examine its current entries and templates, and then post your item. More likely, though, you will use wiki software to develop a collaborative project for the course itself—bringing together research on a specific academic topic. A wiki might even be used for a service project in which participants gather useful information about nutrition, jobs, or arts opportunities for specific communities.

As always with electronic projects, you need to learn the software—which will involve not only uploading material to the wiki but also editing and developing texts that classmates have already placed there.

Make videos and podcasts to share information.   With most cell phones now equipped with cameras, digital video has become the go-to medium these days for recording just about any event or for sharing ideas and information. In a sociology or government course, you might want to record important interviews; in a biology or engineering course, a video might be the best way to demonstrate a complex procedure. Software such as Movie Maker or iMovie can help you tell a

For a tutorial on audio editing, see **macmillanhighered.com/howtowrite3e.**
Tutorials > Digital Writing > Audio Editing with Audacity

story or make an argument; you can edit and mix digital scenes, refine the sound, add special effects and captions, and so on. If your subject is better served by animation, software such as Blender gives you different choices. You can construct nonnarrative kinds of video writing by combining text, film clips, still photos, and music using software such as Animoto, Soundslides, or Camtasia.

Podcasts remain a viable option for sharing downloadable audio or video files. Playable on various portable devices from MP3 players to tablets, podcasts are often published in series. Academic podcasts usually need to be scripted and edited. Producing a podcast is a two-step process. First you must record the podcast; then you need to upload it to a Web site for distribution. Software such as GarageBand can do both.

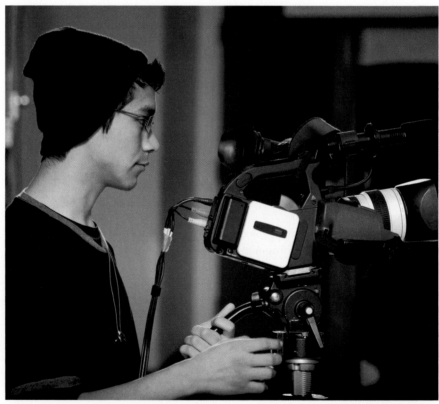

Hill Street Studios/Getty Images.

Use maps to position ideas.   You use mapping services such as Google Maps whenever you search online for a restaurant, store, or hotel. The service quickly provides maps and directions to available facilities, often embellished with links, information, and images. Not surprisingly, Google Maps, the related Google Earth, and other mapping software are finding classroom applications.

Multimedia maps also make it possible to display information such as economic trends, movements of people, climate data, and other variables graphically and dynamically, using color, text, images, and video/audio clips to emphasize movement and change across space and time. Even literary texts can be mapped so that scholars or readers may track events or characters as they move in real or imaginary landscapes. Mapping thus becomes a vehicle for reporting and sharing information, telling personal stories, revealing trends, exploring causal relationships, or making arguments.

Use appropriate digital formats.   Digital documents come in many forms, but you will use familiar word-processing, presentation, or spreadsheet software for most of your academic work. Compatibility is rarely an issue today when you move materials across computer platforms (PC to Mac) or download a presentation in a classroom for an oral report. Still, it never hurts to check ahead of time if, for example, you use Keynote or Prezi for a report rather than the more common PowerPoint.

Occasionally you need to save digital files in special formats. Sharing a file with someone using an older version of Word or Office may require saving a document in compatibility mode (.doc) rather than the now-standard .docx mode. Or moving across different applications may be easier if you use a plain text (.txt) or rich text format (.rtf)—in which case your document will lose some features, though the text will be preserved. When you want to share a document exactly as you wrote it and send it successfully across platforms, choose the .pdf mode. Files in .pdf form arrive exactly as you sent them, without any shifts in headings, alignments, or image locations; just as important, they cannot be easily altered.

Even if you have only a limited knowledge of differing image file formats (such as JPG, GIF, or TIFF), you probably understand that digital files come in varying sizes. The size of a digital-image file is directly related to the quality, or resolution, of the image. Attach a few high-resolution 26-megapixel photos to an e-mail and you'll clog the recipient's mailbox (or the e-mail will bounce back).

English instructor Hala Herbly asked students to map the movements across Europe of the monster from Mary Shelley's novel *Frankenstein.* © 2010 Google. Google and the Google logo are registered trademarks of Google, Inc., used with permission. Map data © 2010 Europa Technologies, PPWK. TeleAtlas-Hala Herbly.

For most Web pages and online documents, compressed or lower-resolution images will be acceptable. On the other hand, if you intend to print an image—in a paper or brochure, for example—use the highest-resolution image (the greatest number of pixels) available to assure maximum sharpness and quality.

Edit and save digital elements.   Nonprint media texts often require as much revising and editing as traditional written ones. In fact, the tools for manipulating video, audio, and still-image files are among the most remarkable accomplishments of the digital age. Even the simplest image-editing software, for example, enables users to adjust the tint, contrast, saturation, and sharpness of digital photographs or crop them as needed. If you are developing a podcast, an audio file can be tweaked a dozen ways using an audio editor like GarageBand or Audacity; such programs can also be used to create or refine musical clips. Comparable software is available for editing video clips.

Do keep careful tabs on any electronic content you collect for a project. Create a dedicated folder on your desktop, hard drive, or online storage and save each item with a name that will remind you where it came from. Keeping a printed record of images, with more detailed information about copyrights and sources, will pay dividends later, when you are putting your project or paper together and need to give proper credit to contributors.

Image-editing software offers numerous options for enhancing picture files. Look for these options on format tabs, palettes, or dropdown menus.
John J. Ruszkiewicz.

Respect copyrights.   The images you find, whether online or in print, belong to someone. You cannot use someone else's property—photographs, Web sites, brochures, posters, magazine articles, and so on—for commercial purposes without permission. You may use a reasonable number of images in academic papers, but you must be careful not to go beyond "fair use," especially for any work you put online. Search the term "academic fair use" online for detailed guidelines. Be prepared, too, to document images in academic research papers.

> **Your Turn**   Most of the software programs mentioned in this chapter have Web sites that describe their features, and some sites even include sample projects. Explore one or two of these programs online to learn about their capabilities. Then describe a new media project you would like to create using the software.

For a tutorial on photo editing, see **macmillanhighered.com/howtowrite3e.**
Tutorials › Digital Writing › Photo Editing Basics with GIMP

49

Tables, Graphs, and Infographics

display data

Just as images and photographs are often the media of choice for conveying visual information, tables, graphs, and other "infographics" are essential tools for displaying numerical and statistical data. They take raw data and transform it into a story or picture readers can interpret.

Most such items are created in spreadsheet programs such as Excel that format charts and graphs and offer numerous design templates—though you will find basic graphics tools in Word and PowerPoint as well. More elaborate charts and graphs can be drawn with software such as Adobe Illustrator.

Creating effective tables and graphs is an art in itself, driven as always by purpose and audience. A table in a printed report that a reader will study can be rich in detail; a bar graph on screen for only a few moments must make its point quickly and memorably. Function always trumps appearance. Yet there's no question that handsome visual texts appeal to audiences. So spend the time necessary to design effective items. Use color to emphasize and clarify graphs, not just to decorate them. Label items clearly (avoiding symbols or keys that are hard to interpret), and don't add more detail than necessary.

In academic projects, be sure to label (*Fig.*, *Table*), number, and caption your important graphic items, especially any that you mention in your text. Both MLA and APA style offer guidelines for handling labels; the APA rules are particularly detailed and specific.

Use tables to present statistical data. Tables can do all kinds of work. They are essential for organizing and recording information as it comes in, for example, daily weather events: temperature, precipitation, wind velocities, and so on. A table may also show trends or emphasize contrasts. In such cases, tables may make an argument (in a print ad, for example) or readers may be left to interpret complex data on their own—one of the pleasures of studying such material.

Tables typically consist of horizontal rows and vertical columns into which you drop data. The axes of the chart provide different and significant ways of presenting data, relating x to y: for example, in Table 1, lifetime earnings are connected to education level.

In designing a table, determine how many horizontal rows and vertical columns are needed, how to label them, and whether to use color or shading to enhance the readability of the data. Software templates will provide options. Good tables can be very plain. In fact, many of the tables on federal government Web sites, though packed with information, are dirt simple and yet quite clear.

Use line graphs to display changes or trends. Line graphs are dynamic images, visually plotting and connecting variables on horizontal x- and vertical

Table 1
Expected Lifetime Earnings Relative to High School Graduates, by Education Level

	Total Lifetime Earnings	Total Earnings Relative to High School Graduates	Present Value of Total Lifetime Earnings (3% Discount Rate)	Present Value Earnings Relative to HS Graduates (3% Discount Rate)
Not a High School Graduate	$941,370	0.74	$551,462	0.75
High School Graduate	1,266,730	1.00	738,609	1.00
Some College, No Degree	1,518,300	1.20	878,259	1.19
Associate Degree	1,620,730	1.28	943,181	1.28
Bachelor's Degree	2,054,380	1.62	1,189,836	1.61
Master's Degree	2,401,565	1.90	1,427,392	1.93
Doctoral Degree	3,073,240	2.43	1,748,716	2.37
Professional Degree	3,706,910	2.93	2,123,309	2.87
Bachelor's Degree or Higher	2,284,110	1.80	1,312,316	1.78

Sources: U.S. Census Bureau, 2006, PINC-03; calculations by the authors.

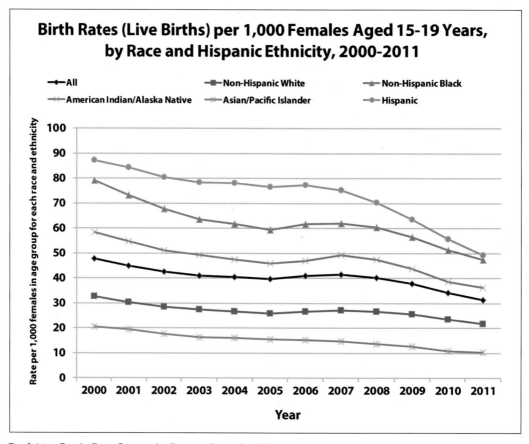

Fig. 1. Line Graph. From Centers for Disease Control and Prevention. Hamilton BE, Martin JA, Ventura SJ. *Births: Preliminary data for 2010.* National Vital Statistics Reports, 2011; 60(2): Table S-2.* Hamilton BE, Martin JA, Ventura SJ. *Births: Preliminary data for 2011.* National Vital Statistics Reports. 2012; 61(5). Table 2, Hyattsville, MD: National Center for Health Statistics, 2012.

y-axes so that readers can see how relationships change or trends emerge, usually over time. As such, line graphs often contribute to political or social arguments by tracking fluctuations in income, unemployment, educational attainment, stock prices, and so on.

Properly designed, line graphs are easy to read and informative, especially when just a single variable is presented. But it is possible to plot several items on an axis, complicating the line graph but increasing the amount of information it offers (see fig. 1).

Use bar and column graphs to plot relationships within sets of data.
Column and bar graphs use rectangles to represent information either horizontally (bar graph) or vertically (column graph). In either form, these graphs emphasize differences and can show changes over time; they enable readers to grasp relationships that would otherwise take many words to explain. Bar and column graphs present data precisely, if their x- and y-axes are carefully drawn to scale. In Figure 2, for example, a reader can determine the number of major

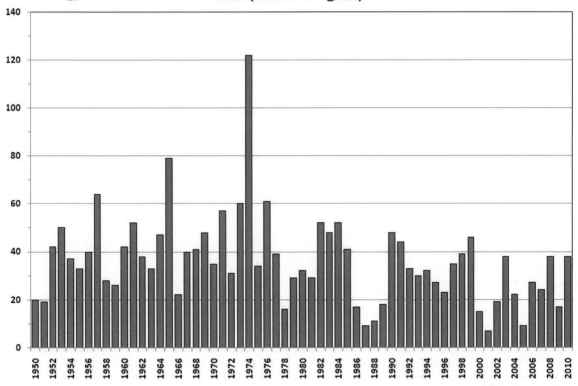

Fig. 2. Number of Strong to Violent (EF3–EF5) Tornadoes. From NOAA Satellite and Information Service. National Oceanic and Atmospheric Administration and the Department of Commerce.

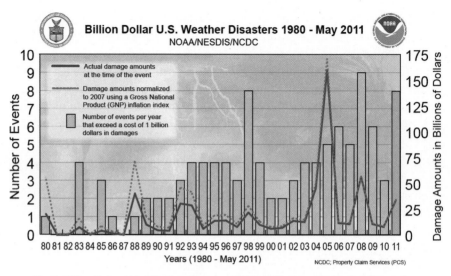

Fig. 3. Billion Dollar U.S. Weather Disasters 1980–2011. From NOAA Satellite and Information Service. National Oceanic and Atmospheric Administration, National Environmental Satellite, Data and Information Service, and the National Climatic Data Center.

tornadoes in any of more than fifty years and also note a slight trend toward fewer severe storms.

But it is easy to ask a single graphic image to do too much. For example, many readers probably find Figure 3 hard to interpret. Is the chart about the number of storms, their growing frequency, or their actual and adjusted costs? Storm effects in the background of the graphic just add to the clutter.

Use pie charts to display proportions.   A typical pie chart is a circle broken into segments that represent some proportion of a whole. Such charts illustrate which parts of that whole have greater or lesser significance, but they do not display precise numbers well. Note in Figure 4, for example, that without the actual sales percentages attached to the chart, you could not easily tell which auto brand sold the most cars in the United States in 2012—Mercedes or BMW. Since the segments in a typical pie chart need to total 100 percent, you sometimes have to include a segment called "Others / Don't know" to account for items not actually present in the major categories.

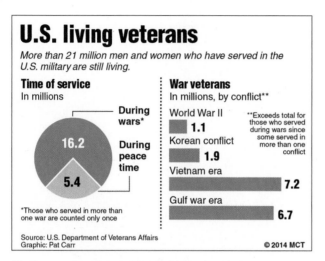

Fig. 4. A combined pie and bar chart uses pale green, a color associated with military fatigue uniforms, to show numbers of veterans in terms of their time of service, as well as the conflicts in which they served. Carr/MCT/Newscom.

Pie-chart sections can be cut only so thin before they begin to lose clarity. Figure 4, for instance, uses a pie chart for double-digit figures, and a bar chart for smaller numbers. If you wanted to use a pie chart to depict dozens of items—say the payrolls of all thirty major league baseball teams—you'd find yourself with slivers readers couldn't interpret confidently. Better to transfer the data to a bar graph that could incorporate more detailed information.

Explore the possibilities of infographics.   Under the rubric of "infographics," many organizations and information specialists create data-driven visual texts about subjects from climate change to trends in music. Such presentations part ways with traditional academic conventions to tell lively but information-rich stories (see fig. 5). One writer calls these focused presentations—freely combining charts, tables, timelines, maps, and other design elements—"visual essays." But many infographics are, in fact, "visual arguments" that use the medium to support particular claims or points of view: They combine images and data to dramatize an issue.

Various tools are available online to support the creation of infographics, including Many Eyes, Google Public Data Explorer, Wordle, and StatPlanet. For more about infographics and many examples, search the term online.

Fig. 5. The Summer Surge. From George-town University Center on Education and the Workforce. Georgetown Center on Education and the Workforce, the Summer Surge.

Your Turn   Study Figure 5, "The Summer Surge." Then look online for additional examples of infographics. (They are readily available on sites such as VizWorld or Cool Infographics.) When you have sampled enough such items to have a sense of what the genre does, try to define the term "infographics" on your own. What do these charts have in common? What are their distinctive features?

Designing Print and Online Documents

think
visually

Much advice about good visual design is common sense: *Of course*, academic and professional documents should look uncluttered, consistent, and harmonious. But it is not always easy to translate principles into practice. Nor are any visual guidelines absolute. A balanced and consistent design is exactly what you want for research reports and government documents, but brochures or infographics may need more snap.

Understand the power of images.   Most of us realize how powerful images can be, particularly when they perfectly capture a moment or make an argument that words alone struggle to express. The famous "Blue Marble" shot of the Earth taken by *Apollo 17* in 1972 is one such image—conveying both the wonder and fragility of our planet hanging in space.

Science Source.

Visual texts can be important elements in your own work. Use photographs to tell arresting stories or use videos to underscore important points in an argument. In fact, you can craft the style of any page or screen—its colors, shapes, headings, type fonts, and so on—to make a text more visually appealing, focused, and accessible.

Be sure, though, to identify or caption any photos, videos, or audio files in your project. Captions, in particular, help readers appreciate the significance of the specific texts you have included. If you also number these items in longer papers (e.g., *Fig. 1*; *Table 4*), you can direct readers to them unambiguously.

For a tutorial on using Word and similar tools, see **macmillanhighered.com/howtowrite3e**.
Tutorials › Digital Writing › Word Processing

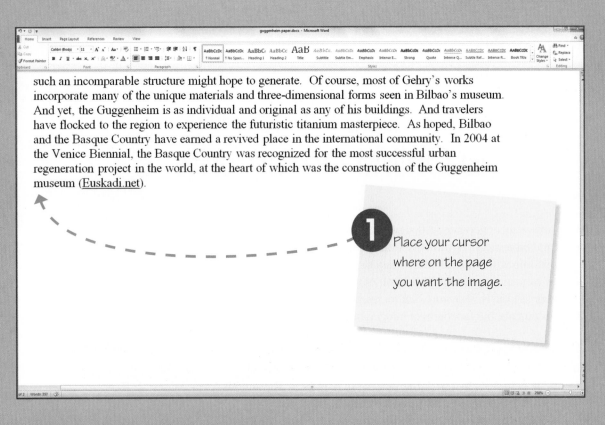

such an incomparable structure might hope to generate. Of course, most of Gehry's works incorporate many of the unique materials and three-dimensional forms seen in Bilbao's museum. And yet, the Guggenheim is as individual and original as any of his buildings. And travelers have flocked to the region to experience the futuristic titanium masterpiece. As hoped, Bilbao and the Basque Country have earned a revived place in the international community. In 2004 at the Venice Biennial, the Basque Country was recognized for the most successful urban regeneration project in the world, at the heart of which was the construction of the Guggenheim museum (Euskadi.net).

1 Place your cursor where on the page you want the image.

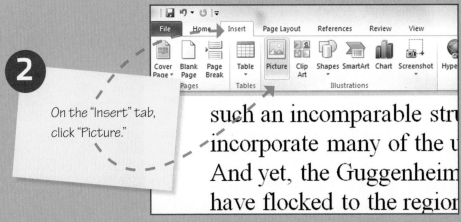

2 On the "Insert" tab, click "Picture."

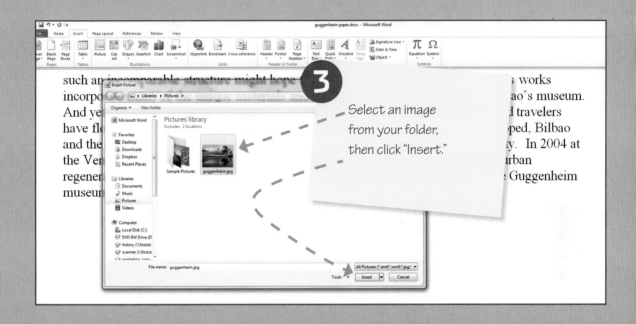

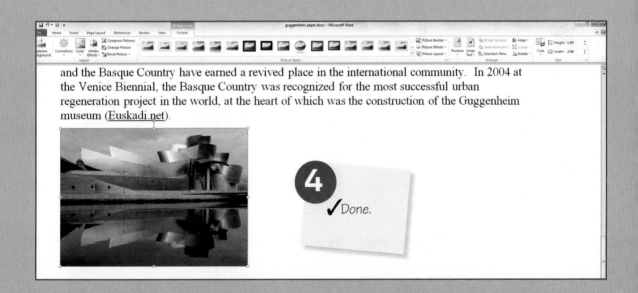

Keep page designs simple and uncluttered. Simple doesn't mean a design should be simplistic, only that you shouldn't try to do more on a page than it (or your design skills) can handle. You want readers to find information they need, navigate your document without missteps, and grasp the structure of your project. Key information should stand out. If you make the basic design intuitive, you can present lots of information without a page feeling cluttered.

Consider, for example, how cleverly Anthro Technology Furniture uses design cues as simple as *Step 1*, *Step 2*, and *Step 3* to guide consumers on a Web page through the complex process of configuring a workstation. Readers simply move left to right across a page, making specific choices. They don't feel overwhelmed by the options, even though the material is detailed.

Horizontal header guides reader across page.

Configuring the piece of furniture is broken into four easy steps.

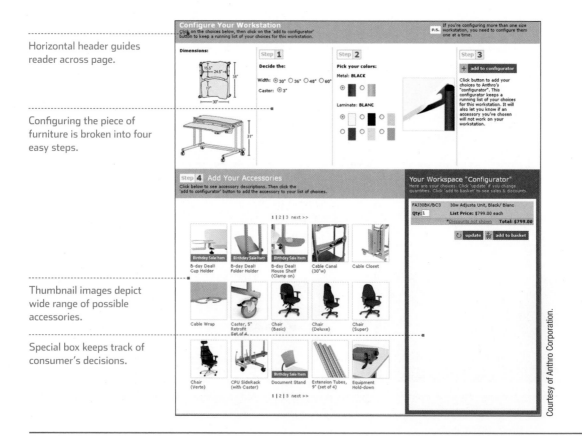

Thumbnail images depict wide range of possible accessories.

Special box keeps track of consumer's decisions.

Courtesy of Anthro Corporation.

Keep the design logical and consistent.   Readers should grasp the logic of a design quickly and then understand how its elements operate throughout a document—especially on Web sites, in PowerPoint presentations, and in long papers.

Look to successful Web sites for models of logical and consistent design. Many sites build their pages around distinct horizontal and vertical columns that help readers find information. A main menu generally appears near the top of the page, more detailed navigational links are usually located in a narrow side column, and

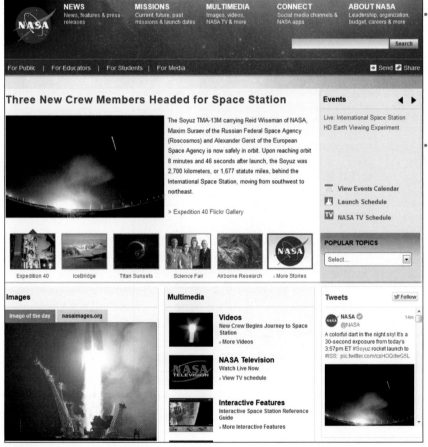

NASA's information-rich page has a consistent horizontal orientation. The eye moves left to right to explore major options. Yet distinct horizontal sections also break the page into visually coherent segments.

Images (many of them thumbnail sized) are carefully aligned to convey information appealingly.

Full screen (not reproduced here) offers more than sixty links or options. Color scheme throughout the site is consistent: white, black, and shades of blue.

NASA home page. Courtesy NASA/JPL-Caltech.

Home page of the *Pittsburgh Post-Gazette*, July 17, 2014. Copyright ©, *Pittsburgh Post-Gazette*, 2014, all rights reserved. Reprinted with permission.

Larger headline size gives impact to this international story.

To attract readers, interior section previews top the simple masthead.

Local human-interest story dominates the news, its importance signaled by its special headline, its placement, and a large color photo.

Below the fold, a unique headline style is used to set off an interesting color photo of a local event.

featured stories often appear in wide columns in the center. To separate columns as well as individual items, the site designers use headlines, horizontal rules, images, or some combination of these devices. Handled well, pages are easy to navigate and thick with information, yet somehow they seem uncluttered.

Keep the design balanced.   Think of balance as an operative term—what you hope to achieve *overall* in a design. You probably don't want many pages that, if split down the middle, would show mirror images. Strive instead for dynamic designs, in which, for example, a large photograph on one side of a document is offset on the other by blocks of print and maybe several smaller images. The overall effect achieved is rough symmetry, even though various page elements may all differ in size and shape.

You can see conventional design principles at work on the front pages of most newspapers (print or online), where editors try to come up with a look that gives impact to the news. They have many elements to work with, including their paper's masthead, headlines of varying size, photographs and images, columns of copy, screened boxes, and much more. The pages of a newspaper can teach you a lot about design.

But you can learn, too, from the boundaries being pushed by designers of Web infographics (see Chapter 49), who use elaborate media effects to present information efficiently yet imaginatively. Unlike newspapers, magazines, or full Web sites, which must follow consistent specifications for page after page, a typical infographic focuses on a single theme or subject, and its creator chooses the media tools best suited to the topic, whether graphs, flowcharts, maps, images, diagrams, or cutaways.

Use templates sensibly.   If you have the time and talent to design all your own documents, that's terrific. But for many projects, you could do worse than to begin with the templates offered by many software products. The Project Gallery in Microsoft Office, for example, helps you create business letters, brochures, PowerPoint presentations, and more. It sets up a generic document, placing the document's margins, aligning key elements and graphics, and offering an array of customizations. No two projects based on the same template need look alike.

If you resist borrowing such materials from software, not wanting yet another part of your life packaged by corporate types, know that it is tough to design documents from scratch. Even if you intend to design an item yourself, consider examining a template to figure out how to assemble a complex document. Take what you learn from the model and then strike out on your own.

Coordinate your colors.   Your mother was right: Pay attention to shades and patterns when you dress and when you design color documents. To learn elementary principles of color coordination, try searching "color wheel" on the Web, but recognize that the subject is both complicated and more art than science. As an amateur, keep your design palettes relatively conventional and model your work on documents that you find particularly attractive.

For academic papers, the text is always black and the background is white. Color is fine in graphs and illustrations if the paper will be reviewed onscreen or printed in color. But be sure that no important elements are lost if the document is printed in black and white: A bar graph that relies on color to display differences might become unreadable. For Web sites and other projects, keep background shades light, if you use them at all, and maintain adequate contrast between text and background. Avoid either bright or pale fonts for passages of text.

Use headings if needed.   Readers appreciate headings as pathways through a text. In academic work, they should be descriptive rather than clever. If you have prepared a good scratch or topic outline, the major points may provide you with almost ready-made headings. ○ Like items in an outline, headings at the same level in a project should be roughly parallel in style. ○

A short paper (three to five pages) doesn't require much more than a title. For longer papers (ten to twenty pages), it's possible to use top-level items from your outline as headings. For some projects, especially in the sciences, you must use the headings you're given. This is especially true for lab reports and scientific articles, and you shouldn't vary from the template.

Choose appropriate fonts.   There are probably dozens or even hundreds of fonts to work with on your computer, but simple is generally best. Here is some basic information to help you choose an appropriate font for your needs.

order ideas
p. 377

help with common
errors p. 566

Serif fonts, such as Times New Roman, show thin flares and embellishments (called serifs; circled in the illustration on p. 565) at the tops and bottoms of their letters and characters. These fonts have a traditional look. In contrast, *sans serif* fonts, such as Helvetica, lack the decorations of serif fonts. They are smoother and more contemporary. On the sample newspaper front page (see p. 562), serif fonts dominate, but sans serif fonts are used for several minor items.

Serif fonts are more readable than sans serif for extended passages of writing, such as papers. Headings in a sans serif font can offer welcome contrast in a document that uses a serif font for its text. Some designers prefer sans serif fonts for Web sites and PowerPoint presentations, especially for headings.

For typical academic projects, all text, headings, and other elements—including the title—are set in one font size, either 10 or 12 point. The standard font is Times New Roman. In professional or business projects, however, such as résumés, newsletters, or PowerPoint slides, you may want to vary fonts and type sizes in order to set off headings, captions, and headlines from other elements.

You can boldface words and phrases selectively to make them stand out clearly on a page. But boldfaced items or headings close together can make a page look heavy and cluttered. Such items should be rare. Never use boldface as the regular text throughout a project. If you want an emphatic font, find one that looks that way in its regular form.

Fonts described as *display* and *decorative* are designed to attract attention (see, for example the masthead of the *Pittsburgh Post-Gazette* on p. 562). You should avoid them for academic and professional writing, but you may want to explore their use when creating posters, brochures, or special PowerPoint presentations. Never use them for extended passages of writing.

Times New Roman

Times New Roman, a serif font.

Helvetica

Helvetica, a sans serif font.

Common Errors

part nine

51 Capitalization

Spring or
spring?

In principle, the guidelines for capitalizing seem straightforward. You surely know to capitalize most proper nouns (and the proper adjectives formed from them), book and movie titles, the first words of sentences, and so on. But the fact is that you make many judgment calls when capitalizing, some of which will require a dictionary. Here are just a few of the special cases that can complicate your editing.

Capitalize the names of ethnic, religious, and political groups. The names of these groups are considered proper nouns. Nonspecific groups, however, are lowercase.

South Korean	Native Americans	native peoples
Buddhists	Muslims	true believers
Tea Party	Democrats	political parties
the Miami City Council		the city council

Capitalize modifiers formed from proper nouns. In rare cases, such as *gargantuan* or *french* (in *fry* or *toast*), the expressions have become so common that the adjective is not routinely capitalized. When in doubt, consult a dictionary.

PROPER NOUN	PROPER NOUN USED AS MODIFIER
French	French thought
Navajo	Navajo rug
Jew	Jewish lore
American	American history

Capitalize all words in titles except prepositions, articles, or conjunctions.

This is the basic rule for the titles of books, movies, long poems, and so on.

Dickens and the Dream of Cinema

In the Company of Cheerful Ladies

The variations and exceptions to this general rule, however, are numerous. MLA style specifies that the first and last words in titles always be capitalized, including any articles or prepositions.

The Guide to National Parks of the Southwest

To the Lighthouse

Such Stuff as Dreams Are Made Of

APA style doesn't make that qualification, but does specify that all words longer than four letters be capitalized in titles—even prepositions. (Note that this rule applies to titles mentioned within articles and essays themselves not titles in APA-style documentation, discussed below.)

A Walk Among the Tombstones

Sleeping Through the Night and Other Lies

In all major styles, any word following a colon (or, much rarer, a dash) in a title is capitalized, even an article or preposition:

True Blood: All Together Now

The Exile: An Outlander Graphic Novel

Finally, note that in APA style *documentation*—that is, within the in-text citations and on the references page, titles are capitalized differently. Only the first word in most titles, any proper nouns or adjectives, and any word following a colon are capitalized. All other words are lowercase:

Bat predation and the evolution of frog vocalizations in the neotropics

Human aging: Usual and successful

Take care with compass points, directions, and specific geographical areas.

Points of the compass and simple directions are not capitalized when referring to general locations.

north	southwest
northern Ohio	eastern Canada
southern exposure	western horizons

But these same terms *are* capitalized when they refer to specific regions that are geographically, culturally, or politically significant (keep that dictionary handy!). Such terms are often preceded by the definite article, *the*.

the West	the Old South
the Third Coast	Southern California
Middle Eastern politics	the Western allies

Understand academic conventions.

Academic degrees are not capitalized, except when abbreviated.

bachelor of arts	doctor of medicine
MA	PhD

Specific course titles are capitalized, but they are lowercase when used as general subjects. Exception: Languages are always capitalized when referring to academic subjects.

Organic Chemistry 101	Contemporary British Poetry
an organic chemistry course	an English literature paper

Capitalize months, days, holidays, and historical periods.

But don't capitalize the seasons.

January	winter
Monday	spring
Halloween	summer
the Enlightenment	fall

Apostrophes 52

Like gnats, apostrophes are small and irritating. They have two major functions: to signal that a noun is possessive and to indicate where letters have been left out in contractions. Apostrophes always need careful review.

Use apostrophes to form the possessive. The basic rules for forming the possessive aren't complicated: For singular nouns, add 's to the end of the word:

the wolf's lair

the photographer's portfolio

IBM's profits

Bush's foreign policy

Some possessives, while correct, look or sound awkward. In these cases, try an alternative:

ORIGINAL	REVISED
the class's photo	the class photo; the photo of the class
Alicia Keys's latest hit	the latest hit by Alicia Keys
Kansas's budget	in the Kansas budget; in the budget of Kansas

it's or
its?

571

For plural nouns that do not end in *s*, also add *'s* to the end of the word:

men's shoes   the mice's tails   the geese's nemesis

For plural nouns that do end in *s*, add an apostrophe after that terminal *s*:

the wolves' pups

the Bushes' foreign policies

three senators' votes

Use apostrophes in contractions.   An apostrophe in a contraction takes the place of missing letters. Edit carefully, keeping in mind that a spell-checker doesn't help you with such blunders. It catches only words that make no sense without apostrophes, such as *dont* or *Ive*.

DRAFT   Its a shame that its come to this.

CORRECTED   It's (It is) a shame that it's (it has) come to this.

DRAFT   Whose got the list of whose going on the trip?

CORRECTED   Who's (Who has) got the list of who's (who is) going on the trip?

Don't use apostrophes with possessive pronouns.   The following possessives do not take apostrophes: *its, whose, his, hers, ours, yours,* and *theirs*.

DRAFT   We photographed the tower at it's best angle.

CORRECTED   We photographed the tower at its best angle.

DRAFT   The book is her's, not his.

CORRECTED   The book is hers, not his.

DRAFT   Their's may be an Oscar-winning film, but our's is still better.

CORRECTED   Theirs may be an Oscar-winning film, but ours is still better.

There is, inevitably, an exception. Indefinite pronouns such as *everybody, anybody, nobody,* and so on do show possession via *'s*.

House of Cards was everybody's favorite.

Why it was so successful is anybody's guess.

Commas  53

The comma has more uses than any other punctuation mark—uses that can seem complex. The following guidelines will help you handle commas in academic writing.

Use a comma and a coordinating conjunction to join two independent clauses.   An independent clause can stand on its own as a sentence. To join two of them, you need both a coordinating conjunction *and* a comma. A comma alone is not enough.

need to
connect
ideas?

> Fiona's car broke down. She had to walk two miles to the train station.

> Fiona's car broke down, so she had to walk two miles to the train station.

There are several points to remember here. Be certain that you truly have two independent clauses, and not just a compound subject or verb. Also, make sure to include both a comma and a coordinating conjunction (*and, but, for, nor, or, so, yet*). Leaving out the coordinating conjunction creates an error known as a comma splice (see p. 577).

Use a comma after an introductory word group.   Introductory word groups are descriptive phrases or clauses that open a sentence. Separate these introductions from the main part of the sentence with a comma.

For an activity on commas, see **macmillanhighered.com/howtowrite3e.**
Tutorials > LearningCurve Activities > Commas

573

> Within two years of getting a degree in journalism, Ishan was writing for the *Wall Street Journal*.

For very brief introductory phrases, the comma may be omitted, but it is not wrong to leave it in.

> After college I plan to join the Marines.

> After college, I plan to join the Marines.

Use commas with common connective words and phrases. These would include items such as the following: *however; therefore; consequently; finally; furthermore; nonetheless; specifically; as a result; in addition; for instance; in fact; on the other hand; that is.* If a transitional word or phrase opens a sentence, it is usually followed by a comma.

> Furthermore, medical reports suggest that trans fats lower the amount of good cholesterol found in the body.

> On the other hand, studies of cholesterol have been notoriously controversial.

When used within a sentence, expressions such as *however* and *for example* should be set off by a pair of commas.

> Big payrolls mean success in professional sports. In baseball, for example, teams from New York and Boston are almost always competitive. There are, however, notable exceptions.

Be especially careful with punctuation around *however* and *therefore*. A common error is to place commas around these connective words to link a pair of related sentences. This move produces an error called a comma splice (see Chapter 54 for more details). Here's what that error looks like:

COMMA SPLICE   In baseball, teams with big payrolls are almost always competitive, however, there are notable exceptions.

To correct this type of comma splice, you can place a semicolon before *however* or create two separate sentences:

> In baseball, teams with big payrolls are almost always competitive; however, there are notable exceptions.

> In baseball, teams with big payrolls are almost always competitive. However, there are notable exceptions.

Put commas around nonrestrictive (that is, nonessential) elements.
You'll know that a word or phrase is functioning as a nonrestrictive modifier if you can remove it from the sentence without obscuring the overall meaning of the sentence.

> Cicero, ancient Rome's greatest orator and lawyer, was a self-made man.
>
> Cicero was a self-made man.

The second sentence is less informative but still makes sense. See also the guideline on page 576, "Do not use commas to set off restrictive elements."

Use commas to separate items in a series.   Commas are necessary when you have three or more items in a series.

> American highways were once ruled by powerful muscle cars such as GTOs, Road Runners, and Gran Sports.

Do not use commas to separate compound verbs.   Don't confuse a true compound sentence (which has two independent clauses) with a sentence that simply has two verbs.

DRAFT   They rumbled through city streets, and smoked down drag strips.

CORRECTED   They rumbled through city streets and smoked down drag strips.

They rumbled through city streets is an independent clause, but *and smoked down drag strips* is not, because it doesn't have its own subject. To join two verbs that share a common subject (in this case, *they*), all you need is *and*. When you have three or more verbs, however, treat them as items in a series and do separate them with commas. Compare the following examples:

TWO VERBS   Muscle cars guzzled gasoline and burned rubber.

THREE VERBS   Muscle cars guzzled gasoline, burned rubber, and drove parents crazy.

Do not use a comma between subject and verb.   Perhaps it's obvious why such commas don't work when you notice one in a short sentence.

DRAFT   Keeping focused, can be difficult.

CORRECTED   Keeping focused can be difficult.

When a subject gets long and complicated, however, you might be more
tempted to insert the comma. It would still be both unnecessary and wrong.
The commas in the following sentences should be omitted.

UNNECESSARY COMMA   Keeping focused on driving while simultaneously trying to
operate a cell phone, can be difficult.

The excuses that some people come up with to defend their
bad habits on the road, sound pathetic.

Do not use commas to set off restrictive elements.   Phrases you cannot
remove from a sentence without significantly altering meaning are called *restrictive* or *essential*. They are modifiers that provide information needed to understand the subject.

Only nations that recognize a right to free speech and free press should be
eligible for seats on international human rights commissions.

Students who have a perfect attendance record will earn three points for class
participation.

Delete the blue phrases in the above examples and you are left with sentences
that are vague or confusing. Put commas around the phrases and you create the
false impression that they could be removed.

Comma Splices, Run-Ons, and Fragments

54

The sentence errors marked most often in college writing are comma splices, run-ons, and fragments.

Identify comma splices and run-ons. A *comma splice* occurs when only a comma is used to join two independent clauses (an independent clause contains a complete subject and verb).

need a complete sentence?

Identify a comma splice simply by reading the clauses on either side of a doubtful comma. If *both* clauses stand on their own as sentences (with their own subjects and verbs), it's a comma splice.

COMMA SPLICES   Officials at many elementary schools are trying to reduce childhood obesity on their campuses, research suggests that few of their strategies will work.

Some schools emphasize a need for more exercise, others have even gone so far as to reinstate recess.

A *run-on* sentence resembles a comma splice, but this somewhat rarer mistake doesn't even include the comma to mark a break between independent clauses. The clauses just slam together, confusing readers.

For an activity on run-ons and comma splices, see **macmillanhighered.com/howtowrite3e.**
Tutorials > LearningCurve Activities > Run-Ons and Comma Splices

577

Common Coordinating
Conjunctions

and	or
but	so
for	yet
nor	

RUN-ON SENTENCES   Officials at many elementary schools are trying to reduce childhood obesity on their campuses research suggests that few of their strategies will work.

Some schools emphasize a need for more exercise others have even gone so far as to reinstate recess.

Fix comma splices and run-ons.   To repair comma splices and run-ons, you have many options. The first is to connect the two independent clauses by inserting *both* a comma and a coordinating conjunction between them.

Officials at many elementary schools are trying to reduce childhood obesity on their campuses, but research suggests that few of their strategies will work.

Some schools emphasize a need for more exercise, and others have even gone so far as to reinstate recess.

A second fix is to use a semicolon alone to join the two clauses.

Officials at many elementary schools are trying to reduce childhood obesity on their campuses; research suggests that few of their strategies will work.

Some schools emphasize a need for more exercise; others have even gone so far as to reinstate recess.

Less frequently, colons or dashes may be used as connecting punctuation when the second clause summarizes or illustrates the main point of the first clause.

Some schools have taken extreme measures: They have banned cookies, snacks, and other high-calorie foods from their vending machines.

Along with the semicolon (or colon or dash), you may wish to add a transitional word or phrase (such as *however* or *in fact*). If you do, set off the transitional word or phrase with commas. ○

Officials at many elementary schools are trying to reduce childhood obesity on their campuses; research, however, suggests that few of their strategies will work.

Some schools emphasize a need for more exercise — in fact, some have even gone so far as to reinstate recess.

Alternatively, you can rewrite the sentence to make one of the clauses clearly subordinate to the other. To do that, introduce one of the clauses with a

connect ideas
p. 387

subordinating conjunction so that it can no longer stand as a sentence on its own. Compare the two corrected versions to see your options:

DRAFT	Officials at many elementary schools are trying to reduce childhood obesity on their campuses, research suggests that few of their strategies will work.
CORRECTED	Although officials at many elementary schools are trying to reduce childhood obesity on their campuses, research suggests that few of their strategies will work.
CORRECTED	Officials at many elementary schools are trying to reduce childhood obesity on their campuses, even though research suggests that few of their strategies will work.

> **Common Subordinating Conjunctions**
>
> | | |
> |---|---|
> | after | once |
> | although | since |
> | as | that |
> | because | though |
> | before | unless |
> | except | until |
> | if | when |

Finally, you can simply use end punctuation to create two independent sentences. Here, a period between the clauses eliminates either a comma splice or a run-on.

> Officials at many elementary schools are trying to reduce childhood obesity on their campuses. Research suggests that few of their strategies will work.

Identify sentence fragments.   A sentence fragment is a word group that lacks a subject, verb, or possibly both. As such, it is not a complete sentence and is usually not appropriate for academic and professional writing. (You will find fragments routinely in fiction and popular writing.)

FRAGMENT	Climatologists see much physical evidence of climate change. Especially in the receding of glaciers around the world.

Fix sentence fragments in your work.   You have two options for fixing sentence fragments. Attach the fragment to a nearby sentence with appropriate punctuation, often a comma:

COMPLETE SENTENCE	Climatologists see much physical evidence of climate change, especially in the receding of glaciers around the world.

For an activity on fragments, see **macmillanhighered.com/howtowrite3e.**
Tutorials > LearningCurve Activities > Fragments

Turn the fragment into its own sentence:

COMPLETE SENTENCE   Climatologists see much physical evidence of climate change.
They are especially concerned by the receding of glaciers
around the world.

Watch for fragments in the following situations.   Often a fragment will
follow a complete sentence and start with a subordinating conjunction.

FRAGMENT   Climate change seems to be the product of human activity.
Though some scientists believe sun cycles may explain the
changing climate.

COMPLETE SENTENCE   Climate change seems to be the product of human activity,
though some scientists believe sun cycles may explain the
changing climate.

Participles (such as *breaking, seeking, finding*) and infinitives (such as *to break, to
seek, to find*) can also lead you into fragments.

FRAGMENT   Of course, many people welcome the warmer weather. Upset-
ting scientists who fear governments will not act until global
warming becomes irreversible.

COMPLETE SENTENCE   Of course, many people welcome the warmer weather. Their
attitude upsets scientists who fear governments will not act
until global warming becomes irreversible.

Use deliberate fragments only in appropriate situations.   You'll find
that fragments are common in advertising, fiction, and informal writing. In personal e-mail or on social networking sites, for example, expressions or clichés
such as the following would probably be acceptable to your audience.

In your dreams.   Excellent!

Not on your life.   When pigs fly.

Subject/Verb Agreement

Verbs take many forms to express changing tenses, moods, and voices. To avoid common errors in choosing the correct verb form, follow these guidelines.

Be sure the verb agrees with its real subject. It's tempting to link a verb to the noun(s) closest to it (in purple below) instead of the subject, but that's a mistake.

DRAFT	Cameras and professional lenses that cost as much as a small **car** makes photography an expensive hobby.
CORRECTED	Cameras and professional lenses that cost as much as a small car make photography an expensive hobby.
DRAFT	Bottled water from convenience **stores** or **groceries** usually cost far more per ounce than gasoline.
CORRECTED	Bottled water from convenience stores or groceries usually costs far more per ounce than gasoline.

Some of the indefinite pronouns described as variable (see chart on p. 583) are exceptions to the rule. Whether they are singular or plural depends on the nouns that follow them (see p. 583).

none are or *none is?*

For an activity on subject/verb agreement, see **macmillanhighered.com/howtowrite3e**.
Tutorials › LearningCurve Activities › Subject-Verb Agreement

581

In most cases, treat multiple subjects joined by *and* as plural. But when a subject with *and* clearly expresses a single notion, that subject is singular.

> Hip-hop, rock, and country are dominant forms of popular music today. [subject is plural]
>
> Blues and folk have their fans too. [subject is plural]
>
> Rock and roll often strikes a political chord. [subject is singular]
>
> Peanut butter and jelly is the sandwich of choice in our house. [subject is singular]

When singular subjects are followed by expressions such as *along with, together with,* or *as well as,* the subjects may feel plural, but technically they remain singular.

DRAFT   James Blake, as well as Kendrick Lamar, Macklemore & Ryan Lewis, Kacey Musgraves, and Ed Sheeran, were competing for Best New Artist at the 2014 Grammys.

CORRECTED   James Blake, as well as Kendrick Lamar, Macklemore & Ryan Lewis, Kacey Musgraves, and Ed Sheeran, was competing for Best New Artist at the 2014 Grammys.

If the corrected version sounds awkward, try revising the sentence.

CORRECTED   James Blake, Kendrick Lamar, Macklemore & Ryan Lewis, Kacey Musgraves, and Ed Sheeran were all competing for Best New Artist at the 2014 Grammys.

When compound subjects are linked by *either . . . or* or *neither . . . nor,* make the verb agree with the nearer part of the subject. Knowing this rule will make you one person among a thousand.

> Neither my sisters nor my mother is a fan of Kanye West.

When possible, put the plural part of the subject closer to the verb to make it sound less awkward.

> Neither my mother nor my sisters are fans of Kanye West.

Indefinite Pronouns

Singular	Plural	Variable
anybody	both	all
anyone	few	any
anything	many	more
each	others	most
everybody	several	none
everyone		some
everything		
nobody		
no one		
nothing		
one		
somebody		
someone		
something		

Confirm whether an indefinite pronoun is singular, plural, or variable.
Most indefinite pronouns are singular, but consult the chart on this page to double-check.

> Everybody complains about politics, but nobody does much about it.

> Each of the women expects a promotion.

> Something needs to be done about the budget crisis.

A few indefinite pronouns are obviously plural: *both, few, many, others, several.*

> Many complain about politics, but few do much about it.

And some indefinite pronouns shift in number, depending on the prepositional phrases that modify them.

> All of the votes are in the ballot box.

> All of the fruit is spoiled.

Most of the rules are less complicated.

Most of the globe is covered by oceans.

None of the rules make sense.

On the Security Council, none but the Russians favor the resolution.

Be consistent with collective nouns.   Many of these words describing a group can be treated as either singular or plural: *band, class, jury, choir, group, committee.*

The jury seems to resent the lawyer's playing to its emotions.

The jury seem to resent the lawyer's playing to their emotions.

The band was unhappy with its latest release.

The band were unhappy with their latest release.

A basic principle is to be consistent throughout a passage. If *the band* is singular the first time you mention it, keep it that way for the remainder of the project. Be sensible too. If a sentence sounds odd to your ear, modify it:

AWKWARD   The band were unhappy with their latest release.

BETTER   The members of the band were unhappy with their latest release.

Irregular Verbs

Verbs are considered regular if the past and past participle—which you use to construct various tenses—are formed by simply adding -*d* or -*ed* to the base of the verb. Below are several regular verbs.

Base Form	Past Tense	Past Participle
smile	smiled	smiled
accept	accepted	accepted
manage	managed	managed

Unfortunately, the most common verbs in English are irregular. The chart on page 586 lists some of them. When in doubt about the proper form of a verb, check a dictionary.

lie or *lay*?

Base Form	Past Tense	Past Participle
be	was, were	been
become	became	become
break	broke	broken
buy	bought	bought
choose	chose	chosen
come	came	come
dive	dived, dove	dived
do	did	done
drink	drank	drunk
drive	drove	driven
eat	ate	eaten
get	got	gotten
give	gave	given
go	went	gone
have	had	had
lay (to put or place)	laid	laid
lie (to recline)	lay	lain
ride	rode	ridden
ring	rang, rung	rung
rise	rose	risen
see	saw	seen
set	set	set
shine	shone, shined	shone, shined
sing	sang, sung	sung
sink	sank, sunk	sunk
speak	spoke	spoken
swear	swore	sworn
throw	threw	thrown
wake	woke, waked	woken, waked
write	wrote	written

57

Pronoun/Antecedent Agreement

You already know that pronouns take the place of nouns. Antecedents are the words pronouns refer to. Pronouns share some of the same markers with nouns, such as gender and number.

SINGULAR/FEMININE   The nun merely smiled because she had taken a vow of silence.

SINGULAR/MASCULINE   The NASCAR champion complained that he got too little media attention.

their or *his* or *hers?*

SINGULAR/NEUTER   The chess team took itself too seriously.

PLURAL   Members of the chess team took themselves too seriously.

PLURAL   They seemed awfully subdued for pro athletes.

PLURAL   The bride and groom wrote their own marriage vows.

PLURAL   Many in the terminal resented searches of their luggage.

The basic rule for managing pronouns and antecedents couldn't be simpler: Make sure pronouns you select have the same number and gender as the words they stand for.

DRAFT   When a student spends too much time on sorority activities, they may suffer academically.

CORRECTED   When a student spends too much time on sorority activities, she may suffer academically.

As always, though, there are confusing cases and numerous exceptions. The following guidelines can help you avoid common problems.

Check the number of indefinite pronouns.   Some of the most common singular indefinite pronouns—especially *anybody, everybody, everyone*—may seem plural, but they should be treated as singular in academic or formal writing. (For the complete list of indefinite pronouns, see the chart on p. 583 in Chapter 55.)

DRAFT   Has **everybody** completed **their** assignment by now?

CORRECTED   Has **everybody** completed **his or her** assignment by now?

If using *his or her* sounds awkward (and it almost always does), revise the sentence.

Have **all students** completed **their** assignments by now?

Correct sexist pronoun usage.   Using either *his* or *her* alone (instead of *his or her*) to refer to an indefinite pronoun can be considered sexist unless the pronoun clearly refers only to males or females. The principle also applies to *he* and *she* when the pronouns are similarly exclusionary. ○ You usually have several options for avoiding sexist usage.

DRAFT   Don't trust a driver using **her** cell phone on the freeway.

CORRECTED   Don't trust a driver using **his or her** cell phone on the freeway.

CORRECTED   Don't trust drivers using **their** cell phones on the freeway.

Treat collective nouns consistently.   Collective nouns—such as *team, herd, congregation, mob*, and so on—can be treated as either singular or plural.

The Roman **legion** marched until **it** reached **its** camp in Gaul.

The Roman **legion** marched until **they** reached **their** camp in Gaul.

Just be consistent and sensible in your usage. Treat a collective noun the same way, as either singular or plural, throughout a paper or project. And don't hesitate to modify a sentence when even a correct usage sounds awkward.

AWKWARD   The **team** smiled as **it** received **its** championship jerseys.

BETTER   **Members** of the team smiled as **they** received **their** championship jerseys.

respect your
readers p. 408

Pronoun Reference

58

A pronoun should refer back clearly to a noun or pronoun (its *antecedent*), usually the one nearest to it that matches it in number and, when necessary, gender.

> Consumers will buy a **Rolex** because **they** covet **its** snob appeal.
>
> Nancy Pelosi spoke at the news conference instead of **Harry Reid** because **she** had more interest in the legislation than **he** did.

If connections between pronouns and antecedents wobble within a single sentence or longer passage, readers will struggle. The following guidelines can help you avoid three common problems.

Clarify confusing pronoun antecedents. Revise sentences in which readers will find themselves wondering who is doing what to whom. Multiple revisions are usually possible, depending on how the confusing sentence could be interpreted.

CONFUSING	The batter collided with the first baseman, but he wasn't injured.
BETTER	The batter collided with the first baseman, who wasn't injured.
BETTER	The batter wasn't injured by his collision with the first baseman.

sure what *it* means?

Make sure a pronoun has a plausible antecedent. Sometimes the problem is that the antecedent doesn't actually exist—it is only implied. In these cases, either reconsider the antecedent/pronoun relationship or replace the pronoun with a noun.

CONFUSING   Grandmother had hip-replacement surgery two months ago, and it is already fully healed.

In the above sentence, the implied antecedent for *it* is *hip*, but the noun *hip* isn't in the sentence (*hip-replacement* is an adjective describing *surgery*).

BETTER   Grandmother had her hip replaced two months ago, and she is already fully healed.

BETTER   Grandmother had hip-replacement surgery two months ago, and her hip is already fully healed.

Be certain that the antecedent of *this*, *that*, or *which* isn't vague. In the following example, a humble *this* is asked to shoulder the burden of a writer who hasn't quite figured out how to pull together all the ideas raised in the preceding sentences. What exactly might the antecedent for *this* be? It doesn't exist. To fix the problem, the writer needs to replace *this* with a more thoughtful analysis.

FINAL SENTENCE VAGUE

The university staff is underpaid, the labs are short on equipment, and campus maintenance is neglected. Moreover, we need two or three new parking garages to make up for the lots lost because of recent construction projects. Yet students cannot be expected to shoulder additional costs because tuition and fees are high already. This is a problem that must be solved.

FINAL SENTENCE CLARIFIED

How to fund both academic departments and infrastructure needs without increasing students' financial outlay is a problem that must be solved.

Pronoun Case

In spoken English, you know it when you run into a problem with pronoun case.

> "Let's just keep this matter between **you** and . . . *ummmm* . . . **me**."
>
> "To **who** . . . I mean, uh . . . **whom** does this letter go?"
>
> "Hector is more of a people person than **her** . . . than **she** is."

Like nouns, pronouns can act as subjects, objects, or possessives in sentences, so their forms vary to show which case they express.

I or *me*? *who* or *whom*?

Subjective Pronouns	Objective Pronouns	Possessive Pronouns
I	me	my, mine
you	you	your, yours
he, she, it	him, her, it	his, her, hers, its
we	us	our, ours
they	them	their, theirs
who	whom	whose

Unfortunately, determining case isn't always easy. Here are some strategies for dealing with these common situations.

Use the subjective case for pronouns that are subjects. When a pronoun is the lone subject in a clause, it rarely causes a problem. But double the subject and suddenly there's trouble.

> Sara and me . . . , or is it Sara and I? . . . wrote the report.

To make the right choice, try answering the question for each subject separately, one at a time. You will then probably recognize that *Sara* wrote the report, and so did the subjective form of the pronoun, *I: I* wrote the report. (*Me*, the objective pronoun, sure didn't.) So the revision is simple:

> Sara and I wrote the report.

Use the objective case for pronouns that are objects. Again, choosing one objective pronoun is generally easy, but with two objects, the choice becomes less clear. How do you decide what to do in the following sentence?

> The corporate attorney will represent both Geoff and I . . . Geoff and me?

Again, deal with one object at a time.

> The corporate attorney will represent Geoff.
>
> The corporate attorney will represent me.

The sentence needs the objective form of the pronoun:

> The corporate attorney will represent Geoff and me.

Or, to be more concise:

> The corporate attorney will represent us.

Note that *us* is also an objective form of the pronoun. The subjective form *we* would not work here at all.

Use *whom* when appropriate. One pronoun choice brings many writers to their knees: *who* or *whom*. The rule, however, is the same as for other pronouns: Use the subjective case (*who*) for subjects and the objective case (*whom*) for objects. In some cases, the choice is obvious.

DRAFT   Whom wrote the report?

CORRECTED   Who wrote the report?

DRAFT   By who was the report written?

CORRECTED   By whom was the report written?

But this choice becomes tricky when you're dealing with subordinate clauses.

DRAFT   The shelter needs help from whomever can volunteer three hours
               per week.

The previous example may sound right because *whomever* immediately follows the preposition *from*. But, because the pronoun is the subject of a subordinate clause, it needs to be in the subjective case.

CORRECTED   The shelter needs help from whoever can volunteer three hours
               per week.

When in doubt, prefer *who* to *whom*. Even when you err, you won't sound ridiculous.

Finish comparisons to determine the right case.   Many times when writers make comparisons, they leave out some understood information.

    I've always thought John was more talented than Paul.

    (I've always thought John was more talented than Paul *was*.)

But leaving this information out can lead to confusion when it comes to choosing the correct pronoun case. Try the sentence, adding *him*.

DRAFT   I've always thought John was more talented than him.

               I've always thought John was more talented than him *was*.

CORRECTED   I've always thought John was more talented than he.

If it sounds strange to use the correct pronoun, just complete the sentence.

CORRECTED   I've always thought John was more talented than he was.

Don't be misled by an appositive.   An *appositive* is a word or phrase that amplifies or renames a noun or pronoun. In the example below, *Americans* is the appositive. First, try reading the sentence without it.

DRAFT	Us Americans must defend our civil rights.
APPOSITIVE CUT	Us must defend our civil rights. [*Us* can't be a subject.]
CORRECTED	We Americans must defend our civil rights.

Note that when the pronoun is contained within the appositive, as in the examples that follow, the pronoun uses the case of the word or words it stands in for. This rule makes more sense when seen in an example.

SUBJECTIVE	The runners leading the marathon, Matt, Luci, and I, all had trained at Central High School.
OBJECTIVE	The race was won by the runners from Central High, Matt, Luci, and me.

In the first example, *runners* is the subject of the sentence. Since *Matt, Luci, and I* merely rename that subject, they share its subjective case. In the second example, *the runners* have become the object of a preposition: *by the runners*. So the threesome now moves into the objective case as well: *Matt, Luci, and me*.

Misplaced and Dangling Modifiers

In general, modifiers need to be close and obviously connected to the words they modify. When they aren't, readers may become confused—or amused.

are your descriptions clear?

Position modifiers close to the words they modify.

MISPLACED   Layered like a wedding cake, Mrs. DeLeon unveiled her model for the parade float.

Mrs. DeLeon is not layered like a wedding cake; the model for the parade float is.

REVISED   Mrs. DeLeon unveiled her model for the parade float, which was layered like a wedding cake.

Place adverbs such as *only, almost, especially,* and *even* carefully.
If these modifiers are placed improperly, their purpose can be vague or ambiguous.

VAGUE   The speaker almost angered everyone in the room.

CLEARER   The speaker angered almost everyone in the room.

AMBIGUOUS   Joan only drove a pickup.

CLEARER   Only Joan drove a pickup.

CLEARER   Joan drove only a pickup.

Don't allow a modifier to dangle. A modifying word or phrase at the beginning of a sentence should usually be followed by a subject to which it connects clearly. When it doesn't, the modifier is said to dangle, especially when there is no other word in the sentence it can logically describe.

DANGLING   Arriving at sunset, the Grand Canyon was awash in golden light.

Nothing in the sentence is actually modified by the opening phrase. Revision is necessary.

REVISED   Arriving at sunset, we beheld the Grand Canyon awash in golden light.

Don't, however, confuse dangling modifiers with *absolutes*, which are phrases that can, in fact, modify entire sentences without connecting to particular words or subjects. Here are some examples:

All things considered, the vacation was a success.

To be honest, our hotel room at the park left much to be desired.

Parallelism

When items in sentences follow similar patterns of language, they are described as parallel. Parallel structure makes your writing easier to read and understand.

When possible, make compound items parallel. Don't confuse your readers by requiring them to untangle subjects, verbs, modifiers, or other items that could easily be parallel.

making a list?

NOT PARALLEL	Becoming a lawyer and to write a novel are Casey's goals.
PARALLEL	Becoming a lawyer and writing a novel are Casey's goals.
NOT PARALLEL	The college will demolish its aging stadium and bricks from it are being sold.
PARALLEL	The college will demolish its aging stadium and sell the bricks.
NOT PARALLEL	The TV anchor reported the story thoroughly and with compassion.
PARALLEL	The TV anchor reported the story thoroughly and compassionately.

Keep items in a series parallel.   This means that once you start a series, all the items in it should share the same form or structure. You might have a series of adjectives (*tough, smart,* and *aggressive*), adverbs (*slowly* and *carefully*), participles (*kicking, screaming,* and *giggling*), infinitives (*to break the siege* and *to free the hostages*), and so on.

NOT PARALLEL	She was a fine rookie teacher — eager, very patient, and gets her work done.
PARALLEL	She was a fine rookie teacher — eager, very patient, and conscientious.
NOT PARALLEL	We expected to rehabilitate the historic property, breaking even on the investment, and earn the goodwill of the community.
PARALLEL	We expected to rehabilitate the historic property, to break even on the investment, and to earn the goodwill of the community.
PARALLEL	We expected to rehabilitate the historic property, break even on the investment, and earn the goodwill of the community.

Keep headings and lists parallel.   If you use headings to break up the text of a document, use a similar language pattern and design for all of them. It may help to type the headings out separately from the text to make sure you are keeping them parallel. Items in a printed list should be parallel as well.

Acknowledgments

Michael Barone. Excerpt from "The Beautiful People vs. the Dutiful People," *US News & World Report,* January 16, 2006. Copyright © 2006 US News & World Report. By permission of Michael Barone and Creators Syndicate, Inc.

Sven Birkerts. Excerpt from "Reading in a Digital Age," *The American Scholar,* Spring 2010. Copyright © 2010.

Peter Bregman. Excerpt from "Diversity Training Doesn't Work," *Psychology Today* Magazine, March 12, 2012. Copyright © 2012 Sussex Publishers, LLC. Reprinted with permission.

David R. Brower. Excerpt from "Let the River Run Through It," *Sierra,* March/April 1997. Copyright © 1997.

Robert Bruegmann. Excerpt from "How Sprawl Got a Bad Name," from *American Enterprise,* Volume 17, issue 5, June 16, 2006. Copyright © 2006.

Nicholas Carr. Excerpt from "Does the Internet Make You Dumber?" *Wall Street Journal,* June 5, 2010. Reprinted with permission of the Wall Street Journal. Copyright © 2010 by Dow Jones & Company, Inc. All rights reserved worldwide. License number 3434970912672 and 3434971079436.

Michael Chorost. Excerpt from *Rebuilt: How Becoming Part Computer Made Me More Human* by Michael Chorost. Copyright © 2005 by Michael Chorost. Houghton Mifflin Harcourt Publishing Company.

Paula Marantz Cohen. "Too Much Information: The Pleasure of Figuring Things Out for Yourself." Reprinted from *The American Scholar* blog of June 11, 2013. Copyright © 2013 by the author.

Ann Coulter. Excerpt from *Godless: The Church of Liberalism* by Ann Coulter. Copyright © 2007 by Ann Coulter. Three Rivers Press.

Lacy Crawford. Excerpt from "Writing the Right College Entrance Essay," *Wall Street Journal,* August 24, 2013. Reprinted with permission of the Wall Street Journal. Copyright © 2013 by Dow Jones & Company, Inc. All rights reserved worldwide. License number 3434971255426 and 3434971363906.

Clive Crook. Excerpt from "John Kenneth Galbraith, Revisited." Copyright © 2006 The Atlantic Media Co., as first published in the *Atlantic Magazine,* May 15, 2006. All rights reserved. Distributed by Tribune Content Agency, LLC.

William Deresiewicz. "Great Expectations: What Gatsby's Really Looking For," *The American Scholar,* June 23, 2013. Copyright © 2013 by William Deresiewicz. Reprinted by permission of the author.

Emily Dickinson. "I felt a Funeral, in my Brain." Reprinted by permission of the publishers and the Trustees of Amherst College from *The Poems of Emily Dickinson,* edited by Thomas H. Johnson, Cambridge, Mass.: The Belknap Press of Harvard University Press. Copyright © 1951, 1955, 1979, 1983 by the President and Fellows of Harvard College.

Roger Ebert. Excerpt from review of *The Lake House,* from rogerebert.com, posted June 15, 2006. Copyright © 2006.

Joseph Epstein. Excerpt from "Plagiary: It's Crawling All Over Me." Copyright © 2006 by Joseph Epstein. Originally published in the *Weekly Standard* (March 2006). Reprinted by permission of Georges Borchardt, Inc., on behalf of the author.

"Fast Food: Ads vs. Reality." From the *West Virginia Surf Report.* Copyright © 2007. Reprinted by permission.

Kendrick Frazier. Excerpt from *People of Chaco: A Canyon and Its Culture* by Kendrick Frazier. Copyright © 1999, 1986 by Kendrick Frazier. W. W. Norton & Company.

Thomas L. Friedman. Excerpt from "A Well of Smiths and Xias," *New York Times,* June 7, 2006. Copyright © 2006 The New York Times. All rights reserved. Used by permission and protected by the Copyright Laws of the United States. The printing, copying, redistribution, or retransmission of this Content without express written permission is prohibited.

James P. Gannon. "America's Quiet Anger," from the *American Spectator,* March 30, 2010. Copyright © 2010. Reprinted by permission of the *American Spectator.*

Malcolm Gladwell. Excerpt from "Troublemakers." First appeared in the *New Yorker,* February 6, 2005. Copyright © 2005 by Malcolm Gladwell. Used with the permission of the author.

Jonah Goldberg. "Global Warming and the Sun," from the *National Review Online,* September 2, 2009.

Index

Missing something? Instructors may assign the online materials that accompany this text. For access to them, visit **macmillanhighered.com/howtowrite3e**.

Inside LaunchPad for *How to Write Anything: A Guide and Reference*

Multimodal Readings
- Narrative: Katerina Cizek, *Out My Window* [MULTIMEDIA DOCUMENTARY]
- Report: UNICEF, *Innovations for Child Health in Uganda* [VIDEO REPORT]
- Argument: 5 Gyres, *Understanding Plastic Pollution through Exploration, Education, and Action* [INTERACTIVE WEB SITE]
- Evaluation: Ivan Penn and the *Tampa Bay Times, Mandarin Chinese, Rosetta Stone Style* [PRODUCT TEST]
- Causal Analysis: *TheAtlantic.com, Think Again* [MULTIMODAL PROJECT]
- Proposal: Michael Pollan, *Celebrate School Lunch* [VIDEO]
- Literary Analysis: Erik Didriksen, *Pop Sonnet: Royals* [PARODY]
- Rhetorical Analysis: Nickolay Lamm, *The History of Music* [INFOGRAPHIC]

Tutorials
Critical Reading
- Active Reading Skills
- Reading Visuals: Purpose
- Reading Visuals: Audience

Documentation and Working with Sources
- Do I Need to Cite That?
- How to Cite an Article in MLA Style
- How to Cite a Book in MLA Style
- How to Cite a Database in MLA Style
- How to Cite a Database in APA Style
- How to Cite a Web Site in MLA Style
- How to Cite a Web Site in APA Style

Digital Writing
- Photo Editing Basics with GIMP
- Audio Editing with Audacity
- Presentations
- Word Processing
- Online Research Tools
- Job Search/Personal Branding

LearningCurve
- Critical Reading
- Topic Sentences and Supporting Details
- Topics and Main Ideas
- Working with Sources (MLA)
- Working with Sources (APA)
- Commas
- Fragments
- Run-Ons and Comma Splices
- Active and Passive Voice
- Appropriate Language
- Subject-Verb Agreement